# SOCIAL

# PROBLEMS

JOHN J. KANE

# SOCIAL
# PROBLEMS

A SITUATIONAL-
VALUE APPROACH

**PRENTICE-HALL, INC.,** *Englewood Cliffs, N. J.*

for

Marianne

# Preface

T he field of social problems has long occupied the attention of American sociologists and their students. It continues to be one of the most commonly taught subjects on the undergraduate level in colleges and universities, and more recently it has found its way in a limited fashion into high school social studies courses under such titles as "problems of democracy" or others. Among the public at large, whose knowledge of sociology is meagre and whose understanding of the sociologists' function slight, the field of social problems is usually believed to be the exclusive content of sociology, and remedies for social problems its major concern. If this were ever entirely true, it has long since ceased to be so. Sociology is not merely the study of society's problems; it is the study of group relationships and the phenomena resulting from such. As the late Professor James H. S. Bossard frequently stated in his classes, no student of medicine would attempt to understand the structure and function of the human body by confining himself to pathology. One must understand the "normally" functioning human organism in order to establish a criterion of pathology. However, as in the study of medicine pathology cannot be neglected, in the study of sociology, a

vii

knowledge of society's problems is essential to a full understanding of all aspects and functions of society.

Sociologically, the very definition of what constitutes a social problem is contingent upon the dominant values of a society. Such values will vary from place to place and time to time. Values are part of the culture, and cultures differ widely. Even within the same society, social change results in alterations in value systems and alterations in value systems result in social change. In the past, American sociologists have been very sensitive about values; to label a statement "a value judgment" was to condemn it completely, even though this condemnation may have been a value judgment itself. Recently, however, American sociologists have evinced greater interest in the subject of values, although as sociologists they feel no need to approve or disapprove of the values studied. There is today a full awareness that values influence perception and perception influences behavior.

The approach to social problems utilized in this book, the *situational-value approach*, attempts to take into account both majority and minority value systems. When social situations appear to threaten a society's welfare according to its dominant value system, such a situation is considered an overt social problem. But what about the values of minorities? The term minorities, as used here, refers to both numerical and sociological minorities. Looked at in one way, the values of a minority may be interpreted as a dominant value within a society. For example, some of the reputedly dominant values in American society are really upper-middle-class values, not shared at all, or shared to a lesser degree, by other social classes which combined are more numerous and some of which enjoy more power and prestige than the upper-middle class. Yet there is some justification for treating upper-middle-class values as dominant, especially in a book written for college students who are generally members of this social class. They can readily grasp the significance as a social problem of a social situation contrary to their value systems.

There is, however, a limitation in this type of presentation unless it is made clear that these are not the only value systems within American society. The same is true of what has been termed in this book, a *covert* social problem. This is described as an emerging social situation which is now a social problem or is likely to become one in the near future according to a numerical minority of experts or scholars, although presently it is not so recognized by most of the public.

Religion has an impact upon value systems, both in the perception of them and in the resultant behavior. In fact, religion may be considered, in one aspect at least, as a system of values. In the United States, a country with over two hundred and fifty different denominations, sects, and cults, variations in values stemming from religion are tremendously diverse. Even if one had adequate knowledge of all these diverse value systems, it would require volumes to explore them. For the most part in this book, where religious values are associated with social problems—as they are in many cases—efforts have been made to utilize Christian and Judaic values, which have much in common, with particular concentration upon Catholic values. The obvious reason for this is that Catholicism is my religion and the probable religious background of most students who will study this book. An equally cogent reason is the hope that Protestant and Jewish students who read this book may gain a fuller and more accurate knowledge of Catholic values in the areas discussed. Hopefully, this may help dispell some of the hazy notions of Catholic values regarding some aspects of social problems. It should also indicate that Catholic opinion on social situations which are not actually matters of faith and morals is far from monolithic. Although major emphasis is upon Catholic values, I have introduced Protestant and Jewish values when pertinent and feasible, as well as values of some Asiatic and African religions.

This is not, however, a text in religion. The orientation is sociological and social-psychological. Religion, philosophy, and theology are introduced only when and where I believe such an inclusion essential.

Emphasis has been upon the description and analysis of problems, although remedial measures have been cited and suggested. I feel that remedies for social problems are the function of the social philosopher and ultimately, in a democracy, the decision of its citizens. Such functions and decisions may well be facilitated by the explanations and views offered by sociologists.

In any book the author is compelled to determine what problems to include and what problems to omit. His decisions rarely enjoy universal approval. In this book the omission of chapters on communism, as well as on political and economic institutions, may arouse criticism. Communism has been discussed briefly, and voting behavior has been examined, but due to limitations of length, a thorough treatment of these topics has not been included. Similarly I found it necessary to omit a discussion of the American Indian and Puerto Rican, and I suggest that this book be supplemented by outside readings in these areas.

On the other hand, two topics not treated in most books of social problems have been included, that of the aging and the aged and that of the American Catholic minority. The first has already become an important social problem. The second is a problem not yet entirely admitted, despite events which clearly indicate it is a social problem, and one which may become more urgent in the immediate future.

The interest of students and the public in social problems is not difficult to understand. Social problems are the subject of news in daily papers, are found on radio and television, and are often treated in books and lectures. Some are highly dramatic, controversial, and packed with human interest. They are problems which threaten the welfare of society and every citizen should be aware of them. Educated persons have a special responsibility to acquire accurate knowledge of the incidence and causal factors of such problems, both to allay the "alarmists," and to take the initiative as community leaders in the alleviation of such conditions without being deceived by the simple, single-causation approach or the easy, short-cut methods of solution dear to many people. Furthermore, liberally educated students should have a thorough knowledge of the society in which they live, and this includes both its "normal" and "abnormal" aspects. It is my earnest hope that this book will make such a contribution to readers and students.

I wish to acknowledge the courtesy and kindness of the many authors and publishers who have granted permissions to use quotes, charts, tables, and graphs. I feel especially indebted to William R. O'Brien, M.D., a practising psychiatrist and analyst in Philadelphia, for his comments on the chapter on alcoholism and other chapters; to Mr. Edward Kane, Comptroller of Women's Medical College and Hospital of Pennsylvania, for his criticism of certain chapters; to Mrs. Harriet Graf, who typed most of the manuscript; and to my wife and daughters, who materially assisted in assembling charts and arranging reference material.

I, of course, assume full responsibility for all statements in this book, as well as for any errors or omissions.

John J. Kane

# Contents

xi

# SOCIAL
# PROBLEMS

# PART ONE

# Introduction

T HE first section of this book attempts to define social problems, and to analyze and apply this definition. Since a situational-value approach is employed, Chapter 1 contains a brief survey of some situational aspects of American society, and particularly emphasizes the influence of social change upon social problems. It is pointed out, however, that social change likewise involves alterations in value systems, and these too can create, modify, or reduce the perception of problems. A distinction is made between *overt* social problems—i.e., those that are usually well recognized—and *covert* social problems—i.e., those which have only a limited recognition. Relationships between sociology and social psychology on the one hand and social philosophy, philosophy, and theology on the other, are explored, and it is indicated that the frame of reference of this book is largely sociological. However, since texts in social problems generally discuss remedial measures, and since this book is no exception, it is necessary to introduce some social philosophy, because remedies are in the province of this discipline rather than in that of sociology. In other words, what is sometimes termed "applied sociology" is really social philosophy hopefully based upon the empirical evidence provided by social science.

1

In the second chapter, some of the traditional approaches to social problems are described, their advantages and limitations noted, and the situational-value approach set forth. These do not exhaust all the possible methods of analyzing social problems, and students are encouraged to use others available in the literature of the field and to exercise their ingenuity in the development of still further approaches to specific problems—or to all problems.

# 1

# Social Problems and

# American Society

I T is relatively simple to illustrate a social
problem. It is far from simple to define it.
Juvenile delinquency, adult criminality, divorce, poverty, unemployment, war, and physical and mental illness are obvious illustrations of what are commonly
termed social problems, and are all topics usually treated
in any textbook dealing with this subject. Furthermore,
there is some interrelationship among these topics. Unemployment over a long period of time will result in
poverty for most persons; and in the wake of war there is a
statistical increase in the rates of divorce, juvenile delinquency, and mental illness. In fact, it is generally accepted
that social problems are interdependent, and it has almost
become a maxim that in order to alleviate one, there must
be a general, all-out attack on all of them. It is likewise
believed that the solution of one social problem may
merely give rise to another, since the ultimate results of
social change are both far-reaching and unknown. These

are propositions generally accepted in sociological circles *about* social problems. Yet an entirely adequate *definition* of a social problem is difficult.

The difficulty in defining social problems is that despite their reputed relationship to each other, there does not seem to be any common denominator allowing a simple statement which describes and analyzes them. Approaches to this topic likewise vary. Among the more common ones are: the social problems approach; the social disorganization approach; the cultural lag approach; the value-system approach; and the community approach.[1] Each of these will be considered in detail in the next chapter. Here they are listed merely to indicate part of the difficulty in defining a social problem.

Definitions of a social problem often contain three elements. The first element holds that it is a condition involving a relatively large number of persons—although just how many persons no one seems quite prepared to say. The second element maintains that this condition is a threat to the welfare of the respective society when measured by the value system apparently held by most persons within that society. The third element assumes that this condition is amenable to collective action.

There is certainly merit in these elements, but they leave some questions unanswered. While a social problem may exist *objectively*, it does not exist *subjectively* until society (or at least many members of a society) becomes aware of it. How is this accomplished? In the day of the "hidden persuader" and the "soft sell," propaganda techniques may be fruitfully used to emphasize some problems and de-emphasize others. Collective action is also contingent upon the ability of leaders and organizations to persuade the public. For instance, the fact that Franklin D. Roosevelt was a polio victim undoubtedly facilitated the "March of Dimes," and ultimately aided the discovery of the Salk vaccine. But credit too must go to the dynamic leadership of Basil O'Connor, who headed the movement.

The National Safety Council, established to reduce traffic fatalities and accidents, used to display a small cross every fifteen minutes on television programs during holiday weekends. Each cross represented a death predicted by this organization during the period on the basis

---

[1] John E. Nordskog, Edward C. McDonagh, Melvin J. Vincent, *Analyzing Social Problems* (New York: The Dryden Press, 1956), p. 2.

of statistical calculation. Many communities use a large sign to list the number of traffic deaths during the current year as compared to the same period of the previous year.

These are two examples of how the public may be made aware of a social problem and galvanized into some kind of action. At the same time there are other social problems which have not yet been so dramatically, so widely, or so effectively publicized, although they may actually be at least as much if not more critical than those cited. Subjectively, then, a social problem depends upon the public's awareness of it, and remedial measures are contingent upon the effective mobilization of public opinion against it.


## VALUES

Inherent in the definition of social problems under discussion is the notion that the social condition must be seen as a threat to society. In other words, it is not merely the presence of a particular social condition which is important but how it is defined. Men perceive situations against the background of their values, attitudes, and motives, or what Theodore Newcomb has termed the "intervening variable." A *motive* is energy mobilized and directed toward a goal which is drive-reducing—a hunger drive, for example, creates the food motive. An *attitude* is a tendency to react for or against something. A *value*, which is really the most important of the three elements under discussion—and in fact shapes attitudes and motives —is a firm conviction or belief which is very strongly held.

Among some of the values which appear to be widely held in American society are: belief in democracy (albeit the specific meaning of this term shows variations), the profit motive, private property, sacredness of human life, formal education, desirability of upward vertical mobility (i.e., "getting ahead in life"—although this is more pronounced in the middle and upper classes), freedom of worship, monogamy, and the superiority of what is called "the American way of life." America is also a youth-centered society and until quite recently relatively little attention has been paid to the aged.

As a consequence any social condition which is perceived as a threat to these or certain other values commonly held is apt to be considered a social problem. The key term here, however, is *perceived*. Crime is a threat to private property and in some cases to life itself. Juvenile delinquency also threatens life and property, and since it involves youth in a youth-centered society it is not only seen as a social problem but one which is rather emotion-arousing.

In 1954 the U.S. Supreme Court held that racially segregated public education was illegal and ordered the gradual integration of public schools along racial lines. In some sections of the country this has resulted in violence and various devices, including the closing of public schools by state authority, to avoid such integration. A public referendum in Norfolk, Virginia even supported the closing of schools in preference to racial integration. To some Americans racially segregated schools seem to constitute a social problem; to others, racially integrated schools are a social problem. Probably all of these Americans, whether they support or oppose racially integrated schools, would maintain that they believe in democracy. It is not merely the value system, but the way in which one perceives a situation and so interprets it against his value system, that determines whether or not a particular situation is considered a social problem.

## THE EXTENT OF SOCIAL PROBLEMS

Problems may be personal, social, or both, but the test of a social problem must ultimately rest on whether the condition is considered a true threat to social organization. It may likewise rest upon the assumption that the incidence of a given condition is increasing rapidly and may ultimately threaten social organization. The basis for such a claim, however, should be examined critically before it is accepted.

The number of persons involved in a social problem may or may not be important in the recognition of the problem. In the case of unemployment, there is no doubt that when it rises beyond a given point and affects a sizable proportion of the population either nationally or locally it is recognized formally by the federal, state, and city governments and informally by the public at large, particularly those who are unemployed. Statistics on unemployment, while probably not entirely accurate as to the economic conditions—since there are always a certain number of perennial "unemployables" in a society who may be included—at least give approximate accuracy compared to some other statistics. Narcotic addiction and alcoholism are considered social problems, and estimates are given of the actual number involved. Yet it is doubtful if such figures can even approximate accuracy. This is equally true of crime. Perhaps no set of statistics produced in any area is less correct than those labeled "crimes known to the police"—and these are the best possible statistics that can be provided in this area!

Private councils, conferences, or foundations dedicated to the reduction or elimination of certain social conditions such as prejudice, discrimination, or alcoholism exist on the basis of contributions. These contributions in turn depend upon arousing the public to the seriousness of the specific situation. Such organizations are not usually given to underestimation of a problem, although no claim is made that willful deceit is practiced.

An individual who is a narcotic addict has a personal problem. But is narcotic addiction a social problem today? Are enough persons involved or likely to become involved that such addiction will prove a true threat to society? In 1959 the Federal Bureau of Narcotics estimated the number of active drug addicts in the United States at 45,391, which is about half the number believed to have existed a generation ago.[2] Other estimates are much higher, and the New York Police claimed 90,000 addicts in that city alone.[3] In a population of about 180,000,000 it is difficult to believe, if the Narcotic Bureau figures were correct, that this should be considered a social problem on the basis of numbers. Yet most textbooks on social problems will include a discussion of drug addiction.

## THE DEFINITION OF A SOCIAL PROBLEM

At this point it is proposed that social problems can only be defined according to two categories: *overt* social problems and *covert* social

[2] Federal Bureau of Narcotics, *Traffic in Opium and Other Dangerous Drugs* (Washington, D.C.: Government Printing Office, 1960), p. 37.

[3] Marshall B. Clinard, *Sociology of Deviant Behavior* (New York: Holt, Rinehart & Winston, Inc., 1957), p. 268.

problems. An overt social problem is a social condition about which collective remedial action is taken by the state or private agencies or both because the public has been made aware of it and has come to believe or has been persuaded that this condition constitutes a threat to society according to the value systems of the society.

Under the overt heading can be found most of the social problems usually encountered in sociology textbooks—crime, delinquency, alcoholism, poverty, and such. On the other hand there are certain social problems of a covert nature which have not yet been recognized for a variety of reasons, about which no remedial collective action is taken, but which still constitute a threat to society—at least in the minds of a segment of the public and/or a number of competent observers.

The terms overt and covert do not imply that one kind of social problem is real and the other imagined. Rather, they are used to indicate that while an actual problem may exist, it does not appear to exist until public awareness is aroused and collective action is taken in an effort to remedy it.

## COVERT SOCIAL PROBLEMS

Since social problems do depend upon the perception of the situation via the individual's or group's value system, it becomes obvious that what is considered a social problem and the degree to which a condition is considered serious must depend on these value systems. Within the United States there are many kinds of groups with divergent and sometimes conflicting value systems. First, there are different social classes and, as Richard Centers demonstrated, one of the important criteria of social class is the value system.[4] Of the two hundred and fifty different religious denominations, many have extremely variant value systems. While large-scale immigration practically ceased in the late twenties, many persons of foreign birth and their immediate descendants have values which show variations from the dominant American culture.

To some of the Amish, compulsory school laws requiring attend-

---

[4] Richard Centers, *Psychology of Social Classes* (Princeton, N.J.: Princeton University Press, 1949), p. 153.

ance beyond the eighth grade present a social problem for them. Seventh Day Adventists may refuse to work on Saturday. Christian Scientists will not accept medical care; at times courts must intervene to compel essential operations on their children. Some Jews have objected strenuously to the celebration of Christmas in public schools if it involves religious aspects. Years ago the U.S. Supreme Court forbade the practice of polygamy among the Mormons. In certain areas of the south, state police have used force to prevent snake handling among some religious cults. While little of this ever finds its way into a text on social problems, such difficulties represent value conflicts and problems for the persons involved.

Many of these problems are regional, and few involve large numbers of persons. However, there are certain other covert social problems which do involve large numbers of people and which either receive scanty treatment in many social problems texts or none at all. There are also problems for which *collective* remedial action has yet to be mobilized. Among the former, there is that of abortion. Here, no accurate figures are obtainable, but conservative estimates claim 250,000 a year. Among the latter problems is the matter of divorce. Here and there a court of domestic relations has made efforts to reconcile the parties, and private marriage counselors are available in most large cities; but to date, the public has expressed less concern about this problem than it appears to warrant. It is true that collective action on the part of the state does control divorce, since it is treated as a legal matter; but real collective *remedial* action has yet to be realized.

Another problem only recently recognized in some texts has been that of Protestant-Catholic relationships in America. For almost ten years after the close of World War II, interreligious tensions between these two large bodies of Christians seemed to be mounting. In fact, Bishop G. Bromley Oxnam and Cardinal Francis Spellman stated so publicly.[5] The proposed appointment of a Vatican envoy poured fuel on what was already a fairly brisk fire. Of course, it is inevitable that a certain lag necessarily exists between the emergence of an overt social problem and its inclusion within a text.

The important point for the student to remember is that all social problems are not necessarily found within the covers of a text, no

---

[5] John J. Kane, *Catholic-Protestant Conflicts in America* (Chicago: Henry Regnery Co., 1955), p. 7.

matter how voluminous it may be. This is one reason for the distinction made between overt and covert social problems.

## THEOLOGY, PHILOSOPHY, AND SOCIAL PROBLEMS

Another reason for distinguishing between the overt and covert social problem is the inevitable question: are social problems moral problems? Such a claim has been made but it cannot be accepted without further distinctions. Those who subscribe to an absolute code of morality, i.e., who insist that objectively speaking a specific act is always and everywhere morally wrong, make a distinction in terms of the moral guilt of the person involved. Female infanticide is practiced among certain preliterates. Objectively, this act is wrong. Subjectively, there is doubt whether or not persons practicing infanticide violate the moral code. To put it simply, they may not know better.

Even in highly developed societies infanticide occurs occasionally. A feebleminded mother may put her infant to death. Again this act is objectively wrong, but mental deficiency has robbed this mother of the ability to tell right from wrong. In this case the act is both a moral and a psychological problem. Many social problems are moral problems despite the exceptions noted above. But if social problems are to be treated as moral problems this is a task for the theologian, not the sociologist. Since there are so many different religious denominations in this country, and since their theological systems are by no means uniform, the varieties of social problems would prove tremendous.

Suppose social problems are treated as ethical problems. Since ethics is a division of philosophy, social problems then become a task for the philosopher. But whose system of philosophy shall be used? For some religious denominations, of course, this presents no problem; but even then, social problems become a study in philosophy, not sociology. The basic question is: what does a sociological approach to social problems offer?

The function of the sociologist is the scientific analysis of group phenomena by means of empirical methods. The empirical method, loosely defined, is the inductive method in which one moves from the particular to the general. Philosophy and theology are deductive. They move from general principles to the particular. Ethics and theology are concerned with what "ought to be," sociology with "what is." Philosophy is concerned with ultimate ends, sociology with proximate ends. Theology is based upon supernatural revelation, tradition, and the teachings of the Church; sociology employs methods and techniques on the purely natural level.

Obviously all three disciplines should complement each other. Unfortunately in the past, and to some extent even in the present, there has been some antagonism between philosophy and theology on one hand and sociology on the other. It is likewise true that clashes occur between systems of philosophy and theology. Even within a given system, all philosophers and theologians do not always agree. Neither have sociologists been noted for singleness of mind.

But in the application of principles, the theologian must call upon other disciplines for assistance. A diseased uterus which constitutes a threat to life may be removed, even though it sterilizes the patient. No theologian would depend upon theology to determine whether or not a uterus was diseased. Ecclesiastical marriage courts sometimes consult psychiatrists before they reach a decision, because theology does not teach a man how to diagnose a psychosis.

When a social philosopher talks of the living wage, he can only reach a determination of just what this may be in a specific case through knowledge provided by the social sciences, particularly economics, sociology, and social psychology. On the other hand the sociologist should not attempt to behave as a philosopher on the basis of his knowledge and training in social science. This too has been done.

The major contribution of the sociologist in the social problems course of study is an analysis of the factors which, on the basis of empirical evidence, seem to produce social problems. Many methods are employed, including questionnaires, schedules, participant or non-participant observation, statistical measurements, case histories, content analyses, and combinations of these approaches. Thus the sociologist should be able to provide some reasonably accurate idea of the incidence of a problem, its origin and development, and the sociological factors apparently associated with it, particularly those which appear to exert a causal effect.

## APPLIED SOCIOLOGY

The social-problems course has been called "applied sociology," since originally it was largely reformative. Today this aspect of sociology has passed over to social work and what is sometimes called "social engineering." The major function of sociology is analysis, but in social problems this may be extended to an examination of the collective remedial action employed to reduce or eliminate problems.

Social work or social service is an independent discipline concerned with "helping people to help themselves." The case worker may engage in counseling of various types, investigate families which apply to adopt children, operate in the field of probation and parole, and perform functions similar to all of these in a personal setting by working with an individual. Group work may be illustrated by recreation directors in playgrounds, boys' clubs, and like organizations. Social service administration is a field concerned with the actual executive work of community chests, the Red Cross, and other organizations of this type.

*Social engineering* is an attempt to apply sociological rules and principles to a situation in order to effect changes in the structure and thus remedy a condition. The term has not acquired wide usage. Perhaps the word "engineering" carries some unfortunate connotations implying that persons can be handled like machinery.

## AMERICAN SOCIETY AND SOCIAL CHANGE

The kind of social problems which beset a society tend to be influenced by the nature of that society. The United States is a large, complex, urbanized, and industrialized nation characterized by rapid social change. Within the last fifty years this country has passed through two major wars and a severe depression—not to mention the Korean conflict and several recent recessions—and it is now involved in an apparently interminable "cold" war. Before 1920 most

Americans did not live in cities. Radio, television, and airplanes were unknown at the turn of the century.

Changes in social relationships have been just as revolutionary. American women could not vote until the third decade of this century. Dating, as now practiced, was unknown. The structure and function of the family have been radically altered. The *conjugal family*, consisting of two generations (parents and children), has replaced the *consanguineal family*, made up of three or more generations, more common in the past. The family used to be an economic producing unit; now it is usually a consuming unit. Clothing was made at home and food was raised on the farm, some of it being preserved for the rest of the year. A large family was an economic asset on the farm, where sons could help in the fields and daughters in the kitchen. The large family is an economic liability within the city. Furthermore, sons and daughters today are supported in whole or in part at least through high school, and not infrequently through college and graduate or professional school. In the past fewer persons went to high school and even fewer to college. Most boys began work in their early or middle teens, as was also the case to some extent with girls.

Labor unions on a large scale—and particularly the industrial union, which like the United Automobile Workers, organizes within one general industry regardless of craft—is a relatively recent organization, born during the depression of the thirties when legislation favorable to unions was introduced. Today unions must be thought of as social institutions which exert a strong influence not only on the economy but also on politics and, to some extent, community life. The ultimate weapon of labor unions is the strike, which can often literally paralyze a city.

More Americans in proportion to the population now claim affiliation with a religious denomination than at any time in our history. There is a reputed religious revival occurring in the United States. Yet a spirit of secularism seems to pervade the American scene. External manifestations of religious belief and action seem to be belied by the crime rate, scandals in government, incidence of absolute divorce, failure to observe Sunday as the Sabbath, and a heightened concern over wealth and material goods.

In the last century when the Pennsylvania Railroad had to run a train on Sunday, it apologized publicly for so doing. In 1887 the divorce rate was 0.5 per 1,000 persons; in 1955 it had reached 2.3 per 1,000 persons. Crime and lawlessness have never been conspicuous by their absence from American life, nor were scandals in high government unknown. The inaccuracy of statistics on past and present crime make a scientific historical comparison impossible, but in the last century scandals in government were actually considered scandalous. Today they tend to be viewed with almost ambivalent feelings.

Emphasis on wealth and material goods is in part a heritage of our Puritan forerunners, and has been considered an aspect of the Protestant ethic as defined by Max Weber. Today it seems to be part of the American ethos. There is much of Thorstein Veblen's "conspicuous consumption," i.e., the tendency for persons to buy and exhibit material items considered valuable by the society's standards, such as expensive cars, furs, jewelry, homes, and clothing. These items are usually external symbols of high status, and are avidly sought, acquired, and often paid for through long-term installment plans with perhaps more anxiety than money in the long run. Arguments over money are the most common type of family quarrel in the United States. All of this runs counter to the virtues of prudence and humility usually associated with religious ideals. Church membership and the reputed religious revival notwithstanding, secularism at least vies with if not outdistancing religion in many areas of American life.[6]

On the other hand, the picture is not altogether negative. The charity of the American people in times of catastrophe and distress is remarkable. The economic recovery of Europe and Asia after World War II resulted in no small part from American aid, not only through official government assistance paid for by U.S. taxes, but also through various private agencies, which have provided money, food, and clothing from individual voluntary contributions.

Another apparently emerging change in this country is the "welfare state." This term is generally considered an invidious one, but it has become so generally accepted that it is used here. A welfare state is one in which the government through taxation provides certain free services to all citizens: education, medical and dental care, extra family allowances for children, unemployment compensation, old-age

---

[6] "Unchanging Duty in a Changing World," Statement of the American Bishops, Annual Meeting, Nov. 17, 1961, *Our Sunday Visitor*, 50 (1961), pp. 10-11.

assistance, and others, as well as material help for those unable to support themselves. Slum clearance, erection of low-cost housing, and social security are also functions of the so-called welfare state.

It should be said at the outset that in the United States many of these measures have already been adopted, notable exceptions being medical and dental care and family allowances. For this reason persons usually labeled "conservative" claim that the United States has already declined into a welfare state. Those usually labeled "liberals" would object that this country has failed to adopt some of the essential measures and has not yet adequately or extensively carried out some of the measures already adopted.

There seem to be two major objections to the welfare state. First, it is considered contrary to what has been termed "rugged individualism," upon which, it is said, this country was established and upon which it has flourished. This represents a basic value conflict. Second, and perhaps more important, fears are expressed that such a situation would lead to government domination of life itself, and the "Big Brother" of George Orwell's *1984* would become a reality. Another objection, not expressed as much as the two mentioned above but by no means suppressed, is the concern that such welfare provisions would result in impossible taxation that would prove ruinous, at least to the more prosperous.

Some aspects of this matter will be discussed later under family, mental and physical health, and economic problems. Here it is introduced to illustrate another facet of social change in America and the significance of such change for the field of social problems.

Finally, one of the most important social changes occurring within the twentieth century has been the emergence of the United States as a major world power. While most Americans would accept this statement without question, its full impact does not yet seem to have reached them. In some quarters a certain provincialism typical of nineteenth-century American thinking still prevails. But the pressure of circumstances will inevitably force an awakening, as shown by the fact that this same century has seen the establishment and overthrow of two ideologies, fascism and Nazism, and the establishment and spread of a third, communism.

Ultimately all of these "isms" might once have been described— and in fact have been described—as merely economic systems. In reality all three were much more. They should best be described as political, economic, and social systems dominated by a special philosophy of life. Socialism, which has a number of varieties, was spelled out by Karl Marx and Friedrich Engels during the last century, but the actual forms which fascism, Nazism, and communism took had little relationship to the classical notions of Marx and Engels.

In Germany Nazism developed under Adolf Hitler, being derived chiefly from his book *Mein Kampf.* In Italy, Benito Mussolini seized control of the government after his famous "march on Rome" during the unrest following World War I. Lenin in Russia was able to wrest control away from the revolutionary government that had supplanted the Czar during World War I. A notable characteristic of Hitler's reign was racism, which resulted in first the expulsion and later the virtual extermination of Jews in Germany and the countries conquered by Hitler's armies. All three systems depended heavily upon physical force to impose themselves on the German, Italian, and Russian peoples.

The United States shares its position as the leading world power today with the Union of Soviet Socialist Republics. Germany has been split in half, with West Germany allied to the western powers and East Germany under communist control. Italy is now a republic, and fascism as an important force does not appear to exist in that country. The conflict of East and West, with Russia and her satellites on one hand and the United States and her allies on the other, is probably the most significant fact of contemporary history. Its effects in America, in terms of social problems, are tremendous.

The military factor has also influenced American life. For example, compulsory military service has been continued, and millions of American young men have been inducted into the armed services during the last fourteen years, although with the exception of the Korean conflict the country is supposedly at peace. The full implications of this have not yet been adequately explored. Educational, professional, and business careers have been interrupted or delayed. Families have been separated, and marriages between American men and foreign women have increased. International incidents have occurred with our allies as a result of certain crimes committed by some American servicemen in foreign lands. Feelings in this country have run strongly against the alleged imposition of foreign laws on American servicemen.

Communist propaganda has seized upon every incident to whip

up world opinion against this country. The Little Rock episode in 1957 was an excellent example of this. The race to launch the first satellite into orbit was won by Russia, and this has resulted in vigorous criticism of American education and the initiation of crash programs to change it. Charges of communist infiltration of the federal government, especially the State Department, have rocked the American public and produced hysterical partisans on both sides. Taxes to provide aid for allies and for research and development of rockets, satellites, and other armaments dip deeply into American purses. At the same time government spending for armaments is a factor in inflation and cutbacks in such spending facilitate recessions.

During all of this, grave doubts have haunted many citizens regarding U.S. status in the cold war, and one former Communist has stated that Christianity has lost out to communism. While this claim is more than merely debatable, it should now be clear that the American-Soviet battle for world supremacy strongly influences U.S. society and cannot be divorced from some of the domestic social problems which it helps create.

## VALUE CHANGE

While these items by no means exhaust the spectrum of social change, they are sufficient to illustrate some of the more important characteristics of American society today, as compared with the past. But social change depends on more than inventions and discoveries, wars and depressions. The system of values within a society likewise undergoes change, and a condition that might not have been considered a social problem may become one, while one formerly viewed as a social problem may gain acceptance.

It has already been indicated that an overt social problem exists only when as a result of public awareness it is collectively dealt with because it is perceived to constitute a threat to society in terms of a given society's values. An interesting example of a value change in American society is collective bargaining.

A century ago the right of workingmen to form labor unions for the purpose of bargaining collectively with employers for better wages and working conditions was rather generally denied. The first large labor union that lasted for a relatively long period of time in the United States was The Knights of Labor, founded in 1869 in Philadelphia. At first it was a secret organization, partly because this was an era of secret societies but mainly because of employer opposition. Furthermore, in the past many employers required a prospective employee to sign what was known as a "yellow dog contract." This was an agreement not to join a union.

Rather slowly, opposition to collective bargaining weakened, but never disappeared entirely until the 1930's, when federal legislation, notably the Wagner Act, gave impetus to the labor movement and gained for it a much wider—in fact an almost general—acceptance. This is an example of a value change resulting from collective social action.

Other examples of value changes are easily provided. Opposition to artificial contraception was so strong in the past that legislation known as the Comstock Law was passed to exclude information on this subject from the U.S. mails. Today contraception is believed to be widespread, except among Catholics and a few other religious denominations. Divorce was vigorously opposed by some Protestant denominations which today accept or at least tolerate it. The Suffragettes who fought for the female voting franchise were ridiculed as "unsexed creatures" by both men and women. Today, the right of women to vote is established and accepted. Child labor was once defended. Today it is illegal.

Since social problems are contingent upon the value system, it is clear that what constitutes an overt social problem will change from time to time. Such changes are not entirely divorced from inventions and discoveries, wars and depressions. The rate of change is accelerated during certain periods of history, particularly during wars and depressions. An invention or discovery may alter the whole perspective in which a situation is viewed. Hospital mortality rates in the last century were so high that to many persons the hospital was a place to which one went to die. With the advent of asepsis, anesthetics, and improved medical and surgical care, the horror of hospitals has practically disappeared.

There are certain conditions and practices in contemporary society about which there is no unanimity. In the future there may be greater agreement, and such matters may be generally considered serious social problems. One is the effect of radioactive fallout from nuclear weapons. Another is the relationship between cigarette smoking and lung cancer as well as the possible ill effects on humans from automobile exhaust fumes. Whether or not any of these eventually become accepted as social problems, it is quite certain that the social problems of tomorrow will not be identical with those of today. Discovery, invention, wars, depressions, and changes in the value system will continue to redefine the social problem.

## REVIEW QUESTIONS

1. Define "social problem." Analyze and evaluate the validity of this definition.
2. How do social problems come to the attention of the American public? Is the acuteness of a problem determined by the public's degree of awareness of it?
3. What is the difference between a "covert" and an "overt" problem? Give examples of each.
4. Is absolute divorce a social problem in American society? Explain your answer in detail.
5. What is the relationship between social problems and social philosophy?
6. What is the relationship between social problems and philosophy and theology?
7. What is "social engineering?"
8. Exemplify and discuss how certain social changes in the material aspects of American culture contribute to social problems.
9. How have changes in American value systems altered the types of situations considered to be problems?
10. In what way does it appear likely that future social change will result in new social problems?

## SELECTED READINGS

*Articles*

Augusta, Sister Maria, "Theoretical Conversions in the Analysis of Social Change," *American Catholic Sociological Review*, 21 (Winter 1960), 290-310.

Cronin, John F., "The Catholic Approach to Social Action," *American Catholic Sociological Review*, 10 (Oct. 1949), 152-58.

Fitzpatrick, Joseph P., "Catholics and the Scientific Knowledge of Society," *American Catholic Sociological Review*, 15 (Mar. 1954), 2-5.

Furfey, Paul Hanly, "On Defining Sociology," *American Catholic Sociological Review*, 9 (Mar. 1948), 19-25.

————,"Value Judgments in Sociology," *American Catholic Sociological Review*, 7 (Mar. 1946), 83-95.

————, "The Humanitarian Philosophy and the Acceptance of Sociological Generalizations," *American Catholic Sociological Review*, 15 (June 1955), 117-22.

————, "The Social Philosophy of Social Pathologists," *Social Problems*, 2 (Oct. 1954), 66-77.

Kane, John J., "Are Catholic Sociologists a Minority Group?" *American Catholic Sociological Review*, 14 (Mar. 1953), 2-12.

Kolb, William A., "The Impingement of Moral Values on Sociology," *Social Problems*, 2 (Oct. 1954), 66-70.

Lynch, Sister Miriam, "Communication between Philosophers and Sociologists," *American Catholic Sociological Review*, 19 (Oct. 1958), 290-309.

Pepper, George B., "Leslie A. White's Theory of Cultural Evolution," *The American Catholic Sociological Review*, 21 (Winter 1960), 319-30.

Pierce, Albert, "Empiricism and the Social Sciences," *American Sociological Review* (Feb. 1956), 135-37.

Scheuer, Joseph F., "The Use of Analogical Conceptualization in Sociology," *American Catholic Sociological Review*, 10 (June 1949), 107-19.

Schnepp, Gerald J., "Social Progress, 1931-1946—An Estimate of a Papal Document," *American Catholic Sociological Review*, 7 (June 1949), 107-19.

# 2

# The Theoretical Orientation
# for Social Problems

T HE purpose of this chapter is to describe and
evaluate some of the most common theories
or approaches employed to explain social
problems. Scientifically it would be desirable, if possible,
to discover a single basic theory that would provide a
framework for the explanation of all social problems. To
date such a theory has not been found. Instead, five "approaches" are commonly utilized, although most authors
are content with fewer. They are: the social problems
approach, the social disorganization approach, the culture
lag approach, the community approach, and the value
system or value structure approach.

## THE SOCIAL PROBLEMS APPROACH

The social problems approach is the oldest and the one
most frequently used. Herman Abbot has pointed out that

it may take either of two forms: a survey in which an effort is made to examine a very large number of problems, or the intensive investigation of a single problem such as suicide or crime.[1]

This approach provides wide knowledge of the incidence, causal factors, and impact upon society of each specific problem, as well as detailed knowledge of remedial action and an evaluation of it. In fact, it becomes something of an encyclopedia of social problems, and of social action for reducing or eliminating them. As such it does have considerable value, particularly for the student who is beginning the study of sociology or the student who elects such a course to learn something of a society's problems.

But three serious limitations exist in such an approach. First, it is quite difficult to retain continuity or to hold the course together. Each new problem introduced seems to create another and quite different course. Second, the variety of theories upon which causal factors are based becomes bewildering. Third, as pointed out in the first chapter it is believed that social problems are interrelated and interdependent. If so, such an impression is ultimately lost in the social problems approach. Even when a single problem is treated there is a tendency to neglect its interrelationship with other problems.

But there is no single cause of all social problems. Today multiple causation is the usual sociological approach, and efforts to explain the tremendous variety of social problems in terms of a unilateral cause are considered futile. Professor Abbott believes that there are common elements in at least the early stages of all social problems, but admits that this is no single-causation theory. For example, he cites the expansion of industries and cities as a basic condition which results in the breakdown of family life and neighborhood controls, as well as the invasion of cities by racial and ethnic minorities seeking employment. These may ultimately result in crime, race riots, and a less stable family system.[2]

Where race riots, for example, have occurred, Negro invasions of cities and the resultant competition for housing and jobs have been common elements. Yet sometimes these common elements exist and race riots have not occurred. It is quite as important to explain the

---

[1] Herman P. Abbott, *An Approach to Social Problems* (Boston: Ginn & Co., 1949), pp. 9-10.
[2] Abbott, *op. cit.*, pp. 9-10.

absence of race riots under these conditions as it is to discover the common elements themselves.

## THE SOCIAL DISORGANIZATION APPROACH

This concept was developed by W. I. Thomas and Florian Znaniecki in *The Polish Peasant in Europe and America*. Charles H. Cooley also made contributions to this theory. According to Thomas and Znaniecki, social disorganization is a "decrease of the influence of the existing social rules of behavior upon individual members." [3] As a result there developed individuation and a lack of social cohesiveness. From this came social problems. Cooley showed that the breakdown of institutional stability increased the incidence of social problems.

Social disorganization may be thought of as a process which will inevitably create social problems, but the factors that are behind social disorganization must be found. In the case of the Polish peasant who migrated to the United States, transition to a new culture offering none of the stability of the old produced as it has in many immigrants the "marginal man," who threw off the controls of his old culture and did not take on those of the new. He was caught between cultures. The problem was particularly acute for the children of immigrants.

Social disorganization may also occur as a result of numerous immigrants coming to a large city from a farming or rural area. It can occur as secondary group contacts replace primary group contacts. The anonymity of metropolitan areas may be another factor. In other words, any situation which breaks or weakens the ties of the individual to his group and its institutions without his acceptance by or allegiance to new groups and institutions would bring about, or may bring about social disorganization.

But the late Professor Richard C. Fuller raised a serious question about certain social problems reputedly associated with social disorganization. A boy may be an integral part of a gang which engages in delinquent behavior. He adheres closely to the behavior rules

---

[3] W. I. Thomas and Florian Znaniecki, *The Polish Peasant in Europe and America*, Vol. 2 (New York: Alfred A. Knopf, Inc., 1927), pp. 1127-33.

of the delinquent gang. Therefore, he can only be said to be a victim of social disorganization in terms of the wider society.[4] This is obviously true of other deviants who form groups of their own kind.

Furthermore, can the theory of social disorganization explain all social problems? Some mental disease is organic, some may result from accidents at birth, and some have unknown causes. But an even more severe criticism of the theory is that it is offered as an explanation of social problems but is not actually applied to them.

Despite these limitations, the concept of social disorganization does have value and can be applied to some social problems. It is better than the social problems approach simply because it holds some promise of at least tying certain problems together and emphasizing their interrelatedness.

## THE CULTURE LAG APPROACH

William Fielding Ogburn is the author of this theory, which has been widely quoted but not without challenge. According to Ogburn all parts of a culture do not change at the same rate. Material aspects, such as machines, techniques, and so on, are likely to be altered through invention or discovery more quickly than nonmaterial aspects of a culture, such as family relationships. He termed the difference in the rate of change "culture lag," i.e., one part of the culture lagging behind another and thus causing maladjustments or social problems to occur.

His classic example was workmens' compensation laws. In earlier days when machinery was relatively simple, accidents were fewer. When they did occur, employers took care of medical costs. Because industry was apt to be small, employers and employees had a face-to-face relationship. The owner had a personal interest in his employees and took care of them during this crisis. As industries became larger, employer-employee relationships became more distant and formalized, but industrial accidents were still taken care of in the same way.

When agitation began for workmens' compensation laws, employers opposed them. Eventually, however, they were passed. The

---

[4] Richard C. Fuller, "Sociological Theory and Social Problems," *Social Forces*, 15 (May, 1937), p. 497.

period between that in which industrial machinery was becoming more and more dangerous and employers were taking little personal interest in employees, and the passage of workmens' compensation laws, illustrates what Ogburn terms culture lag.

Generally, Ogburn's concept means that changes in policy are necessitated by changes in the material culture. Failure to initiate such policy changes results in social problems. A current example of such lag is in the control of commercial airlines. Policies and methods adopted when air traffic was far less significant were not changed when air traffic increased and recently pilots testified that grave danger existed at certain airports for this reason.

Culture lag is most useful in dealing with those social problems in which technological change renders former attitudes obsolete—for example, the belief that distance and oceans separating the United States and foreign countries offer a protection in war. If modern airplanes did not dispel this notion then jets and rockets must.

Ogburn has been criticized because he apparently seemed to place too much emphasis upon technological change. It is claimed that he made technology a tail that wagged the dog (culture), failing to place enough emphasis on resistances to change within a culture and appearing to treat technology as though it itself were not a part of a culture.[5]

## THE COMMUNITY APPROACH

Strictly speaking the community approach is not actually intended to be an approach to social problems at all. Rather, it is a survey of a specific community, which investigates various social institutions using anthropological methods. *The Yankee City* series by Professor W. Lloyd Warner and his associates, *Elmtown's Youth* by the Hollingsheads, *Middletown* and *Middletown in Transition* by the Lynds— all are examples of community surveys which employed the methods of anthropology.[6]

[5] William F. Ogburn, *Social Change* (New York: The Viking Press, 1950), pp. 200-83. For one criticism of Ogburn's theory see Abbott, *op. cit.*, pp. 31-34.

[6] Robert S. Lynd and Helen M. Lynd, *Middletown* (New York: Harcourt, Brace & World, Inc., 1929).

The Lynds' study is particularly valuable because they investigated a midwestern town both before and during the depression of the thirties. On their second visit, they tried to discover whether or not values had changed significantly as a result of this drastic economic change. Actually it was found that they had not changed.

*Elmtown's Youth* was a study of high school students and youth of high school age and was oriented largely around social class. It was clear that the values and behaviors of these youths were a function of their social class values. *The Yankee City Series* is the most thorough and detailed of these surveys, and among other things it devoted special attention to ethnic groups and management-labor relations. It too concerns itself with social class and the values inherent in social classes.

All of these studies have made contributions to the field of social problems. Warner and his associates were able to show how absentee ownership of shoe factories altered social relationships within a factory and contributed to the strike in progress when the study was made. The major advantage of using this type of approach is that social problems are readily viewed as interrelated, and can be spelled out in great detail within the confines of the specific community.

But the major social problems are national in scope, and a study of crime in Middletown is by no means the same as a study of crime in a large metropolitan area such as New York City or Chicago. Certain social problems such as drug addiction might not even be found in some of the small communities under study. Perhaps the best use of this approach is to provide theories and illustrations of certain problems in detail. This is no criticism of these studies because, as pointed out above, they were never intended to be exclusively an investigation of social problems.

---

Robert S. Lynd and Helen M. Lynd, *Middletown in Transition* (New York: Harcourt, Brace & World, Inc., 1937).

W. Lloyd Warner and Paul S. Lunt, *Social Life of a Modern Community* (New Haven: Yale University Press, 1941).

W. Lloyd Warner and Paul S. Lunt, *The Status System of a Modern Community* (New Haven: Yale University Press, 1942).

W. Lloyd Warner and Leo Srole, *The Social System of American Ethnic Groups* (New Haven: Yale University Press, 1945).

W. Lloyd Warner and J. O. Low, *The Social System of the Modern Factory* (New Haven: Yale University Press, 1947).

August B. Hollingshead, *Elmtown's Youth* (New York: John Wiley & Sons, Inc., 1949).

## THE VALUE SYSTEM APPROACH

This approach has been termed the "value structure," the "value conflict," and the "value-scheme" approach. Values are the ideals, beliefs, or norms which a society—or the large majority of a society's members—holds. As pointed out in the first chapter they are responsible for the definition of a problem; they may help create a problem and they may also interfere with its solution.

Professor Fuller has explained it in detail. He claims that a common sociological orientation to social problems may be found in the conflict of values characterizing every social problem.

> These conflicts are mirrored in the failure of people to agree that a given condition is a social problem, or assuming such agreement, failure to reach an accord as to what should be done about it. It is exactly this disagreement in value-judgments that is the root cause of all social problems, both in the original definition of the condition as a problem and in subsequent efforts to solve it.[7]

Fuller and Myers made a three-fold distinction among social problems on the basis of the different levels of their relationships to these value schemes. Physical problems, such as floods, droughts, earthquakes, and similar phenomena are regarded as threats to social welfare by practically everyone. But they reason that such conditions should not be regarded as social problems since they are not the result of value conflicts. No one argues about how to prevent such gigantic natural phenomena as earthquakes, hurricanes, or volcanic eruptions—although it must be admitted that some steps can and have been taken to prevent such disasters. Conflicts in values about whether or not to spend the money needed to erect levees, dams and such to control floods would appear to put floods and a few other similar conditions in the area of social problems, at least indirectly. Once a disaster has occurred, conflicts in values will hamper decisions on how to relieve the condition, how much to spend on relief, and other policy decisions. But cultural factors do not enter into the actual hurricane or earthquake as such.

---

[7] Richard C. Fuller and Richard R. Myers, "Some Aspects of a Theory of Social Problems," *American Sociological Review, 6* (Feb. 1941), p. 27.

The second relationship involves what remedial measures should be taken to reduce or eliminate a social problem. While all "right thinking" citizens agree in their opposition to crime, they do not agree on how to prevent it or how to handle those committing crimes. The same may be said of many other social problems such as traffic fatalities, psychoses and mental deficiency.

The third relationship Fuller and Myers term the "moral" problem. It is a condition about which no unanimity of opinion prevails throughout a society. In other words many persons doubt that this type of condition represents a problem at all. "With the moral problem we have a basic and primary confusion which goes much deeper than the question of solution which troubles us in the ameliorative problem." [8] In fact, some conditions, such as divorce and race prejudice, fall into this category.

Professor Goode has illustrated this moral problem incisively in an article on divorce. He compared the plight of the social engineer brought to a community to help reduce the divorce rate with a civil engineer asked by a community to erect a bridge. Upon his arrival the social engineer would discover that persons within the community could not agree upon the seriousness of divorce, upon the policies they would accept to relieve it, or indeed even agree that they wished to relieve it. If a civil engineer came to a community and found that people did not know where they wanted a bridge built, how much they wished to spend, or even whether they wanted a bridge at all, he would leave in disgust.[9]

What Fuller and Myers have termed the "moral" problem has been defined as a covert social problem in this text. It should also be pointed out that the term " 'moral' problem" was used by Stuart A. Queen and Jennette R. Gruener in their *Social Pathology*. It is placed in quotes to indicate that these authors did not define it as pertaining to fundamental questions of right and wrong.[10]

Herman Abbott has criticized the values approach because it tends

---

[8] Fuller & Myers, *op. cit.*, p. 27.

[9] William J. Goode, "Social Engineering and the Divorce Problem," *The Annals*, 272: pp. 86-94. (Note: All reference to *The Annals* throughout this book refer to *The Annals of the American Academy of Political and Social Science*.)

[10] Stuart A. Queen and Jennette Rowe Gruener, *Social Pathology* (New York: Thomas Y. Crowell Co., 1940), pp. 38-42.

to play down the situational aspects involved in a social problem and fails to deal adequately with the social change which is implicit in it.[11]

## THE APPROACH OF THIS TEXT

An adequate approach to social problems requires both a sociological and social-psychological approach. Sociology deals with phenomena arising from group relationships. It is concerned with social change, and the impact of such change upon a society. For example, the very size of a group alters relationships within it. Sociologists speak of the primary group—the family, the neighborhood, and the play group—all of which are relatively small, involve face-to-face relationships, are characterized by informality, and reveal the individual in many aspects of life.

The secondary group, on the other hand, is large, formal, and meets at stated times for definite purposes. Within it the individual displays only a few facets of his personality and behavior. Examples are large urban schools, labor unions, professional societies, and similar organizations.

Of course, size alone is not the sole criterion of primary and secondary groups. The nature of the bond is quite important. One is "tied" to the family because of the nature of the bond. Children do not choose their families. Later, however, they will choose or be chosen by some secondary groups for membership. Husbands and wives do choose each other, but their union is based upon mutual vows of a religious nature, or at least of a legal nature if they are married in a nonreligious ceremony. Marriage is reputedly for life, although millions of Americans do obtain divorces.

The bonds of the neighborhood and play group are less binding than those of the family but more binding than most of the secondary groups or associations. Certain circumstances usually dictate where one lives and with whom one cultivates friendships. Custom, sentiment, and close, frequent contact are influences cementing the bonds of the neighborhood and play group.

In contrast, membership in a secondary group is largely by choice,

---

[11] Abbott, *op. cit.*, p. 11.

albeit nominal membership may be required because of school laws, labor union regulations, and such. These are among the factors that make social relationships within these two categories of groups different, and which illustrate the sociological approach. There are, of course, many other factors, such as the religious, economic, educational, racial, ethnic, residential and others which are of interest to the sociologist. All of these situational aspects merit consideration in the analysis of social problems.

Social change has already been discussed and its impacts, as pointed out, are far-reaching, intensive, and may create social problems. One result of social change in large cities has been to multiply secondary groups at the expense of primary groups. As individuals relinquish or are denied the security of the primary group relationship, the sense of *anomie*, or not belonging, becomes pervasive. A number of studies have found that the incidence of schizophrenia, a psychosis, is much greater in the area of a city inhabited by homeless men. This does not mean that schizophrenia is *caused* by lack of membership in primary groups but it appears to be associated with it.

It should also be noted that not all social change is the result of discovery, invention, or technology. During the depression of the thirties some Negroes moved from the South to the North, not to find jobs, which were practically non-existent, but simply because lessened racial discrimination made it easier to obtain public relief. The Negro invasion of the District of Columbia was a result of the federal government's policies toward the employment of Negroes.

SOCIAL PSYCHOLOGY

While sociology deals mainly with group phenomena, social psychology is concerned with the individual as a member of a group. Strictly speaking, sociologists do not neglect the study of the individual; but the emphasis is largely on the group itself. Social psychology emphasizes the behavior of the person as it is influenced by the group. Behavior refers to both *covert behavior* (how the individual perceives, thinks and feels) and *overt behavior* (how he acts).[12]

---

[12] S. Stansfeld Sargent and Robert C. Williamson, *Social Psychology* (New York: The Ronald Press Company, 1958), p. 3.

Motives, attitudes, and values are the special focus of the social psychologist and were defined in the first chapter. There it was pointed out that an individual's behavior depends on how he defines a situation, i.e., how he perceives it. This he does against his system of values. Because values are so important, social psychology seems vital to establishing a theoretical orientation for the study of social problems.

## THE SITUATIONAL-VALUE APPROACH

The situation refers to those influences outside of himself which impinge upon an individual. These are the sociological factors already listed, among which are education, religion, income, residence, and ethnic or racial background. Furthermore, these situational factors are interrelated and interdependent and are organized as a unit in their focus on the individual involved.[13]

In *The Jack Roller*, a famous study by Clifford Shaw, the impact of situational factors is amply attested by the delinquent Stanley's own story of his career. He was poor, lived with his father and stepmother, who showed him little affection, associated with a gang, and was encouraged to steal by his stepmother. He learned the code of his gang, especially not to "squeal" when apprehended by the police, and specialized in robbing intoxicated men. He had relatively little formal education, played truant from school, and had been in the reformatory.[14]

Stanley's delinquency cannot be viewed solely as the result of having a stepmother, or lack of affection, or poverty, or gang membership. Rather it was a complex of these various situational factors impinging upon him as a unit. But even if one of these factors were attempted as an explanation of Stanley's delinquency, another dimension would have to be introduced. It is not merely the situational factors but how Stanley perceived and reacted to them that must be considered.

---

[13] James H. S. Bossard, *Sociology of Child Development* (New York: Harper & Brothers, 1954), p. 3.

[14] Clifford Shaw, *The Jack Roller* (Chicago: University of Chicago Press, 1930).

Stanley had acquired a set of values against which his delinquent behavior seemed the "right and proper" thing to do. Status in the gang was contingent upon his ability to act as a lookout for the police when his gang was engaged in robbery, by his ability to withstand police questioning, and later to engage in the successful "rolling" of intoxicated men. In other words, an understanding of Stanley involves a grasp of both his social situation and his value system.

The approach attempted in this text will be a combination of the situational and the value approach. Social change will be used to cover alterations in both the situation and in the value systems. There is one obvious deficiency in this method. The influence of heredity, a factor within the organism, is omitted. How serious is such a deficiency?

Some social problems, such as mental deficiency, are the result of heredity. But the amount of feeblemindedness inherited is a matter of dispute. Certain physical diseases and defects are also inherited, but they are relatively rare. So far as it is known today, the majority of social problems simply cannot be traced to heredity. Poverty, alcoholism, delinquency, crime, racial, religious and ethnic group prejudice, and war can scarcely be attributed to physical inheritance.

Furthermore, even some of the conditions which can be traced to heredity, such as mental deficiency and physical defects, are social problems because of the value system of the culture. Certain preliterate societies execute twins at birth or murder children because of their pigmentation. The Spartans destroyed defective children at birth by leaving them on hillsides to die of exposure. Among Americans such behavior would be considered barbarous. The major difference here is not traceable to physical inheritance but to the value systems of the respective cultures.

However, omission of heredity in a discussion of social problems still presents a difficulty. There is reason to believe, as will be pointed out later, that certain vices such as alcoholism and drug addiction may be associated with personality structure. How much of a person's personality depends upon heredity? This is merely a rephrasing of the perennial question of "heredity versus environment" or "nature versus nurture."

On the basis of contemporary research there is fairly wide but not universal agreement that with the exception of temperament, personality is not inherited, but acquired. True enough the physical basis of personality is inherited, i.e., the nerve structure and such, but personality is formed throughout life, particularly during infancy, childhood, and adolescence. Temperament is rooted in the physiology of the organism and seems to be inherited. It refers to such characteristics as moodiness, cheerfulness, the energy with which one acts, and similar qualities. But at best, temperament refers to how one behaves, not what one does.[15] Omission of heredity as an important factor in most social problems seems justified for these reasons.

## THE INTERRELATIONSHIP OF SOCIAL PROBLEMS

Will a situational-value approach adequately reveal the interrelationship of social problems? This can only be determined by the student after he has read this book. But at the outset it must be admitted first that all causal factors involved in a given social problem are not known. In addition, problems are grouped because the relationship of some problems to others is obvious. For example, alcoholism, drug addiction, and suicide do have something in common. All are types of escape from tension and conflict. Suicide is the final and extreme escape from the problems of this world for the individual involved. Alcoholism and drug addiction are temporary escapes but like suicide seem in the last analysis to create more problems than they solve. Persons involved in any of these are at the very least emotionally disturbed, sometimes neurotic, and in some cases undoubtedly psychotic.

But when one gets beyond such generalizations great differences are found in the rates of suicide and alcoholism. Catholics have a very low rate of suicide. The Protestant rate is higher, and recently the Jewish rate has risen. On the other hand, Jews have a very low rate of alcoholism while Catholics, especially Irish Catholics, have a much higher rate. While these problems show some interrelationship in that all are traceable to tensions and conflict, the actual outlet used varies in terms of many sociological factors such as age, religion, ethnic composition, and, especially, cultures and sub-cultures.

Certain other social problems show a much greater interrelation-

---

[15] Sargent and Williamson, op. cit., p. 53.

ship. There is an *association* between crime and poverty, poverty and slum living, race and poverty. But no sociologist claims that poverty *causes* crime. It may in some cases but it is not accepted as a general explanation. White-collar crime, i.e., the type carried on in a man's business or professional career, may be committed by persons in relatively high economic brackets. Negroes may be forced to live in slum, or at least rundown, areas not through lack of money but because of discrimination.

While the general interrelationship of social problems is usually taken for granted, it may never have been spelled out entirely since with the present level of sociological knowledge it is not possible to do so. Where such relationships exist and can be proved, they will be indicated. The advantage of the situational-value approach is simply a common theoretical orientation, against which each problem may be analyzed and a continuity provided.

## PREDICTION OF FUTURE SOCIAL PROBLEMS

The covert social problem was defined as a social condition about which no collective *remedial* action has been taken because the public has not come to accept it as a condition threatening society's welfare, although a segment of the public and/or competent observers may so consider it. This raises a question inherent in the field of social problems. Should social scientists be able to detect social problems that will unfold in the future?

An ounce of prevention is reputedly worth a pound of cure. Social change is like a pebble cast into a pond. Its ripples ultimately reach out to the farthest shore. To date the long-range effects of a specific social change have not been known. Yet it would be better to foresee and forestall a social problem, if possible, than to suffer its ravages, and then belatedly spend time and money in an effort to halt or remedy it.

With the benefit of hindsight it is possible to criticize some of the failures of the past. In 1909 Professor Lichtenberger stated that the increasing divorce rate should not appall anyone. It merely meant that behavior standards expected in marriage would be raised and the ultimate effect would be greater family stability. But by 1947 the ratio of divorce to marriage in a given year was one-to-three. Since then it has declined slightly. Americans obtain more divorces than any nation in the world, and actually outdo Canada and most of western Europe combined.

Efforts today center more on the individual than on the problem itself. Parole, marriage, and delinquency prediction scales exist. Success in predicting future delinquents is claimed in 80 per cent to 90 per cent of the cases studied in New York. Premarriage counseling is available, but probably not widely used. Debates wax hot over parole prediction scales and generally the decision to parole is made exclusively by parole boards, some of which exist as a result of political expediency rather than criminological acumen.

But the possibilities of predicting future social problems are not unrealistic. Some economists have been able to predict depressions and recessions; demographers have been able to project population statistics—not always correctly, admittedly; and sociologists have indicated the likelihood of racial and minority group tensions in certain communities.

Today there are sufficient data from demographers to indicate some of tomorrow's social problems, assuming that present trends continue. In 1980 it is estimated that there will be 22 million persons over sixty-five years of age in the United States. In 1900 there were only three million. Financial support and nursing care of the aged are problems of tomorrow predictable today.

Providing adequate schools and teachers for the education of America's youth is a problem already facing elementary schools because of the postwar birth rate. It will soon confront high schools and then colleges and universities. With it go problems of taxation, since until 1940 the proportion of younger persons had dropped and the proportion of older persons increased. In other words the number of persons with taxable incomes will be relatively small until the babies of the forties begin earning their own living.

If present trends in juvenile delinquency continue, this may constitute an even more serious problem in the future. At present, the number of delinquent persons in the ten-to-eighteen age bracket— the usual age when one may be legally adjudged a delinquent—is relatively low. Within a few years the percentage of all youths in this age category will have increased greatly.

These are some possible future problems. With more adequate

statistics and a study of trends others could probably be predicted. Of course conditions can change, or society can try to change conditions. In either case some of the problems can be avoided. But collective remedial action is not likely to be taken unless the public is made aware of the problem. While the social scientist may attempt to predict future social problems and call society's attention to them, remedial measures are usually beyond their scope or function.

## SOLVING SOCIAL PROBLEMS

The viewpoint that sociologists are not directly involved in the solution of social problems is one commonly challenged and deprecated.[16] But again, the function of the sociologist is analysis. This is a sufficiently difficult task and actual solution or remedial measures are the responsibility of an entirely separate host of disciplines, such as social work, social philosophy, law, and others. In an age of specialization, progress has been achieved by dividing up tasks. The sociologist's contribution is an understanding of the causal factors in a given social problem. He may, against this background, make evaluations of certain approaches being proposed to reduce or eliminate a problem. But in the last analysis, the general public—of which the sociologist is, of course, a member—must make the decisions regarding remedial measures. This is particularly true within a democratic society. As a citizen the sociologist should be interested in resolving social problems, but this is not his major professional concern.

## THE FRAMEWORK OF THIS BOOK

Various social problems are grouped together when they seem to have close relationships. In each case the history and incidence of the problem is explained. The situational-value approach is used to

---

[16] Robert S. Lynd, *Knowledge for What?* (Princeton, N.J.: Princeton University Press, 1939).

provide a theoretical orientation, and an evaluation is made of the more common methods employed to combat overt social problems.

The same general pattern will be followed for covert problems, but in this case particular efforts are made to determine whether or not such problems may be justifiably identified as such, and if so why the public at large has not yet so accepted them.

## REVIEW QUESTIONS

1. What is meant by an "approach" to social problems?
2. List three approaches and evaluate each, indicating its assets and liabilities.
3. What is meant by a "situation?" Illustrate. Does it act alone upon an individual or group?
4. How can social psychology contribute to an understanding of social problems?
5. What is a "value?" How does it influence perception?
6. Should physical disasters such as hurricanes and earthquakes be considered social problems?
7. What are the limitations of the situational-value approach to social problems?
8. Can you suggest approaches to social problems not mentioned in this chapter which would prove fruitful?

## SELECTED READINGS

*Articles*

Blumer, Herbert, "Attitudes and the Social Act," *Social Problems, 3* (Oct. 1955), 59-65.

Bowman, Claude C., "Must the Social Scientists Foster Moral Skepticism?" *American Sociological Review, 10* (Dec. 1945), 709-15.

————, "Is Sociology Too Detached?" *American Sociological Review, 21* (Oct. 1956), 563-67.

Furfey, Paul Hanly, "The Sampling Problem," *American Catholic Sociological Review, 8* (Dec. 1947), 258-65.

Gorden, Raymond L., "Inter-action between Attitude and a Definition of the Situation in the Expression of Opinion," *American Sociological Review, 17* (Feb. 1952), 50-58.

Queen, Stuart A., "Social Participation in Relation to Social Disorganization," *American Sociological Review*, 14 (Apr. 1949), 251-56. See also the discussions of Albert A. Cohen, Ernest R. Mower, and Stuart A. Queen, pp. 259-62 of the same issue.

Schneider, Joseph, "Cultural Lag: What Is It?" *American Sociological Review*, 10 (Dec. 1945), 786-91.

Timasheff, N. S., "Sociological Theory Today," *American Catholic Sociological Review*, 11 (Mar. 1950), 25-33.

Vogt, Evon Z. and Thomas F. O'Dea, "A Comparative Study of the Role of Values of Social Action in Southwestern Communities," *American Sociological Review*, 18 (Dec. 1953), 645-53.

*Books*

Carr, Lowell Jilliard, *Situational Analysis*. New York: Harper & Brothers, 1948.

Lynd, Robert S., *Knowledge For What?* Princeton, N.J.: Princeton University Press, 1939.

———— and Helen M. Lynd, *Middletown*. New York: Harcourt, Brace & World, Inc., 1929.

Warner, W. Lloyd, *Social System of the Modern Factory*. New Haven: Yale University Press, 1947.

————, *Social Systems of American Ethnic Groups*. New Haven: Yale University Press, 1945.

————, *Social Life of a Modern Community*. New Haven: Yale University Press, 1941.

————, *Status System of a Modern Community*. New Haven: Yale University Press, 1942.

————, *The Living and the Dead*. New Haven: Yale University Press, 1959.

# PART TWO

# Problems of Population,

# Health, and Gerontology

T HE expression "population explosion" has almost become a colloquialism in the United States. Scholars and popular authors have written on it extensively and it has been the theme of television programs, as well as many lectures. Disagreement among the experts is marked, and the average citizen, if not confused, tends to embrace one or the other extreme view on the matter. The problem is dramatic, controversial, and charged with emotion. It is the first problem discussed in this book because it is basic to the other problems covered in this section—physical health and medical care, mental illness, and the aging and aged.

The treatment of the population problem here is somewhat unusual because it heavily emphasizes religious attitudes and practices in the area of birth control, as well as situational factors. For millions of people, their religious convictions constitute a major factor in their value systems. Even those who do not subscribe to the religious tenets of any denomination, sect, or cult must still reckon with such values when they propose population policies. Furthermore, population problems are most acute in those parts of the world where Christianity, Protestant or Catholic, has little impact, with the exception of Latin America. For this reason, religious values of some of the Asiatic and African denominations have been considered in detail, along with Christian and Judaic attitudes. The actual impact of religion upon fertility patterns in the United States has been considered from available empirical evidence.

Where population problems have occurred they have been the result of public health measures and medical care, which have prolonged life. Therefore, the next topic deals with this matter, although it is largely limited to the United States. The incidence of mental illness is also associated to some degree with length of life. Senility, a type of psychosis, is found only among older persons, and certain functional psychoses may not develop until later years. Consequently, consideration of mental illness seems appropriate to this section.

The number of persons sixty-five or over has increased more rapidly in the United States since the turn of the century than the entire population itself. Their social, economic, political and health adjustments are emerging as a major social problem. Obviously, this situation is closely associated with population growth and physical and mental health. For this reason the problem of aging and the aged was included in Part Two. By grouping these problems together, their interrelationship and interdependence should become clear.

# 3

# The Population Explosion:

# Fact or Fallacy?

T HROUGHOUT the world today more than
80 persons are added to the population each
minute, about 5,000 each hour, 120,000 each
day, and 44 million each year. United Nations demographers have repeatedly increased their estimates for
1980. In 1951 they expected the 1980 world population
to be between 2,976 to 3,636 million. Seven years later
this had been revised upward to 3,850 to 4,280 million.[1]

It took 200,000 years for the world's population to
reach 2500 million, it will take a mere 30 years to add
another 2000 million. With the present rate of increase, it can be calculated that in 600 years the
number of human beings on earth will be such that
there will be only one square meter for each to live on.
It goes without saying that this can never take place;
something will happen to prevent it.[2]

[1] Richard M. Fagley, *Population Explosion and Christian Responsibility* (New York: Oxford University Press, Inc., 1960),
pp. 15-16.
[2] "*World Population Review*," *Population Bulletin*, Population
Reference Bureau, Inc., 15, No. 2 (Mar. 1959), p. 22, (As
quoted from the Preface of the United Nations Report,
"Future Growth of World Population.")

41

The term "population explosion" has rather recently come into common usage to describe this very rapid increase of persons on the face of the earth. Whether one regards this as a useful expression to describe the present and prospective increase of human beings on this planet, or thinks of it as scare psychology and a heavily loaded term, depends upon a number of factors. First among these is the individual's knowledge of demography and his ability to understand and appreciate demographic projections for the future. Relatively few, it may be noted, have either the knowledge or motivation for careful analysis of population predictions. Furthermore, the "man in the street" is quite understandably confused by the fact that the experts cannot reach agreement either on the future size of the world's population or the world's ability to support such a population.

The perception of the population situation is necessarily influenced by the individual's system of values, particularly philosophical and religious values—as Dr. Frank Lorimer has suggested. He states: "The treatment of the population question has been distorted by cultural conflicts, involving the confused interplay of scientific, religious, political and personal elements." [3] This is especially true in the controversy between those advocating contraception and exponents of Roman Catholic doctrine. But he continues: "The difference has been sharpened or embittered by incongruous political alliances, by intensification of in-group loyalties and out-group prejudices, and by impetuous actions that hamper cooperation of sincere persons seeking common goals." [4] The population problem thus presents three aspects of disagreement: over the probable future size of the world population, over ability to feed this population, and over methods of controlling population growth.

Population may increase in a specific nation for one or all of the following reasons: a decrease in the death rate, an increase in the birth rate and/or in immigration, and through annexation of territory. On the other hand a decrease in the birth rate or an increase in the death rate or less immigration would lower the population. *Fecundity* is the potential reproductive power of a people. *Fertility* is the actual reproduction. The latter is measured by the *crude birth*

[3] Frank Lorimer, "An Inquiry Concerning Some Ethical Principles Relating to Human Production," *Cross Currents*, 8 (Winter 1958), pp. 24-42.
[4] Lorimer, *op. cit.*

*rate* or the *net reproduction rate.* The crude birth rate refers to the number of births per 1,000 persons at a given period of time. The *specific* or *refined birth rate* is the number of births to 1,000 women in their childbearing period—usually between the ages of 15 and 44. The *net reproduction rate,* which is superior to the crude or refined birth rate, refers to the average number of daughters that will be born to every 100 female infants if birth and death rates at various age levels do not change. In speaking of fertility, the age and sex structure of a population is important. Since women bear children, the *sex ratio* at any given time influences the number of marriages that will occur. The *sex ratio* refers to the number of men for every 100 women in the population. The sex ratio most favorable for a maximum number of marriages is 120 to 140 men per every 100 women. But since women do not generally bear children after the age of about 44, a high proportion of women in age categories beyond 44 would mean a lowered fertility rate.

The *crude death rate* refers to the number of deaths per 1,000 persons in a population. Just as specific birth rates may be computed by considering age, sex, and other factors, so too *specific death rates* may be obtained. The third factor, *immigration,* refers to the number of persons who move into a country to take up permanent residence. Many factors are involved here, such as the willingness of the host country to receive immigrants, occupational opportunities there, poor economic or other undesirable conditions in the immigrants' native land, and other factors. Immigration, of course, is countered by *emigration.* This refers to the number of persons who move out of the country to take up permanent residence elsewhere. Emigration from Ireland during the last century reduced the population of that land, whereas heavy immigration increased the population of the United States.

However, there is no disagreement over the factors responsible for the present rapid increase in world population. In relatively recent years life expectancy has increased considerably. In ancient Egypt, Greece, or Rome the life expectancy of the average infant was only 30 years. By 1880 the life expectancy of a baby born in Massachusetts was 40 years. Today in Europe and other economically advanced areas infants have a life expectancy of about 70 years. It is possible to increase life expectancy most remarkably in those areas of the world which are underdeveloped. For example, the death rate in Ceylon has been cut in half since the end of the Second World War, and death rates in India, Malaya, and Thailand, as well as many other countries, have been cut by a third.[5] Since the drop in mortality rates has not been offset by a decline in the birth rates, populations continue to grow. In Ceylon the population is increasing at the rate of 2.8 per cent per year, which is a much higher rate of increase than was ever recorded in most European countries and sufficient to more than double the population every 25 years.[6]

The basic reasons for the decline in mortality are public health measures combined with better medical care. An excellent example of both of these measures is the control and treatment of malaria. Malaria was known in ancient Rome and came to be associated with low-lying swamplands. It was believed to be caused by breathing a miasma which arose at night from low, swampy areas. It was not until 2,000 years later that a French Army surgeon, Charles Louis Alphonse Laveran, discovered that malaria is caused by a specific parasite called plasmodium which invades the red blood cells. But the question remained as to how this parasite entered human blood cells. About 17 years later a British medical officer working in Calcutta, Sir Ronald Ross, was able to prove that the mosquito was the intermediate host for the plasmodium of malaria.

For a long time the principal means of treating malaria was a drug, quinine. This was first used by a Jesuit missionary in Peru in 1600. The principal source of this drug was Malaya, a Dutch possession. The chichona bark from which quinine is derived became unavailable to the Allies because of the Japanese occupation during World War II. As a result other medications were derived, particularly attabrine. This drug became the major treatment for malaria during the war. Since then research has provided several more drugs which are even more effective: chloroquine, amodiaquine, and pyrimethanine.

But public health measures have been even more fruitful in reducing the incidence of malaria. French attempts to build the Panama Canal were sorely handicapped by deaths from yellow fever and malaria. When this country undertook construction of the canal, Dr. William C. Gorgas, a major in the United States Army Medical

---

[5] *Population: An International Dilemma* (New York: The Population Council, 1958), pp. 3-6.
[6] *Population: An International Dilemma*, p. 6.

Corps, drained swamps and stagnant pools in which the mosquitoes bred, or poured oil upon them. As a result he decreased the malaria rate, which in 1906 was 821 per 1,000 workers, to 76 per 1,000 workers in 1913.[7]

The discovery of DDT, an insecticide which killed not only mosquitoes but flies and other disease-carrying insects, had a revolutionary impact on malaria and certain other diseases. In 1946 Ceylon's death rate was 20.2. In that year there were 12,578 deaths from malaria. But through the use of DDT, Ceylon's death rate had declined to 9.8 by 1956. In that year there were only 144 deaths from malaria.[8] While malaria has been used as an example of public health measures and medical care, many others could be provided along similar lines.

Maternal and infant mortality rates have been drastically reduced in many parts of the world by better prenatal care, asepsis measures, improved surgical techniques, and superior medical care. The infectious diseases of childhood have for the most part been brought under control, as well as the plagues that periodically killed off large numbers of people. While famine has not come under complete control, it is less frequent in most of the world than in the past.

## FOOD SUPPLY

The most famous, albeit neither the first nor the most original writer on the problem of population and food supply, was Thomas Robert Malthus, who published his first essay on this topic in 1798. The full title of the first edition is "An Essay on the Principle of Population as It Affects the Future Improvement of Society, with Remarks on the Speculations of Mr. Godwin, M. Condorcet, and Other Writers." A revised edition of this essay appeared in 1803. Malthus was a clergyman in the Church of England and became a Fellow at Cambridge University.

The major theme of his essay can be briefly summarized. He believed that the world's food supply increased in arithmetic progres-

[7] "World Wide War on Malaria," *Population Bulletin*, Population Reference Bureau, Inc., *14*, No. 1 (Mar. 1958), pp. 2-9.
[8] "World Wide War on Malaria," *Population Bulletin*, pp. 2-9.

sion—that is, one, two, three, four, etc.—while population increased by geometric progression—one, two, four, eight, etc. Thus, theoretically at least, the population could ultimately outrun the food supply. However, he believed that there were two types of factors which checked population growth: positive checks, such as poverty, disease, misery, and war; and preventive checks, such as delayed marriage, moral restraint, continence, and any other prudential restraint except birth control. While his essay was undoubtedly pessimistic, it sold very widely and was and still is considered an important contribution by some authorities. Malthus has been criticized because he did not see that food supply could be increased tremendously through technology, scientific farming, and better distribution. Neither was he aware of the fact that there is a tendency for the size of families to be reduced as they achieve a better standard of living. Nevertheless, it is theoretically possible that the population could outrun the food supply, and it is just this aspect of the population problem that has aroused so much controversy today.

At the present time, it is claimed, that about two-thirds of the world's population are underfed and as yet no way has been found to give them an adequate diet. It is true that the United States has considerable food, but if one year's U.S. surplus were distributed, it would only mean the equivalent of two teacupfuls of rice every 17 days for each of the 1.8 billion people who are hungry. This would mean only about 90 additional calories to their present per capita diet. Even if the entire world food supply, estimated at 800 million metric tons in 1956, were equitably distributed, every person in the world would be on short rations.[9] The Food and Agricultural Organization of the United Nations (FAO) surveyed the nutritional content of food available to more than half of the world's population in 1952. It stated:

> Today more than one-half of the people of the world do not get enough food for a healthy existence. They not only get too little food but their diet consists mainly of cereals and starchy foods. The average family in many countries cannot afford food such as meat, eggs and milk. The most serious deficiency in their diet is the lack of good quality protein. Protein malnutrition is the greatest single source of death in children between the ages of 1 and 5. Many adults die each year of deficiency diseases, such as beri-beri;

[9] "The World Food Supply," *Population Bulletin*, 15, No. 1 (Feb. 1959), p. 1.

others survive but show the results of malnutrition in their stunted growth, lack of energy, and low resistance to disease. In these parts of the world average life expectancy is about 30 years.[10]

In 1957 the United Nations published its report on the world social situation. It indicated that there will have to be a dramatic increase in food supplies to feed the populations of the world at current levels of consumption about 25 years from now. Supplies of cereals would have to be increased by some 300 million tons, or 43 per cent, and supplies of protective foods by even higher percentages. Some allowance will also have to be made for probable improvement in food consumption levels, and this will make the matter more difficult.[11]

Whether or not food supplies can be increased to this extent is not readily answered. There is little doubt that through technology the world's bread basket may yield even more food than it does today. Probably more cropland can be brought into cultivation, but since the best land is now under cultivation, new land which is less suitable can be cultivated only at a higher cost. Millions of acres of land are lost each year through soil erosion and others are taken out of agriculture for industry and expanding cities. Still, more efficient harvesting of the seas—for instance, algae farming—the use of solar energy for agriculture production, more efficient land use, and improved fertilization may help.[12] Huge quantities of food are lost between harvest and dinner table through insects, rodents, birds, and bacteria. The FAO states that in the United States alone insects, weeds, and plant diseases cause farmers a loss of 13 billion dollars each year, and in the entire world the quantity of rice and grain destroyed annually by rodents and insects equals the amount put on the world market.[13]

## OTHER NEEDS FOR A GROWING POPULATION

While attention is centered upon food supply—and this undoubtedly is the basic need—certain other factors are needed to

---

[10] "The World Food Supply," *Population Bulletin*, p. 8.
[11] "The World Food Supply," *Population Bulletin*, p. 11.
[12] "The World Food Supply," *Population Bulletin*, p. 1.
[13] "The World Food Supply," *Population Bulletin*, p. 12.

accommodate a growing population. One of these is housing. Another is schooling. As pointed out above, the population expansion has been most rapid in underdeveloped countries. The decline in infant and childhood mortality rates means that the proportion of children under 16 to older persons becomes greater in this part of the world than in the Western nations. When a population has a birth rate of 40 per 1,000 persons each year, the ratio of children under 16 to older persons becomes 40:60 rather than 25:75, as it is in most western nations. If these countries attempt to spend as much on the nurture and development of each child as developed countries do, the economic burden is impossible. It is met by cutting down expenditures on each child for his food and necessities, and compels children to begin productive labor at an earlier age. This naturally limits the child's educational achievements.[14]

The problem of a rapidly expanding population in underdeveloped areas is well expressed in the U.N. report on the world social situation:

> Rapid growth of population may complicate the problem of the economic and social development of underdeveloped countries in three principal ways. First, it can increase the pressure of population on land that is already densely settled and so retard increases in the productivity of agricultural labor. This effect is seen not only in agricultural countries where nearly all the cultivatable land is now occupied, but also in many under-developed countries where the density of population in cultivated areas is high, although large amounts of potentially productive land lie unused because of land ownership systems, lack of capital or techniques to exploit the land, or for other reasons.
>
> Second, accelerating population growth can aggravate the problem of capital shortage, which is one of the most important obstacles in the economic development of nearly all under-developed countries. The faster the population grows, the larger share of each year's income which must be invested in increasing the stock of productive equipment merely to maintain the existing level of equipment for workers. The larger the investments required for this purpose, the smaller the share of annual income that will be available either to raise the level of current consumption per capita, or to make investments which would increase the productivity and permit higher levels of consumption in the future.

[14] *Population: An International Dilemma* (New York: The Population Council, 1958), pp. 10-11.

Third, the high birth rate of under-developed countries creates a heavy load of dependent children for the working population. The percentages of children under 15 years of age in less developed countries of Asia, Africa, and Latin America are generally in the order of 40% or more of the total population, while the range of this ratio in European countries is from 20% to 30%. This difference is the consequence of higher birth rates in the former areas. The necessity of supporting so many children puts the workers of the under-developed countries at an added disadvantage in their efforts to save and invest in economic development. It also complicates the problem of providing the children with the education that is essential for social and economic advancement in the long run.[15]

In view of this evidence it appears clear that in certain parts of the world there is a serious population problem. Death rates have declined and reproduction rates have remained unchanged but more infants survive than in the past. When these children mature, the population growth will be accelerated because there will be more people living to an age when they can reproduce. Food supply is already short in some areas of the world and even if improved methods of agriculture succeed in raising food production considerably, this is not the only need such persons have. Housing, schooling, medical care, and many other kinds of needs will have to be met. It is a disservice to speak as though the only problem were food supply.

## CONTROL OF POPULATION GROWTH

Efforts to control the growth of population are not new. In primitive societies—even in ancient Greece and Rome—*infanticide* (the killing of infants, especially girl infants, by exposure or other methods) existed. Certain types of contraceptives were apparently known even to ancient peoples. On the other hand some nations at times have attempted to raise their rates of reproduction, notably Nazi Germany and Italy under Mussolini. The culture of a people or the culture of the period in which they live may strongly influence the birth rate. For example, in medieval Europe certain factors

---

[15] Robert C. Cook, ed., "Report from the World Social Situation," (New York: United Nations Bureau of Social Affairs, 1957), 15: pp. 32-33.

operated which limited fertility. Universal marriage was not required because of prevailing social conditions, nor did they impel men and women to have children as early as possible or reward large families. In the absence of an extended family the individual husband assumed full responsibility for the support of his wife and children, and there were strong social pressures against improvident marriages. Those who entered military life had to postpone marriage and those who entered religious orders had to forego it. Sons who would inherit the land were not encouraged to marry young and servants were expected to remain single. In fact, there were often rules against the marriage of domestics. In the 16th and 17th centuries edicts existed in many German states against the marriage of paupers.[16]

At the time of the potato famines in Ireland during the 1840's the country was seriously overpopulated. As a result millions emigrated, reducing the population to such an extent that Ireland still has fewer persons than it had in the middle of the last century. In 1941, 63 per cent of the women between 25 and 29 years of age in Ireland were still unmarried.[17] On the other hand in some parts of the world, notably Asia, early marriage is common. In most of Asia the traditional family is the extended or joint family. In such cultures the procreation and nurture of a son who will eventually take over his father's prerogatives is required, and this is often a religious obligation. Girls are married about the time of puberty and childbearing begins shortly afterward. But the practice of family limitation is a highly individual matter, adopted by the people themselves for personal motives and not for reasons of national advantage.[18] In other words, fertility cannot be divorced from the cultural values stemming from religious, economic, political, and social factors. So it still remains a moot question whether any of the family-limitation methods urged by advocates of birth control will really function in certain cultures.

Among the methods of birth control in use throughout the world today are artificial contraception, the rhythm method, abortion and sterilization, and coitus interruptus. More recently the discovery of a pill, Enovid, which controls the menstrual cycle, may come into general use. *Artificial contraception* involves the use of mechanical

[16] *Population: An International Dilemma*, pp. 16-17.
[17] *Population: An International Dilemma*, p. 21.
[18] *Population: An International Dilemma*, pp. 24-25.

or chemical methods to prevent the union of ovum and sperm. None of these are absolutely foolproof, some of them are expensive, and all of them require adequate knowledge of their use. The *rhythm method* requires abstinence from sex relations during that period of the month when the woman is likely to become pregnant. Among women who menstruate regularly, who keep careful track of their menstrual periods, and who, along with their husbands, are willing to practice abstinence during the required periods, the rhythm method is relatively effective. But it is doubtful that it is feasible in backward countries where persons are poorly educated and unable to keep track of the menstrual cycle. Even when devices such as colored beads are used to indicate the safe period, rhythm has been something less than satisfactory.

*Abortion* in this context refers to the destruction of a viable fetus before it "comes to term" (can live outside the womb) by means of an operation. In Japan the government permits abortions and the number reported rose from 246,000 in 1949 to 1,068,000 in 1953. It is believed that if the unreported abortions were added, the total may have been much higher than that of live births. In 1934 in Moscow, when the Communists permitted abortions, there were 270 per 1,000 births. The abortion clinics were closed in 1936.[19]

*Sterilization* in the male involves a somewhat simple operation called a "vasectomy," which makes the passage of sperm impossible. In the female it is somewhat more complicated and involves an abdominal operation in which the fallopian tubes are tied off. In Puerto Rico more than 10 per cent of the mothers arrange for sterilization after having borne their third, fourth, fifth, or later child.[20] *Coitus interruptus* refers to the interruption of the sex act to prevent deposit of sperm before it can reach the ovum.

RELIGIOUS   ATTITUDES   TOWARDS
FAMILY   LIMITATION

When world population problems are discussed, the Roman Catholic Church frequently suffers criticism because of her stand on

[19] *Population: An International Dilemma*, p. 29.
[20] *Population: An International Dilemma*, p. 24.

artificial contraception, sterilization, and abortion. The Catholic Church considers artificial contraception contrary to natural law because it frustrates the end of the act, which is the union of ovum and sperm. However, this does not mean that in every sex relationship the sperm must impregnate the ovum. Rather it means that no artificial barriers must be put in the way of this occurrence. Under these circumstances the Church permits rhythm when there is an adequate reason. The Catholic Church considers abortion willful murder and direct sterilization an unjustifiable mutilation.

But in terms of world population growth, the stand of the Catholic Church has had little impact. Those areas of the world in which the greatest population pressures exist, with the exception of Latin America, are India, Ceylon, China, Japan, and parts of Africa, where Christianity—Protestant or Catholic—is relatively weak numerically and where the important religious bodies are Hinduism, Buddhism, and Mohammedanism. Therefore, in discussing religious values and population growths it is necessary to include the positions of Hinduism, Buddhism, and Mohammedanism towards marriage and parenthood.

There are probably about 300 million Hindus in the world. Within this religion there are strong pro-fertility elements and a male-centered view of life, with a belief in reincarnation—which makes sons important because they must pray for their ancestors and deliver them from hell. At the same time it tends to relegate women chiefly to their childbearing functions. However, there are elements such as asceticism which urge men to rise above desire for sons, wealth, and domination. Gandhi was strongly opposed to birth control, with the exception of complete abstinence, and considered contraception morally equivalent to prostitution. He seemed to regard periodic continence the same way.[21] Today, however, there is evidence that Indian opinion moves toward the support of family limitation. Buddhism has somewhere between 300 and 350 million members. It does not deal much with the doctrine of parenthood, at least in terms of family limitation. In fact, its viewpoint seems calculated to discourage fertility.

Mohammedans number between 350 and 400 million persons. They are found in Asia and northern Africa, and at the present time

---

[21] Fagley, *op. cit.,* pp. 96-98.

this religion seems to be spreading faster than Christianity in many parts of Africa. Islam is rooted in the patriarchal tradition and in the past afforded almost unrestricted marital opportunities for the Arab male. Fagley believes that parenthood in the ethos of Islam might generally be described as "procreation unlimited." Recently as a result of population pressures, efforts have been made by some Islamic scholars to find evidence to support voluntary family limitation. In March, 1953, the Fatwa Committee of Azher University in Cairo, an influential group of scholars of Moslem canon law stated:

> The use of medicine to prevent pregnancy temporarily is not forbidden by religion, especially if repeated pregnancies weaken the woman due to insufficient intervals for her to rest and regain her health. The Koran said 'Allah desireth for you ease; he desireth not hardship for you . . .' But the use of medicine to prevent pregnancy absolutely and permanently is forbidden by religion.[22]

While communism strictly speaking is not a religion, and in fact is antireligious, its values have been accepted by or imposed upon millions of persons. Since at present it is the dominant system of thought in China, it at least deserves mention. Karl Marx attacked Malthusianism as a product of decadent capitalism. But countries under communist control have followed myriad and changing patterns regarding family limitation. In 1954 when it became clear that the Chinese population was increasing at the rate of about 12 million per year, talk of family limitation began. By 1958 the new theory of population was under attack. Whatever population policy the communist countries ultimately settle upon will be of extreme importance to population growth in the future.

### JUDAISM AND CHRISTIANITY

In the Western world, Judaism has had a tremendous impact upon Christianity. In early Hebrew times there was strong emphasis upon fertility, and celibacy was excluded. Some indications of this can be seen in the custom of the *levirate*, by which a brother had to marry the widow of an older brother if he died childless. This was true

---

[22] Fagley, *op. cit.*, pp. 103-4.

even if he were already married and had to divorce his wife. There was strong emphasis upon the family name and a burning desire that it should not die out in Israel, a type of immortality achieved through preserving the family name. Throughout the Old Testament there are injunctions to be fruitful and multiply, first given to Adam, repeated to Noah, and then to Jacob. For a woman, being barren was considered a divine reproach or at least an affliction. The action of *Onan*, probably coitus interruptus, was strongly condemned—in fact the Lord slew him for it. All authorities do not agree with this interpretation but some believe this attitude was the result of the early plight of the Israelites, when their numbers were few, their enemies many, and their land poor. Be that as it may, the older tradition of Judaism strongly favored fertility.

Even in later Judaism the pro-fertility orientation of the Old Testament is continued. Maurice Kertzer in his book *What is a Jew?* says that a home without children is believed by the Jews to be a home without blessing. Rabbi Hertz stated that celibacy is contrary to nature.[23] As a result of urbanization, however, certain changes have occurred among Jews. Today it is apparently sufficient for a family to have two children. But in the Orthodox viewpoint, according to Willey Hochman, "Jewish tradition and viewpoint cannot consider planned parenthood for social or economic reasons." [24] The Conservative and Reformed rabbis, however, do consider such reasons.

The Rabbinical Assembly, the conservative body in the United States, stated in 1935:

> Careful study and observation have convinced us that birth control is a valuable method for overcoming some of the obstacles that prevent the proper functioning of the family under present conditions. . . . Proper education in contraception and birth control will not destroy, but rather enhance, the spiritual values inherent in the family and will make for the advancement of human happiness and welfare.[25]

The Catholic position has been ably explained by Rev. John L. Thomas, S.J. He states that in a world established by creative intelligence and revealed in the inherent purpose of things, this purpose is discovered by observing their normal tendencies and operations.

[23] Fagley, *op. cit.*, pp. 119-21.
[24] Fagley, *op. cit.*, p. 122.
[25] Fagley, *op. cit.*, p. 122.

Man is a creature endowed with reason and will achieve development and perfection of his nature by choosing things in accordance with the order established by the Creator. God alone is the author and source of life, and He did not give man faculties for furnishing the co-principles of life, and then keeping them entirely under his absolute dominion. Sex has been entrusted to man for the good of the species and right reason demands that it be employed accordingly. But it is also a manifestation of conjugal love and creativity. Birth control, and by this he means artificial contraception, is considered wrong not because its effect is the prevention of conception, but because the act is considered contrary to right reason. "Marriage partners who use birth control do not act as reasonable persons since they will to perform an act essentially implying the fulfillment of this initial stage, yet at the same time they do not will its fulfillment." He considers this action a contradiction of practical order and a violation of right reason.

In writing of sterilization he distinguishes two types—direct and indirect. Direct sterilization is considered morally wrong by Roman Catholics. However, indirect sterilization is a different matter and the principle of totality applies here. By totality he means that an individual has the right to use the services of his organism as a whole and consequently may allow individual parts to be destroyed or mutilated when and to the extent necessary for the good of his entire being. In other words, in the face of cancer or some other serious condition it would be possible to operate, removing the malignancy as the first purpose, even though the second result would be the sterilization of the person involved.

Against this background it is possible to discuss the use of the so-called fertility pill. To date no official position has been taken by the Church on this matter, although many theologians have written about it. Thomas believes that if the pill were used for purposes of direct sterilization, the action would be morally wrong; but if the use of the pill resulted in indirect sterilization, the principle of totality would apply. For example, he believes that the pill could at least be legitimately used to eliminate malfunctions or pathological conditions in the human system, even if the secondary effect were temporary or permanent sterilization.

The Catholic Church is also opposed to abortion. This includes therapeutic abortion. However, in the case of an ectopic pregnancy, where the ovum is fertilized, remains in the fallopian tubes, and cannot come to terms, it is possible to operate and remedy a diseased condition, even though the ultimate fate of the fertilized ovum is extinction.[26]

Pius XII has indicated that rhythm may be practiced temporarily, or even perhaps permanently for grave reasons such as health of the wife or certain serious social indications (and by this it is generally construed to mean the family already has more children than it can reasonably support). The justification for rhythm is based upon the fact that it does not artificially interfere with the end of the act. Roman Catholic teaching is that the ends of marriage are the procreation of the human race, the rearing or education of children, and the development of mutual affection between spouses. The primary end of marriage, however, is the procreation and education of children. Procreation takes priority in the end of the marital act. Here there is a divergence in some of the Jewish thought cited, and a divergence in some of the Protestant thought that will be cited.

While this may seem like rather elaborate causistry to the non-Catholic, it is based upon very logical development from the early days of the Church. As Thomas has put it,

> The different aspects of a man's personality tend to be interrelated: one cannot except the important area of sexual activity from control while expecting the individual to display these same qualities in other sectors of human behavior. The control of man's basic drive is according to the order of reason and constitutes a necessary pre-condition both of personal development and productive social endeavor.[27]

In concluding these remarks on the Catholic position (which out of necessity have been considerably streamlined), it is not a position of irresponsible parenthood, nor does the Roman Catholic Church forbid birth control. The rhythm method is likewise a type of birth control, and under certain conditions, if both husband and wife agree, they may live in complete continence. Admittedly, this is extremely difficult and for the vast majority of couples entirely unlikely.

It is rather difficult to explain the Protestant position because as Dr. John Bennett has put it, Protestants can be expected to dis-

---

[26] John L. Thomas, *Daedalus*, 88 (Summer 1959), pp. 444-50.
[27] Thomas, *op. cit.*, pp. 450-451.

agree on many issues. Usually they favor the use of contraceptives, but advise married couples to use them conscientiously, and although they have given much less thought to this aspect of the problem, they generally favor government policies making effective contraception available to the population as a whole. They likewise believe that in the two purposes of the marital act—the expression of love between a husband and wife, and the procreation of the children—one should not be subordinated to the other. In other words, the expression of love shall not be subordinated to procreation. But neither do Protestants believe that birth control should be practiced as an escape from parenthood in normal marriage.[28]

Among American Protestant denominations—including the Methodist, the United Lutheran Church, and the Augustana Lutheran Church—there have been decisive statements on this matter. But the Anglican bishops have gradually changed their position. On the basis of the Lambeth Conferences in 1908, they spoke out strongly against the use of contraceptives. In 1920, while still opposed, Bishop Kirk, a leading Anglican authority on moral theology, sensed the beginnings of permissiveness on this subject. By 1930 the bishops had given clear permission for the conscientious use of contraceptives, and spoke out even more forthrightly in 1958 in presenting the case for birth control.[29]

The 1958 report of the Lambeth Conference states that marriage has three functions: "the procreation of children, the fulfillment and completion of husband and wife in each other, and the establishment of a stable environment in which the deepest truths about human relationship can be expressed and communicated and children can grow up seeing and learning what mature life is really like."[30] The relative importance of the three functions is not quite clear from the report, but it does state that all other duties and relationships in marriage are not to be subordinated to procreation. So it seems to be critical of a tradition which it had taught for a long time, i.e., that procreation was the sole or principal purpose of marriage. In approving family planning in 1928 the Conference stated that it should be done in ways acceptable to both husband

---

[28] John Bennett, *Daedalus*, 88 (Summer 1959), pp. 456-57.
[29] Bennett, *op. cit.*, p. 457.
[30] Rev. D. Sherwin Bailey, "The Lambeth Conference and the Family," *Eugenics Review*, 50, No. 4 (Jan. 1959), p. 239.

and wife, in Christian conscience. Induced abortions, however, are forbidden unless dictated by strict and undeniable medical necessity.

Dr. Bennett believes that in principle Protestants would support state laws for the sterilization of those whose genetic unfitness is clear. But at the same time he admits the danger in this type of human engineering as it gains momentum. He believes it could constitute a threat to individual liberty.

To summarize these statements, it seems that Hinduism and Islam both lean toward the pro-fertility orientation, although certain changes are now occurring. The position of the Buddhists regarding family limitation seems to be a passive one. Orthodox Jews seem generally opposed to family limitation, although the Conservative and Reformed bodies appear to accept it within limits. Roman Catholics—and, incidentally, Orthodox Catholics as well—still oppose contraception, whereas Protestant bodies have changed their original positions for the most part and now approve of family planning. Regardless of an individual's own conviction in these matters, it must be noted that any attempts to urge contraception, sterilization or abortion will run counter to some of the world's great religions. Furthermore, as noted earlier, such techniques will not be sufficient to control population growth unless supported by social and economic measures to provide more food, education and other essentials of life.

On the basis of available scientific estimates, it seems clear that there is a population problem and that it is acute in certain parts of the world. There is no point in denying this although there seems little point in exaggerating it or trying to employ scare techniques. Interreligious relations and world problems will not be improved by the type of bitter controversy which has sometimes prevailed in some quarters. In a democratic society, we must be prepared to tolerate the values of those with whom we do not agree, unless the toleration of such values would result in disaster. Although many Protestant denominations have supported the use of contraceptives in family planning, it should be emphasized that none of them have done so without a word of caution. They all seem to believe that parenthood should be one of the purposes of marriage and that such parenthood should be responsible. The position of the Roman Catholic Church is that parenthood should normally be the purpose of marriage, and such parenthood should also be responsible.

## THE IMPACT OF RELIGION ON FERTILITY

So far the philosophical and theological positions of the various religious denominations regarding birth control have been explored. To what extent do such values influence the birth rate of married couples? This will be viewed in two ways: first, the extent to which any kind of birth control is employed, including periodic abstinence or rhythm; and second, the actual family size in terms of religious background. This material is based upon interviews with 2,713 white married women between the ages of 18 and 39 (inclusive) living with their husbands or separated on a temporary basis because of the husband's being in the Armed Forces.[31]

The two factors which show the closest association with the family planning patterns of American couples are religion and education. While the majority of couples—Catholics, Protestants or Jews—have used some method of avoiding conception, the number is highest among Jews, next highest among Protestants, and lowest among Catholics. Among all Catholic wives in the study, 41 per cent had never practiced birth control and 28 per cent had used rhythm only, although 31 per cent had used other methods in addition to rhythm.[32] While the proportion of those who use some form of birth control is considerably lower among Catholics than among Protestants in all age groups, the difference decreases as age increases. In mixed religious marriages the religion of the wife is more closely associated with birth control practices. In a Catholic wife-Protestant husband marriage, the number who use some form of contraception is close to that of Catholic couples. In the opposite situation, the proportion of those using some form of birth control is some-

---

[31] From *Family Planning, Sterility, and Population Growth* by Ronald Freedman, Pascal Whelpton, and Arthur A. Campbell. Copyright 1959. McGraw-Hill Book Company, Inc. (p. 10). Used by permission.
[32] Freedman, Whelpton, and Campbell, *op. cit.*, p. 210.

what closer to that of Protestant couples. In view of this, the wife's religion was used as the index of religious affiliation for the couple in most of this study. Another interesting aspect is that Catholics who attend church regularly are less likely to use some form of birth control than those who do not. On the other hand, Protestants who attend church regularly are more likely to employ some form of birth control. The authors of this study believe that Catholics who attend church regularly come in contact with religious leaders and laity who express values unfavorable to family limitation, and particularly to artificial birth control. Protestants who attend church regularly are less likely to hear this issue discussed, and insofar as there is discussion it is likely to be favorable to family planning.

The theory that Catholic-Protestant differences over the use of family limitation methods merely indicate differences in economic or educational status, and that Catholic fertility practices will approximate those of Protestants as Catholics ascend the socio-economic scale, is not supported by the findings of this study. It was also found that Jewish Users began the practice of family limitation earliest, Protestant Users earlier than Catholics, and Catholic Users relatively late.[33]

Many other sociological factors were investigated in this study, such as the education of wife and husband, the husband's income and occupation, whether the wife worked outside the home, and the type of community involved; but religion, along with education, remained the most important factor in determining whether the family used some type of family limitation.

While Catholic wives used some form of family limitation to a lesser extent than Protestant and Jewish wives, the average number of births among Protestant and Catholic wives born between 1916 and 1920 was identical—2.6. This was also true for Protestant and Catholic wives born between 1931 and 1937, the average number of births in 1955 being 1.1. However, the most likely expected lifetime total births of these women will vary. Catholic wives born in the period 1916-1920 will most likely have an average of 3.1 total births, while Protestant wives will have 2.8. Among the wives born between 1931-37, Catholic wives will average 3.8 births, to 2.9 among

---

[33] Freedman, Whelpton, and Campbell, *op. cit.*, pp. 107-10.

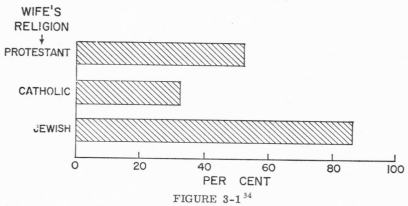

PERCENTAGE OF USERS
BEGINNING CONTRACEPTION
BEFORE FIRST PREGNANCY

FIGURE 3-1 [34]

Protestants. The reason that Catholic wives had not borne more children than Protestant wives at the time of the interview was due primarily to their later marriages. They tended to be an average of 1.5 years older than Protestants and as a result had been married a shorter period of time.[35]

## THE EDUCATIONAL IMPACT ON FERTILITY

The degree of association between the use of some type of birth control and education is more pronounced among Protestant wives than among Catholic wives, although differentials do exist among the latter. For example, among college graduates only 10 per cent of Protestant wives had never used any type of birth control compared with 38 per cent of Catholic wives in this category. Only 4 per cent of Protestant wives compared to 42 per cent of Catholic wives who had completed college used rhythm. On the other hand, in this category 86 per cent of Protestant wives but only 20 per cent of Catholic,

[34] Adapted from Freedman, Whelpton, and Campbell, *op. cit.*, p. 110.
[35] Freedman, Whelpton, and Campbell, *op. cit.*, p. 275.

wives had used other methods of contraception, meaning rhythm and others. Among those wives who had completed high school 74 per cent of Protestants had used other methods of contraception compared to 29 per cent of Catholic wives. Among Protestant wives with 1 to 3 years of high school, 63 per cent have used other methods, among Catholic wives in this category, 38 per cent was the figure. On the grade school level 46 per cent of Protestant wives but only 25 per cent of Catholic wives have used other methods of contraception.[36] Among Catholic wives it is interesting that the greatest conformity to the teachings of the Church regarding birth control is found among college-educated women. The least conformity is found among those who have attended high school for 1 to 3 years, rather than among grade school women.[37]

But all wives who attend high school for 1 to 3 years had an average of 2.1 births by 1955, compared to an average of 1.8 both for wives who had completed college and wives who had completed high school. On the other hand the wives who had only completed grade school had an average of 2.9 births in 1955.

## INCOME AND OCCUPATIONAL IMPACT ON FERTILITY

Most couples in all income groups practiced some type of family limitation, but the number increased with the husband's annual income. However, it should be remembered that income generally increases with age, and age is also associated with the use of preventive measures. The greatest difference in the number of persons who used birth control measures and those who did not occurred between the lowest income group, earning under $3,000 a year, and the next higher group.

For example, 79 per cent of those wives whose husband's income was $6,000 or more employed some type of family limitation; in the $5,000-$5,999 category, 76 per cent; in the $4,000-$4,999 category, 72 per cent; in the $3,000-$3,999 category 69 per cent; and those under

---

[36] Freedman, Whelpton, and Campbell, *op. cit.*, pp. 200-201.
[37] Freedman, Whelpton, and Campbell, *op. cit.*, p. 199.

TABLE 3-1[38]

PERCENTAGE WHO ARE USERS, FOR ALL COUPLES AND FECUND
COUPLES, BY WIFE'S AGE, BY HUSBAND'S INCOME

| Wife's age | Total | Husband's income | | | | |
|---|---|---|---|---|---|---|
| | | $6,000 or more | $5,000-$5,999 | $4,000-$4,999 | $3,000-$3,999 | Under $3,000 |
| | | | *All couples* | | | |
| Total | 70 | 79 | 76 | 72 | 69 | 58 |
| 18-24 | 68 | 82 | 78 | 72 | 73 | 62 |
| 25-29 | 73 | 84 | 79 | 72 | 74 | 59 |
| 30-34 | 73 | 82 | 77 | 78 | 70 | 59 |
| 35-39 | 65 | 75 | 72 | 68 | 60 | 52 |
| | | | *Fecund couples* | | | |
| Total | 83 | 93 | 90 | 85 | 83 | 71 |
| 18-24 | 71 | 87 | 82 | 75 | 76 | 64 |
| 25-29 | 84 | 93 | 90 | 83 | 86 | 73 |
| 30-34 | 90 | 94 | 92 | 94 | 91 | 79 |
| 35-39 | 90 | 95 | 98 | 93 | 81 | 86 |

$3,000, 58 per cent. The earlier initial use of birth control measures
was likewise associated with higher income.[39]

While there were differences in the number of births according to
the husband's income, these differences were small. By 1955, wives
whose husbands made $7,000 or more annually averaged 2.3 births;
those whose husbands made under $3,000 a year averaged 2.0 births.
Even if the average number of births most likely to be had by such
couples is computed, the difference is still not great. In the $7,000-a-
year-or-more category, 2.9 is the most likely average number of births,
whereas for those under 3,000 it is 3.2.[40]

The best way to determine differentials in birth rates associated
with occupations would be to examine the size of the families of
men engaged in specific occupations. In this study the sample was too
small to do this. Therefore, the investigators set up five categories of
workers; upper-white-collar—which included proprietors, managers,
officials and professional workers; lower-white-collar—salesmen, clerks,

---

[38] Adapted from Freedman, Whelpton, and Campbell, *op. cit.*, p. 124.

[39] Freedman, Whelpton, and Campbell, *op. cit.*, p. 124.

[40] Freedman, Whelpton, and Campbell, *op. cit.*, pp. 295-96.

and kindred workers; upper-blue-collar—craftsmen, foremen, and kindred workers; lower-blue-collar—operatives and kindred workers, service workers, and non-farm laborers; and farm workers—which included farmers, farm managers, and farm laborers.

TABLE 3-2[41]

PERCENTAGE WHO ARE USERS, FOR ALL COUPLES AND FECUND COUPLES, BY WIFE'S AGE, BY HUSBAND'S OCCUPATION

| Wife's age | Total | Husband's occupation | | | | | |
| | | Upper white collar | Lower white collar | Upper blue collar | Lower blue collar | Farm | Others |
|---|---|---|---|---|---|---|---|
| | | | | All couples | | | |
| Total | 70 | 81 | 76 | 69 | 62 | 63 | 70 |
| 18-24 | 68 | 81 | 72 | 68 | 66 | 58 | 64 |
| 25-29 | 73 | 87 | 82 | 69 | 65 | 67 | 71 |
| 30-34 | 73 | 82 | 86 | 70 | 64 | 64 | 83 |
| 35-39 | 65 | 76 | 60 | 68 | 53 | 60 | — |
| | | | | Fecund couples | | | |
| Total | 83 | 92 | 90 | 84 | 77 | 73 | 75 |
| 18-24 | 71 | 81 | 76 | 74 | 67 | 58 | 69 |
| 25-29 | 84 | 94 | 92 | 81 | 77 | 78 | 80 |
| 30-34 | 90 | 93 | 98 | 91 | 84 | 83 | — |
| 35-39 | 90 | 95 | 97 | 93 | 86 | 74 | — |

Eighty-one per cent of the wives whose husbands were upper-white-collar workers used some type of family limitation, 76 per cent of those whose husbands were lower-white-collar, 69 per cent of the upper-blue-collar, 62 per cent of the lower-blue-collar, and 63 per cent of farm workers. On this basis it seems clear that, except between the lower-blue-collar workers and the farm workers, there is a steady increase in the number of wives who use some form of birth control as the status of the husband's occupation increases.[42]

Once again, however, the average number of births for wives whose husbands are in the various occupational categories noted above was

---

[41] Adapted from Freedman, Whelpton, and Campbell, *op. cit.*, p. 133.

[42] Freedman, Whelpton, and Campbell, *op. cit.*, pp. 132-33.

not very great. By 1955, wives of the upper-white-collar workers had an average of 1.9 births, and the same figure was true for the lower-white-collar category. In the lower-blue-collar category by 1955 there had been an average of 2.2 births, and among the farm workers, 2.7.[43]

The working wife has become common since World War II. The proportion of wives in the labor force increased from 21 per cent in 1947 to 30 per cent in 1956. Even among mothers of pre-school children the percentage of wives in the labor force increased from 11 per cent to 16 per cent during that period. Thirty-six per cent of mothers of school age children were working in 1956. When a wife is employed outside the home it is highly likely that she will have a completely planned fertility. "Among Fecund Users, 42 per cent of the working wives but only 25 per cent of the non-working wives have completely planned fertility. The proportion with such planned fertility also increases with the number of years the wife has worked since marriage."[44]

It is interesting to note that couples with working wives are much more likely to have completely planned fertility, and this is not the result of other factors such as the wife's education, the husband's income, or the wife's religion. It seems clear that a large number have avoided pregnancy because the birth of a child would interfere with the wife's employment outside the home.[45]

## SITUATIONAL-VALUE APPROACH

From the previous discussion, situational factors producing an expanding population are clear. First, there has been a relatively sudden and sharp decrease in the mortality rate because of public health measures and better medical care. This applies particularly to underdeveloped or newly developing countries in which the life expectancy was formerly quite low. At the same time there was no change in the birth rate. In the United States following the close of World War II, millions of men returned home to resume family life, and millions

[43] Freedman, Whelpton, and Campbell, *op. cit.*, p. 306.
[44] Freedman, Whelpton, and Campbell, *op. cit.*, pp. 137-38.
[45] Freedman, Whelpton, and Campbell, *op. cit.*, pp. 137-38.

who had delayed marriage because of service in the Armed Forces now took brides. Furthermore, the average age at marriage for both American males and females had decreased by about two years since the early forties. With the number of marriages high and the age at marriage lower, the birth rate increased.

In certain Asian, African, and Latin American countries there has always been a fairly high birth rate because of the prevailing value systems. Hindus, as was pointed out, consider the birth of a son to be a religious obligation. Furthermore, they have strong prohibitions against family limitation. The same has been true of Mohammedans. Current conditions in the United States, however, are less readily explained. During the 1930's and because of the economic depression, marriages were delayed and the values of the middle and upper classes were largely in favor of family limitation. The birth control movement (later the Planned Parenthood movement) became relatively prevalent.

Since the close of World War II, there have been indications that young married couples, while not entirely opposed to family limitation, have changed their attitudes toward the size of the family desired. Today, three, four, and even more children are acceptable. Whether this will continue cannot presently be determined. There is as yet no indication of a sizable decrease in the American birth rate.

An expanding population requires more food, more housing, and more extensive educational and medical facilities. In a country capable of supplying such, an economic boom results. In a nation unable to meet these requirements, there may be a serious overpopulation problem.

## REMEDIAL MEASURES

Many approaches to an overpopulation problem, where it exists, may be undertaken. Obviously, increased production of food, better distribution of food supplies, more housing, and more educational and medical facilities must be provided. For certain countries where the situation is now critical or promises to become so in the immediate future on the basis of children already born, some morally permissible methods of family limitation may have to be employed temporarily. But no single approach to overpopulation is in itself adequate. Those who focus attention exclusively upon family limitation are employing a unilateral approach just as are those who talk of nothing but increasing the food supply. In either case, there is always the danger that a combination of approaches essential to the reduction or solution to any social problem will be overlooked while propaganda and action programs centering upon one aspect of solution are emphasized to the detriment of others.

One hopeful approach to overpopulation rests in emigration from such countries to those areas of the world where population density is much lower. However, there are certain problems in this solution which render it something less than a panacea.

The argument that even large-scale emigration would fail in the long run to relieve population pressure depends mainly upon the premise that the death rate in poverty-ridden, heavily populated countries is kept at a high level partly by the excessive size of the population, which hinders the attainment of the per capita income level necessary for the maintenance of health. If the pressure of numbers upon population is alleviated by emigration, the argument runs, the relief will be only temporary, for a falling death rate and the rising rate of natural population growth will eventually replace the immigrants with as many more survivors. It is claimed that the birth rate may rise as the result of emigration.

Such arguments are not universally accepted because some writers maintain that emigration from the countries under consideration will not only reduce the population by the actual number of emigrants but will also tend to reduce the amount of natural increase in the remaining population, since emigrants usually belong to the most fertile age groups. So far as practical obstacles to large-scale immigration are concerned there is less room for disagreement. It is difficult to persuade the desired number of people to emigrate, even though their condition in the homeland is poor and they are offered substantial assistance in re-establishing themselves elsewhere. It is also difficult to find suitable areas in which immigrants are welcome. Everywhere there are restrictions on immigration, and the countries that desire immigrants are anxious to receive persons with certain skills and occupational aptitudes that are in very short supply in the poorest and most densely populated countries. No country is willing to accept large numbers of immigrants within a short period. Yet only a very large volume of immigration can significantly alter the rate of population growth and the social and economic conditions in many of the more heavily populated countries. Millions would have to emigrate from India and China every year to neutralize the natural increase. But the practice of countries of immigration to select immigrants from certain ethnic groups further limits the immigration outlets. Few countries welcome large-scale immigration, for example, from Asian or Caribbean countries.

Some believe that a program of emigration combined with other means of checking population growth and increasing economic opportunities may be of real assistance. Davis claims that if in the next 30 years 6 million persons could emigrate annually from India and 2 million annually from Pakistan, the natural increase of population in those countries would be cancelled during that period. This would provide for these countries to industrialize without the hindrance of a constant increase in the number of mouths to be fed, and would create conditions favorable to a falling birth rate. But in the long run emigration would have to help bring the birth rate under control in order to have a lasting effect upon the standard of living. Davis admits that emigration on the scale hypothesized is a practical impossibility.

## REVIEW QUESTIONS

1. Under what circumstances do populations increase and under what circumstances do populations decrease in various countries?
2. In using measurements of population increase or decrease, why is the reproduction rate superior to the crude or refined death rates?
3. What are the major reasons for the present overpopulation in certain parts of the world?
4. Who was Thomas Robert Malthus? What was his analysis of the population problem?
5. How did Malthus propose to relieve overpopulation?
6. To what extent could surplus food in America satisfy the world demand?
7. What specific methods could be employed to increase world food supply?
8. What are the most common methods of birth control in use today in the world?

9. Discuss the attitudes of the world's great religions toward family limitation, including those of Roman Catholicism, Protestantism, Judaism, Hinduism, Mohammedanism and Buddhism.
10. What is the attitude of communist countries toward birth control?
11. What appear to be the most important factors influencing family limitation in the United States?
12. Evaluate emigration from overpopulated countries as a possible solution to overpopulation.

## SELECTED READINGS

*Articles*

Burch, Thomas K., "Post-War Japan: A Case Study in Population Policy in Social Disorganization," *American Catholic Sociological Review*, 19 (Mar. 1958), 45-53.

Canisia, Sister Mary, "Family Size of the Catholic Graduate," *American Catholic Sociological Review*, 10 (June 1949), 101-6.

Dinkel, Robert M., "Occupation and Fertility in the United States," *American Sociological Review*, 17 (Apr. 1952), 178-82.

Dougherty, Frederick J. and C. J. Nuesse, "Differentials in Catholic Opinion on the Admission of Displaced Persons," *American Catholic Sociological Review*, 12 (Dec. 1951), 202-16.

Durand, John B., "Mortality Estimates from Roman Tombstone Descriptions," *American Journal of Sociology*, 65 (Jan. 1960), 365-73.

Hauser, Philip N., "Demography in Relation to Sociology," *American Journal of Sociology*, 65 (Sept. 1959), 169-73.

——, "Present Status and Prospects of Research of Population," *American Sociological Review*, 13 (Aug. 1948), 371-82.

Mayer, Albert J. and Sue Marx, "Social Change, Religion, and Birth Rates," *American Journal of Sociology*, 62 (Nov. 1956), 338-90.

Mulvaney, B. G., "Post-Depression Fertility in the United States," *American Catholic Sociological Review*, 14 (June 1953), 84-93.

Westoff, Charles F., Eliot G. Mishler, and Lowell Kelly, "Preferences in Size of Family and Eventual Fertility 20 Years After," *American Journal of Sociology*, 62 (Mar. 1957), 491-97.

Woofter, T. J., "Factors Sustaining the Birth Rate," *American Sociological Review*, 14 (June 1949), 357-66.

"World Population in Transition," *The Annals*, 237 (Jan. 1955). Students are to refer to the population bulletins published by Population

Reference Bureau, Inc. "Statistical Abstracts of the United States" are published yearly by the U.S. Dept. of Commerce, Bureau of the Census, and are recommended for current data on U.S. population. (Note: All references to *The Annals* throughout this book refer to *The Annals of the American Academy of Political and Social Science*.)

## Books

Fagley, Richard M., *The Population Explosion and Christian Responsibility*. New York: Oxford University Press, Inc., 1960.

Freedman, Ronold, Pascal Whelpton, and Arthur A. Campbell, *Family Planning, Sterility and Population Growth*. New York: McGraw-Hill Book Co., Inc., 1959.

Mead, Margaret, *Male and Female*. New York: William Morrow & Co., 1959.

Phelps, Harold A. and David Henderson, *Population in Its Human Aspects*. New York: Appleton-Century-Crofts, Inc., 1958.

*Population: International Dilemma*. New York: The Population Council, 1958.

Stycos, J. Mayone, *Family and Fertility in Puerto Rico*. New York: Columbia University Press, 1955.

Thompson, Warren S., *Population Problems*. New York: McGraw-Hill Book Co., Inc., 1953.

# 4

# Physical Health and

# Medical Care

T O maintain or recover good health has been
the goal of mankind for centuries. Preliterate
peoples had their witch doctors or medicine
men, primitive surgery and dentistry were known in ancient
Egypt, and the Greeks produced "the father of medicine,"
Hippocrates, whose oath graduates of medical schools continue to take. The names of the great physicians and scientists who have contributed to medical knowledge are still
remembered and revered because good health, both physical and mental, is essential to the very existence of a
society. In 430 B.C., it is claimed that the black death, a
plague, brought to an end the golden age of Athens. It
broke out again in 14th-century Europe and had a profound impact on the feudal system.[1] For two years beginning in 1845, a potato blight caused a famine in Ireland, in
which about one million persons starved to death. Those

---

[1] Jessie Bernard, *Social Problems at Mid-Century* (New York:
The Dryden Press, 1957), pp. 183-84.

who escaped starvation became highly susceptible to infectious diseases, particularly tuberculosis. Millions of Irish emigrated to the United States and as a result a sharp increase in tuberculosis mortality occurred in Philadelphia, New York, and Boston around 1850.[2] In 1918 an influenza epidemic killed millions of people and seriously disrupted life both in the United States and abroad.

As the above paragraph indicates, health is a social fact and thus the concern of social scientists as well as the physicians, dentists, nurses, statesmen, and all other citizens. But in the present context of American thinking, health is apt to be considered more a matter of individual or at best family concern than social concern. This attitude triggers criticism of proposals for compulsory health insurance, usually described by its opponents as "socialized medicine," and tends to relegate the matter of medical care to a private affair between physician and patient. But, while the privacy of physician-patient relationships must be respected as far as possible, there are definite limits to it. For example, physicians are licensed by the respective states in which they practice. They are required by law to report the discovery of certain infectious diseases and to provide for the quarantine of such patients. Children must be vaccinated against smallpox before admission to school. Persons entering the United States from certain foreign countries must also be vaccinated. In an epidemic of serious proportions, such as the influenza epidemic of 1918, the state immediately closes schools, churches, theatres, and other places where large numbers of persons assemble. Governments at various levels employ other provisions to safeguard public health, including the enforcement of the Pure Food and Drug Act, the collection of garbage, the testing of drinking water, and the pasteurization of milk. In other words American attitudes toward health are ambivalent. Health as a social fact is recognized by the public health measures enacted into law, but the treatment of illness by a physician, with the exceptions noted above, is a matter of private rather than public concern.

This tendency to consider an individual's health his own business, to be handled through his own initiative, has probably hampered the development of preventive medicine. Closely associated with this

---

[2] Rene Dubos, *Mirage of Health* (New York: Harper & Brothers, 1959), pp. 83-84.

attitude is the belief that the decreased incidence of death from infectious diseases has been the result of both scientific discovery and individual therapeutic care by a physician. This is not entirely accurate. A great deal of this decrease resulted from simple public hygiene measures, such as the removal of filth. Barcelona and Alicante did not suffer yellow fever after the anti-filth campaigns of 1804 and 1827. With sanitary measures typhus morbidity and mortality decreased. Yet these measures were carried out by boards of health and other civic bodies which accepted neither the idea of contagion or the germ theory of disease. The incidence of tuberculosis has been reduced through rest and good food in healthful surroundings. In fact, death from a number of infections had begun to decline in Western Europe and North America before the introduction of specific methods of therapy and even before the demonstration of the germ theory of disease.[3] While the remarkable strides made in scientific medicine are not to be deprecated, it is clear that public social measures in preventive medicine made a contribution for which they are not usually given credit.

## AMERICAN HEALTH PATTERNS

The health level of Americans is not easily determined, but at least two approaches may be used: *mortality rates*—that is, the death rate —and *morbidity rates*—that is, rates of illness. The *crude mortality rate*—i.e., the number of deaths recorded during the calendar year per 1,000 persons—has in the United States declined from 17.2 in 1900 to an estimated 9.2 in 1954. This decline was temporarily interrupted in 1918 as a result of the influenza epidemic but otherwise it shows a progressive decrease. The crude mortality rate ignores such important factors as age, sex, and cause of death.

It can be seen from the chart in Figure 4-1 that females have consistently had lower rates of mortality than males since the turn of the century. But two basic factors of mortality measurement should be considered: "First, crude mortality is affected by the age-sex dis-

---

[3] Dubos, *op. cit.*, pp. 125-26.

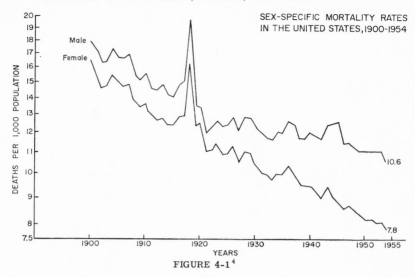

FIGURE 4-1[4]

tribution of a population; second, rate of decline depends a great deal on the particular stage of health development in a given country." [5] He continues: "Since women have a lower mortality rate than men, a population in which females considerably outnumber males would have a lower over-all mortality rate. Furthermore, a country with a low standard of living and inadequate medical facilities could make very sharp reductions in its crude mortality rate by means of sanitation or disease-control through immunization. Today only about 20 per cent of the world's population has a crude mortality rate under 15, and approximately 40 per cent of all people live under conditions resulting in a rate of 30 or over. . . . Three times the rate of countries with relatively high standards of living." [6] One factor that has reduced American mortality rates is the 80 per cent decline in deaths per 1,000 infants less than one year old. It is believed that future declines in mortality depend largely on progress in diagnosis and treatment of the two leading causes of death, heart disease and cancer.[7]

Today communicable diseases have almost been eliminated as

---

[4] Adapted from *Sex Specific Mortality Rates, 5*, No. 1 (New York: Health Information Foundation, Jan. 1954), p. 2.

[5] *Sex Specific Mortality Rates*, p. 2.

[6] *Sex Specific Mortality Rates*, p. 2.

[7] *Sex Specific Mortality Rates*, p. 3.

leading causes of death. Between 1900 and 1954 death rates from pneumonia-influenza declined 86 per cent, from tuberculosis, 94 per cent, and from diarrhea and other gastro-intestinal conditions, 96 per cent. Diphtheria has become virtually extinct, declining 99 per cent since 1900. On the other hand, heart disease, the leading cause of death today, was responsible for over 550,000 deaths in 1954, its rate rising from 137.4 per 100,000 in 1900 to 315 per 100,000 in 1954. The next most common cause of death in the United States in 1954 was cancer, followed by vascular lesions, which include cerebral hemor-

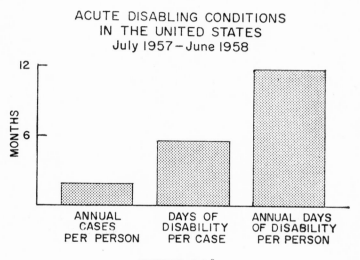

ACUTE DISABLING CONDITIONS
IN THE UNITED STATES
July 1957 – June 1958

FIGURE 4-2 [9]

rhages. The vascular lesion rate has remained relatively constant for the past 50 years. Accidents are the fourth most common cause of death in the American population but they rank first among the causes of death for ages one through twenty-four years.[8]

While dramatic decreases in the U.S. mortality rate are one indication of the nation's health, and a heartening one, rates of illness must also be considered. Some diseases may not result in death, or may only

---

[8] *Changes in Leading Causes of Death*, 5, No. 3 (New York: Health Information Foundation, Mar. 1956), pp. 2-3.

[9] Adapted from *Acute Illness in Two Surveys*, 8, No. 10 (New York: Health Information Foundation, Dec. 1959).

result in death after a long period of time. They can, however, disable or handicap an individual. A National Health Survey was carried out between July 1957 and June 1958 by the Health Information foundation. It investigated the civilian noninstitutional population. "The average annual frequency of acute disabling conditions recorded in the National Survey was 2,041 per 1,000 population, or just over 2 cases per person."

It is possible that the national health survey data overstates the normal illness picture by as much as one-third because of the Asian influenza epidemic of that year.[10] Certain other factors may also enter into this picture. The individual may now be more aware of the need to seek treatment, even for minor illnesses, and he may be taking advantage of more liberal sick-leave policies and the use of health insurance against loss of income from illness.

Another indication of American health—at least that of young males—was the high armed forces rejection rate during the Second World War. Toward the end of the war 16 million youths had been examined and half of them had been found unfit for military service. Five million were rejected outright, 1,500,000 were inducted and their defects corrected, and another 1,500,000 were inducted only to be discharged later for mental and physical defects not acquired in the service.[11] Another study conducted in 1952 ("The President's Commission on the Health Needs of the Nation"), stated that one survey in Baltimore showed almost 12 per cent of the men and 17 per cent of the women interviewed had a major chronic disease. In San Francisco 63 per cent of some 4,000 longshoremen who took various medical tests were found to be suffering from some defect.[12]

An earlier National Health Survey, conducted in the winter of 1935-36 to determine the prevalence of certain chronic diseases, estimated that one out of every six persons in the United States suffered from some type of prolonged sickness, and the total number of persons affected was about 23 million.[13]

---

[10] *Acute Illness in Two Surveys,* 8, No. 10 (New York: Health Information Foundation, Dec. 1959), p. 2.

[11] John F. Cuber, Robert A. Harper, and William F. Kenkel, *Problems of American Society: Values in Conflict* (New York: Holt, Rinehart & Winston, Inc., 1956), p. 93.

[12] Cuber, Harper, and Kenkel, *op. cit.,* p. 94.

[13] Minna Field, *Patients Are People* (New York: Columbia University Press, 1958), p. 24.

Disabling illness means a loss of productivity among most of the population and may mean a loss of salary, particularly if prolonged. In the National Health Survey of 1957-58, the total annual disability days per person was 11.4.[14] In the 1935-36 National Health Survey it was estimated that a total of a billion days was lost from work each year as a result of prolonged illness.[15] While a certain amount of illness is almost inevitable, the question is whether the incidence of illness in the United States can be lowered. One of the striking aspects of this problem is that 1,500,000 young males were inducted into the service in World War II despite defects which were later corrected at government expense. The 1935-36 National Health Survey found that the rate of illness among families close to relief level was 42 per cent higher than in families with incomes above $3,000 a year. However, it is not certain whether illness resulted in low incomes or low incomes resulted in illness. But certain kinds of physical conditions are known to be associated with low economic conditions such as tuberculosis. Inadequate diet and failure to seek medical attention— or a delay in seeking it—are likewise associated with low income.[16]

## COST OF MEDICAL CARE

In 1953 Americans spent 10.2 billion dollars on health care, which was 85 per cent of the total cost. The balance was paid by federal, state and local governments. Thirty-seven per cent of all personal health care expenditures in 1953 went for physicians' services. Hospital costs took 20 per cent, dental costs, 16 per cent, medicines, 15 per cent, and appliances and other goods and services 13 per cent of the total family medical expense. The average family spent 4 to 5 per cent of its income on medical care. Personal consumption expenditures in 1953 for recreation, alcoholic beverages, tobacco, the purchase and maintenance of automobiles, clothing and accessories, housing, household operating expenses, and food each exceeded the amount of money spent for medical care.[17]

---

[14] *Acute Illness in Two Surveys,* p. 2.
[15] Field, *op. cit.,* p. 30.
[16] Field, *op. cit.,* p. 32.
[17] *What Americans Spend for Personal Health Services,* 5, No. 7 (New York: Health Information Foundation, Sept. 1956), pp. 1-2.

The fact that Americans spend more money on recreation, drinking, smoking, and automobiles has been used by some to defend the high cost of medical care. It is maintained that if one is willing to spend this much on luxuries, one should be willing to spend this much on a necessity such as medical care. However, it should be noted that Americans increased their spending for medical care at a higher rate between 1929 and 1950 than for tobacco, alcoholic beverages, recreation, or personal care.[18] But there are certain aspects of the cost of medical care that deserve serious consideration. First of all, the occasions and types of medical needs cannot usually be known in advance. It is true that a family might budget for medical care; but how much should be saved? In 1953, 8 per cent of the families surveyed had no medical expenses at all; but 11 per cent of the families incurred 43 per cent of the total personal health services billed.[19]

Certain revolutions have occurred in medical care which have already increased the price—as all prices indeed have increased because of inflation. It seems probable that these costs will be raised even more in the future. Not too long ago the family physician dispensed almost all the medical care that an individual received. Hospitals were used infrequently, and usually for terminal cases only. Today, the use of various diagnostic tests such as X rays, electrocardiographs, encephalograms, and others have undoubtedly raised the level of medical attention but they have likewise raised its cost. The use of hospitals and surgery has increased. Among physicians there is a much greater tendency toward specialization and the general practitioner is less hesitant to refer patients to them than he may have been in the past. Furthermore, the future physician usually spends four years in college, four years in medical school, and one or two years of internship. If he decides to specialize, he may spend one to three or four years in residence. During all or most of this period, he has little or no income. Quite understandably, he is obliged to charge more for his services than the general practitioner of the past who may have entered medical school after only four years of secondary education.

This, then, is the challenge facing the American people. If they

[18] Michael M. Davis, *Medical Care for Tomorrow* (New York: Harper & Brothers, 1955), p. 18.
[19] *What Americans Spend for Personal Health Services*, p. 2.

want better medical care, and it may be assumed that the vast majority do, they will have to be prepared to pay for it. But just how they shall pay for it is a matter of dispute. The very poor may make use of free clinics, or if on relief, seek help through public welfare. The very wealthy have no problem about medical bills. But this leaves the vast majority of the American people in a position where they may readily meet ordinary medical expenses but find it difficult, if not impossible, to pay the extraordinary bills which may arise. It is clear that some type of health insurance is necessary. The unresolved question is whether such insurance of the voluntary type is adequate or whether a national compulsory health insurance is necessary.

## VOLUNTARY HEALTH INSURANCE

In 1956 about 110 million Americans—that is about 70 per cent of the population—were covered by some type of voluntary health insurance. Of this number almost all had insurance for hospitalization, 94 million had protection against surgery costs, 58 million had policies covering in-hospital physicians' fees, and 7 million were insured against major medical expenses. The best known of these insurance plans is Blue Cross-Blue Shield. Blue Cross was organized in the 1930's to help insure persons against hospital costs. Blue Shield followed shortly after to protect persons chiefly against surgical and obstetrical expenses. But between 1951 and 1952 other insurance companies have exceeded Blue Cross-Blue Shield in total enrollment, although they have paid out less in hospitalization insurance benefits per insured individual. In 1955 for example, these companies paid $11.33 per insured person while Blue Cross-Blue Shield paid $17.15 per person.[20]

Voluntary health insurance now covers more Americans than before and likewise pays increasingly large parts of the insured persons' bills for hospitalization, surgery, and other health services. In 1956, "insurance paid for more than half the cost of all hospital services to insured and uninsured persons, more than 40 per cent of the cost of

---

[20] *The Growth of Voluntary Health Insurance*, 5, No. 9 (New York: Health Information Foundation, Nov. 1956), pp. 1-2.

PER CENT OF U.S. POPULATION PROTECTED BY HOSPITAL
SURGICAL AND MEDICAL EXPENSE INSURANCE
1940–1956

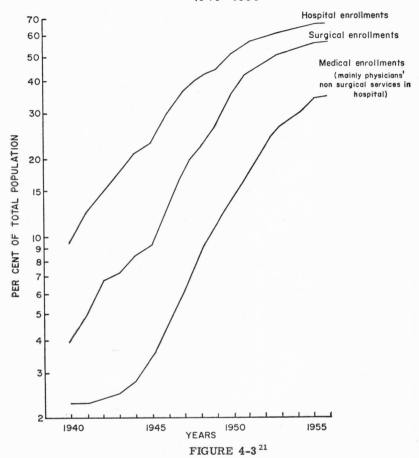

FIGURE 4-3 [21]

all surgical operations and more than 25 per cent of physicians' fees
in maternity cases." [22]

Voluntary health insurance plans generally cover hospital and
physicians' services only while in the hospital. However, many families

[21] Adapted from *The Growth of Voluntary Health Insurance, op. cit.,* p. 1.
[22] *Growth of Voluntary Health Insurance,* p. 2.

have high charges for other medical services. For example, 6 per cent of all families had changes amounting to more than $200 for doctors' services other than surgical or obstetrical. These involved home calls and office consultations, generally not covered by insurance. Four per cent of the families had dental charges of more than $200 and 2 per cent paid more than that amount for medicines.[23] The percentage of families covered also varies in terms of income. Only 41 per cent of families with earnings below $3,000 a year have some type of health insurance, whereas 71 per cent of those whose incomes range from $3,000 to $5,000 have it. When income is above $5,000 a year, 80 per cent of the families have such coverage. Variations are also found on the basis of residence. In urban areas 64 per cent of the families are insured, whereas in rural farm areas the percentage drops to 38 per cent.[24] It is well known that persons over 65 years of age are much less likely to be covered by insurance plans than those in the younger groups.

While voluntary health insurance plans are being extended to more persons, and the extent of protection increased, it is clear that they by no means cover all of the health cost. It is interesting to note that persons who are covered by health insurance usually pay more for health services than those who do not. One explanation, of course, is that such persons are more likely to seek medical attention than those who lack insurance. Furthermore, health insurance is more likely to cover nearly all the costs of the lower income groups than of higher income groups. Here again is an indication that persons with less money simply fail to secure medical attention unless all or most of it is covered by their insurance plan. It is a safe conclusion that while voluntary health insurance has helped considerably, it has by no means solved the problem of health care in the United States.

There are certain other types of health insurance, such as group health plans in which physicians are on a salary. They provide a considerably greater amount of physicians' services than do the Blue Shield plans. One of the best examples of this is the Health Insurance Plan of Greater New York (H.I.P.). However, group arrangements

---

[23] *Health Insurance Benefits on the American Family,* 6, No. 2 (New York: Health Information Foundation, Feb. 1957), pp. 1-3.
[24] Odin Anderson, with Jacob J. Feldman, *Family Medical Costs and Voluntary Health Insurance: A Nationwide Survey* (New York: McGraw-Hill Book Co., 1956), pp. 14-16.

are quite different from the usual American practice, which involves private, individual handling of medical care.[25]

## NATIONAL COMPULSORY HEALTH INSURANCE

Efforts have been made to establish a national compulsory health insurance in the United States. Specific plans differ somewhat, but generally they would employ the Federal Old Age and Survivors Insurance as a basis, with health insurance provisions being added to the present insurance features. Ultimately, this plan involves a comprehensive coverage involving care through general practitioners, specialists, nurses, hospitalization, diagnostic tests, medicines, and those appliances which are highly expensive. Up until now this proposal has been vigorously opposed by the American Medical Association on the grounds that the Federal Government would ultimately have complete control of medical practice. Concern is also expressed that the patient would not have the right to select his own physician, that clerical costs would be tremendous, and that the individual doctor would be compelled to spend a great deal of time making out reports. Furthermore, it is claimed that costs would be astronomical. At present it is simply impossible to determine whether such objections are valid or not. Similar types of compulsory health insurance have long existed in Europe, and more recently in England, where they were initiated under the Labor Government and maintained when the Tory Party took power.

Regardless of the statements for or against national compulsory health insurance, it is quite clear that federal, state, and local governments are already heavily involved in the business of medical care. It was pointed out above that such governments already pay about 15 per cent of the costs of annual health care in this country. The federal government provides large amounts of money for medical research. Under the Hill-Burton Act it assists in the construction of hospitals and operates military and Veteran's Administration hospitals. In view of these and other trends to be mentioned later, it seems likely that some type of compulsory health insurance may ultimately be enacted.

---

[25] Anderson, with Feldman, *op. cit.*, p. 7.

## DISTRIBUTION OF MEDICAL SERVICE

In 1958 there were 230,600 physicians in the United States, excluding Alaska and Hawaii. Dentists totaled 98,540 and nurses 460,000.[26] On this basis it appears that there was about one physician for every 785 persons in the United States. This would be a very high ratio except for the fact that a large number of physicians are not engaged in the practice of medicine. Some work exclusively in research, others are employed by large industries or are residents in various hospitals taking post-graduate training. Among those engaged in the actual practice of medicine, some are in the armed services and thus generally not available to civilians other than close relatives of service personnel. Another large group of physicians limits its practice to specialization. Probably only about two-thirds of physicians are in private practice, and thus available to meet the medical needs of the American public. The real physician-patient ratio in this country is probably about one doctor for every 1,200 Americans.

Dr. Dwight H. Murray, a former president of the American Medical Association, claimed that reports of a shortage of physicians were inaccurate. He stated that the nation's medical schools were producing a sufficient number of doctors to handle health needs adequately.[27] The argument that the supply of physicians is adequate points to the drop in the general mortality rate, in the maternal, infant and communicable disease death rates, and an increase in the length of life, all of which it is claimed indicates that the physician supply has been adequate. Automobile transportation makes the physician more accessible to the patient than in the past and a doctor today can do more in the same number of hours because of better drugs, instruments, laboratory facilities, professional, and technical assistance than he could have done in the same time in the past.[28]

There is, however, the assumption in this statement that all physi-

---

[26] *Statistical Abstract of the United States, 1960*, Bureau of the Census, Washington, D.C., 1960, p. 73.

[27] Lawrence Bloomgarten, "How Many Doctors?" *The Commonweal*, 66 (Sept. 13, 1957), pp. 583-86.

[28] Michael M. Davis, *Medical Care for Tomorrow* (New York: Harper & Brothers, 1955), p. 55.

cians possess the skill, facilities, and assistance which are in fact possessed by only a few.[29] The production of physicians has remained relatively constant over the last 40 years. Dr. Howard A. Rusk of the New York University College of Medicine states that recent advances in medicine increase the need for physicians rather than lessen it because they encourage better standards of care and thus require physicians to spend more time on their cases. Another indication of a physician shortage is that one out of every four of the positions for house doctors in approved hospitals cannot be filled. As a consequence, it is necessary to recruit doctors from outside the country and hospital administrators regularly advertise in foreign medical journals and send representatives abroad to recruit physicians. Out of 22,000 resident physicians in American hospitals today, 8,000 are graduates of foreign medical schools, here on temporary visas. In addition to this, 22 per cent of the budgeted positions for doctors in city and state health departments are vacant. Few new medical schools have been founded in recent years, nor have existing schools been expanded to any extent. As a result over 7,000 young Americans who have successfully completed premedical college training are refused admission to medical college for lack of room.[30]

It is very difficult to determine what is an adequate ratio of physicians to population. Medical care is still more a matter of patient demand than of patient need. During the Second World War, the War Manpower Commission stated that the absolute minimum physician-patient ratio was one doctor for every 1,500 persons, and if it dropped below this civilian health would suffer. Since Americans apparently desire more than an absolute minimum ratio, it seems clear that the desirable ratio would be somewhat below this. But this problem is further complicated by the distribution of physicians in the United States. In 1952 in the state of Mississippi, there was one doctor for each 1,500 persons. In New York State, the ratio was 1 to 510.[31] The ratio of patients to physicians is, of course, much higher in rural than in urban areas. In other words, it is not the overall national ratio of physicians to patients that matters so much as the actual ratio in specific areas.

Only in communities of under 2,500 people do general practitioners

---

[29] Davis, *op. cit.*, p. 56.
[30] Bloomgarten, *op. cit.*, p. 584.
[31] Cuber, Harper, and Kenkel, *op. cit.*, p. 103.

make up five-sixths or more of the physicians as they did two generations ago. The physician today is usually an urban man, just as are
other Americans. But while slightly more than half the people live in
metropolitan areas, 70 per cent of the physicians are found there. In
fact, only 4 per cent of the physicians live in counties with towns no
larger than 2,500 population, while 8 per cent of the population
dwells in such counties. This is even more true of the specialist.
Seventy-five per cent of all pediatricians in private practice in 1946
were located in cities with a population of over 50,000 persons; but
90 per cent of the 3,073 counties in the United States had no pedia-
trician at all.[32]

Reasons for this poor distribution of physicians are not difficult to
find. Specialists tend to locate in large cities with good hospital facilities. Usually, patients do not go directly to a specialist but are referred to them by general practitioners. Thus, their logical location
is a relatively large population center. While this is less true of
general practitioners, it is not entirely untrue of them either. They
are likely to select a locality with both a large population and adequate hospital and other facilities. Recently, smaller towns and rural
localities have attempted to attract physicians by providing them
with offices and equipment for which there is no charge during the
beginning period of the physician's practice.

But economic factors play a part in the physician's selection of a
location. The doctors in the Middle West have the highest net
median earnings of any region in the country. The charges for office
visits, house visits, obstetrical cases, appendectomies, and tonsillec-
tomies show considerable variation throughout the nation. In Kansas
City the general practitioner's average charge for an office visit was
$3.00 and in Los Angeles it was $5.33. In Philadelphia a general
practitioner charged about $4.17 for a house visit, while in San
Francisco he charged $7.83. An obstetrical case in Scranton cost
$78.50, in Los Angeles $175.00. In this latter city an appendectomy
cost $233.33 on an average, whereas in Baltimore it was $129.17. Ton-
sillectomies varied from $52.00 in Minneapolis to $100.00 in Los
Angeles.[33] However, income and costs also show variations from
city to city and the net profit of the physician or surgeon in the respective localities may not vary so much as these prices seem to

[32] Davis, op. cit., pp. 46-47.
[33] Statistical Abstract of the United States, 1960, p. 339.

indicate. Still as the Bureau of Medical Economics of the American Medical Association has pointed out, the distribution of physicians is most affected by the amount of income a population is able to spend. In other words, physicians locate where there is a demand for their services rather than simply a need.[34]

HOSPITALS

The distribution of physicians, as pointed out, is associated to some extent with the presence of adequate hospital facilities within a community. How then do hospital facilities measure up to the health needs of the American public nationally? In the United States, hospitals are provided by the federal and state governments largely to care for long term disabilities such as tuberculosis and mental illness. Religious, voluntary, and local government hospitals are usually general hospitals which take care of relatively short-term illnesses, as well as surgery, maternity, and emergency treatment. In 1955, out of 21 million Americans newly hospitalized, 95 per cent were treated in general hospitals, while about 2 per cent were admitted to mental and psychiatric institutions. The remaining 3 per cent entered other specialized treatment centers.

In the last 20 years there has been both a very great increase in the number of hospitals and hospital facilities and in the number of Americans making use of such institutions. Almost three times as many Americans are admitted to hospitals today as 20 years ago. For example, six out of every 100 Americans were hospitalized in 1935, but 20 years later 13 out of every 100 were admitted, and in the future the increase promises to be even greater. This does not mean that more Americans were ill in 1955 than in 1935, but rather that they now tend to make fuller use of scientific and technological developments. While the building of new hospitals and additions to those already in existence has increased, the number of beds available has barely kept pace with population growth. Fortunately, patients today remain hospitalized for less time than in the past because of various medical advances. So it is not purely a matter of the ratio of beds per 1,000

---

[34] Michael M. Davis, *op. cit.*, p. 47.

HOSPITAL BEDS PER 1,000 U.S. POPULATION
1909-1955

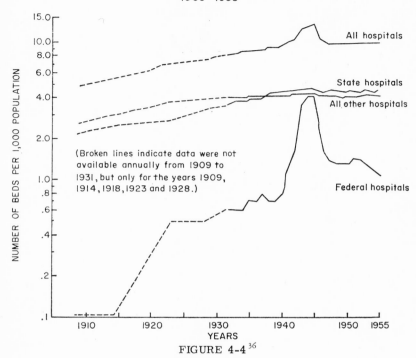

FIGURE 4-4 [36]

persons in the population that counts, but rather the length of time a patient occupies these beds.[35]

The suggested Hill-Burton Act standard for general hospitals is a ratio of 4.5 beds to each 1,000 persons in the population. In 1955 the national average was 4.2 beds per 1,000 persons, and 21 states were below this ratio. Twenty-nine states were below the recommended 4.5 ratio. The District of Columbia, California, Massachusetts, Nevada, New Mexico, Oregon and Utah actually suffered a net loss of hospital beds between 1940 and 1955. Nevertheless, nationally the number of general hospital beds increased by 200 per cent between

[35] The Growth of American Hospital Facilities (New York: Health Information Foundation, Oct. 1956), pp. 1-2.

[36] Adapted from The Distribution of American Hospital Facilities (New York: Health Information Foundation, Dec. 1956), p. 3.

1909 and 1955 when the population was increasing by only 80 per cent.

One of the radical changes in American hospitals is the number of personnel now required to staff them:

> The most striking change of the past 10 years, however, is the great increase of nearly 60% in the number of personnel employed to maintain the quality and scope of today's hospital care. An average of 95 persons is now employed for the care of every 100 patients in all types of hospitals, or 22 more than were employed as recently as 10 years ago. For short term, general hospitals the figure rises to 203 employees for every 100 patients in bed, an increase of 37% over the 1946 figure of 148 employees per 100 patients.[37]

At the same time the average wages of full-time hospital personnel increased 107 per cent from $1,329 in 1946 to $2,754 in 1955. While this was a much greater increase than that received by persons in manufacturing industries, the average hospital employee in 1946 had received 47 per cent less a year than the average worker in such industries. Hospital personnel still earn 37 per cent less than industrial workers. As hospital personnel become unionized, it is probable that the gap between their salaries and other workers will be closed. But this also means that the cost of maintaining hospitals will be increased.

Despite remarkable progress made in hospital facilities during recent years, it is still apparent that in most states the recommended Hill-Burton Act standard has yet to be achieved. It is also obvious that the cost of administering hospitals will become greater as salaries of personnel are increased. But there are other aspects to an adequate distribution of hospital facilities; for example, how large should a small-community hospital be? Generally speaking, it is agreed that no community should build a hospital with fewer than 50 beds unless advised by experts to do so. Furthermore, an adequate X-ray, laboratory and other treatment facilities may attract physicians to a community; but small communities may not find it economically possible to provide all of the resources required for complete patient care. It is almost impossible for them to secure the services of all the types of specialists required. Under these circumstances, it is apparent that

---

[37] *The Growth of American Hospital Facilities* (New York: Health Information Foundation, Oct. 1956), p. 3.

small communities will have to join together in the building and maintenance of hospitals. Perhaps it will always be necessary for patients with certain illnesses to travel relatively long distances to medical centers for treatment. But at this time, it is apparent that more can be done to provide adequate hospital facilities in many American communities.

## ATTITUDES TOWARDS THE MEDICAL PROFESSION

Physicians have long enjoyed high status in American life. They have been glamorized in novels, stage shows, and motion pictures, "immortalized" in paintings, and glorified in the advertisements of pharmaceutical houses. Certainly the physician of the past—especially the rural general practitioner—was something of a hero to most Americans. But among contemporary Americans the halo of the doctor is now less apparent than some of his practices. In research carried on for the American Medical Association by Rollen Waterson and Ernst Dichter, it was found that patients resented the tendency of some physicians to behave like deities. There seemed to be a tendency on the part of the doctor to talk down to the patient, to refuse to answer his questions, and generally to treat him as a child.[38] The unwillingness, failure, or reluctance of physicians to communicate with patients and their families is brought out very clearly in a study by Fred Davis, "Uncertainty in Medical Prognosis, Clinical and Functional." In this case parents of children who had been stricken with paralytic poliomyelitis were unable to discover from the attending physician whether their children would be permanently crippled or not, or to what extent they could expect complete or partial recovery. Physicians tended to postpone telling the parents by claiming they had only three minutes in which to speak to them. This was done even at that period of prognosis when the physician could inform the research teams rather reliably what the actual condition of the child would be. Part of this reluctance was due in the beginning to the real uncertainty of the prognosis; but their reticence con-

---

[38] Sidney Shallet and J. Robert Moskin, "Why You Can't Afford to Be Sick," *Women's Home Companion* (July 1956), p. 87.

tinued even when the outcome could be reasonably well predicted. Physicians argued that they thus evaded severe emotional reactions on the part of parents, preferring to let them learn the truth in a natural way—by which they apparently meant the ultimate acceptance of what they were forced to observe over a very long period of time.[39]

To the sociologist, the failure of physicians to communicate the true nature of an illness or its probable prognosis might well be explained in terms of culture lag. The American public today is better educated than in the past and by means of newspapers and magazines considerably better informed about some diseases. Doctors seem to think in terms of the past when the public had less education, less information, and perhaps considerably more trust and confidence in the physician's advice. Of course, in every instance the decision as to what, how, and when to communicate will have to be made in terms of a patient's personality and social background, both of which are more matters of psychology and sociology than of medical science.

Patients also reported that physicians were increasingly unwilling to make night calls. In addition, they complained about overcharging, fee splitting, unnecessary surgery, and failure to rid the profession of those physicians who have been convicted of malpractice.

## SITUATIONAL-VALUE APPROACH

Basic to any discussion of physical health and medical care is the concept set forth at the beginning of this chapter that health is a social affair. While society has been forced to conclude that it must protect itself in the event of epidemics and safeguard itself against impure food and water, it has not yet come to realize—at least in the United States—that the health of every American is a very important issue. When an individual contracts a highly communicable and dangerous disease and is detected, he would be compelled to undergo quarantine and treatment. On the other hand, individuals suffering from a serious illness may delay medical attention through lack of money. The loss of an individual's productivity and the resulting distress—psychological and economic—to his family, may be less critical

---

[39] Fred Davis, "Uncertainty in Medical Prognosis, Clinical and Functional," *American Journal of Sociology*, 66 (July 1960), pp. 41-47.

to society at large than the threat of infection, but it is still a social problem because it may involve large numbers of people.

The values of the American Medical Association have been such that it has in the past opposed the Blue Cross Plan, fought group insurance plans, and only reluctantly and rather recently appeared to accept the idea of health insurance at all. When former President Truman proposed compulsory health insurance, the American Medical Association claimed it could find a satisfactory solution to problems of physical health and medical care without it, but it failed to come up with such a plan. To date this association seems so dedicated to the private practice of medicine on a fee basis it fails to take into consideration some of the great social changes that have occurred in the United States. On the other hand the American Medical Association has made excellent contributions to American health and medical care. It was largely responsible for the establishment of better medical schools and it certainly should have a great deal of influence in shaping any future programs of medical care and health insurance. But the health standards of the United States concern all Americans, and not simply physicians who are members of the American Medical Association.

## REMEDIAL MEASURES

At this point it appears that a thorough, careful, and extensive study of physical health in the United States and the level of medical care should be carried out. Only when this is done can there be a definite answer to many of the questions in this field. On the basis of present research, it seems that the level of medical care could be raised, the health of Americans improved, more men and women trained in medicine, and hospital facilities raised to the Hill-Burton Act standard.

There is also a need to alert Americans to the symptoms of the more serious diseases, especially cancer, and to get them to seek medical attention as early as possible. The student physician should be taught that his future profession involves not only natural science but also social science. This is particularly true in the field of preventive medicine, which needs considerably more emphasis than it has so far received. Finally, it must be possible for all Americans to obtain adequate medical, dental and hospital services. If this goal cannot be achieved without some type of national compulsory health insurance, then this too will have to be accepted, but hopefully the nature of the program would be such that the best interests of both physician and patient will be protected.

## REVIEW QUESTIONS

1. Why is health considered "a social fact"?
2. To what extent does the state now control medical care?
3. What are the two indices employed to determine American health patterns? How reliable are data on such indices?
4. To what changes can the decline in the American mortality rates since the turn of the century be mainly traced?
5. Evaluate the rejection rate of draftees during World War II as an index of health standards among young American males.
6. Americans spend a larger percentage of their incomes on alcohol and tobacco than they do on medical care. Is this not an indication that efforts to secure compulsory health insurance are unnecessary?
7. Evaluate the present status of voluntary health insurance in the United States. Discuss particularly the extent of its benefits and coverage.
8. What are the major objections to national compulsory health insurance? Evaluate these objections against your knowledge of American health patterns.
9. Does the United States have an adequate number of practicing physicians?
10. Are present hospital facilities in the United States adequate? Discuss this in terms of the number of beds, the distribution of hospitals and the Hill-Burton standards.
11. What are American attitudes toward the medical profession?
12. From the situational-value approach, analyze health and medical care as a social problem in this country.

## SELECTED READINGS

*Articles*

*Acute Illness in Two Surveys*, New York: Health Information Foundation, 8, No. 10 (Dec. 1959).

Bloomgarten, Lawrence, "How Many Doctors?" *The Commonweal* (Sept. 13, 1957), pp. 583-86.

Ben-David, Joseph, "Roles and Innovations in Medicine," *American Journal of Sociology*, 65 (May 1960), 557-68.

*Changes and Leading Causes of Death.* New York: Health Information Foundation, 5, No. 3 (Mar. 1956).

Davis, Fred, "Uncertainty in Medical Prognosis, Clinical and Functional," *American Journal of Sociology*, 66 (July 1961) 41-47.

Dinkel, Robert N., "Factors Underlying the Location of Physicians Within Indiana," *American Sociological Review*, 11 (Feb. 1946), 16-25.

*The Distribution of American Hospital Facilities.* New York: Health Information Foundation, 5, No. 10 (Dec. 1956).

Freidson, Eliot, "Client Control in Medical Practice," *American Journal of Sociology*, 65 (Jan. 1960), 374-418.

*The Growth of American Hospital Facilities,* New York: Health Information Foundation, 5, No. 8 (Oct. 1956).

*The Growth of Voluntary Health Insurance.* New York: Health Information Foundation, 5, No. 9 (Nov. 1956).

*Health Insurance Benefits on the American Family.* New York: Health Information Foundation, 6, No. 2 (Feb. 1957).

Hoffer, Charles R. and Edgar A. Schuler, "Measurement of Health Needs and Health Care," *American Sociological Review*, 13 (Dec. 1948), 719-24.

Shallet, Sidney and J. Robert Moskin, "Why You Can't Afford to Be Sick," *Woman's Home Companion* (July 1956).

*What Americans Spend for Personal Health Services.* New York: Health Information Foundation, 5, No. 7 (Sept. 1956).

## Books

Apple, Dorrian, *Sociological Studies of Health and Sickness.* New York: McGraw-Hill Book Co., Inc., 1960.

Anderson, Odin with Jacob J. Feldman, *Family Medical Costs and Voluntary Health Insurance: A Nation-wide Survey.* New York: The Blakiston Division, McGraw-Hill Book Co., 1956.

Becker, Howard S., *Boys in White: Student Culture in Medical Schools.* Chicago: University of Chicago Press, 1961.

Davis, Michael M., *Medical Care for Tomorrow.* New York: Harper and Brothers, 1955.

Dubos, Rene, *Mirage of Health.* New York: Harper and Brothers, 1959.

Faulkner, Edwin J., *Health Insurance.* New York: McGraw-Hill Book Co., Inc., 1960.

Field, Minna, *Patients Are People*. New York: Columbia University Press, 1958.

Freidson, Eliot, *Patient's Views of Medical Practice*. New York: Russell Sage Foundation, 1961.

# 5

# Mental Health

I N 1957 there were 167,697 first admissions to hospitals for mental illness. At the end of 1958 there were 612,111 patients in such hospitals. This was a rate of 357 persons per every 100,000 in the population.[1] But this by no means represents the total number of mentally ill persons in the United States. Some are out-patients, some are treated privately in the office of a psychiatrist, and it is probable that a large number of the mentally ill have never been diagnosed. The per capita cost of maintaining patients in state mental hospitals—which involves salaries of personnel, purchase of provisions, fuel, light, water, and so on—rose from $301 in 1940 to $1,324 in 1957.[2] Today between one-half to two-thirds of all hospital beds are occupied by patients who are mentally ill, and estimates claim that at some time in their lives about one out of every ten persons will be institutionalized for mental illness. But it is not certain whether the incidence of mental disease is increasing or

[1] *Statistical Abstract of the United States, 1960*, Bureau of the Census, Washington, D.C., 1960, pp. 78 and 79.
[2] *Statistical Abstract of the United States, 1960*, p. 80.

not. Certainly, in an urban society persons with severe mental disabilities are more likely to be noted, brought to the attention of a psychiatrist, and diagnosed. When the United States had an agrarian economy, the tempo of life was slower, and the eccentric behavior of an individual was more readily overlooked. Nevertheless, the incidence of mental illness, the cost of maintaining hospitals, and the short supply of psychiatrists contribute to make this a serious overt social problem.

## TYPES OF MENTAL ILLNESS

Mental illness is divided into *psychoses* and *neuroses*. The former is a severe type of mental disease in which the patient periodically or usually is out of contact with reality. The latter are milder emotional disturbances which tend to make adjustment in certain areas of life difficult or almost impossible. Psychoses are further divided into the *organic* and the *functional*. Organic psychoses are those for which there is a recognizable physical basis, such as a brain tumor, paresis, or trauma. The functional psychoses are those for which to date no recognizable physical basis has been discovered. Mental illness may also be divided into *acute* and *chronic* stages. The former is transitory, that is it may be reversed; the latter is of relatively permanent duration.

*Paresis* is the result of infection from syphilis, which is caused by a microorganism, *treponemum pallidum*. Only a small number of untreated syphilitics develop paresis. Sometimes symptoms of it do not appear until 20 years after the initial infection. Among these symptoms are defects in reflex actions, particularly in the pupillary reflex to light, tremors of the lips and tongue with disturbance in speech function, and difficulty in writing. The prognosis of paresis depends upon the extent of brain damage that has occurred prior to medical treatment. *Fever therapy* is used, that is, the person's temperature is raised to a degree at which the syphilitic spirochete cannot survive. Penicillin is also used, but to date it has not been effective when used alone.[3]

---

[3] James C. Coleman, *Abnormal Psychology and Modern Life* (Chicago: Scott, Foresman and Co., 1956), pp. 428-36.

Brain tumors are the result of a growth within the brain itself. They may be of a malignant nature and destroy other tissue, or non-malignant. In either case, since the skull is a bony structure unable to expand, pressure results. Symptoms of this disease vary with the location, size, and growth of the tumor, as well as the personality of the patient. But eventually, most patients show symptoms of some mental disorder as the result of brain damage, or develop neurotic or psychotic behaviors. Treatment is by surgery, and the prognosis for some cases is complete recovery. In others certain symptoms may remain, as well as partial paralysis.[4] In addition to the two types of organic psychoses described, there are those which are caused by brain damage from blows or accidents, toxic conditions resulting from certain infectious diseases—notably diphtheria, pneumonia and typhoid fever—as well as disorders resulting from prolonged alcoholism.[5]

## FUNCTIONAL PSYCHOSES

The functional psychoses are of particular interest to sociologists because to date no organic basis for them has been discovered. Even in the organic psychoses, there is some association between symptoms and the behavior of the individual prior to his illness. But in the functional psychoses, since there seems to be no physical basis, psychiatrists, psychologists, and sociologists have been especially interested in the social and psychological backgrounds of the individual.

The three major functional psychoses are schizophrenia, formerly known as *dementia praecox*, since it was believed to attack only the young; manic-depressive psychoses; and paranoia. Four types of schizophrenia are usually distinguished: simple, hebephrenic, catatonic, and paranoid. *Simple schizophrenia* is a retreat from reality or from life. The individual ceases to have an interest in anything, including his work, his studies, his personal appearance, his family, and his friends. "Pep talks" to motivate him are useless, and in fact do not really reach him. Still, many of these individuals are not admitted to mental hospitals because somehow or other they get by. *Hebe-*

---

[4] Coleman, *op. cit.*, pp. 441-45.
[5] Coleman, *op. cit.*, pp. 447-57.

*phrenic schizophrenia* is much more severe in its manifestations. The individual shows all the symptoms of simple schizophrenia plus considerable word distortion ("word salad"), silly behavior, and a peculiar laugh.

*Catatonic schizophrenia* is perhaps the most dramatic of all. In extreme cases an individual may sit in a chair and rock the entire day with a vacant expression on his face, never uttering a word. The individual may also assume an immobile position and, if his hand is raised above his head, may retain it this way for hours despite physical discomfort. He completely neglects personal hygiene and must be taken care of. The paranoid schizophrenic becomes highly suspicious of family, friends, and neighbors. He sometimes believes that persons are attempting to kill him, or are constantly following and criticizing him. He may likewise develop delusions of grandeur, believing that he is God, George Washington, or Napoleon.

*Paranoia* also involves delusions of persecution or grandeur. However, some patients seem to have a completely logical explanation of their situation. A stranger meeting and talking with a paranoid may be convinced that the individual is by no means psychotic and is being detained in the hospital for other reasons. The rate of admissions to hospitals for this condition is quite low, and it is believed that many escape diagnosis entirely unless they prove troublesome.

The *manic-depressive* psychoses, sometimes called *affective-reactions* may constitute a type of cyclical behavior. At one time the patient is highly elated, excitable, and talkative. On another occasion he may be completely depressed, silent, and withdrawn. In other cases some patients exhibit only one of these stages of behavior. Delusions and hallucinations are not uncommon.

## ETIOLOGY OF FUNCTIONAL PSYCHOSES

The actual causes of functional psychoses are by no means clear. They range over biological, constitutional, psychological, and sociological factors. Generally speaking, it is agreed that biological factors do not directly cause any of the functional psychoses mentioned here. While there is some evidence that the incidence of mental disorders may be somewhat higher in families in which one member has succumbed to a functional psychosis, this is not sufficient to support a biological theory of causation. One could just as readily argue on this basis that it was the similarity in early environment that brought about the mental illness. Neither is there any proof that constitutional factors such as somatotypes revealed any direct association between body build and functional psychoses. Recently, through the injection of certain chemicals, a schizophrenic state has been brought about in normal individuals. This has stimulated a search for constitutional factors in this disease. However, even if constitutional factors are discovered, psychological and sociological factors cannot be ruled out.[6]

One of the basic factors believed important in the functional psychosis is parent-child relationships during the early years. Everyone requires an adequate amount of love, affection, and security. Children also need an opportunity to grow up and gradually assume responsibility. But such conditions are not found in every American home. There are some parents who reject children, sometimes even physically abandoning them, but more frequently in a psychological sense neglecting them. The rejected child lacks the sense of security essential to his normal development. He finds it difficult to learn to love other persons because he has never been loved himself. Such youngsters may give early indications of disturbed personalities through antisocial acts in school or ultimately in juvenile delinquency. The opposite of this is the child who is over-protected and thus prevented from maturing. Certain infantile types of behavior, not uncommon at certain stages of life, persist into later childhood and youth. The dominant parent, with a stern, narrow concept of discipline, may arouse exaggerated feelings of guilt in his children. The over-indulgent parent creates the impression that the world is the child's "oyster," and everyone must wait on him. Thus, a selfish, egocentric personality may develop. However, it is not merely what happens to the child that matters but how he interprets the situation. This may explain why some children exposed to very adverse circumstances of this type do not become mentally ill. Furthermore, there is always the possibility that constitutional factors may play some part in facilitating or impeding psychoses and neuroses.

The contemporary values of American society may contribute to

---

[6] Coleman, *op. cit.*, p. 276.

the traumas which children suffer. A certain amount of trauma, of course, is inevitable. The point is that the trauma should not be so severe and extensive that the child cannot handle it. The psychological rejection of children today stems in part from rapid social change. Very strong demands are made upon parents not only to feed, clothe, and educate children but also to observe the multitudinous child-rearing techniques put forth by authorities, many in direct conflict with each other. Arnold Green has said that much of the literature on child rearing seems to claim that parents have a combined culinary, nursing, and psychiatric function and nothing more. But in our society cooks, nurses, and psychiatrists are paid for what they do and parents are not—at least in a monetary sense.[7] Today's children do not usually help a family to get ahead materially. Yet this is one of the great goals of American life, especially in the middle class. In some families they may be viewed as serious liabilities, and thus tend to be rejected.

On the other hand they may be used as vicarious instruments to attain status. Parents may attempt to bask in the reflected glory of a child's achievements, real or otherwise. A boy may be pushed into making the football team, an honor society, a fraternity, or to a level of education of which he is incapable. The reward in this case for being a good and successful boy is parental love. Failure to conform and achieve causes withdrawal of parental love. For the middle-class American child, parental love is a sine qua non. The loss or threatened loss of it almost inevitably arouses feelings of insecurity. Girls, too, may suffer similar parental propulsions into a highly competitive world in which parental expectations simply cannot be realized. Even if parents charitably overlook such failures, a sense of guilt is likely to burn within the youthful breast because of the pressure of the middle-class sub-culture.

## SOCIOLOGICAL FACTORS IN MENTAL ILLNESS

The sociological approach to mental illness has involved studies of ecology, social disorganization, and social stratification. Dunham

---

[7] Arnold W. Green, "Why Americans Feel Insecure," in *Readings in Sociology*, ed. Edgar A. Schuler, *et al.* (New York: Thomas Y. Crowell Co., 1960), p. 818.

and Faris investigated the distribution of schizophrenic and manic-depressive illness in Chicago. They found the highest rates of schizophrenia were concentrated in interstitial areas characterized by social disorganization. This was true of both men and women. High rates of paranoid and hebephrenic schizophrenia were likewise found in socially disorganized communities, but high rates for catatonic schizophrenia existed mainly in foreign-born and Negro communities. At that time it was not certain whether selective migration was responsible for this high incidence of schizophrenia.[8] Data was obtained from four state hospitals and eight private institutions. In the same study, however, there was no typical distribution for the manic-depressive psychoses.

This distribution of schizophrenia was explained on the basis of tendencies toward social isolation by certain segments of the population. Faris said, "Any form of isolation that cuts the person off from intimate social relations for an extended period of time may possibly lead to this form of mental disorder."[9] This hypothesis was later studied by Melvin L. Kohn and John A. Clusen. Their sample consisted of 45 schizophrenic and 13 manic-depressive patients first admitted to mental hospitals in Maryland between 1940 and 1952. They found that a larger proportion of patients than of the control group (made up of persons sharing the same social economic factors but not being schizoid) recalled that their mothers had been angered, were more dominating, more anxious for their children to get ahead, less likely to be satisfied with the children's behavior, and more restrictive than their fathers. But only about one-third of the schizophrenic and manic-depressive patients showed evidence that they had been socially isolated at the age of 13 or 14. Neither could they find any evidence that these patients were prevented from interacting with their peers through lack of playmates, excessive horizontal mobility, illness, or parental restriction. In other words, they found no evidence of an association between social isolation and familial relationships. Their interpretation of the situation is that certain inadequacies in social relationships either within or without

---

[8] H. Warren Dunham, "The Ecology of the Functional Psychoses in Chicago," *American Sociological Review*, 2 (Aug. 1937), 467-69; and Robert E. L. Faris, "Cultural Isolation and the Schizophrenic Personality," *American Journal of Sociology*, 40 (Sept. 1934), pp. 155-64.

[9] Faris, *op. cit.*, p. 157.

the family caused these individuals to feel they did not belong to their peer groups. They concluded: "In any case, isolation does not seem to be the crucial experience in predisposing the individual to illness." [10]

While it is clear that the incidence of schizophrenia is unduly high in interstitial areas, an entirely satisfactory explanation of this phenomena has not been found. Professors August Hollingshead and Fredrick C. Redlich examined the question of social stratification and psychiatric disorders. Their investigation covered the city of New Haven and surrounding towns of East Haven, North Haven, West Haven, and Hamden with a total population of 250,000 persons in 1950.

TABLE 5-1[11]

DISTRIBUTION OF NORMAL AND PSYCHIATRIC POPULATION
BY SOCIAL CLASS

| | Normal Population* | | Psychiatric Population | |
| Social Class | Number | Per cent | Number | Per cent |
| --- | --- | --- | --- | --- |
| I | 358 | 3.1 | 19 | 1.0 |
| II | 926 | 8.1 | 131 | 6.7 |
| III | 2500 | 22.0 | 260 | 13.2 |
| IV | 5256 | 46.0 | 758 | 38.6 |
| V | 2037 | 17.8 | 723 | 36.8 |
| Unknown** | 345 | 3.0 | 72 | 3.7 |
| Total | 11,422 | 100.0 | 1,963 | 100.0 |

Chi square = 408.16, P less than .001.

* These figures are preliminary. They do not include Yale students, transients, institutionalized persons, and refusals.

** The unknown cases were not used in the calculation of chi square. They are individuals drawn in the sample, and psychiatric cases whose class level could not be determined because of paucity of data.

Their first hypothesis was that the diagnosed prevalence of psychiatric disorders is significantly related to a person's position in

[10] Melvin L. Kohn and John A. Clusen, "Social Isolation in Schizophrenia," *American Sociological Review,* 20 (June 1955), pp. 265-73.

[11] Adapted from August B. Hollingshead and Fredrick Redlich, "Distribution of Normal and Psychiatric Population by Social Class," *American Sociological Review, 18,* No. 2 (Apr. 1953), p. 167.

the class structure. The table (5-1) above, reveals that this hypothesis was substantiated. Class I was composed of families with inherited wealth who live in the best areas of the city. The heads of these families are leaders in business and professional occupations. Class V consisted mainly of semi-skilled factory workers and unskilled laborers. Most of them did not complete elementary school. They lived in the very poor section of their cities and few belonged to community institutions. On the basis of the above table, 3.1 per cent of the community's population is in Class I, but only 1.0 per cent of the psychiatric cases; 17.8 per cent of the community's population is in Class V, but constitutes 36.8 per cent of the psychiatric patients. They concluded that there is a definite association between particular types of social environment as measured by social class and particular kinds of psychiatric disorders as measured by psychiatric diagnosis. At this point it is not possible to determine what these associations are, nor how they are related to a particular type of mental illness in a given individual. It should be recalled that this study dealt only with persons who had been diagnosed as mentally ill.[12]

A more selective investigation of occupational differences in mental disorders was conducted by Herman R. Lantz and involved 1,000 U.S. Air Force officers and enlisted men from World War II, both white and Negro, between the ages of 16 and 44. They had been referred to a mental hygiene clinic between May 1943 and April 1944. This study included neuroses as well as psychoses, but for present purposes the discussion is limited to the 62 patients who were schizophrenic. Their civilian occupations were broken down as follows: 8.4 per cent were in a professional and managerial category, 3.2 per cent were in clerical and sales, 5.9 per cent in service occupations, 4.2 per cent were in agriculture, 3.0 per cent were skilled workers, 10.4 per cent were semi-skilled workers, 11.5 per cent were unskilled workers, 12.5 per cent performed odd jobs (that is, held jobs of less than one year's duration), and 2.9 per cent were students. Lantz concluded that persons who were diagnosed as psychotic ranked high in civilian occupational areas with low prestige. However, a possible opposite conclusion (i.e., a person in civilian life with high occupational

---

[12] August B. Hollingshead and Fredrick C. Redlich, "Social Stratification in Psychiatric Disorders," *American Sociological Review*, 18, No. 2 (Apr. 1953), pp. 163-69.

prestige ranking low in psychoses) could not be ruled out by this study because of the nature of the sample, and other factors.[13]

## THE NEUROSES

The terms *neurosis* and *psychoneurosis* are interchangeable. They are mild personality disorders of a functional rather than an organic nature for which confinement in a hospital is rarely necessary. They may be considered a psychological maladjustment of a person to specific circumstances at a specific time. Furthermore, they are a matter of degree. There is a popular belief that everyone is "a little bit crazy." This seems to be the folk way of saying that at times nearly everyone may be somewhat maladjusted. Furthermore, the Army popularized the idea that every man has a breaking point. Contingent upon one's physical and psychological resources, it is possible for anyone to reach a point where he may break neurotically or psychotically. On the other hand, certain persons whose physical and psychological resources are not very great may live well-adjusted lives so long as they remain in an environment in which stress is not great. The incidence of neuroses in the United States simply cannot be determined. Dr. Strecker estimated that three-fourths of all patients consulting general practitioners have psychiatric disturbances of one type or another.[14]

While accurate statistics on the number of neurotics cannot be established, general opinion is that this condition is far more common than usually believed. Depending on the degree of neurotic reaction, such conditions represent a serious overt social problem. First, they interfere with an individual's satisfactory adjustment to his family, his friends, his occupation, and his life in general. Second, they place considerable strain on almost all of his interpersonal relationships. To some extent at least—although the exact extent is unknown—they contribute to alcoholism, the divorce rate, juvenile delinquency, and adult crime. On the other hand, the word "neurotic"

---

[13] Herman R. Lantz, "Occupational Differences in Mental Disorders," *Social Problems*, 2, No. 2 (Oct. 1954), pp. 100-103.
[14] Sol Wiener Ginsburg, "The Neuroses," *The Annals*, 286 (Mar. 1953), pp. 55-64.

has become a colloquialism which is carelessly tossed about by the public.

The more familiar clinically significant types, as Dr. Ginsburg has pointed out, are anxiety, hysteria, and compulsive-obsessional neuroses. There are, of course, many others, and for a thorough discussion of them the student is referred to books on the psychology of the abnormal. Feelings of anxiety are a common symptom of emotional disturbance. However, an important distinction must be made. At one time or another all persons undergo feelings of anxiety: on the eve of an important examination, just prior to marriage, or when any highly important or dangerous event is about to occur. But neurotic feelings of anxiety do not stem from a present and recognized danger. Rather they represent worries about events which may never occur at all or whose occurrence is very doubtful, or concern about something in the past over which the individual now has no control. They should be distinguished from fear, which is a normal emotion, sometimes quite helpful, alerting us to a "clear and present" danger. Very often the individual is anxious but really does not know what he is anxious about.

Anxiety may be chronic or acute. In some cases it is always present, and at times it erupts into a sharp, acute attack. The individual is filled with a sudden apprehension, his pulse beats quickly, his blood pressure rises, his palms perspire, the gastro-intestinal tract is disturbed, and he may suffer dizzy spells. At times, these may awaken a person from a deep sleep.[15] Feelings of anxiety may involve a grave concern about health. A headache is identified as a brain tumor, a pimple is diagnosed by the patient as cancer. Vague pains in the back, chest, arms, or elsewhere are experienced. The sense of anxiety may likewise be induced by the presence of a certain person, a visit to a specific place, crowds, or great heights. It may occur even when the individual seems otherwise entirely normal.[16] One of the most startling manifestations of neuroses is *hysteria*, or what was formerly termed "conversion hysteria." On the unconscious level, hysteria is the method by which an individual solves a problem but at the same time "saves face." An individual's arm may become paralyzed, or he may go blind, although no organic basis for the paralysis or blindness can be discovered. Under deep hypnosis,

[15] Coleman, *op. cit.*, pp. 175-76.
[16] Ginsburg, *op. cit.*, p. 60.

blindness or paralysis resulting from hysteria can be corrected. No reputable practitioner would do this, however, because the relief of one symptom of a neurosis normally causes another to appear in its place. These individuals should not be thought of as malingerers because, on the conscious level, the arm is actually paralyzed and the eyes actually do not function.

Another type of neurosis is *compulsive-obsessional* behavior. This is not necessarily abnormal, but such behavior may be termed neurotic when it becomes utterly compulsive. A good example from literature is Lady Macbeth's constant hand-washing. Of course, the obsession-compulsions are often of a much more serious nature, such as an urge to kill or to commit rape. One of the characteristics of a neurotic which Karen Horney pointed out is *rigidity*, i.e., the inability to alter behavior to situations. She believed that conflict was extremely important in neuroses and described three types of personalities: those who move toward people, those who move against people, and those who move away from people. Those who move toward people suffer a desperate need of feeling secure. They try to be kind and loving in order that others will be kind and loving to them. This seems to be perfectly natural and desirable behavior, but actually it is motivated not by altruism but rather by the selfish wish to enhance their own ego. Similarly those who move against people believe that they had better strike first before they are hurt. Finally, those who move away from people try to create the impression that they are above it all. Actually, the fear that other people may injure them is at the bottom of their motivation. Unfortunately, they are unable to change their behavior, because of the rigidity basic to neurosis.[17]

ETIOLOGY OF NEUROSES

Much of what already has been written in this book about the etiology of psychoses, aside from the organic psychoses, is applicable

---

[17] Karen Horney, *Our Inner Conflicts* (New York: W. W. Norton and Co., 1945), p. 34, and pp. 40-95.

to neuroses. To date no biological basis for neurotic conditions has been found, although neurotic conditions do contribute to physiological ills as the result of sleeplessness, loss of appetite, and, probably, stress. Psychiatrists have attempted to explain the origin of neuroses partly in terms of the highly competitive culture of the United States, in which some individuals suffer feelings of inferiority and attempt to over-compensate. More commonly, faulty parent-child relationships are offered as an explanation. As pointed out above, Horney places the blame on the various types of conflicts that occur in life, such as the inability to live up to one's aspirations, the failure to control dangerous impulses, or the general frustrations of life itself. Today, however, it is generally recognized that while childhood experiences may predispose an individual toward neuroses the stress and conflict of his adult life must also be taken into consideration.

On the basis of sociological research, the incidence of neuroses is higher among persons in the upper social classes and the higher occupational categories. During the First World War, shell-shock—really a kind of hysteria—was found more frequently among enlisted personnel than among officers. This was not true in the Second World War. The reasons for this difference are by no means clear, but it has been suggested that as interpersonal relationships and life conditions become more complex and difficult, neurotic reactions increase. The higher the individual's occupational and social status, the greater the degree of personal responsibility he must assume and the more complicated the relationships in which he must engage.[18]

## TREATMENT OF MENTAL ILLNESS

The functional psychoses are attacked with electrically or chemically induced shock treatments, drugs (more recently including tranquilizers), surgery, and, particularly, psychotherapy, which is really a type of counseling. Strictly speaking, shock treatments are not direct therapy but rather methods employed literally to shock the individual

---

[18] Coleman, *op. cit.*, p. 224; Lantz, *op. cit.*, p. 101; Fredrick C. Redlich. *op. cit.*, p. 167.

into a rational state so that the psychiatrist can carry on psychotherapy. Tranquilizers are used to decrease emotional disturbances such as anxiety and may make it possible to treat patients in the physician's office. Certain types of surgery, such as pre-frontal lobotomy, are rather extreme measures generally employed only when other methods fail. At present the chief method of treating mental illness is discussion between the psychiatrist and the patient, in which, hopefully, the patient may gain new insights, understand his condition, and recover. Psychoanalysis employs free association and interpretation of dreams toward this end. Psychotherapy is a time-consuming task. The number of psychiatrists required for this work is far in excess of the 10,000 or so psychiatrists practicing in this country. Even with the aid of clinical psychologists and psychiatric social workers, the number of mentally ill persons is too great to be handled by existing personnel.

For example, the American Psychiatric Association established as a desirable standard one psychiatrist for every 95 patients. Today, a psychiatrist in a typical state mental hospital cares for from 150 to 400 or more patients. The ratio of nurses to psychiatric cases is one to 100, whereas it should be one to 15. In some states the ratio is from one to 700 or 800. Clinical psychologists care for double the number of patients that the standards of the American Psychiatric Association have called for.[19]

At present there are about 750,000 beds and about 600 hospitals for the mentally ill. To meet the national need, this number would have to be expanded by almost 50 per cent. Many of these buildings are old and badly deteriorated. Some of the smaller private institutions are so bad that they were described as "snake pits" by an inmate who had recovered. Salaries for attendants are quite low, and in some places the type of personnel attracted to these jobs is questionable. In *The Shame of the States*, Albert Deutsch has pointed out the serious overcrowding in mental institutions, the tendency to use restraints more than apparently necessary in better hospitals, and the low average daily per capita expenditure for patients in state mental hospitals. At present the lack of personnel coupled with the lack of adequate facilities makes the treatment of the mentally ill on an adequate scale impossible, not to mention the prevention of mental illness.

---

[19] Coleman, *op. cit.*, p. 623.

## SITUATIONAL-VALUE APPROACH

The average layman's attitude toward mental illness is a compound of fear and ignorance. If a family member contracts a psychosis, efforts are made to conceal the fact, because there is a widespread belief that mental disease is hereditary. Almost invariably the truth becomes known and the family suffers embarrassment. As pointed out earlier, there is no conclusive proof that mental illness is hereditary. Many people because of ignorance believe that all mentally ill patients are dangerous maniacs. Actually, the vast majority are harmless. Some of these attitudes are carried over from earlier times when the mentally ill were brutally treated. For example, in England it was customary for ladies and gentlemen to visit asylums to be "entertained" by the plight of the inmates. At other periods of history, psychotics were believed to be possessed by the devil. Some of the poor deluded women in colonial New England who confessed that they were witches were very likely suffering from mental illness. Philippe Pinel in 18th century France began unchaining the mentally ill and removing them from their dungeons. This was a radical innovation, but he proved that these patients were generally not dangerous. His example was followed by Dr. Benjamin Rush in Philadelphia's Pennsylvania Hospital in 1783. Still later, Dorothea Dix aroused the American public to the barbarous conditions in mental institutions. Despite these notable advances, and although public attitudes toward mental illness have improved, the myths and legends of the past do not die easily.

Mental illness is no rare condition involving a tiny fraction of the population. On the contrary, as pointed out earlier well over half a million persons were hospitalized for it in 1958. It is estimated that about 10 per cent of the U.S. population may at some time suffer severe mental illness. This does not include the large number of neurotics, about whom no accurate estimate is possible. Mental illness should be viewed as if it were just another kind of disease. It may strike anyone. So long as the demented are considered a strange, alien group, public interest in the treatment and prevention of psychoses and neuroses cannot increase.

In 1946 the National Mental Health Act was passed. It provides for research into all phases of mental illness under the direction of a National Institute of Mental Health. Students who qualify may be trained in psychiatry, clinical psychology, psychiatric nursing, and mental health. Research funds are available, as well as grants and aid to states and territories for programs outside of mental hospitals and institutions.

In addition to this, there is a national group known as the National Association for Mental Health. It too supports research, provides for training personnel, and arouses public opinion in behalf of better mental hospitals. It has helped set up mental health clinics in various communities, and carries on a program of public education. The National Mental Health Act and the National Association for Mental Health are hopeful signs that public fear, ignorance, and apathy toward the mentally ill is being changed in the United States.

## REMEDIAL MEASURES

The approach to the problem of mental illness should be a three-pronged one. It must involve, first of all, the adequate treatment of the mentally ill. To do this there is a need for more personnel and for more and better facilities. Extensive research into present therapeutic measures is likewise called for. Second, there should be more thorough and extended research into the prevention of mental illness. Third, the American public should be made aware of the true nature and incidence of mental illness, and the possibilities for treatment and prevention, so that they will actively support such measures.

It seems entirely unlikely that an adequate number of psychiatrists can be produced in the near future. Nevertheless, qualified young men and women should be encouraged to enter this field. But it requires about seven to eight years of training after college to complete both medical school and a residence in psychiatry. Therefore, attention should be given to the possibilities of using clinical psychologists, psychiatric social workers, and other qualified professional people to assist the present psychiatrists in their work. However, under no circumstances should this approach be allowed to lower the standards of psychiatric care. Although qualified professional persons may be available, hospital facilities must be considerably expanded and research and experimentation with new treatments should be initiated, especially to help decrease the amount of time mental patients must spend in hospitals. This is particularly true of schizophrenia, where the hospital-observation period is very long.

Prevention of mental illness, if it can be achieved, is even more important than treatment. Present research has barely scraped the surface of the problem. While sociological studies, as pointed out, do reveal some association between mental illness and socio-economic status, much more needs to be done. Present research is considerably more descriptive than analytical. Association does not necessarily mean causality. It is merely a clue indicating possible avenues of future investigation.

Finally, all of these programs will cost money. The fact is, however, that if more efficient methods of treatment, and, particularly, better methods of prevention are discovered, the ultimate cost should be below the present expense. To gain support for these programs, various educational facilities should be utilized, such as the National Association for Mental Health. Mental illness is a serious social problem. Because of its proportions, it must be dealt with in an organized way, and organized support can only come when the American public is made keenly aware of the problem.

## REVIEW QUESTIONS

1. What is the estimated incidence of mental illness in the United States?
2. How does a psychosis differ from a neurosis?
3. What are some causes of organic psychosis?
4. Why does the sociologist have a particular interest in the functional psychoses?
5. Can biological factors be definitely ruled out as causes of functional psychosis?
6. Evaluate the following statement: "Psychosis and neurosis in American society are largely produced by acute competition."

7. What do ecological studies reveal about the distribution of functional psychosis?

8. Do psychoses and neuroses reveal any associations with social class?

9. What are the most common methods of treating mental illness?

10. Analyze mental illness in the U.S. by means of the situational-value approach, indicating the situational factors and values which hamper treatment of the mentally ill.

11. What is the difference between a clinical psychologist and a psychiatrist?

## SELECTED READINGS

*Articles*

Cameron, Norman, "The Paranoid Pseudo-Community Revisited," *American Journal of Sociology*, 65 (July 1959), 52-8.

Clark, Robert E., "Relation of Schizophrenia to Occupational Income and Occupational Prestige," *American Sociological Review*, 13 (June 1948), 325-29.

Cohn, Melvin L., and John A. Clusen, "Social Isolation and Schizophrenia," *American Sociological Review*, 20 (June 1955), 265-73.

Dunham, H. Warren, "The Ecology of the Functional Psychosis in Chicago," *American Sociological Review*, 2 (Apr. 1937), 467-79.

Farris, E. L., "Cultural Isolation and a Schizophrenic Personality," *American Journal of Sociology*, 40: 155-64.

Fromm, Eric, "Origins of Neurosis," *American Sociological Review*, 9 (Apr. 1944), 380-84.

Ginsburg, Sol Weiner, "A Neurosis," *The Annals*, 286 (Mar. 1955), 55-64.

Green, Arnold W., "Why Americans Feel Insecure," in *Readings in Sociology*, eds. Edgar A. Schaler, *et al.* New York: Thomas Y. Crowell Co., 1960, pp. 812-21.

————, "The Middle Class Child and Neurosis," *American Sociological Review*, 11 (Feb. 1946), 31-41.

Herr, Vincent E., "The Loyola National Institute of Mental Health-Seminary Project," *American Catholic Sociological Review*, 21 (Winter 1960), 331-36.

Hollingshead, A. B., R. Ellis, and E. Kirby, "Social Mobility and Mental Illness," *American Sociological Review*, 18 (Apr. 1953), 163-69.

———— and Fredrick C. Redlich, "Social Stratification and Psy-chiatric Disorders," *American Sociological Review*, 18 (Apr. 1953), 163-69.

Lantz, Herman R., "Occupational Differences in Mental Disorder," *Social Problems*, 2 (Jan. 1955), 100-103.

Linn, Erwin L., "Patient's Social Economic Characteristics and Re-lease from a Mental Hospital," *American Journal of Sociology*, 65 (Nov. 1959), 280-86.

McKeown, James E., "The Behavior of Mothers of Normals, Neu-rotics and Schizophrenics," *The American Catholic Sociological Review*, 18 (Mar. 1956), 33-40.

Simmons, Ozzie G., and James A. Davis, "Interdisciplinary Col-laboration in Mental Illness Research," *American Journal of Sociology*, 63 (Nov. 1957), 297-303.


## Books

Averback, Alfred, *Schizophrenia*. New York: The Ronald Press Company, 1959.

Coleman, James C., *Abnormal Psychology in Modern Life*. Chicago: Scott, Foresman and Co., 1956.

Dunbar, Flanders, *Mind and Body: Psychosomatic Medicine*. New York: Random House, 1947.

Dunham, H. Warren, *Sociological Theory and Mental Disorder*. Detroit: Wayne State University Press, 1960.

Faris, Robert E. Lee, *Mental Disorders in Urban Areas: An Ecologi-cal Study of Schizophrenia and Other Psychoses*. New York: Hafner Pub-lishing Company, 1960.

Farnsworth, Dana L., *Mental Health in College and University*. Cambridge, Mass.: Harvard University Press, 1957.

Fein, R., *Economics and Mental Illness*. New York: Basic Books, Inc., 1958.

Halliday, James A., *Psychosocial Medicine: A Study of the Sick Society*. New York: W. W. Norton & Co., 1948.

Hollingshead, August B., *Social Class and Mental Illness*. New York: John Wiley and Sons, Inc., 1958.

Horney, Karen, *The Neurotic Personality of Our Times*. New York: W. W. Norton and Co., 1937.

————, *Our Inner Conflicts*. New York: W. W. Norton & Co., 1945.

Linton, Ralph, *Culture and Mental Disorders*. Springfield, Illinois: Charles C. Thomas, Publisher, 1956.

*Mental Health Education: A Critique*, Pennsylvania Mental Health, Inc., cosponsored by the American Psychiatric Association and the National Association for Mental Health, Inc., 1960.

Vanderveldt, James and R. Odenwald, *Psychiatry and Catholicism*. New York: McGraw-Hill Book Co., Inc., 1952.

# 6

# The Aging and the Aged

S INCE the turn of the century the population of the United States has doubled, but
the number of persons 65 years of age and
over has more than quadrupled. At present there are
about 15 million men and women in this age category.
Their number is increasing at the rate of more than
400,000 a year.[1] But the social problem of aging is not
merely the result of numbers. It has been compounded by
the transition from a rural economy to an urban, industrialized one. In 1850 only 16 per cent of the U.S.
population lived in communities of 2,500 or more. By
1950, 59 per cent lived in urban areas. In the past, the
farmhouse was large enough to accommodate a three-
generation family. When grandfather reached 65, he did
not retire. The more strenuous work was carried on by his
sons but he could always do something to help or at
least give direction.

Today most American workers face compulsory re-

---

[1] "Studies of the Aging and Aged, Selected Documents, Vol.
XI," *Fact Book on Aging*, Committee on Labor and Public
Welfare, U.S. Senate (Washington, D.C.: Government
Printing Office, 1957), p. 1.

tirement at 65. For American men especially, their occupation has been of major importance in their lives. It has enabled them to care for a wife and children, has provided a certain status within the community, and has been a source of friends and acquaintances. Compulsory retirement sharply and suddenly alters this situation. The status of a retiree is an ambivalent one for many Americans, particularly when they have not been prepared for it. Time may hang heavily on their hands and their wives sometimes complain that they get underfoot at home. In some societies the aged are respected as repositories of wisdom. This is not true in the United States because rapid social change has created a wide gulf between generations and older methods of doing and thinking have been rendered obsolete by new ones with which older persons may not have kept up. Sometimes it seems that a pitying tolerance is the most characteristic attitude of many persons toward the aged.

Because the older person is no longer employed, he may feel functionless. Because his income is apt to have been reduced considerably, he may not have enough money to live in reasonable comfort. Because of his advanced years, the problem and costs of medical care increase. For some, adequate housing is lacking. To alleviate or eliminate some of these difficulties, a new discipline known as *gerontology* has been developed.

> Gerontology is a scientific study of the phenomena of aging. By aging, we mean the progressive changes which take place in the cell, tissue, and organ system, a total organism, or a group of organisms with the passage of time. All living things change with time in both structure and function, and the changes which follow with the general trend constitute aging.[2]

The social problem of the aged is moving from the covert to the overt stage. As the number of aged in the population grows and as the public becomes increasingly aware of their social, economic, psychological, and medical problems, more attention is focused upon them. Failure to recognize the existence of this problem in the past was partly because the percentage of the aged in the population was not so great as it is today, and partly because of the youth-orientation of American society.

In the United States, concern about youth has been expressed

---

[2] Nathan W. Shock, *Trends in Gerontology* (Stanford, Calif.: Stanford University Press, 1957), p. 1.

through laws regarding their education, the establishment of a public school system, and legislation governing the age at which children may work and their working conditions. Some of the greatest strides in medicine have been made in the elimination and treatment of childhood diseases. Vocational counseling and premarriage

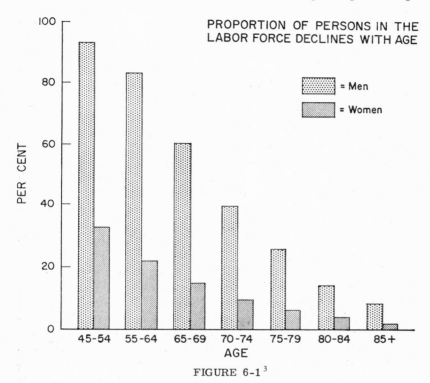

FIGURE 6-1 [3]

counseling have dealt almost exclusively with youth. While all of this is desirable, it merely underscores a fact that American society has until recently been preoccupied almost exclusively with youth. By 1975 it is estimated that there will be more than 20 million persons 65 years of age and over, and this will mean more attention for the older persons in the future.

[3] Adapted from *Housing for the Elderly, A Fact Book*, Housing and Home Finance Agency, Office of the Administrator, Washington, D.C., June 1959.

The chart in Figure 6-1 indicates that more than two out of every three men 65 years of age and over are either unable to work or are not working for other reasons. Among these other reasons would be both the inability to obtain a job and compulsory retirement. Of the women in this age bracket, more than nine out of ten are either unable to work or do not work for some other reason. Most of these women are not in the labor force, probably because they are housekeepers—but some of them have also retired. Many workers, particularly men, are forced into retirement by a period of unemployment just prior to the age of 65. A survey carried on by the Old Age and Survivors' Insurance Office of the Department of Health Education and Welfare in 1941-42 found that only 5 per cent of the men receiving benefits said they had retired and filed for benefits while they were in good health. More than half had already been laid off and about one-third retired because of illness or failing health.[4] In fact, even at the age of 40 or 45, many men find it very difficult to secure a job. During the depression of the thirties both very young and very old persons had the most difficult time obtaining work. During the Second World War a severe labor shortage resulted in expanded employment of older persons. At the conclusion of the war older women tended to drop out of the labor force while older men remained in it.

While the popular feeling is that the older worker is less productive than the middle-aged worker, research does not bear this out. Dr. Breen and Mr. Spaeth studied samples of matched pairs of workers in four Chicago companies: a steel mill, a men's-clothing factory, a radio-and-television factory, and a photographic-equipment plant. Their findings revealed that there was no significant difference in the main productivities scores between the two age groups studied. They concluded that as far as their research project was able to measure these differences, the older group produced as much and as consistently as the younger group.[5] Their findings were in agreement with other research done in this field. Discrimination in em-

---

[4] Ewan Clague, "Aging and Employability" in *Living Through the Older Years, Proceedings of the Charles A. Fisher Memorial Institute on Aging,* ed. Clark Tibbitts (Ann Arbor: University of Michigan Press, 1951), p. 144.

[5] Leonard Z. Breen and Joe L. Spaeth, *Journal of Gerontology,* 15 (1960), pp. 68-70.

ployment against older workers seems to be a fact and this has led Professor Breen to speak of the aged and aging in the United States as a minority group. However, there are great differences in the attitudes of various categories of workers toward retirement. Generally speaking, unskilled and semi-skilled steel workers want to continue work to a much lesser extent than, say, physicians. The meaning of work, therefore, is associated with social class. Dr. Havighurst has pointed out that the meaning of work varies among people. To the extent that older people can maintain their self-esteem and status in the community and as retirement plans are able to meet the economic needs of older people, voluntary retirement is likely to increase.[6]

## INCOME

One of the major problems affecting the older worker or retiree is the lack of an adequate income. In 1957 the median income of families with a head between ages of 55 and 64 was $4,773. But for those families with a head 65 years and over the median income was $2,490. While it is true that the median income for older men had increased from about $1,000 in 1948 to $1,247 by 1952, it must be noted that it is not the actual amount of cash received but rather what food and services such money can buy. For example, in 1955 $50 was required to buy the same goods and services that could be purchased with $26.50 in 1940.[7] Even those who have set aside a sum for the proverbial rainy day find that this sum is less adequate than it was just a few years ago.

According to government estimates it cost an elderly couple in October, 1950 from $1,602 a year (in New Orleans) to $1,908 (in Milwaukee) in order to maintain a modest but adequate level of living in an urban area. But in 1954 almost half of the families with heads 65 years of age or over had cash incomes of less than $2,000, and a fifth had less than $1,000. In the same year about

---

[6] E. A. Friedmann and R. J. Havighurst, *The Meaning of Work and Retirement* (Chicago: University of Chicago Press, 1954), p. 183.

[7] Shock, *op. cit.*, pp. 34-36.

TABLE 6-1[8]

TOTAL MONEY INCOME OF ALL FAMILIES IN THE UNITED STATES, AND OF FAMILIES WITH HEADS AGED 55 AND OVER, 1957

| Total money income | All families | Age of head of family | |
| | | 55 to 64 | 65 and over |
| --- | --- | --- | --- |
| Number (in thousands) | 43,714 | 6,629 | 5,818 |
| Per cent | 100.0 | 100.0 | 100.0 |
| Under $500 | 3.0 | 3.9 | 4.7 |
| $   500 to $  999 | 3.4 | 3.9 | 10.3 |
| 1,000 to  1,499 | 4.0 | 4.1 | 12.7 |
| 1,500 to  1,999 | 4.5 | 5.0 | 12.1 |
| 2,000 to  2,999 | 9.6 | 10.9 | 17.9 |
| 3,000 to  4,999 | 25.9 | 25.2 | 20.0 |
| 5,000 to  6,999 | 24.8 | 21.3 | 11.3 |
| 7,000 to  9,999 | 16.3 | 15.2 | 6.3 |
| 10,000 and over | 8.4 | 10.5 | 4.6 |
| Median income | $4,971 | $4,773 | $2,490 |

Bureau of the Census, Current Population Reports, Consumer Income, Series P-60, No. 30, December 1958.

two-thirds of all persons 65 years of age or over living alone or with nonrelatives had a cash income of less than $1,000.[9]

In December, 1955, about 29% of all persons 65 years of age and over were receiving income from employment either as an earner or the wife of an earner. Forty-three per cent were getting Old Age and Survivors Insurance benefits; 12% were getting benefits from the special retirement systems for railroad and government workers or the veterans program. Eighteen per cent were on public assistance. Eleven per cent were living solely on other types of incomes (investments, commercial annuities, industrial pensions and so forth), or support from relatives.[10]

---

[8] Adapted from *Housing for the Elderly, A Fact Book, op. cit.*
[9] "Studies of the Aging and Aged," *op. cit.*, pp 1-2.
[10] "Studies of the Aging and Aged," *op. cit.*, p. 29.

## HOUSING

Despite recent improvements and governmental help, housing for the aged is today still inadequate. In 1950 94.3 per cent of persons 65 and over lived in some type of household with their spouse, other relatives, nonrelatives or alone. 5.7 per cent lived in quasi-households such as institutions, hotels, or similar residences.

Perhaps it is ironic but one problem of housing results from the fact that 68 per cent of nonfarm families in which the head is 65 or over own their own home. A man's home is his castle, and there is an undeniable sentimental attachment to the house in which one has lived most of his life. But this same house may have little but emotional value for the aged, and may even be a hazard to them. First, it is likely to be large, having two stories and a basement, with all the peril that stairs present to those in their late 60's and 70's. The care of such a home and its grounds is too taxing for some older persons. Not infrequently it is located in an area that has now become marginal and is hemmed in by taverns, hot dog stands, and rooming houses, and smothered by the noise and fumes of heavy traffic. In about two-thirds of the cases this large home has only one, or at most two, occupants.

One solution to this problem is for the aged to move in with their children. Sometimes this works out quite satisfactorily. Often it does not. Newer housing is apt to be smaller, bedroom and bathroom facilities are taxed, tempers become short, and the aged have a sense of imposing on their children and a not entirely unfounded feeling in some cases that they are unwanted. Some older persons prefer to enter a convalescent home or an institution for the aged, such as those maintained by communities of Catholic nuns, fraternal organizations, or, if necessary, the state. Standards in private convalescent homes are spotty. Some are admittedly firetraps, many are relatively expensive, and few will accept the bed-ridden. Church and fraternal organization homes are apt to be better than many private establishments and frequently offer good recreational and medical facilities. They generally provide for married couples, single persons, widows, and widowers. Some have been criticized for their failure to

TABLE 6-2[11]

LIVING ARRANGEMENTS OF PERSONS AGED 65 YEARS AND OVER,
BY AGE AND SEX, 1950

(Percentage distribution, based on $3\frac{1}{3}$ per cent sample)

| | Age | | | | | | | | |
|---|---|---|---|---|---|---|---|---|---|
| | 65 and over | | | 65 to 74 | | | 75 and over | | |
| Living arrangement | Total | Male | Fe-male | Total | Male | Fe-male | Total | Male | Fe-male |
| Total | 100.0 | 100.0 | 100.0 | 100.0 | 100.0 | 100.0 | 100.0 | 100.0 | 100.0 |
| Living in households | 94.3 | 93.8 | 94.7 | 95.3 | 94.5 | 96.0 | 92.1 | 92.1 | 92.1 |
| Own households | 68.9 | 75.9 | 62.8 | 74.8 | 80.2 | 69.6 | 56.3 | 65.7 | 48.6 |
| Married and living with spouse | 43.9 | 58.5 | 31.1 | 51.1 | 64.5 | 38.9 | 28.3 | 44.7 | 14.8 |
| Living with relatives other than spouse | 10.6 | 7.1 | 13.6 | 10.0 | 6.2 | 13.3 | 11.8 | 8.8 | 14.4 |
| Living alone or with nonrelatives | 14.4 | 10.3 | 18.1 | 13.7 | 9.5 | 17.4 | 16.2 | 12.2 | 19.4 |
| Not in own households | 25.3 | 17.9 | 31.9 | 20.7 | 14.2 | 26.4 | 35.8 | 26.4 | 43.3 |
| Living with relatives | 21.1 | 13.5 | 28.0 | 16.5 | 9.9 | 22.4 | 31.3 | 21.7 | 39.0 |
| Living with nonrelatives | 4.2 | 4.4 | 3.9 | 4.2 | 4.3 | 4.0 | 4.5 | 4.7 | 4.3 |
| Living in quasi-households | 5.7 | 6.2 | 5.3 | 4.7 | 5.5 | 4.0 | 7.9 | 7.9 | 7.9 |
| In institutions | 3.1 | 3.0 | 3.2 | 2.1 | 2.2 | 1.9 | 5.3 | 4.8 | 5.8 |
| Other quasi-households | 2.6 | 3.2 | 2.1 | 2.6 | 3.3 | 2.1 | 2.6 | 3.1 | 2.1 |
| Total | 100.0 | 100.0 | 100.0 | 100.0 | 100.0 | 100.0 | 100.0 | 100.0 | 100.0 |
| In families (1 or more relatives present) | 76.5 | 79.9 | 73.4 | 78.4 | 81.6 | 75.6 | 72.2 | 76.1 | 68.9 |
| Not in families (no relatives present) | 23.5 | 20.1 | 26.6 | 21.6 | 18.4 | 24.4 | 27.8 | 23.9 | 31.1 |

Bureau of the Census, United States Census of Population: 1950, Vol. 4, Special Reports, pt. 2.

segregate the senile from those not mentally ill. It is depressing for an older person to see others suffering from senility and to fear that tomorrow he may also be a victim. As more and more states move to enact legislation on the standards for such homes conditions should improve.

[11] Adapted from *Housing for the Elderly, A Fact Book, op. cit.*, Table 26.

But many older persons, even though alone in the world, would like to maintain a home of their own. Scandinavia, Germany, and Holland have done a great deal in housing the aged. Units for couples and single persons have been built without stairs, or with elevators and safeguards such as bathtub bars and nonskid floors.

The United States Government, through the Housing Act of 1956, has facilitated the purchase of housing by older persons by financing rental projects designed particularly for the aged and by making public low-cost rentals more available to them. For instance, it is now possible for persons 60 or over to purchase a home with a 30-year mortgage even when, because of age, financial, or physical condition, they cannot otherwise qualify by having a third party sign with them. Another provision makes it possible for church, fraternal, or labor groups to secure F.H.A. mortgage insurance for construction of eight units or more specifically designed for the aged. The F.H.A. also allows full cost for such items as central dining room facilities, recreation rooms, infirmaries, and similar accommodations essential to elderly people. Low-cost public housing is also available to older persons, and in New York State 10 per cent of all state-financed public housing is set aside for them. But today less than half of the states have such housing projects, despite the need for them.

Housing developments for the aged have been established in Arizona, Florida, and some other southern states. Entire towns have been erected with individual homes or apartments exclusively for older persons. The trailer camp is another location to which some older persons have moved. Certain camps are designed solely for them, while others reserve a specific section. Some couples move to a southern camp for winter months, coming north to be with their children during the summer. Others have their trailers set up permanently in one place. Certain questions may be raised about the advisability of some of the present developments. Is there a danger that senior citizens will find they are segregated? Is it entirely wise to exclude younger persons from some of these communities in which their parents have decided to live? At present this may be the result of a dearth of housing for the aged, but association with children and grandchildren should not be denied.

One of the changes in housing for older persons is that of location. Formerly it was common to locate homes for the aged in rural areas. Inexpensive land was undoubtedly a factor but more than one oldster has remarked that it made him feel he was being turned out to pasture. Today there is a tendency to erect housing in or near the center of the city so that older persons may walk to church, theaters, clubs, museums and such, or at least have access to public transportation. This likewise makes feasible day visits to their children and friends in the same city. Medical and hospital facilities are readily accessible.

Another problem closely associated with housing is that of meals. Older persons, particularly those living alone, sometimes fail to provide adequate food for themselves. There is a temptation to subsist on cold snacks and to neglect hot meals altogether. Others lack the strength to prepare a regular dinner. Some communities have inaugurated volunteer agencies known as "meals on wheels" which bring a completely prepared hot meal to the homes of aged persons. Charges for such services are based on the ability of the aged to pay for them. They are usually quite low and periodic examinations of persons who receive such services show an improvement in both their physical and psychological health.[12]

### HEALTH

Since the beginning of the century life expectancy at birth for white males has increased from 48 to 63 years; for white females from 51 to 73 years. Nonwhite males born in 1956 have a life expectancy of 61 years; nonwhite females almost 66 years.[13]

Over the centuries the life expectancy of human beings has shown a remarkable increase. In ancient Rome, for example, the life expectancy for males at birth was between 15 and 20 years; for females about one year longer.[14] Increased life expectancy has largely been the result of improved sanitation, a decrease in infant and maternal mortality rates, and the conquest of childhood diseases within the last half century. On the other hand the death rate for heart disease

---

[12] Shock, op. cit., p. 112.
[13] Summary of Health and Vital Statistics, U.S. Department of Health, Education and Welfare, Washington, D.C., June 1958, p. 26.
[14] John D. Doran, "Mortality Estimates from Roman Tombstone Inscriptions," American Journal of Sociology, 65 (1960), 365; and Shock, op. cit., p. 11.

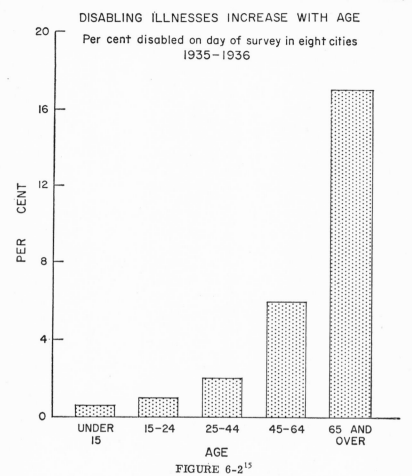

DISABLING ILLNESSES INCREASE WITH AGE

Per cent disabled on day of survey in eight cities
1935—1936

FIGURE 6-2[15]

has increased from 137.4 per 100,000 population in 1900 to 360.5 in 1956. Deaths from cancer have more than doubled in the same period. These latter increases in deaths from heart diseases and cancer reflect the increased number of aged persons in the population.

As persons age the prevalence of disabling illness increases. In 1950 6 out of every 100 persons between 45 and 64, and 17 out of every 100 persons 65 and over, had a long-term disabling illness.

[15] Adapted from *Fact Book on Aging, op. cit.*, p. 41.

The incidence of such illness is likely to increase because in 1956 white males age 65 had a life expectancy of 12.9 years; white females at the same age 15.5 years.[16] While older people need medical attention and hospitalization to a greater extent than younger persons, they usually have much less money with which to purchase them. This introduces one of the most controversial questions in the field of health in the United States today.

Recently, various legislation has been introduced in the U.S. Congress to help defray the cost of medical care, hospitalization, and medicines. The best known of these is the Forand Bill, which would increase employee and employer contributions for social security and provide medical care for those 65 years of age or over. Its opponents claim it would cost a fantastic sum of money, some estimates going as high as 2 billion or more a year, and the most vigorous objections have been brought by the American Medical Association, which terms it a type of socialized medicine. On the other hand it has received the very strong support of labor. At present it appears unlikely that the Forand Bill will be passed but very likely some type of provision for medical care of the aged will eventually be enacted by Congress. Ultimately, however, as the number of older persons in American society increases, legislative fear of their political power will probably result in more adequate medical provisions for them.

## PSYCHOLOGICAL AND PHYSIOLOGICAL FACTORS IN AGING

Dr. Wilma Donahue has pointed out that the general age curves for psychological functions have a parabolic shape. During the first third of the curve from birth to the late teens or early twenties there is a sharp acceleration to a peak. This is followed by a long period during which a person functions at maximum efficiency or begins a very slow decline into the late 40's or 50's. In the later years there is a more rapid decline in the curve, which represents

---

[16] *Summary of Health and Vital Statistics, op. cit.,* p. 27.

decreased efficiency. Actually the decline in the physiological aspects of aging is much greater than in the psychological area.[17]

It is well known that both visual and auditory acuity tend to decrease with the years. There is also some indication that scores obtained by older persons on general intelligence tests such as those for vocabulary show very little decline or none at all with increased age. But here again there is a matter of individual differences. The decline in the case of an individual who has high intellectual endowments and considerable education is much less steep than it is among persons lacking these. Reaction time is likewise somewhat slower for older persons than for youth. Theoretically, this should mean that older persons would have more automobile accidents than younger persons. The contrary is true. The older person is able to compensate for his slower reflexes by the use of greater prudence and judgment. Older persons, however, do show increased inability to learn nonsense syllables or to recall isolated facts. Here again it is not possible to determine whether it is a lack of motivation or a real decline in mental efficiency.

Certain personality changes may occur in the later years as the result of physiological changes. The idea that older people tend to be stubborn, lack flexibility and adaptability, and are conservative and reactionary may be the result of their social situation. Cowdry has stated:

> Feeling inferior and inadequate as social beings, they (older persons) find a sense of security and support in old established beliefs and practices insofar as these affect the environment with which they must interact. To put it another way, the aging person is likely to have an emotional need of finding the world as unchanging and predictable as the infant finds his completely subsidized world.[18]

Various tests have been conducted on the relationship between ability to learn and age. Generally, they reveal that learning ability rises definitely until about age 25 and then begins a slow decline. Present evidence seems to indicate, however, that no one should

---

[17] Wilma Donahue, "Changes in Psychological Processes" in *Living Through the Older Years, Proceedings of the Charles A. Fisher Memorial Institute on Aging,* ed. Clark Tibbitts (Ann Arbor: University of Michigan Press, 1952), pp. 69-70.

[18] E. V. Cowdry, "Problems of the Aging," as quoted in Donahue, *op. cit.,* p. 79.

hesitate to learn a new task, because of age, at least up until 50 or 55 years of age. Motivation is an important factor in learning, and the inability of adults to learn may be due to an original lack of mental capacity or factors other than age. The older person simply may not be sufficiently motivated to learn a new task, or he may fear ridicule by others, which would inhibit the learning process. There is evidence that memory is less keen at age 65 than at age 50, but so far it is impossible to determine whether this loss in memory represents a small loss in many or a great loss in a few. Intelligence tests attempting to measure innate mental capacity show less decline with age if speed is not a factor. Basically, it appears that when intellectual activities and interests are continued, comprehension, reasoning and judgment are maintained at a relatively constant level.[19]

Physiological changes in the sensory and mental apparatus of older people appear to be related to a reduced supply of oxygen to the cortical tissue. Studies reveal that older persons show a decreased ability to memorize several series of unrelated words. While the average college student can remember about 8 out of 10, their professors, who were between 55 and 60, averaged a recall of only 4 to 5 words. However, when the supply of oxygen to these young men was reduced, their ability to recall was about the same as that of their professors.[20] The results of such experiments are most meaningful to industry.

Among the advantages enjoyed by older workers is decreased absenteeism, although admittedly only those older persons in relatively good health are apt to be employed. When the older worker is disabled, he does tend to require a longer period of time before his return to work and/or more medical attention. But turnover among older workers is considerably less than that among younger workers. Since it requires a considerable period of time to train workers for certain positions, the relative permanency of older workers is an asset to industry. Again, it should be repeated that all of this must be considered on an individual basis. Age cannot be computed ex-

[19] Ross A. McFarland, "The Psychological Aspects of Aging," *Problems of Aging*, ed. Robert L. Craig (New York: The New York Academy of Medicine, 1956), pp. 17-19.
[20] McFarland, *op. cit.*, pp. 20-21.

clusively in chronological time but rather in terms of the physiological and psychological condition of the specific individual.[21]

For a long time it has been more or less customary to explain emotional or mental illness in old age by *senility*, that is, an organic type of psychosis resulting from arteriosclerosis of the brain. This, of course, is not uncommon; but Dr. Francis J. Braceland, a well-known American psychiatrist, has called attention to the fact that some mental illness in old age is functional. He points out that during the aging process there is a gradual impairment of the body's capacity to maintain itself, associated with tissue changes of a degenerative nature. He believes that emotional pressures themselves contribute to this type of breakdown. Old age is a period of great stress for many people and, as they utilize strong adaptive measures and their physical and mental capacities wane, the sense of security disappears. They may rebel against the social and economic problems of aging, and even those who do not face such problems are still unable to accept their situations. Rebellion against them aggravates their already precarious positions. This view that emotional disturbances in old age may be of a functional nature is relatively new. Dr. Braceland considers cerebral arteriosclerosis a normal component of aging, and he feels that it only infrequently leads to an organic psychosis. Even when it does, psychological and sociological factors may be quite important.

Dr. Braceland also points out that manic-depressive psychotics now tend to live longer and to have additional attacks in old age. Furthermore, since many more persons now live to 65 and beyond, they may experience severe emotional problems and anxieties, with the result that even mild brain damage can stimulate a psychotic reaction. Fortunately, the prognosis is good. These are disorders that can be treated, and if they are not recognized and treated, suicide may result. Such persons may suffer periods of depression, but anxiety, hypochondria, and compulsive symptoms may be so obvious that the depression goes unnoticed. He believes that some patients suffering functional psychosis in old age do so because the latent potentiality toward such a psychosis is brought out by the biological, psychological, and, probably, sociological stresses of aging. Among these he cites the bereavement of friends, retirement from work,

---

[21] McFarland, *op. cit.*, pp. 23-24.

and decreased satisfaction with life. This is especially noticeable among those who attach considerable importance to their occupations. He notes that individuals who are most susceptible to depression in their latter years are likely to be persons who had been rigid, stubborn, or overly conscientious and meticulous. In other words, their basic insecurity is increased by physical and mental handicaps common in older years.

One of his most interesting observations is that the very qualifications that brought success to these persons during their middle years may hinder adjustment in later years. Accustomed to a role of authority and superordination, they react negatively to a passive and subordinate role. Although they are less frequent, paranoia and hallucinations also occur. They are more marked among women than men. These persons try to solve the problem of age and approaching death by establishing an environment in which they can live out their infantile strivings. Prognosis in such cases is poor.

However, increased experience in dealing with the psychiatric disorders of the aged has altered the notion that these persons are poor subjects for intensive psychiatric effort. Dr. Braceland's statements should do much to assure the aged that their situation is far from hopeless even when complicated by emotional or mental disorders, should stimulate them to seek psychiatric attention, and should encourage psychiatrists to expend the necessary time and effort on them.

## SOCIOLOGICAL FACTORS

To some extent the sociological factors, or at least most of them, have already been cited. To review them briefly, retirement, lowered income, mental and physical health problems, inadequate housing, loss of friends and relatives through death, as well as a general feeling that they are no longer loved or wanted—all contribute to the problems of the aging. Much of this is intensified by the fact that American society, as pointed out earlier, is youth-centered. The role of the aging and aged has yet to be defined adequately. Thus they find themselves at once in a role which is generally undesirable or is at best ambiguous. As a result their frustrations are increased at a time of life when a certain amount of frustration is more likely than usual by reason of physiological and psychological factors.

## SITUATIONAL-VALUE APPROACH

The situation of the aging and aged is apt to be one of increasing loneliness. Most of their life has been lived and a relatively short span remains. Not only do they witness the passing of relatives and friends, but they are keenly aware that their own active partici- pation in certain roles must, of pure necessity, decrease. Yet many of these roles have become habitual because they have occupied them during most of their years. For the American male his occupation is usually of paramount importance. But this, usually, is now over. His role as father is a tenuous one since his children are likely to have grown up and married, or at least to have left home. Men, to a lesser extent than women, do not suffer the loss of their spouses. But some do, and this adds to their emotional difficulties.

Women, while they are more likely than not to be widows by age 70 or later, do not necessarily relinquish their occupational roles. Most have been housewives, and they can continue—albeit on a diminished scale—the role of a homemaker, even if only for them- selves. In most cases their world has been one of primary relation- ships, i.e., with a husband and children. Some grandmothers are able to continue the mother-surrogate role with their grandchildren. Frequently, they may live with a daughter and assist materially in housekeeping. At any rate, unless they have been career women they do not face the same kinds of crises that the male usually faces.

Since the values of American society do center around youth—and to a lesser extent middle age—as the more desirable periods of life, the aged come to feel that they are living in a society which places a relatively low value upon their period of life. Some even think of themselves as necessary evils and bitterly resent their position. If circumstances permit, some tend to become domineering and de- manding, while others retreat into a state of apathy. Rapid social change deprives them of the high status they might enjoy in a more static society, where their knowledge of the past and their ex- periences could be passed on to the young.

But certain aspects of social change are already altering both the situational and value aspects of the aging and aged. Old Age and Survivors Insurance means that fewer of them will become dependents. While their income may be slight, they do possess some and no longer prove a complete burden upon children, some of whose economic circumstances limit their ability to provide for parents. The increased number of older persons in American society will inevitably bring about changes in both their situations and in the attitudes taken toward them. Until this occurs, however, their present position in society and society's attitudes toward them make their position difficult and constitute a social problem.

## REMEDIAL MEASURES

Many things have been done and even more can be done to alleviate age as a social problem. The amount and extent of social security benefits will have to be increased so that the aged can enjoy at least a comfortable existence. Adequate housing can be provided for them on a much wider scale. Recreational opportunities and, particularly, the facilitation of association with persons of their own age group will also help. Eventually, a better method of providing medical, hospital, and nursing care will have to be provided.

In 1961, Senate Resolution 266 was proposed by the administration but not passed by Congress. It provided for "the financing of a balanced program of health services, including hospitalization, outpatient laboratory diagnosis, skilled nursing home care, home health services, and, within actuarially feasible limits, part of the cost of medicines, for all retired elderly persons, under a separate insurance fund to be collected and administered by the Social Security Administration." Furthermore, it would have included those not now covered by social security.[22]

The problem of the aging and aged in this respect has already been described and it is sufficient to repeat that they generally have more need of medical attention than others but less money with which to

---

[22] A *Report Made by the Sub-Committee on Problems of the Aging and Aged, of the Committee on Labor and Public Welfare, United States Senate* (Washington, D.C.: Government Printing Office, 1961), p. 2.

pay for it. Certain improvements have been made through voluntary health insurance, notably Blue Cross, which pays at least part of the hospitalization costs—including certain diagnostic tests—and Blue Shield, which is largely for surgical expenses. These are nonprofit organizations. More recently, commercial insurance companies have entered the field and, while enrollment in them has increased, amounts of their payments for hospital care, surgery, and such are considerably less than those of Blue Cross-Blue Shield.

If any group of people really needs health insurance, it is the aged; yet the larger proportion of persons without such insurance are those 65 or over. Some cannot obtain it because they are unemployed; others, though employed, work for companies in which group insurance plans do not exist. Many claim they cannot afford such insurance, while some are indifferent to it or have procrastinated in applying for it. Perhaps the cruelest reason for lack of such coverage among the aged is that it has been cancelled. Senator George R. Metcalf of the New York State legislature reported that a study of nine commercial carriers in that state revealed that eight of them selling individual health insurance policies provided for cancellation due to age or physical condition.[23] Cancellation of or failure to renew an older person's health insurance policy makes it just about impossible for him to obtain this coverage from another company. This situation is improving, and will doubtless be helped by the proposed federal health insurance plan.

But broader extension of voluntary health insurance to the aged and the inclusion of noncancellation clauses are not enough. Benefits from these policies are usually inadequate. Such insurance means very little when it pays $5.00 a day for a hospital bed which actually costs the patient $15.00 or $20.00 a day. Coverage is neither extensive enough in numbers or in benefits. Furthermore, commercial companies operate for profit, and as the incidence of illness and hospitalization among the aged is great, the venture is likely to be profitless. Health insurance for the aged must be based upon a sense of social justice and not the profit of financial enterprise.

One provision of the proposed bill covered nursing homes. This is perhaps the greatest single need of America's aged. A study in

---

[23] Senator George R. Metcalf, *Health Insurance for the Aged: Good News for Later Life,* New York State Joint Legislative Committee on the Problems of the Aging, Legislative document (1958), No. 8, p. 119.

Massachusetts revealed that 40 per cent of the patients who spent more than 30 days in a hospital were there for nonmedical reasons, i.e., they could have been cared for adequately in nursing homes without occupying hospital beds, which are in short supply throughout most of the country. While states vary in their legislation on nursing homes, the national situation is deplorable. Some of these institutions are firetraps, have no resident nurses, fail to segregate the senile from the mentally normal, refuse bed patients entirely, and generally cost more than many older persons can afford. Extension of home care for the aged who are ill or disabled, another measure in a government proposal, would release more hospital beds, open up more space in nursing homes, and, when feasible, permit oldsters to live out their lives in familiar surroundings, sometimes with or near relatives and friends.

There are some objections to the government proposal. The fear of tremendous paperwork on the part of the busy physician, who would probably have to make out triplicate or quadruplicate reports by the dozen, is one. Chiseling and malingering are just about inevitable, and efforts to prevent or stop such abuse could well mean an appeal to elected political officials, always sensitive to constituent pressure. Some older persons, although not many, simply do not need such help and can well afford health care. Estimates of the cost of such health insurance for the aged vary tremendously and seem to be influenced as much by emotion as economics. But the strongest opponent is the American Medical Association, almost inevitably beset by an exaggerated anxiety that any such measure is merely a foreshadowing of "socialized medicine."

It should be noted that the proposed Senate Resolution is actually an insurance plan. Some persons not now included in Social Security will benefit, but in the years ahead, as coverage is extended, older persons can look forward with greater serenity in regard to health problems in later years. A realization that they can obtain and pay for health care through insurance removes the stigma some now suffer of being a charity case. In some states, older persons can only obtain free medical care by what amounts to the taking of a "pauper's oath." The late years of life are usually not easy. Problems run far beyond the matter of health and income, although these presently loom as one of the major areas of difficulty. To the extent that these are adequately met, at least two aspects of frustration and anxiety typical of later life can be removed.

If the medical needs of America's aged are to be heeded, some type of compulsory health insurance seems necessary. To spread the cost equitably, a national plan seems desirable. This should supplement rather than destroy voluntary types of health insurance, at least among those aged who can afford them. The argument that some older persons can pay for medical care and thus should not benefit under compulsory health insurance might just as well be used against the provisions of the Old Age, Disability and Survivors Insurance (Social Security). Few persons today would attempt this.

Equally important is an effort to find an adequate definition of the roles of the aging and aged and to convince them that they have something to contribute to society. Among some of the measures would be changes in compulsory retirement ages. Admittedly, this is difficult because insurance programs are based upon a specific retirement age. But it is at once cruel and wasteful to retire those in good physical and mental health. The loss of some of these people to society is probably incalculable. Preparations for retirement are now made by many companies, and even more of this will be necessary in the future. When the period of old age can be considered one in which individuals may return to activities they have longed to enjoy during most of their lives but have been unable to do so from lack of time and money, this period of life will take on a new meaning. In fact, it has already done so for a number of older people. As the life span increases and the number of those 65 and over becomes greater, society will be compelled to give greater consideration to this segment of human life. Older persons themselves will have to make the adjustments necessitated by diminished strength and vigor, but the degree of such decline in most persons is not so severe as to preclude the living out of a happy, satisfactory life.

## REVIEW QUESTIONS

1. How has the ratio of persons 65 years of age and over changed since the turn of the present century? To what do you ascribe this change?
2. Define gerontology.

3. What are the prevalent American attitudes toward the aging and aged? Contrast these attitudes with other societies.

4. Are older workers less productive than middle-aged workers? Cite empirical evidence for your answer.

5. Compare the incomes of persons 65 or over with those below this age. What specific measures could be taken to increase the income of older persons?

6. How does housing represent a problem to the aged?

7. Has the United States government facilitated purchase of housing by older persons?

8. What is the health status of aged Americans? Be specific and cite actual studies.

9. What is senility? Is this a problem best handled within an institution?

10. To what extent do the predominant American values toward the aged facilitate or hamper the solution of the problems they face?

## SELECTED READINGS

### Articles

Cavan, Ruth, "Family Life and Family Substitutes in Old Age," *American Sociological Review*, 13 (Feb. 1948), 71-82.

Havighurst, Robert J., "The Leisure Activities of the Middle Aged," *American Journal of Sociology*, 63 (Sept. 1957), 152-62.

"Notes on the Economic Situation in the United States." U.S. Bureau of Labor Statistics, Washington, D.C., 1958.

Scott, Frances Gillespie, "Factors in the Personal Adjustment of Institutionalized and Non-institutionalized Aged," *American Sociological Review*, 20 (Oct. 1955), 538-46.

### Books

Barron, Milton L., *The Aging American: An Introduction to Social Gerontology and Geriatrics*. New York: Thomas Y. Crowell Co., 1961.

Biren, James E., ed., *Handbook of Aging and the Individual: Psychological and Biological Aspects*. Chicago: University of Chicago Press, 1960.

Burgess, Ernest W., ed., *Retirement Villages: New Living Patterns for the Later Years. Division of Gerontology*, University of Michigan, Ann Arbor, Michigan, 1961.

Cavan, Ruth S., Ernest W. Burgess, Robert J. Havighurst, and Gerbert Goldhamer, *Personal Adjustment in Old Age*. Chicago: The Science Research Associates, 1949.

Drake, Joseph T., *The Aged in American Society*. New York: The Ronald Press Company, 1961.

Greeley, Ogden, *Private Nursing Homes: Their Role in the Care of the Aged*. New York: Public Affairs Commission, 1960.

Kaplan, Oscar, *Mental Disorders of Later Life*. Stanford, California: Stanford University Press, 1956.

Tibbitts, Clark, ed., *Handbook of Social Gerontology: Societal Aspects of Aging*. Chicago: University of Chicago Press, 1960.

# PART THREE

# Problems of Personal Deviation

I N the next section that which is usually termed "personal deviation" is treated. This includes juvenile delinquency, crime, narcotic addiction, alcoholism, and suicide. Like population problems, juvenile delinquency has become a frequently discussed topic in American society. But these discussions often generate more heat than light. While no effort is made to minimize the problem, students will be able to understand it more adequately if they realize that statistics on this and other problems considered in this section are far from accurate, and that, depending upon one's frame of reference, a strong case can be made either for an alarmist attitude or for taking these problems lightly. They will also learn that the etiology of juvenile delinquency is considerably more complex than usually believed, and that simple, single-causation theories and easy remedies are absurd.

Many adult criminals have a history of delinquency as juveniles, and the chapter on crime and the criminal is in a sense an extension of the chapter on delinquency, although the type of crime may vary and some crimes considered are almost exclusively adult crimes.

Alcoholism and narcotic addiction are also personal deviations but their association with adult crime is somewhat tenuous. Public intoxication is a misdemeanor, but those usually arrested for it are persons from the lower strata of society who create a public nuisance. Possession of narcotics, unless legitimately authorized by a physician for treatment of an illness, is also illegal. But both alcoholism and narcotic addiction are primarily medical and psychological rather than legal problems. The possession of or the drinking of alcoholic beverages by those under twenty-one years of age is against the law in most states and constitutes either an act of delinquency if the person is young enough or a violation of state law if he is between the age of legal delinquency and twenty-one.

The drinking of alcoholic beverages by the young not infrequently results in other antisocial behavior. Drug addiction among teenagers, contrary to popular belief, is not widespread.

Suicide is included in this section because it too is considered deviant behavior but its relationship to delinquency, crime, alcoholism, and narcotics is not notable. But the continuity of this section is not impaired if it is realized that all personal deviation has in common some rejection of the dominant value system, although the motives for such rejection may vary.

# 7

# Juvenile Delinquency

AMONG American social problems perhaps
none has attracted more attention, aroused
greater concern and resulted in more fre-
quent discussions and investigations than juvenile delinquency. For several years a Senate subcommittee studied
the subject, issuing its report in 1961. President Eisenhower has stated:

> Another growing social problem of concern to the na-
> tion is juvenile delinquency. During the last eight years
> there has been a 60% increase in the number of chil-
> dren appearing before our courts. The state and com-
> munities need technical assistance and financial aid to
> help them halt this trend. I therefore renew my re-
> quest that Congress enact legislation promptly to
> authorize federal aid to the states for strengthening
> their services for prevention and treatment of juvenile
> delinquency.[1]

But the first problem in a discussion of juvenile delinquency is an adequate definition of this term. Strictly

---

[1] James H. Bobo, "Juvenile Delinquency in the United States,"
*Federal Probation*, 20, No. 2 (June 1956), p. 35.

speaking, a juvenile delinquent is a youth so adjudged by a court. In most states juveniles are those under 18, but in other states ages vary from those under 16 to those under 21. A delinquent is a person below the legal age designated by the state who has violated a law or who because of other acts or conditions may be brought to juvenile court and adjudged delinquent. These acts and conditions are painstakingly long, as Sol Rubin has pointed out.

In addition to the violation of any law or ordinance the following behavior may cause an individual to be designated a delinquent: immoral or indecent conduct, immoral conduct around school, knowingly associating with vicious or immoral persons, growing up in idleness or crime, wandering in the street at night when not on lawful business in the event there is a curfew, habitual truancy from school, incorrigibility, habitually using vile, obscene, or vulgar language in a public place, smoking cigarettes around a public place, and others. While every state does not have all of these behaviors listed, there is no state in which the law confines itself for a definition of delinquency merely to violations of laws and ordinances.[2]

But while legal delinquents are those so adjudged by a court for one or more of the reasons cited, how shall those children be classified who commit an undetected act of delinquency, or those who are given a "pass" (station adjustment, i.e., a warning) by the police? Lowell Juilliard Carr maintains that there are many different meanings to the term "delinquency." For him "legal delinquents" are those who commit antisocial acts as defined by law, "detected delinquents" are those who show antisocial behavior, "agency delinquents" are those who are detected and reach an agency, "alleged delinquents" are those who are apprehended or brought to court, and "adjudged delinquents" are those found guilty.[3] It is clear that the term "juvenile delinquent" is at best vague and so broad that in some jurisdictions nearly every child would qualify as a delinquent.

[2] Sol Rubin, "The Legal Character of Juvenile Delinquency," *The Annals*, 261 (Jan. 1949), p. 2.

[3] Lowell Carr, *Delinquency Control* (New York: Harper & Brothers, 1941), p. 59.

INCIDENCE OF JUVENILE DELINQUENCY

According to the Federal Bureau of Investigation's Uniform Crime Reports for 1958, arrests of persons under 18 years of age have been increasing by about 10 per cent each year. The arrests of youth were greater than the increase of young people in the population.

> Changes in arrests of youths from 1957 to 1958 ranged from an increase of 33.8% in buying, receiving, or possessing stolen property down to an encouraging decrease of 9.7% in gambling. Perhaps the most significant decrease was that of 7.4% in auto theft; however, this is offset by increases of 7.4% and 7.2% in burglary and larceny, respectively.[4]

Youths under 18 constituted only 12.1 per cent of all persons arrested but as the chart in Figure 7-1 indicates they constituted 64.1 per cent of those arrested for auto theft, 49.9 per cent for burglary, 48.5 per cent for larceny, 30.9 per cent for receiving stolen property, and 22.8 per cent for robbery. It should be noted that the above chart is based upon arrests in 1,580 cities with a population of 52,329,497, a figure which in 1958 was somewhat less than one-third of the U.S. population.

But these statistics can be viewed differently. Since arrests of juveniles are increasing and since a large percentage of crimes listed above are attributed to them, the impression may be created that most delinquency is of a serious nature. This is not true. Taking persons in the 17-year-old category as an example, in the jurisdictions noted, total arrests during 1958 amounted to 62,307. But auto thefts constituted only 5.3 per cent of these arrests; burglary, the next most frequent crime in the chart, amounted to 7.8 per cent of total arrests. The most frequent area of arrests for those 17-year-olds was labeled "all other offenses," which amounted to a total of 14,169 persons in this age group. "All other offenses" includes violations of state or local laws for which no provision has been made in the twenty-seven classifications of the Uniform Crime Reports. These classifications specify, for

---

[4] *Uniform Crime Reports for the United States, 1958,* Federal Bureau of Investigation, U.S. Department of Justice, Washington, D.C., 1959, p. 11.

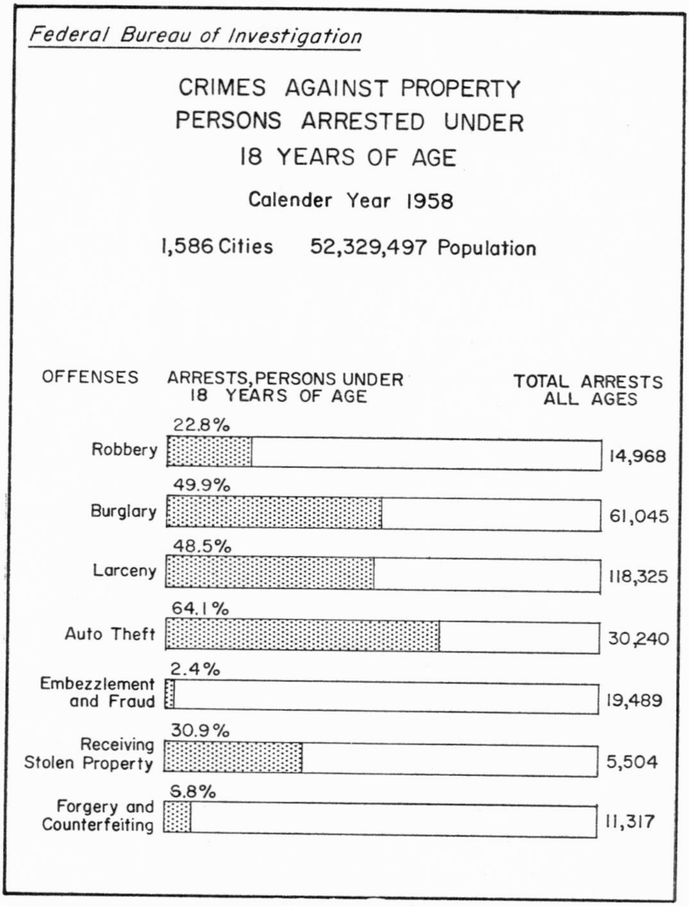

Federal Bureau of Investigation

CRIMES AGAINST PROPERTY
PERSONS ARRESTED UNDER
18 YEARS OF AGE

Calender Year 1958

1,586 Cities    52,329,497 Population

| OFFENSES | ARRESTS, PERSONS UNDER 18 YEARS OF AGE | TOTAL ARRESTS ALL AGES |
|---|---|---|
| Robbery | 22.8% | 14,968 |
| Burglary | 49.9% | 61,045 |
| Larceny | 48.5% | 118,325 |
| Auto Theft | 64.1% | 30,240 |
| Embezzlement and Fraud | 2.4% | 19,489 |
| Receiving Stolen Property | 30.9% | 5,504 |
| Forgery and Counterfeiting | 6.8% | 11,317 |

FIGURE 7-1 [5]

the most part, more serious crimes such as criminal homicide, forcible rape, robbery, larceny, and aggravated assault. A total of 7,316 17-year-olds were arrested for "disorderly conduct," i.e., charges of committing a breach of the peace; 7,099 were arrested for "suspicion," i.e., arrested as suspicious characters but not in connection with any specific offense, being released without any formal charges being placed

[5] Adapted from *Uniform Crime Reports, 1958*, p. 12.

against them. Vagrancy, which involves vagabondage, begging, loitering, etc., accounted for a total of 1,739 arrests in this age category.[6]

Out of a total of 62,307 17-year-olds arrested in 1958, 30,243—or almost half of them—were apprehended for suspicion, vagrancy, disorderly conduct, and "all other offenses," relatively minor charges. Without attempting to minimize the real problem of delinquency, it is clear that many arrests are for minor charges. Furthermore, only about 5 per cent of all persons arrested under study were below eighteen. On the other hand, these figures are for arrests, and it is well known that all delinquency does not result in arrests. The actual number of delinquents in this sense cannot be known, but it is known that the total is greater than arrest statistics indicate.

## IS JUVENILE DELINQUENCY INCREASING?

Statistics on crime are notoriously inaccurate. The best single source is the F.B.I.'s Uniform Crime Reports. This compilation comprises information from city police departments, counties, state police agencies whose authorities extend to criminal matters and assume responsibility for reporting, and 11 departments and territories in other regions administered by the United States. In 1958 reporting departments represented 97.2 per cent of the urban population and 97.1 per cent of the rural population of the United States; but not all of these reports could be used because complete sets for the year were not received or examination showed they had not been correctly prepared. Agencies which sent in reports for the full year covered 87.7 per cent of the population.[7] These statistics are based upon crimes known to the police, and since some crimes never reach the attention of the police, it is probable that the crime rate exceeds the estimates of the F.B.I. Neither are arrest statistics adequate. There is a gap between those arrested and those brought to trial, as there is between those brought to trial and those convicted; thus crime statistics necessarily become "guesstimates." Even if all crimes committed were known to the police, it would be impossible to tell

---

[6] *Uniform Crime Reports, 1958*, pp. 19 and 93.
[7] *Uniform Crime Reports, 1958*, pp. 19-20.

what percentage of them were committed by juveniles unless each criminal were apprehended and convicted.

Nevertheless for the tenth straight year this country has had an increase in juvenile crime. According to figures submitted to the Senate subcommittee by the Children's Bureau of the Department of Health, Education and Welfare, 1958 referrals to the Juvenile Court for delinquency were 175 per cent higher than in 1948. During this same period the juvenile population in this age group increased by only 35 per cent. In 1958 the Children's Bureau reported a total of 700,000 delinquency referrals to the courts, which involved some 600,000 children between the ages of 10 and 17.[8] This is not unique to the United States, occurring throughout most of the Western world. There is a cycle in delinquency, and a study of statistics since 1929 shows that delinquency tends to increase during periods of economic prosperity and to decline during depressions. Delinquency also increases during war and drops in times of peace. The population of the United States has been increasing rapidly since the close of World War II, and consequently the percentage of children between 7 and 17 is also increasing. Today there is and in the future there will be a larger number of potential delinquents simply because there will be more youths in these age brackets. Whether the rate of juvenile delinquency has increased as compared to 30 or 40 years ago is impossible to determine because adequate statistics for past years are unavailable. Certainly there has been an increase in the number of arrests of juvenile delinquents in recent years.[9]

## THE ETIOLOGY OF JUVENILE DELINQUENCY

At the outset certain generalizations about juvenile delinquency are possible. First, its incidence among boys, on the basis of available data, is about ten times as large as it is among girls. Most girl delinquents have been involved in some type of sex offense, although

[8] Senate Committee on the Judiciary, *Juvenile Delinquency*, 86th Cong., 2d sess., 1961 (Washington, D.C.: Government Printing Office, 1961).

[9] Milton L. Barron, "The Delinquent: Society of Juvenile," in *Social Problems in America: A Source Book*, rev., eds. Elizabeth B. Lee and Alfred M. Lee (New York: Holt, Rinehart & Winston, Inc., 1955), p. 308.

they have also been arrested for drunkenness, larceny, vagrancy, assault, disorderly conduct, and suspicion. Boys are more likely to be referred to courts on charges of stealing, traffic violations, and injuries to persons. Rates of delinquency, especially in the case of crimes against property, are higher in urban than in rural areas. Within cities delinquency rates are disproportionately high in certain sections, particularly in the interstitial areas. In proportion to their numbers in the population, Negro youths have a considerably higher rate of juvenile delinquency than white youths. Some authorities believe that the higher incidence of delinquency in the poorer areas of the city and among Negro youths is the result of discrimination against the poor and minorities. Certain offenses, such as malicious mischief, when committed by a middle-class youth in an outlying residential area may result in only a police warning if his father pays the bill. On the other hand, the same offense in a slum area may bring the child to the attention of a juvenile court. Finally, most juvenile delinquency is committed by a group or a gang.

It is generally agreed today that crime and delinquency are not innate, that is, inherited. The theories of Cesare Lombroso, that a criminal could be identified by certain atavistic characteristics such as a receding forehead, abnormally large ears, pronounced prognathism (jutting jaw), and the amount of body hair were repudiated years ago when noncriminals were found to have the same characteristics. Neither have efforts to associate various types of crime with body build proved conclusive. In the earlier part of the twentieth century certain American studies such as *The Kallikak Family, The Jukes,* and *The Smoky Mountain Pilgrims* claimed that criminal behavior was hereditary and associated with a low intelligence quotient. Improvements in IQ tests and more sophisticated investigation disproved this. Today, it is believed that criminal behavior is learned. If constitutional factors play a part, they are at best an indirect factor. Morons are highly suggestible and may be led into crime by others. They may also be more easily apprehended. Certain physical defects may result in feelings of inferiority and, partly as a result of this, some of these individuals may become involved in criminal behavior. Psychotics may commit crime but, of course, cannot be held responsible. If constitutional factors play a direct part in delinquency, it has yet to be proved.

The late professor Edwin Sutherland used the theory of "differential association" to explain delinquency, claiming that this type of behavior was learned, just as other kinds of behavior are learned. In the case of the juvenile delinquent this is a promising approach. Sheldon and Eleanor Glueck, in their study of 500 criminal careers, found that more than half of the families of former inmates of the reformatory had official court records for various offenses before the imprisonment of the men studied. While there was no official record of it they found that 30 per cent of the families were delinquent, and in three-fourths of the 402 families about which they obtained information the parental offenses involved more than drunkenness.[10] In *The Jack Roller*, a famous study of a young delinquent by the late Clifford Shaw, it was found that Stanley, who wrote the autobiography, learned his delinquency by associating with a gang. Some of his delinquency was encouraged by his stepmother. But it must be admitted that all children whose parents or siblings are delinquent do not themselves become so. It is also true that some youngsters living in areas where gangs flourish do not become members of gangs and do not engage in criminal behavior. Obviously, opportunities for and encouragement toward crime do not always elicit delinquency.

Albert K. Cohen speaks of the delinquent sub-culture, which he describes as nonutilitarian, malicious, and negativistic. This, he admits, does not describe all juvenile crime, but it is particularly characteristic of gang behavior. Gangs do not steal in order to acquire articles that they can eat, wear, or sell but rather to cause discomfiture to others. It is a method of gaining recognition in the sub-culture in which they live.[11]

GANGS

Gang activity is an important factor in juvenile delinquency. At the New York hearing, the chairman of the subcommittee on juvenile delinquency stated:

You here in the great city of New York have seen the tragic results of their (gangs) predatory activities in recent weeks. And so too

---

[10] Sheldon Glueck and Eleanor Glueck, *Five Hundred Criminal Careers* (New York: Alfred A. Knopf, Inc., 1930), p. 121.

[11] Albert K. Cohen, *Delinquent Boys, The Culture of the Gang* (New York: The Free Press of Glencoe, Inc., 1955), pp. 25-27.

have indeed citizens of other cities seen it happen in their cities and their communities. For instance, in Washington recently a member of the House of Representatives had to rush to the aid of a citizen who was being attacked on the street by what he called "a pack of wolves." An Air Force sergeant stepped into the night to check his car and ended up dead on a Washington street, shot four times by a gang of young thugs. Broad daylight assaults on innocent victims in Philadelphia and Chicago tell us the same ugly, unhappy, and tragic story. A frightening thing, it seems to me, is that many of these teenage killers seem to be devoid of any feelings of humility, humanity, or sympathy. Neither do they appear to have the usual criminal motivation, such as stealing for gain. A brief look at the files of this sub-committee over the years will show that a west coast gang brutally assaulted a disabled war veteran. In the Midwest several of them strolled into a bar and blinded one of the patrons by smashing a beer bottle across his face. And throughout the southwestern states we have heard reports of chain-wielding gangs who beat their lone victims just for thrills. I guess as they put it "just for kicks." Nor is this scourge peculiar to the United States. I visited in Europe, and from western Europe, Scandinavian countries, and from behind the Iron Curtain come stories of the "Teddy Boys, Rattleboys, Bugbears, Hooligans, and Halbstarkes," wielding switchblade knives, brass knuckles, and bicycle chains. Paris alone reports 10,000 to 12,000 members of "Les Bandes." [12]

One of the most extensive studies of boys' gangs was carried on by Frederick M. Thrasher. Gangs, he found, develop out of play groups, and some attain a high degree of solidarity. Some engage in criminal activities. Such gangs usually have a fairly well-defined territory in which they operate.[13] In the "Tops and Bottoms" areas of West Philadelphia, Negro boys' gangs sprang originally from the association of boys on street corners. The first overt conflict, with its resulting solidarity, occurred when a number of boys from the Bottoms area invaded a dance held by the Tops in their territory and attempted to take their girls. As a result of this the gangs became somewhat more formal in structure (although to the outside observer they always appeared informal), developed leadership, and, when possible, purchased certain types of jackets or insignias. They also acquired esoteric names and some type of hangout such as a restaurant or candy store. They established definite territorial limits which they did not

---

[12] Senate Committee on the Judiciary, *Juvenile Delinquency*, pp. 55-56.
[13] Frederick M. Thrasher, *The Gang* (Chicago: University of Chicago Press, 1927 and 1936).

permit other boys or boys' gangs to invade. In fact, such an invasion was a signal for a fight—a "rumble." They were involved in petty crime, such as stealing junk from railroad yards, and ultimately in some stabbings.

In the case of the poor Negro youth, the gang practically replaced his family. Most families in the Bottoms territory, that is the poorer area, occupied two or three rooms at best, and out of sheer necessity the youngsters spent most of their time on the streets. The gang offered companionship, recreational opportunities, and a certain recognition. In fact, not belonging to a gang in this area made life difficult. Physical security depended in part upon gang membership because the lone boy had no one to back him up when he was attacked.[14] Thrasher found that 652 gangs out of 1,313 had a demoralizing influence on their members, 609 may not have had such influence, although this was not certain, and only 52 clearly did not demoralize their members. While gangs themselves are not a cause of delinquency, they facilitate it by indoctrinating members into methods of crime and by creating a system of values favorable to delinquency.

The city and county of Los Angeles claimed that each has more than 150 gangs. In New York City the Youth Board stated that there are 150 active fighting gangs in the city. But there is a difference, and only about 40 gangs in both the city and county of Los Angeles are of the same nature as the 150 gangs described in New York. The Senate subcommittee describes four types of gangs. First, there is the type which has little structure and organization and is usually rooted in a particular spot where youngsters meet. The basis of their bond is strictly friendship and they manifest little serious antisocial activities. When they do engage in fighting or other antisocial behavior it is strictly on a protective basis. The second kind of gang is the *club* type, which is organized around a specific interest such as athletics and thus may come into greater contact with other groups. They are more likely to be involved in social agency programs and because of their contact with other groups there does exist the potentiality for ganging and other antisocial behavior. The third type of gang is the *conflict group*. While this may have been developed originally around certain specific interests it has banded together aggressively either for protection or aggression. Basically, they are conflict oriented, have

---

[14] John J. Kane, "The Tops and Bottoms," *American Sociological Review*, 9, No. 2 (June 1948), p. 74.

war counselors, carry weapons, and have practices and procedures that would help them in gang fighting. The fourth type of gang is the thoroughly delinquent group. A great deal of the very serious antisocial behavior, such as rapes and assaults, is committed by this group.[15]

The Senate subcommittee found that some gangs had names which are nationwide in their usage. This does not mean that any of the gangs is a national organization, but rather that drives and motivations around self identity are similar, and publicity received in one city is felt in another. Some gangs attain a geographical identity by naming themselves after the neighborhood area or street where they live. Others seek a negative identity to publicize the fact that they are "mean" and thus hopefully produce terror among their enemies. Among names in this last category are "Stompers," "Stone Killers," "Vultures," "Blades," etc. Others use titles associated with their fantasied self-images, such as "Dukes," "Bishops," "Kings," "Royal Knights," "Lovers," etc.[16]

The Senate report states that the size of street clubs or gangs has been exaggerated. The hard core approximates 15 members, but around these there may be from 10 to 30 other boys related in terms of friendship, interest, and history who will only occasionally join with the core in antisocial behavior. The ages of boys' gangs vary tremendously, some being as young as 12 and others as old as 22. Usually, however, gang members tend to be about the same age level, and the average age of street gang members is between 16 and 17. The history of gangs and boys' motivations to join them show similar patterns throughout the country.

> The greater part of these boys come from areas where there is a significant amount of institutional breakdown. The usual avenues for constructive group experience are either not available or are of such a nature that these boys do not make a healthy response to them. In addition, by virtue of familial, cultural and environmental disorganization, these are youngsters who seek and need intense peer group associations. The areas from which they come have traditionally had an excessive amount of club organization, which to one degree or another has been delinquent in orientation. As a result of these factors and others, these are boys who very early became involved in the street club or gang world.[17]

---

[15] Kane, *op. cit.*, pp. 59-60.
[16] Kane, *op. cit.*, pp. 59-62.
[17] Kane, *op. cit.*, p. 63.

## THE FAMILY

A number of observers have mentioned the broken home as a factor in delinquency. The Gluecks found that in 60 per cent of the cases they studied an abnormal home situation existed because of the lengthy or complete absence of one or both parents. In 70 per cent of the cases the home had been broken when the young men studied were 14 or younger.[18] The American family is less stable today than it was in the past partly because of urbanization. Coupled with this is a tendency for both husband and wife to work, with the resulting phenomenon of the "latch key" child. In such cases children who return from school in the afternoon may have no adult supervision within the home until 6 o'clock or later. "Moonlighting," in which a father works at two jobs and may be absent from home as much as 16 hours a day five or six days a week—while technically not a broken home—is at least a "fractured" home. The father is not home long enough to provide emotional support and assist in family discipline. When he does come home he is too tired to do anything but sleep. Of course, this situation can also exist in the middle and upper-middle classes when the father is so involved in professional work, business, or civic affairs that he neglects his family. But whether the broken home or fractured home is a cause of delinquency is debatable. Like the gang, it facilitates rather than causes it. Furthermore, while divorce and separation result in broken homes, the more prevalent cause is death. The disorganized home, in which spouses continually quarrel, neglect or reject children is equally important in facilitating delinquency. As the Gluecks' study indicates it is the type of relationship between parents or between parents and children that is the most important.

Social class membership is associated with juvenile delinquency. The lower-class family generally lives in marginal circumstances. The Gluecks found that 15 per cent of the families of delinquent boys were economically dependent, 56 per cent were in the marginal category, and only 29 per cent in the comfortable group. The vast majority of fathers were skilled, semi-skilled, or unskilled workers.[19]

---

[18] Glueck and Glueck, *op. cit.*, p. 122.
[19] Glueck and Glueck, *op. cit.*, p. 122.

Because of the low income among such families, they are apt to reside in or near slum areas where vice and crime flourish. Thus opportunities for delinquency are multiplied.

## THE SCHOOL

*Truancy* is a violation of the law, and in the case histories of many delinquents, it is commonly found to be the first offense. Most truants simply dislike school and, in the case of the lower-class boy or girl, reasons for it are not difficult to find. American schools tend to be middle-class institutions, staffed by teachers who belong to this class. They stress values dear to the middle class, such as promptness, cleanliness, orderliness, and hard work. Generally, these are not paramount values among lower-class people, and the lower-class child finds that the values of his home and peer-group conflict with the values of the teacher and the school. Compulsory school attendance laws which keep boys and girls in classrooms until 16 years of age or older create problems for educational institutions, teachers, and some pupils. This is particularly true for the child who is a slow learner and for whom no special schools or classes exist. About 95 per cent of lower-class children will never attend college. They realize this and resent the fact that they are compelled to attend school when both they and their families would prefer that they had jobs. As a result they tend to become problem children in the classroom and are resented by teachers, who are likely to consider the quiet, somewhat introverted, well-behaved child as the ideal. This type of situation results in the "blackboard jungle," a term made famous in a book and a motion picture about classroom rebellion.

But truancy is a serious matter for another reason. Truants face the prospect of an entire day with nothing to do. Generally, they cannot go home lest parents or neighbors see them, and the tendency is to disappear into the city, looking for something to do. Some of what they do may very well be delinquent behavior. The unemployed teenager who has left school faces a similar problem, usually with the same results, as James Conant has pointed out in *Slums and Suburbs*.

## COMIC BOOKS, TELEVISION, AND MOTION PICTURES

Recently, certain types of comic books and television programs have been blamed for the increase in juvenile delinquency, just as motion pictures were blamed years ago. The so-called "comic" books, some of which are by no means humorous, were first published in 1933. Today, it is estimated that between 40 and 70 million copies of these books are sold every month, with each one being read by several persons. American children themselves, it is claimed, spend $4,000,000 or more annually on comic books. Some of them are perfectly harmless, dealing with the antics of Mickey Mouse or Donald Duck. Some are educational and depict historical events. Others feature adventure, murder, and suspense. It is these about which complaints are made. Some carry cover illustrations of semi-nude women, chained by men or being beaten by men. They are certainly in poor taste and probably do disturb some adolescents. But to date there is no study that definitely proves a relationship between the reading of such comic books and delinquency. In individual cases, it may be that some comic books have aroused some adolescents sexually and may even have taught them the technique for committing a crime. It should be noted, however, that when a youngster is apprehended for delinquency, he looks for an excuse. Not unaware that comic books are being blamed for crime, he may mention them as the reason for his behavior. This may even be unintentionally suggested by those interrogating him. If comic books are really a cause of delinquency, then considering the millions of readers they have, delinquency ought to be even more widespread than it is. It seems probable that such books have their greatest impact on the emotionally disturbed, who might well get into trouble anyway. Recent efforts have been made to clean up comic books, but parents themselves are the best safeguards against their children's reading those that are objectionable.

Violence seems to have become one of the major, if not the major, television theme. Gun fights, stabbings, hangings, and fist fights are nightly occurrences on all national networks. While the "good guys" almost invariably win and the "bad guys" get their just desserts, the ultimate influence of such shows on youth is not known. While motion pictures have their share of violence too, some of them are completely preoccupied with sex. This is especially true of some of the lurid advertisements for motion pictures which appear in the daily press. Studies of the influence of motion pictures on youth were done years ago and their findings may not be applicable today. However, it was discovered that motion pictures had no adverse effect on most young people unless they were already emotionally upset.

A much more critical factor than comic books, television, and motion pictures is the dissemination of outright pornography. The Senate hearings on juvenile delinquency found that there are well-organized distribution points for such material in many large cities. Such pictures are not only sold to youth but in some cases have included photographs of children committing obscene acts. For adolescents who already have difficulty controlling their sexual impulses, pornography is a serious matter.

Dr. John R. Cavanagh, a naval psychiatrist, believes that some of the aggression built up by frustrations which all children encounter may be drained off by comic books. The child is able to project himself into the story and release his aggressions in the field of fantasy rather than in overt, aggressive behavior. However, he does admit that some comic books are harmful and presumably some television programs and motion pictures as well.[20] At this point it is impossible to determine whether comic books, television, and motion pictures really cause delinquency. For some youngsters they may but for many the worst to be said is that they may facilitate delinquent behavior. Even this is conjectural and until careful objective studies are carried out, parents and others should not become unduly concerned about the charges of alarmists.

### SITUATIONAL-VALUE APPROACH

Emotional maladjustment, membership in antisocial gangs, residence in slum areas, poverty, and broken or disorganized homes may

---

[20] John R. Cavanagh, Sr., "The Comics War" in *The Juvenile Offender*, ed. Clyde B. Vedder (Garden City, New York: Doubleday and Company, Inc., 1954), p. 112.

all contribute to juvenile delinquency. In any single case several of these factors may be in operation. But all of these are situational factors, that is, they are circumstances in which the individual finds himself. Yet there are some children who suffer one or more of these situations and do not become delinquent. Therefore, it is necessary to look at the value approach.

When an individual engages in delinquent behavior, it is because he perceives this action as something desirable. Ultimately, it is a question of the kinds of values that have been presented to the youth and the kinds of values which he accepts which make the difference. Because of rapid social change, the increasing instability of the American family, the impact of urbanization and industrialization, the system of social control today seems to be less effective than in the past. It was pointed out that delinquency tends to increase during periods of war and prosperity. It is just these periods in history when value systems are unsettled. Even when the church, the home and the school attempt to transmit adequate value systems, youth is exposed to quite a different system of values from the gang, the entertainment media, and the example of their elders. In other words, they lack a well-integrated, consistent system of values, and as a consequence their perception of the situation is muddled.

## DELINQUENCY AS A SOCIAL PROBLEM

In view of what has been said, there is no question that juvenile delinquency is an overt social problem in the United States. The arrest rates for those under 18 have been increasing, and more youths commit crimes of a serious nature. A relatively large number of persons is involved—both perpetrators and victims—making crime a threat to the common welfare, and efforts are made to deal with it in an organized way. Furthermore, one of the truly great tragedies of juvenile delinquency is that it frequently forecasts an adult criminal career.

## REMEDIAL MEASURES

Panaceas for the elimination of juvenile delinquency abound in American society. Nearly everyone is a self-proclaimed authority in this area. Some belong to the "treat 'em rough" school and would handle young offenders as older offenders are handled. Some would lower the age at which a person may be considered a juvenile delinquent, while others advocate punishing the parents, stricter discipline of children, and the frequent use of physical punishment. Most of these critics claim that the juvenile is coddled, pointing quite correctly to the fact that when some juveniles are apprehended by the police, they inform the officer of their "rights" as juveniles.

At the other extreme are those who advocate more parks, playgrounds, supervised recreation, child guidance centers, and more extended use of probation, as well as slum clearance. But it must be realized there is no single approach to such a complex problem as juvenile delinquency. Some of the solutions offered by those who would get tough with delinquents have been tried and found wanting. Other approaches which are promising have been carried out piecemeal, and in some places not at all. At times they do not succeed, because of lack of money and personnel.

The argument of those who would get tough with delinquents is that this problem is increasing and the various modern and scientific methods suggested have not halted it. It is argued that since in the past when the woodshed was used, delinquency was less, we should therefore return to it. But England experimented with very harsh punishments for juvenile offenders, even hanging pickpockets. This was apparently small deterrent because on the very days when public hangings occurred there was a rash of pickpocketing in the crowd! A royal commission investigated corporal punishment and concluded that it did more harm than good. A comparison of young offenders who had been beaten with those placed on probation showed that the former to a much greater extent repeated their offenses. In two cities where physical punishment was used 440 out of 574 children who received it were again in court within two years.[21] Various studies of

---

[21] Justine Wise Polier, "The Woodshed Is No Answer," *Federal Probation,* 20, No. 3 (Sept. 1956), pp. 4-5.

delinquents in the United States revealed that they had suffered frequent and severe physical punishment at the hands of their parents. It apparently had little effect.

Another popular theory that delinquency can be reduced by punishing parents, either through fines or imprisonment or both has no basis in fact. Judge Paul W. Alexander of Toledo, whose court practiced the punishment of parents when they contributed to the delinquency of their children, found after ten years' experience that there was nothing to commend it. Delinquency had not been curbed, and the number of parents contributing to it had, in fact, increased. The only value of such punishment would be to satisfy what he described as "the primitive, vindictive appetites of self-righteous, nondelinquent parents, irritated and aggravated public authorities, and a substantial portion of the general public." [22] In New York City, the board of education studied the results of fining parents for their children's truancy. It discovered that the children of such parents showed less improvement and were more frequently returned to court for the continual truancy of their children than in the case of parents who were not punished.[23]

One of the really great problems created by the punishment of children and/or their parents is to rivet attention upon punishment as the only method and to forget about all other possibilities of curbing delinquency. Discipline, of course, is necessary within any home, but discipline need not be interpreted exclusively as physical punishment. At times physical punishment may be necessary, but it is never a panacea. Playgrounds, other recreational facilities, and, particularly, adequate supervision of them are invariably suggested as a method of combatting juvenile delinquency. Urban children do need play space and good supervision can stimulate peaceful and challenging recreation; but juvenile delinquency is not exclusively the result of a lack of playgrounds and recreation. Sometimes such centers do not reach the children who most desperately need them. Even if they do, the child spends only part of his time at a playground, and when he is not there he may well engage in delinquent behavior. Sometimes, in fact, such recreation centers may also become centers at which delinquency is planned or carried out.

Police athletic leagues exist in a number of cities, and the idea

---

[22] Polier, *op. cit.*, p. 5.
[23] Polier, *op. cit.*, p. 5.

behind them is both to provide wholesome recreation for youngsters and to change their attitudes toward police officers. Some of these seem successful but the basic question remains as to whether this should be police work or group social work. Slum clearance is certainly desirable under any circumstances and may indeed help decrease the rate of delinquency. But slum areas should not be thought of merely as places with inferior housing, crowded living conditions, narrow, dirty streets, and such. A slum is also a state of mind. In this sense individuals may live in slums but not really be slum dwellers because they do not share the sub-culture of the slum area. If slum clearance has any meaning in the reduction of juvenile delinquency rates it must involve more than the razing of old buildings, the widening of streets, and the erection of housing projects. It involves a re-education in the living habits and values of people. In this sense slum clearance is an important remedial measure for curbing delinquency.

## THE JUVENILE COURT

The first juvenile court in the United States was opened in Chicago on July 1, 1899. By 1950 every state except one had some type of juvenile court statute. The purposes of the juvenile court are first, to remove child offenders from criminal courts to equity courts so that consideration may be given more to the doer than to the deed; and second, to have the juvenile court give protection and treatment to other children who require both. In common law, children were not criminally liable if they were under eight years of age at the time of their offense. The juvenile court extended this age limitation in most places to those below 18. Because the juvenile court is a court of equity, no stigma is attached to a child who comes to its attention. But a great deal of misunderstanding surrounds the juvenile court in the eyes of the public. Some consider it too easy or too liberal and particularly when a youth has been involved in a serious crime which outrages the public, a demand is made that he be turned over to the regular criminal court. In many states this can be and is done. However, perhaps it is just this type of child that most needs the safeguards of the juvenile court.[24]

---

[24] *The Juvenile Offender*, ed. Clyde B. Vedder (Garden City, New York: Doubleday & Company, 1954), pp. 229-30.

One of the basic difficulties confronting juvenile courts in the United States is the lack of judicial manpower. While the population has increased, and the number of juveniles referred to the courts has grown, additional judges and other essential personnel have not been added. In the District of Columbia, for example, it is claimed that a judge has an average of only 12 minutes to spend on each case. The members of the Senate subcommittee stated, "A juvenile court adjudication with regard to a young child wherein the court does not have the necessary time to study a case to properly determine whether a juvenile should be placed in an institution, a foster home, or put on probation, is worse than no juvenile court hearing at all. Sending a child to a court that is supposed to be treatment-oriented, but which in turn only pretends to offer treatment because in reality it is overworked, is worse than sending him to a purely criminal court, which makes no such pretenses but determines guilt or innocence according to strict rules of evidence and safeguards which are offered an adult criminal." [25]

## THE TREATMENT OF DELINQUENTS

The treatment of delinquents is sorely handicapped by lack of facilities, the need for additional trained personnel in many areas, and excessively high case loads among probation officers. On January 29, 1960, the *Philadelphia Bulletin* stated that a boy who had recently been arrested for theft had been arrested a total of thirty-two times since he was six years old on charges that ranged from carrying a concealed weapon through larceny and burglary to indecent assault. The fact that this child was still roaming the streets indicated that the institutions were so overcrowded that they had to refuse admission even to such a serious offender. This was highlighted by Dr. E. Preston Sharpe, Director of the Philadelphia Youth Study Center, who stated that at the time of the Senate hearings there were 600 fewer beds in Pennsylvania institutions for the care of delinquents than in 1945.[26]

Dr. John Otto Reinemann, director of probation of the municipal

---

[25] Senate Committee on the Judiciary, *Juvenile Delinquency*, pp. 90-91.
[26] Senate Committee on the Judiciary, *Juvenile Delinquency*, p. 23.

court of Philadelphia, in his testimony before the Senate subcommittee stated:

A crying need is found in the lack of treatment facilities for the emotionally disturbed and the seriously psychopathic child. Training schools naturally refuse to accept such children and often they are placed on probation or are spending time in the Youth Study Center pending an opening in a state facility—which occurs only in great intervals. For the defective delinquent there exists now a state institution for the male person above 15 years of age at Huntington. There is nothing for boys under that age, or for girls of any age. I hasten to remark that the State Department of Public Welfare is fully cognizant of this problem, but has been hampered by lack of funds and a traditional lack of coordination of existing intramural facilities for the treating and rehabilitation of young delinquents.[27]

The situations described in Philadelphia are more or less typical of the entire country. In some places conditions are better, in other places they are worse. Regardless of the level of scientific knowledge, the dedication of those involved in the treatment of juvenile offenders, no real progress can be made until the American public squarely faces this problematic aspect of delinquency. Delinquency itself is an overt problem, but the lack of facilities, personnel, and money for both constitutes a covert social problem in American society. In the meantime the public is outraged at the extent and seriousness of crime among juveniles. The short-term solutions, quick and inexpensive, are put forth as panaceas, but the methods of preventing or treating delinquents are quite as complex as the causes of delinquency themselves. Until the American people recognize this fact, a decrease in juvenile delinquency seems unlikely.


## REVIEW QUESTIONS

1. Under what circumstances may a person be adjudged a delinquent? Are the bases for such adjudgment realistic?
2. Discuss the following statement: "Juvenile delinquency has increased considerably in the last 40 years."
3. Name some of the sociological factors apparently associated with juvenile delinquency.
4. Is delinquency physically inherited or socially instilled?

---

[27] Senate Committee on the Judiciary, *Juvenile Delinquency*, p. 23.

5. Discuss the following statement: "Juvenile delinquency is caused by gangs."
6. Evaluate the influence of the family and the school on delinquent behavior.
7. To what extent do the media of entertainment such as radio, television, movies, comic books, etc., contribute to delinquency?
8. How effective in curbing delinquency is the physical punishment of delinquents or their parents by fines or imprisonment?
9. What is a juvenile court and how does it function?
10. How effective are present methods of treating juvenile delinquents?

## SELECTED READINGS

*Articles*

Bobo, James H., "Juvenile Delinquency in the United States," *Federal Probation*, 20 (June 1956), 2.

Corbin, S., "The Conflict of Values in Delinquency Areas," *American Sociological Review*, 16 (Oct. 1951), 653-61.

"Juvenile Delinquency," *The Annals*, 261 (Jan. 1949).

Kane, John J., "The Tops and Bottoms," *American Catholic Sociological Review*, 9 (June 1948), 74-83.

Kohn, Melvin L., "Social Class and Parental Values," *American Journal of Sociology*, 64 (Jan. 1959), 337-51.

Lunden, W. A., "War and Juvenile Delinquency in England and Wales," *American Sociological Review*, 10 (June 1945), 390-93.

Polier, Justine Wise, "The Woodshed Is No Answer," *Federal Probation*, 10 (Sept. 1956), 3.

Rubin, Sol, "The Legal Character of Juvenile Delinquency," *The Annals*, 261 (Jan. 1949), 1-8.

Senate Committee on the Judiciary, *Juvenile Delinquency*, 86th Cong., 2d sess., 1961. Washington, D.C.: Government Printing Office, 1961.

Turner, Ralph H., and Samuel J. Surace, "Zoot-Suiters and Mexicans: Symbols in Crowd Behavior," *American Journal of Sociology*, 62 (July 1956), 14-20.

Vasoli, Robert H., "Parole Outcome in St. Joseph County, Indiana," *American Catholic Sociological Review*, 17, No. 3 (Oct. 1956), 213-24.

*Books*

Carr, Lowell Juilliard, *Delinquency Control*, New York: Harper & Brothers, 1941.

Cloward, Richard A., *Delinquency and Opportunity: A Theory of Delinquent Gangs.* New York: The Free Press of Glencoe, 1960.

Cohen, Albert K., *Delinquent Boys: The Culture of the Gang.* New York: The Free Press of Glencoe, 1955.

Cooper, Clara C., *A Comparative Study of Delinquents and Non-delinquents.* Portsmouth, Ohio: Psychological Service Center Press, 1960.

Glueck, Sheldon and Eleanor Glueck, *Five Hundred Criminal Careers.* New York: Alfred A. Knopf, Inc., 1950.

Martin, John McCullough, *Juvenile Vandalism.* Springfield, Illinois: Charles C. Thomas, Publisher, 1961.

Thrasher, Frederick M., *The Gang.* Chicago: University of Chicago Press, 1927-1936.

Vedder, Clyde B., *The Juvenile Offender.* Garden City, N.Y.: Doubleday & Co., 1954.

# 8

# Crime and the Criminal

F ROM a legal viewpoint, "crime is an intentional act in violation of the criminal law,
committed without defense or excuse, and
penalized by the state as a felony or misdemeanor." [1] A
felony is an offense punishable by death or imprisonment
in a state prison, while a misdemeanor covers all other
types of offenses. Stuart A. Queen has pointed out that
this distinction, once useful, has lost most of its meaning.
Many crimes formerly carrying the death penalty have
had their punishment reduced to prison sentences. In
fact, in some states there is no death penalty. Furthermore, a felony in one state may be a misdemeanor in
another. Studies of felons and misdemeanants among
prison and jail populations show that their social background characteristics are quite similar. [2]

Technically, a criminal is one who has been found
guilty of a crime. Some sociologists have argued that such
a definition of a criminal is unrealistic because large
numbers of persons who have violated criminal law

[1] Paul W. Tappan, "Who Is a Criminal?" *American Sociological Review*, 12, No. 1 (Feb. 1947), p. 100.
[2] Walter C. Reckless, *The Crime Problem* (New York: Appleton-Century-Crofts, Inc., 1955), pp. 16-17.

are never apprehended, and if apprehended, are not convicted. Thus investigation of criminals who are adjudicated offenders deals with only a segment of the criminal population. Except for certain crimes such as murder, these may be atypical of the criminal population in the United States. However, since this is, generally speaking, the only part of the criminal population for study, it must be used. However, discussion of this population should be qualified by the selective factors involved in its arrest and conviction.

CRIME TRENDS

In 1958 the Federal Bureau of Investigation measured crime by a new Crime Index. This is composed of seven separate crime categories as shown in Table 8-1. All categories of negligent manslaughter and larceny under $50 which were previously listed with these seven offenses have been excluded. Statutory rape, in which no force is used and the victim is under legal age of consent, is also omitted, and rape figures have been limited to offenses involving force. As a result of this, these figures are not comparable to totals published in previous years.

TABLE 8-1[3]

| Crime index classification | Estimated number of offenses | | Change | |
| --- | --- | --- | --- | --- |
| | 1957 | 1958 | Number | Percent |
| Total | 1,422,285 | 1,553,922 | +131,637 | +9.3 |
| Murder | 8,027 | 8,182 | +155 | +1.9 |
| Forcible rape | 12,886 | 14,561 | +1,675 | +13.0 |
| Robbery | 66,843 | 75,347 | +8,504 | +12.7 |
| Aggravated assault | 110,672 | 113,530 | +2,858 | +2.6 |
| Burglary | 603,707 | 679,787 | +76,080 | +12.6 |
| Larceny over $50 | 354,972 | 391,550 | +36,578 | +10.3 |
| Auto theft | 265,178 | 270,965 | +5,787 | +2.2 |

In 1958 the estimated number of offenses according to this crime index was 1,553,922, which was an increase of 9.3 per cent over 1957.

[3] Adapted from *Uniform Crime Reports for the United States, 1958*, Federal Bureau of Investigation, U.S. Department of Justice (Washington, D.C., 1959), p. 1.

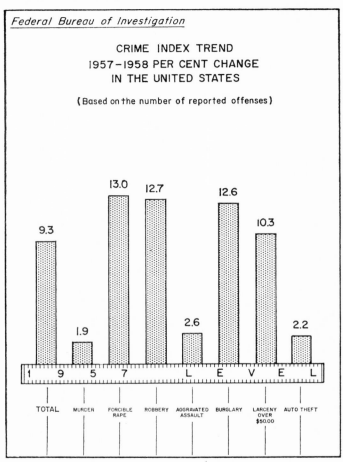

*Federal Bureau of Investigation*

CRIME INDEX TREND
1957–1958 PER CENT CHANGE
IN THE UNITED STATES

(Based on the number of reported offenses)

FIGURE 8-1 [4]

While the estimated population increase in this country between 1957 and 1958 was 1.7 per cent, the percentage increase in the Crime Index was five times as great. Thus crime is growing more rapidly than the general population.

During 1958, robbers using weapons or force committed one-half of their crimes in streets and alleys. One-third of their crimes were

[4] Adapted from *Uniform Crime Reports, 1958*, p. 2.

against places of business. In both of these areas they increased their activity more than 10% over 1957.

Although burglars, as might be expected, operate principally at night, they are also active in the daytime. This is most noticeable in cases involving sneak thievery from homes. Four out of ten residence burglaries occurred during daylight hours. Residence burglaries increased nearly 10% in 1958 over 1957 and accounted for 4 out of every 10 burglaries.

Of all crimes against property, that is, robbery, burglary, auto theft, and other thefts, the latter account for six cases in every ten. Almost one-half (45%) of these common thefts involve accessories or other articles stolen from automobiles.[5]

That crime is a serious social problem involving a large number of persons is evident from these statistics. In 1958, murders in the United States averaged about 22 a day, or almost one per hour. On an average, more than 39 persons suffered forcible rape in the course of a day and more than 206 were robbed. In 1957, almost $480,000,000 worth of property was stolen in 400 cities. The F.B.I. estimates the current annual cost of crime in the United States at about 20 billion dollars.[6]

But the actual amount of crime in this country is not known. The Uniform Crime Reports is based upon crimes known to the police. Certain types of crimes are frequently unreported, such as blackmail, graft, bribery, and certain types of fraud. Even when crimes are reported they are not always cleared by arrests. Generally speaking, crimes against the person more frequently result in arrests than crimes against property.

In 1958, out of every 100 crimes against the person there were 79 arrests. Out of these arrests 69 individuals were held for prosecution. Criminal homicide, forcible rapes, and aggravated assaults generally received more intensive investigation than the more numerous but somewhat less important crimes against property. Out of every 100 robberies in 1958, 48 were cleared by arrests and 42 persons were charged. When robbery and other property crimes such as burglary, larceny, and auto theft are grouped together, the clearance rate drops to 24 for each 100 offenses. The over-all experience for crimes against

[5] *Uniform Crime Reports, 1958*, pp. 5-7.
[6] James H. Bobo, "Juvenile Delinquency in the United States," *Federal Probation*, 20, No. 2 (June 1956). p. 32.

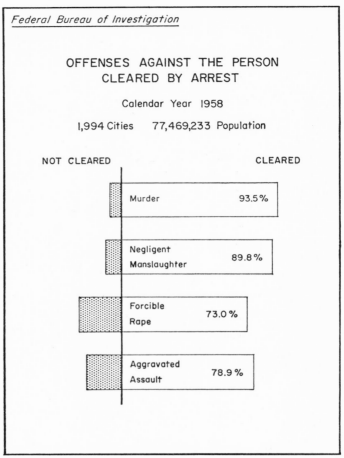

*Federal Bureau of Investigation*

OFFENSES AGAINST THE PERSON
CLEARED BY ARREST

Calendar Year 1958

1,994 Cities     77,469,233 Population

NOT CLEARED                                    CLEARED

Murder                         93.5%

Negligent
Manslaughter            89.8%

Forcible
Rape                    73.0%

Aggravated
Assault              78.9%

FIGURE 8-2[7]

the person and against property was 26 offenses cleared by arrest and 21 persons charged for each 100 offenses.[8]

But only two out of every three persons arrested for the commission of a crime are found guilty. The highest conviction rate is for driving while intoxicated with 81 persons found guilty for each 100

[7] Adapted from *Uniform Crime Reports, 1958,* p. 8.
[8] *Uniform Crime Reports, 1958,* p. 7.

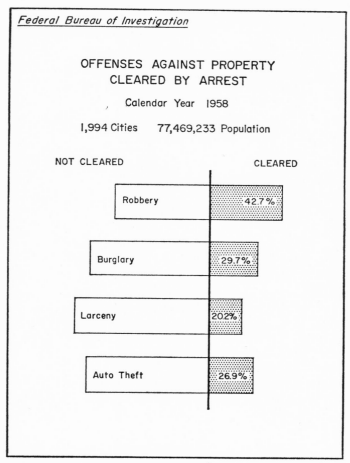

*Federal Bureau of Investigation*

OFFENSES AGAINST PROPERTY
CLEARED BY ARREST

Calendar Year 1958

1,994 Cities    77,469,233 Population

NOT CLEARED                    CLEARED

Robbery          42.7%

Burglary         29.7%

Larceny          20.2%

Auto Theft       26.9%

FIGURE 8-3 [9]

charged. The lowest rate of conviction occurred in negligent man-slaughter where out of every 100 persons charged only 31 were found guilty.[10] Figure 8-4 shows the percentage of persons found guilty among the percentage of persons charged.

___

[9] Adapted from *Uniform Crime Reports, 1958*, p. 9.
[10] *Uniform Crime Reports, 1958*, p. 7.

Federal Bureau of Investigation

### PER CENT OF PERSONS FOUND GUILTY

Calendar Year 1958

198 Cities over 25,000     Total population 38,007,281

| | |
|---|---|
| TOTAL | 66.9% |
| Driving while Intoxicated | 80.8% |
| Drunkenness; Disorderly Conduct; Vagrancy | 73.5% |
| Forgery and Counterfeiting | 72.7% |
| Larceny | 71.0% |
| Liquor Laws | 69.3% |
| Burglary | 67.8% |
| Traffic and Motor Vehicle Laws | 66.7% |
| Narcotic Drug Laws | 65.5% |
| Auto Theft | 64.0% |
| Weapons: Carrying, Possessing, etc. | 63.3% |
| Embezzlement and Fraud | 62.5% |
| Robbery | 60.8% |
| Sex Offenses (Prostitution & Commercialized Vice) | 60.8% |
| Murder | 59.5% |
| Offenses against Family and Children | 59.1% |
| Other Assaults | 52.3% |
| Forcible Rape | 45.6% |
| Stolen Property: Buying, Receiving, etc. | 45.6% |
| Gambling | 45.1% |
| Aggravated Assault | 41.8% |
| Negligent Manslaughter | 30.5% |
| All Other Offenses | 73.8% |

FIGURE 8-4[11]

### THE SOCIAL CHARACTERISTICS OF OFFENDERS

Certain generalizations about the social backgrounds of offenders are possible. First, they are likely to be found in the age group be-

[11] Adapted from *Uniform Crime Reports, 1958*, p. 10.

tween 18 and 25. In all crimes except prostitution, the male rate is almost ten times as high as the female rate. Crimes are more common in urban than in rural areas, and, generally speaking, the larger the city the higher the crime rate. Most offenders, at least on the basis of convictions, come from the lower social and economic classes. They are most likely to be residents of slum areas or poorer sections of the city. The intelligence of serious offenders is comparable to that of the general population but a large proportion of criminals either have not been married or their marriages have failed. Negroes have a higher arrest and conviction rate than white persons, and native-born Americans of foreign-born parents have a higher crime rate than the foreign-born. However, none of these factors should be regarded as a cause of criminality. No race, social class, sex, or age category has a monopoly on crime.[12] But there is reason to believe that younger persons and those who are lower on the social scale are more subject to arrests and conviction than others

AGE

There is a relationship between age and the type of crime committed. Usually such crimes as robbery and aggravated assault require strength and quickness, both of which are more characteristic of younger persons. Certain other crimes, such as fraud, embezzlement, counterfeiting, and forgery require skill, knowledge, and experience, attributes more commonly found among mature adults. Auto theft is a common offense among persons under 25 years of age. In 1958 in 1,586 cities with populations of 2,500 or over, 30,240 persons were arrested for stealing automobiles. Over 20,000 of these were 18 years of age or younger. Only 718 persons were 40 or older.[13] In 1953 over half the robberies, rapes, and larcenies and almost three-fourths of the burglaries were committed by persons under 25 years of age.[14] But while it is true that a large portion of crime is committed by those under 25, distinctions are necessary regarding the type of crime.

---

[12] Ruth Shonle Cavan, *Criminology* (New York: Thomas Y. Crowell Co., 1956), p. 67.
[13] *Uniform Crime Reports, 1958*, p. 93.
[14] *Uniform Crime Reports, 24*, No. 2 (1953), p. 11.

In the distribution of arrests by sex in 1958 in 1,586 cities with over 2,500 people, the only arrests for which the number of women exceeded that of men were prostitution and commercialized vice, the numbers respectively being 5,412 males to 12,060 females. This category includes sex offenses of a commercialized nature, or attempts to commit the same, such as prostitution, keeping a bawdy house, procuring, transporting, or detaining women for immoral purposes. The largest number of women arrested for any single charge was for that of drunkenness—67,517—which was 27.2 per cent of the total arrests of women on various charges.[15] Professor Cavan believes that women may participate in crimes to a greater extent than indicated by statistics on arrests, but their participation may be indirect, in the form of "casing" a store or bank for robbery, the renting of apartments or rooms that can become headquarters for the group, working to get a parole or pardon for men who are arrested, and providing a place to which they may come when released.[16]

### INTELLIGENCE AND EDUCATION

Some early investigators claimed that prisoners had lower IQ's than the general population. Actually, this was an assumption based upon what the IQ of the general population was believed to be because it was not adequately tested—the tests were faulty and the samples inadequate. Earlier emphasis on the heredity of criminality helped to confuse the issue because it was believed that many criminals were feeble-minded. Simon H. Tulchin studied the intelligence scores of 4,748 reformatory men, 5,512 penitentiary men, and 153 penitentiary women in the State of Illinois over a period of 7 years. He concluded:

The percentages of inferior, average, and superior men in a penitentiary and in the army are very similar. The penitentiary has 23.4%

[15] *Uniform Crime Reports, 1958*, pp. 18, 19, and 96.
[16] Cavan, *op. cit.*, p. 53.

inferiors, the army, 25.9%; the penitentiary has 11.8% superiors, the army, 10.6%. In the reformatory only 15.0% of the men rate inferior and 13.0% rate superior.

In general, the distributions by nativity and race as well as the average age of the Illinois army draft compare much more closely with the penitentiary than with the reformatory group, and this fact needs to be considered in any comparison of results.[17]

He also found that the educational background of both reformatory and penitentiary men varied from illiteracy to graduate work in college. Differences in the amount of formal education of army recruits and prisoners in the penitentiary are on the whole very slight. "In the army sample 1.9 per cent of the recruits have had no schooling; in the penitentiary 2.6 per cent of the native whites reported no schooling, but of these 0.7 per cent reported that they could read or even read and write, although they have not attended formal classes." [18]

It seems clear today that the intelligence of those arrested and convicted of crime will show about the same variations as the intelligence of the general U.S. population. Some are morons and some are highly intelligent. Certain types of crime require very careful planning. Confidence men must be intelligent and Loeb and Leopold, convicted of murder, were reputed to have IQ's approaching genius. It should be indicated here that examinations of the intelligence quotient of prisoners may represent a skewed sample, since these people have been apprehended. This may be an indication that in many cases their arrest was associated with a lower IQ. The more intelligent criminals may have been more successful in eluding capture or, when apprehended, eluding conviction and sentence. This is frankly conjectural because chance also enters into this situation.

## MARITAL STATUS

Various studies of prison inmates reveal that they have a lower marriage rate than the population at large and a higher rate of di-

---

[17] Simon H. Tulchin, *Intelligence and Crime* (Chicago: University of Chicago Press, 1939), pp. 152-53. Copyright 1939 by University of Chicago.
[18] Tulchin, *op. cit.*, p. 157.

vorce and separation. To some extent this may be explained by the fact that a large number of inmates are arrested while young, before they have an opportunity to marry. Some come from areas in which the rate of marital instability is quite high and it may be that their divorce and separation rates do not vary much from those of the people among whom they lived before arrest. Naive check forgers had an unusually high rate of divorce and separation, and among the single persons many had been alienated from their families.[19] But marital disruption of offenders may merely be another index of their general instability and maladjustment. In his study of inmates of the Illinois State Penitentiary, Tulchin found that 37 per cent of the population of Illinois was single but 49 per cent of penitentiary inmates were single. Among native-born whites of native-born parents only 38½ per cent of penitentiary inmates were married, compared to 57.4 per cent of the state population. Among the foreign-born more than twice as many of the penitentiary inmates were single as in the general population, while 38 per cent of the inmates were married, compared to 69.6 per cent in the state population.[20]

# RELIGION

Some older European studies, such as that of Gustav Aschaffenburg and W. H. Bonger, claim that Roman Catholics are more criminal than Protestants, and Jews least criminal of the three. Professor von Hentig studied religious affiliation among inmates of juvenile reform schools and prisons. His figures showed that among delinquents and reformatory inmates Catholics were two-and-one-half times more numerous than Protestants. But C. V. Dunn found that in 27 adult prisons and 19 reform schools Protestants were more numerous than Roman Catholics.[21] Of course, the religious affiliations of inmates of a penal institution are meaningless unless they can be compared to the specific religious groups of the population in the state or country. Simon H. Tulchin's study of the religious affiliation of men in the

---

[19] Reckless, *op. cit.*, p. 112.
[20] Tulchin, *op. cit.*, p. 70.
[21] Barnes & Teeters, *New Horizons in Criminology*, 3rd ed. (Englewood Cliffs, N J.: Prentice-Hall, Inc., 1959), p. 614.

Illinois State Penitentiary and the Illinois State Reformatory is presented in Table 8-2.

TABLE 8-2[22]

PERCENTAGE DISTRIBUTION OF MEN IN THE SEVERAL RELIGIOUS
DENOMINATIONS—ILLINOIS STATE PENITENTIARY
AND ILLINOIS STATE REFORMATORY

| Religious Denomination | Native Whites of Native-Born Parents | | Foreign-Born Whites | | Northern-Born Negroes | | Southern-Born Negroes | |
|---|---|---|---|---|---|---|---|---|
| | Penitentiary | Reformatory | Penitentiary | Reformatory | Penitentiary | Reformatory | Penitentiary | Reformatory |
| | Per Cent | Per Cent | Per Cent | Per Cent | Per Cent | Per Cent | Per Cent | Per Cent |
| "None" | 9.9 | 14.9 | 2.9 | 6.8 | 8.3 | 16.3 | 4.3 | 11.0 |
| Baptist | 8.8 | 15.8 | 0.2 | 0.6 | 40.6 | 44.0 | 59.0 | 55.6 |
| Catholic | 30.0 | 18.3 | 69.9 | 67.2 | 15.4 | 7.4 | 9.6 | 4.9 |
| Christian | 7.2 | 14.0 | 1.6 | 0.6 | 0.9 | 1.2 | 0.7 | 0.8 |
| Jewish | 0.8 | 0.3 | 7.0 | 11.6 | 0.0 | 0.0 | 0.0 | 0.0 |
| Lutheran | 3.2 | 2.9 | 9.7 | 5.4 | 0.0 | 0.4 | 0.0 | 0.0 |
| Methodist | 19.2 | 21.4 | 2.0 | 1.5 | 26.5 | 27.2 | 22.5 | 25.1 |
| Presbyterian | 4.9 | 5.0 | 2.2 | 1.5 | 0.0 | 0.8 | 0.6 | 0.6 |
| Protestant Episcopal | 2.3 | 0.0 | 1.2 | 0.0 | 2.5 | 0.0 | 0.3 | 0.0 |
| Protestant Unspecified | 10.1 | 1.8 | 2.2 | 0.6 | 5.5 | 0.8 | 2.1 | 0.6 |
| Miscellaneous | 3.6 | 5.6 | 1.1 | 4.2 | 0.3 | 1.9 | 0.9 | 1.4 |
| Number of Cases | 1,504 | 2,143 | 986 | 336 | 325 | 257 | 955 | 509 |

According to the census about 40 per cent of the church membership in the State of Illinois is classified as Roman Catholic, 10 per cent Methodist, 10 per cent Lutheran, and 10 per cent Jewish, while other denominations range from a fraction of one per cent to 5 or 6 per cent. Among native whites of native-born parents the percentage of Catholics in the penitentiary is below the percentage in the population and in the case of reformatory inmates considerably lower. However, when the foreign-born whites are considered, the number of Catholics exceeds the number in the state population. But in considering the religious affiliation of prison inmates, considerable cau-

[22] Adapted from Tulchin, *op. cit.*, p. 77.

tion is indicated. Practically all inmates claim some religious affiliation but it is probable that for many such affiliation is purely nominal. Furthermore, in the table presented, the percentage of Negroes who claim to be Catholics is far larger than the actual U.S. Negro Catholic percentage in 1939 (when this study was published). At that time only between 3 and 4 per cent of American Negroes were Roman Catholics.

## TYPES OF CRIME

The seriousness and extent of crime in the United States was brought home to American citizens via the Kefauver Senate Crime Committee, which televised its hearings beginning in 1950. It revealed that organized criminal gangs operate in interstate commerce and are located in many large cities. There they have control of various gambling enterprises, including bookmaking, policy, and slot machines, and are involved in other rackets such as narcotics and prostitution. These gangs were originally formed after World War I to cash in on the lucrative bootlegging business. With the repeal of the Volstead Amendment in the thirties, they turned to other enterprises, particularly gambling, managing to secure a monopoly in a city or a section of a city through persuasion, intimidation, violence, murder, and police "pay offs." A criminal organization known as the Mafia operates both domestically and internationally. In this country it is sometimes known as the "Black Hand." Its orders are ruthlessly carried out and those who violate them are usually murdered.

The success of such organized crime can be traced to what is known as the "fix." Sometimes this is done by bribing law enforcement officials, although it may also be carried out by the acquisition of political power, large financial contributions to political organizations, and by purchasing good will through charitable contributions and press relations.[23] The Kefauver Committee found that major organized crime in Philadelphia was the policy, or "numbers" racket. Territories for numbers operators were staked out and, through connivance with some judges, out of thousands of arrests prior to

[23] *The Kefauver Committee Report on Organized Crime* (New York: Didier, 1951), pp. 174-75.

1950 for gambling only two defendants had gone to jail. It was claimed that protection money paid to the Philadephia police in the lower ranks was more than $150,000 a month. Apparently such gambling flourished in Philadelphia with the aid of some police, some judges, and some politicians.[24]

Chicago, the second largest city of the nation, has a strategic location and has been a center for organized crime in the United States. In the 1920's the notorious Torrio-Capone gang terrorized the city. Later, Capone became the head of this illegal empire, which controlled bootlegging, prostitution, gambling, horse racing, and dog racing. In 1924 the gang staffed the polling places during the mayoralty election in Cicero, a Chicago suburb, and as a result this town became the headquarters of the gang's operations. Later, when prohibition was repealed, the gang began to infiltrate legitimate enterprises, including labor unions. Bombings and murders, many of which remain unsolved, have characterized gang activities in Chicago.[25] At the height of his career Capone's take from the rackets was estimated at $6,000,000 a week.[26]

The "protection" racket has proved more profitable than bootlegging ever was to organized gangsters. In this racket, the owner of a legitimate business is approached and informed that he should purchase "protection." Since the owner feels no need for "protection," he may protest. At times, he is quickly convinced. If not, his property is destroyed, his equipment is burned, or he is beaten. Appeals to the police in such cases are usually fruitless because many have already been paid off by the gang.[27]

Organized crime has moved into certain labor unions. Some officials of union locals have criminal records. Under the chairmanship of Senator McClellan, the Senate Crime Subcommittee found that in New York State's Westchester County in 1951 a battle occurred for a share of the $50,000,000 New York garbage removal industry. Through the aid of a local of the Teamsters Union, one carting company was eventually able to secure a monopoly. Stores which did not cooperate were picketed, business men were threatened, and competitors' trucks destroyed. The picketing of stores was particularly

---

[24] *The Kefauver Committee Report on Organized Crime*, pp. 27-30.
[25] *The Kefauver Committee Report on Organized Crime*, pp. 31-32.
[26] Barnes and Teeters, *op. cit.*, p. 21.
[27] Barnes and Teeters, *op. cit.*, p. 21-22.

effective since garbage must be removed promptly because of odors and the danger of disease. There is also a possibility that the health department may close the business if garbage is not disposed of quickly. The struggle did not last very long, and ultimately the victimized carting company had to sell out to the other which then enjoyed a monopoly.[28] Certain labor leaders have stolen union funds. Racketeering has occurred both in labor unions and in management, and the Senate Subcommittee discovered corruption, fraud, kidnapping, dynamiting, larceny, and similar evidence of immoral activity on the part of both management and labor. Victor Reisel, a labor columnist, was blinded by acid thrown at him in 1955, reputedly by a person or persons in the hire of labor bosses.[29]

## WHITE-COLLAR CRIME

*White-collar crime,* a concept developed by the late Edwin H. Sutherland, refers to violations of criminal law by persons of the upper socio-economic class in the course of their occupational or professional activities. Two distinctions about white-collar crime are necessary: first, it is committed by persons who are considered highly respectable in their communities—thus, owners or managers of "fly-by-night" business enterprises with unsavory reputations who violate the criminal code in the course of their occupational activities are not truly white-collar criminals; second, persons of the upper socio-economic classes who commit murder, rape, or similar offenses are not engaging in white-collar crime. Promoters and salesmen of fraudulent stock, misleading and exaggerated advertisements about patent medicines (some of which are actually harmful), illegal abortions by physicians, lawyers who advise organized criminals prior to their offenses as well as those specializing in corporation law who guide criminal or quasi-criminal activities of companies—all are examples of white-collar criminals.[30] A great deal of this type of crime was carried on during the Second World War, when rationing of

---

[28] Robert F. Kennedy, *The Enemy Within* (New York: Popular Library, Inc., 1960), pp. 230-32.

[29] Barnes and Teeters, *op. cit.,* p. 23.

[30] Barnes and Teeters, *op. cit.,* pp. 44-49.

certain commodities, notably some foods and gasoline, was necessary. Black markets flourished, in which individuals were able to purchase restricted goods by paying more than the price established by law, or through the counterfeiting of government coupons required for such goods.

The extent of white-collar crime is just about impossible to determine and a great deal of it goes undetected. Some may be of a petty nature, such as the butcher who short-changes on weights or the businessman who "pads" his expense accounts. The Federal Trade Commission occasionally orders manufacturers to cease and desist from fraudulent advertising. But through prolonged legal delays, the order usually is not immediately obeyed. Even when the order is eventually complied with, however, a new type of advertising, sometimes equally deceitful, often replaces the original. Then the entire legal procedure must be repeated. In the meantime the public continues to be misled. Lack of funds and personnel makes enforcement of such laws as the Pure Food and Drug Act difficult.

## THE PROFESSIONAL CRIMINAL

While crime has become increasingly organized in the United States, and such organized criminals are more and more becoming "professionals," other professional criminals work alone or with one or two confederates. They do not really constitute a "gang" as such, and one or all of them may also be engaged in legitimate enterprises. The basic clue to the professional criminal can be found in his attitude toward crime and society. He and his colleagues live in a sub-culture of their own whose one value seems to be that "only saps work for a living." He views crime as a business matter, takes a calculated risk, and usually plays for high stakes. He looks down upon the pickpocket, the petty thief, the sex criminal, or others who may be termed "situational offenders," that is, those who through force of circumstances occasionally engage in criminal activity.

The characteristics of a profession can be extended to the professional criminal who, through "training," has acquired certain "skills" in his work. He subscribes to a "code," which includes withholding information from the police when apprehended or facing death rather than revealing the names of his colleagues. Generally he feels no sense of shame or regret about his criminal activities.

## THE SEX CRIMINAL

Objective and adequate discussion of sex offenders is extremely difficult. When newspapers publish in horrible detail the sexual assault and murder of a child, public indignation quite naturally is aroused. Reporters use terms such as "sex fiends" and "sex morons" with more emotion than truth. When the public thinks of the sex offender, it usually thinks in these emotional terms, and is persuaded that such crimes are widespread. The Federal Bureau of Investigation categorizes three types of sex offenses; first, *forcible rape*, which includes not only forcible rape but assault to rape and attempted rape; second, *prostitution and commercialized vice*, which involve sex offenses of a commercialized nature—or attempts to commit the same—such as prostitution, keeping a bawdy house, procuring, transporting or detaining women for immoral purposes; and third, *statutory rape*, which amounted to less than 2 per cent of all arrests in the jurisdictions reported.[31] Only about 5 per cent of convicted sex offenders have used force or injury upon a victim. Of course, the fact that such crimes are relatively rare makes them no less reprehensible, but the American public should nevertheless be reasonably well informed both about the real extent and types of sex offenses.

The late Dr. Sutherland found that the possibilities of being murdered by a relative or some other intimate associate were far greater than the danger of murder by an unknown sex offender. Almost 90 per cent of the female victims in his study were murdered by relatives or suitors. About one-fourth of those who murdered women then committed suicide. Among other popular fallacies concerning sex offenders, Paul W. Tappan lists the belief that sex offenders are usually repeaters. Actually, among serious crimes homicide alone has a lower rate of recidivism, or conviction for

---

[31] *Uniform Crime Reports, 1958*, p. 96.

violating the law more than once. He likewise states that the sex offender, contrary to popular belief, does not progress to more serious types of sex crime.[32] Professor Tappan distinguishes two types of sex offenders. The first group includes sexual deviates, whose behavior offends good taste and morals, among which would be listed homosexuals, exhibitionists (peepers), and other minor lewd offenders. The other group, which is composed of dangerous and aggressive offenders who constitute a serious threat to the community, includes aggressive rapists, sadists, sex slayers, and those who attack young children. The second group is much smaller than the first, and it is from this group that the public especially needs protection.[33] A number of states have established what are known as "sexual psychopath laws," under whose provisions sex offenders may be sent to psychiatric centers for diagnosis and treatment. Unfortunately, at this time knowledge of the etiology of sexual abberations is slight. Some persons who commit sex offenses are undoubtedly psychotic, others are neurotic, and still others may be merely emotionally disturbed. Until the very important distinctions among the types of sex offenses and the mental state of the offender are made, the concept of the sexual psychopath will remain a vague, broad catchall.

## TREATMENT OF THE OFFENDER

In their famous operetta *The Mikado*, Gilbert and Sullivan satirized the efforts of contemporary penologists to "make the punishment fit the crime." It was then believed that if the pain suffered in the punishment of a crime were only a little greater than the pleasure derived from committing it, individuals would be deterred from criminal activity. As backward as this may appear today, it was a long step forward in the history of penology. Historically, punishments for even minor offenses were extremely severe, including flogging, branding, amputation of hands, arms, and ears, and similar measures.

---

[32] *The Habitual Sex Offender*, Report and Recommendations of the Commission on the Habitual Sex Offender as formulated by Paul W. Tappan, Technical Consultant, for the New Jersey Commission on the Habitual Sex Offender, pp. 13-14.

[33] *The Habitual Sex Offender*, pp. 17-18.

But even during the Elizabethan period, when punishment was extremely cruel, crime continued to be extremely common.

It would be a mistake to believe that all cruel and barbarous punishments—even though outlawed by the Constitution—have been abolished, or that advocates of such treatment do not still exist. Barnes and Teeters state that floggings within prisons continue today, and deaths have resulted from severe beatings, particularly in southern prison camps and chain gangs. Another method of discipline is suspending prisoners by their hands, with their toes not quite touching the floor.[34] Most states as well as the federal government, continue to use capital punishment. This is carried out in most states by electrocution, in others by hanging and lethal gas. Utah permits a choice between hanging or shooting. However, the number of executions annually continues to decrease, and the crimes for which such punishment is prescribed have been reduced to mainly first-degree murder, forcible rape, and kidnapping.

The chief argument in behalf of capital punishment today is that it deters others from committing such crimes. There is no adequate proof that this is true and in those states which have abolished the death penalty, the rate of homicide is about the same as those states in the same area where the death penalty still exists. Michigan, for example, with no death penalty, has a homicide rate somewhat lower than the adjoining states of Illinois and Ohio which have death penalties.[35] Furthermore, the finality of capital punishment is one of the strongest arguments that can be used against it. There is no means of rectifying such a mistake and at times deathbed confessions of the real offenders have revealed the executed person to have been innocent. Capital punishment may satisfy the public's desire for vengeance, but it seems to perform no other function.

## PRISONS

Today, fines and/or imprisonment are the most common methods of dealing with offenders. Ideally, the function of a prison should be twofold: the protection of society and the rehabilitation of the

---

[34] Barnes and Teeters, *op. cit.*, p. 349.
[35] Barnes and Teeters, *op. cit.*, p. 319.

offender. While the public at large is protected from offenders during their period of incarceration, the best long-term protection occurs when the prisoner has been successfully rehabilitated. But it is a well-established fact that the rate of recidivism is at least 50 per cent among former prison inmates. It is also true that some reformatories and prisons are actually "schools in crime." Instead of rehabilitation, the inmate is inducted into a life of criminality and establishes contacts with the more important leaders of the underworld. This is less true of the better institutions, which use all the resources they can, such as counseling, vocational training, and religious motivation to enable the inmate to lead a decent life when he is released.

But as Professor Vold has pointed out, penal institutions are sorely handicapped in their efforts to treat offenders. When a physician treats a patient, he does so on the basis of a knowledge of causes of the illness. If a prisoner is to be treated rather than punished, the causes for his criminality must be known. Given the present level of such knowledge, this is not always possible, and prison practices are often based upon what was considered relevant at the time such practices were inaugurated. This is just about inevitable because prison administrators cannot await the ultimate development of criminological theory before they establish their procedures.[36]

In many penal institutions, treatment lags far behind what is actually known about crime causation. One reason for this is antiquated buildings, which are seriously overcrowded. There is also a shortage of trained personnel, and even where competent persons exist, the number of inmates with whom they must deal is overwhelming. In some cases, wardens are appointed through political patronage, although they may be woefully ignorant of penology. Work within prisons is essential to rehabilitation. It is one method by which an inmate may acquire skills necessary to support himself when released. But businessmen strongly oppose the sale of products manufactured in penal institutions. Even where the "state system" exists (that is, when goods made in prisons are sold to other state institutions), there is resistance from businessmen and industrialists. In other words, political and economic considerations largely shape penal procedures.

---

[36] George B. Vold, *Theoretical Criminology* (New York: Oxford University Press, Inc., 1958), p. 282.

## PAROLE

*Parole* is a system under which a prisoner is released under supervision prior to the expiration of his sentence. Ideally, every prisoner, if he is to be released at all, should be released on parole. The difficulties in the adjustment of a former prison inmate are tremendous, and he needs help in making this transition. A man released at the expiration of his sentence goes without any sort of supervision or assistance. Parole should not be considered leniency but rather an additional safeguard for the public. But good parole procedures require that adequate personnel exist to supervise the ex-prisoner, and that parole be granted only when indications exist that he is ready for it and has a fair chance of succeeding in the outside world.

In some jurisdictions, parole procedures may be criticized on at least two counts. First, some parole board members, like many wardens, are political appointees. They may serve only a few days each month, have no knowledge whatsoever of the dynamics of human behavior, and be subject to political pressures. Decisions on parole may revolve around their own personal predilections or pet hunches. In the author's observation, one parole board was predisposed to immediately reject applications from inmates convicted of sex crimes or inmates who drank. Parole board decisions are also based in part upon the report of the prison parole officer, and his competency must also enter into their deliberations.

A second criticism of certain parole systems is a lack of well-trained personnel and the heavy case load which each parole officer must therefore carry. In general, the American public is rather poorly informed as to the meaning of parole. Most of its knowledge comes from newspapers which sensationally publicize crimes committed by parolees. They make no mention, of course, of the many parolees who make successful adjustments. In view of the public distrust of parole, the position of parole officer does not enjoy a high status. In many jurisdictions, salaries are pitifully low and well-trained, competent persons are not attracted to these posts. Some officers are completely devoid of training, and the position is often a political plum likely to be lost with the change of administration.

## PROBATION

*Probation* is a system in which a convicted offender is returned to the community under supervision. The important phrase here is "under supervision." A judge may suspend a sentence, or he may suspend the execution of a sentence but unless supervision of the offender is provided for, such procedures should not be considered probation. The most common defense of probation is that it saves the taxpayer money. Today the cost of probation is from $20 to $150 a case. On the other hand the average per capita cost of operating adult penal and correctional institutions, not including jails, is estimated at from $1,000 to $1,500 a year per prisoner. To this must be added the cost of supporting a prisoner's wife and family, if he has them and they are compelled to seek public assistance.[37] But there are also great social advantages associated with probation. It indicates that society is willing to give the offender another chance. He is not separated from his family or his community. Particularly, he avoids the stigma of prison. Of course, probation is no panacea and cannot be extended to all offenders. Probation is not likely to eliminate prisons or the need of parole. However, where it can be employed it saves the state money and generally affords the offender a better hope of successful rehabilitation.

Like parole, probation should not be considered leniency. Rather, it is another method of protecting society and facilitating the offender's rehabilitation. Furthermore, in those jurisdictions which have good probation services, the record of success is fairly high. In the fiscal year ending June 30th, 1954, in the federal system (excluding juvenile delinquents) about 48 per cent of the offenders were imprisoned and about 44 per cent granted probation and suspended sentence. In the following year probation was terminated in 10,246 cases, but only 16 per cent of them through violation.[38]

But some of the criticisms directed at parole may also be directed at probation. Again, there is the matter of adequately trained

---

[37] Austin H. MacCormick, "The Potential Value of Probation," *Federal Probation*, 19:3-4.

[38] MacCormick, *op. cit.*, p. 5.

personnel, careful selection of candidates for probation, and a sensible case load. Such criteria rarely exist, and the rate of successful probation is much lower in those jurisdictions where they do not.

## THE SITUATIONAL-VALUE APPROACH

In the case of the juvenile offender and the adult criminal, a number of situational factors operate which stimulate the violation of law. These have been cited at some length in the chapters on juvenile delinquency and crime and the criminal. These factors involve age, sex, ethnic and racial (or general minority) status, residence in slums or interstitial areas, and types of association—as well as lack of social, educational, and economic opportunities. However, no one of these in itself should be considered a cause of crime. Some delinquents and some adult criminals do not suffer such deprivations, but do commit offenses. Thus it is only possible to generalize that these situational factors, which operate together in many cases as a focus upon the individual, expose him to situations in which he may commit crime and facilitate such behavior.

Many of these situational factors are interrelated and interdependent, such as lack of economic opportunity, minority status, and slum living. Age and sex are factors in delinquency and criminal behavior, partly as a result of the cultural status expectations associated with these factors. In American society adolescents and post-adolescents are in periods of life in which individuals are still attempting to define their roles. The quest for recognition may not readily be satisfied in socially approved ways, and some youths find it within their sub-culture, which may be an anti-social one. This is particularly true of those who belong to delinquent gangs.

Demands of cultural expectations are reflected in the types of crime most common to certain age and sex groups. Violence, vandalism, and similar offenses are typical of youth, not only because they possess the strength and agility for such actions, but because the restraining influences of society have not yet been either adequately transmitted or accepted. While emphasis is placed upon the activities of anti-social gangs, it should be recalled that certain types of gang activity scarcely of an entirely socially acceptable nature are prevalent among college students. Panty-raids, riots preceding or following football games, and mass protests which sometimes take a violent turn are not uncommon in American college life. Serious personal injury—even death—has been associated with some college hazing. There is a transitional period in the lives of most youths in which there is a tendency to rebel against established authority. But generally, the situational factors pressing upon college students are considerably different from those which influence lower-class youths, those who live in slums, and those who suffer minority status. In other words, the actual motivation to engage in such behavior seems common throughout the United States to large numbers of American youth. Its expression, however, will vary.

In the case of the adult criminal, with certain notable exceptions, there is apt to be a history of delinquency in his early years. While some abandon this pattern of life later, others persist in it because the reputed rehabilitation provided in reformatories or in probation programs has been ineffective. This may be traced to some of the systems, to some of the individuals involved, and probably in many cases to both. Some become professional criminals in adulthood, others "occasional" criminals. Still others, who have not been involved with the law in their earlier days, may by reason of critical situational factors in later life become so involved. Such factors can include acute economic circumstances, opportunities for easy— albeit illegal—money, and association with individuals who persuade them to enter crime. All crime, of course, cannot be explained through economic necessity or evil associates.

Certain types of crime such as murder may result from a sudden and unique situation in which an individual finds himself. For example, there are *crimes of passion*. An individual, maddened by jealousy, fear, or hatred, may lose control of himself to such an extent that he kills another. Such murder is not premeditated, and it is for this reason that some murderers have a low rate of recidivism and sometimes prove to be exemplary prisoners, often becoming "trustees." In other words, there are many complex situational factors which operate as a totality and which may facilitate the commission of offenses.

However, beyond situational factors there is a question of how an individual perceives a situation. This is associated with his value system. At the risk of oversimplification, such individuals apparently suffer from a process of inadequate socialization. They have not been thoroughly inducted into the dominant culture of their society. An adequate value system either has not been transmitted or has not been accepted. The family, the school, the church, and the state have either not reached the individual or have not affected him. While constitutional or psychological factors may have deprived an individual of the opportunity to profit from exposure to the dominant value system—as in a case of a moron—it seems probable that relatively little crime can be explained on this basis.

Finally, there is a matter of conflict of values. While within the dominant value system of American society, crime is considered morally and legally wrong, the definition of crime varies from one social class to another, as well as from one region to another—not to mention differences found in ethnic and racial groups. Every type of deviant can find some reinforcement of his value system in large cities and metropolitan areas. In a complex, pluralistic society, this is just about inevitable. In an abstract sense then, crime appears to be the result of some type of deficiency in the individual's social situation—at least as he perceives it—and in a faulty value system or an unfortunate choice of values within his society.

## REMEDIAL MEASURES

The old adage that an ounce of prevention is worth a pound of cure is probably nowhere more true than in the field of criminology. If as much effort and money were spent on crime prevention as is spent on the apprehension, conviction, punishment, and treatment of offenders, the incidence of crime would probably be considerably lower. While some factors in crime causation are clear, others are completely unknown. Perhaps they never will be known. The varieties of crimes and offenders are so great that tremendous research is needed. While the reduction of poverty, elimination of slums, providing of adequate recreational facilities (particularly for youth), and similar measures should be pursued, they in themselves cannot eliminate crime. Of at least equal importance is a change in the value systems of American society. This is no small task, but it is not entirely impossible.

In the last analysis it comes down to the individual and to the individual family. The "get rich quick," "only saps work," and "something for nothing" attitudes so prevalent in American life contribute in no small measure to the high incidence of crime. Glorification of the criminal in newspapers, magazines, and other media and the indifference to political corruption and minor law violations on the part of otherwise respectable citizens lead youth to believe that "everybody's doing it." Until the individual American comes to grips with the reality and consequences of such a philosophy, any change in the present situation is unlikely.

Adequate law enforcement agencies with adequate salaries free of political domination, impartial and speedy justice within the courts, increased use of intelligent probation and parole services, and satisfactory penal procedures will help. One of the hopeful signs is the effort to detect pre-delinquents by means of tests such as the Gluecks have developed. In other words, the techniques of prevention must be emphasized to a much greater extent in the future if there is any hope of reducing America's crime rate.

## REVIEW QUESTIONS

1. What is a crime? What is a criminal?
2. Distinguish between a felony and a misdemeanor. Are these distinctions meaningful today? What is the best source of statistics on criminal offenses? Is this best source an accurate accounting of all crime?
3. Can it be scientifically stated that crime in this country has increased over the rates of 50 or 75 years ago?
4. Discuss the social characteristics of offenders, touching upon age, sex, social class, education, and race.
5. To what extent does religious affiliation seem to be associated with a high or low rate of crime?
6. What is meant by white-collar crime? Does the original definition of white-collar crime seem suitable today?
7. What are the rackets? What are the major sources of information about racketeering in the United States?
8. What is the professional criminal?
9. The sex criminals are highly dangerous to society and have a high rate of recidivism. Evaluate this statement.
10. What are the major methods of treating offenders?

11. How effective is capital punishment as a deterent to very serious crime?
12. What is the difference between probation and parole? What are the advantages and disadvantages of probation and parole?
13. What positive measures can be recommended for the prevention of crime and successful rehabilitation of the offender?

## SELECTED READINGS

*Articles*

Moses, E. R., "Differentials in Crime Rates Between Negroes and Whites," *American Sociological Review*, 12 (Aug. 1947), 411-20.

Tappan, Paul W., "Who Is a Criminal?" *American Sociological Review*, 12 (Feb. 1947), 96-102.

Porterfield, A. L., "A Decade of Serious Crimes in the United States," *American Sociological Review*, 13 (Mar. 1948), 44-54.

Schmid, Calvin F., "Urban Crime Areas, Part I," *American Sociological Review*, 25 (Aug. 1960), 527-41.

———, "Urban Crime Areas, Part II," *American Sociological Review*, 25 (Aug. 1960), 542-49.

Skolnick, Jerome H., "Toward a Developmental Theory of Parole," *American Sociological Review*, 25 (Aug. 1960), 542-49.

Sutherland, E. H., "White Collar Criminality," *American Sociological Review*, 5 (Feb. 1940), 1-12.

———, "Is 'White Collar Crime' Crime?," *American Sociological Review*, 10 (Apr. 1945), 132-39.

*Books*

Abrahamsen, David, *The Psychology of Crime.* New York: Columbia University Press, 1961.

Barnes, Harry Elmer and Negley F. Teeters, *New Horizons in Criminology.* Englewood Cliffs, N.J.: Prentice-Hall, Inc., 1959.

Bensing, Robert C., *Homicide in an Urban Community.* Springfield, Illinois: Charles C. Thomas, Publisher, 1961.

Cavan, Ruth S., *Criminology.* New York: Thomas Y. Crowell Co., 1956.

*The Habitual Sex Offender*, Report and Recommendations of the Commission on the Habitual Sex Offender as formulated by Paul W. Tappan, Technical Consultant for the New Jersey Commission on the Habitual Sex Offender.

Reckless, Walter C., *The Crime Problem*. New York: Appleton-Century-Crofts, Inc., 1955.

Sykes, Greslem M., *The Society of Captives*. Princeton, N.J.: Princeton University Press, 1958.

Tulchin, Simon H., *Intelligence and Crime*. Chicago: University of Chicago Press, 1939.

# 9

# Narcotic Addiction

D RUG addiction is not easily defined, nor is a drug addict readily identified. From the medical viewpoint addiction is a condition resulting from repeated use of any drug to the extent that continued use of it becomes essential in order to retain normal physiological functions, and discontinuance of the drug causes definite physical and mental symptoms.[1]

Generally speaking, however, the term "drug addiction" is restricted to the use of narcotics. In 1950 the Expert Committee on Drugs Liable to Produce Addiction, which is a subdivision of the United Nations World Health Organization (WHO), stated:

> Drug addiction is a state of periodic or chronic intoxication, detrimental to the individual and to society, produced by the repeated consumption of a drug (natural or synthetic). Its characteristics include:
>
> 1. Overpowering desire or need (compulsion) to continue taking the drug and to obtain it by any means;
> 2. A tendency to increase the dose;

---

[1] From *Drug Addiction: Physiological, Psychological and Sociological* Aspects, by D. P. Ausubel. Copyright 1958. (New York: Random House, Inc., 1958), p. 9.

3. A psychic (Psychological and sometimes physical) dependence on the effects of the drug.[2]

The three aspects of drug addiction are tolerance, physical dependence, and euphoria. *Tolerance* refers to the diminishing influence that an equal dose of a drug has upon an individual, which causes him to increase it to regain the desired effect. *Physical dependence* is the physiological state resulting from repeated administration of the drug which makes necessary its continued use to prevent the various painful symptoms of the abstinence syndrome—the pains of drug withdrawal. *Euphoria* is the state of well-being that the drug creates within the individual. Some authorities believe that without euphoria there would be no drug addiction, since it is this condition that the addict wants to achieve.

A distinction may be made between a *habit-forming drug* and an *addictive drug*. Among the common habit-forming drugs are tobacco, coffee, and alcohol. The major difference between an addictive drug and a habit-forming drug is in the withdrawal symptoms. An individual may give up tobacco, coffee, or alcohol and suffer some slight nervousness or intense desire for them but he does not suffer the acute symptoms characteristic of the addict deprived of his narcotic. The addictive drug results in physical dependence upon it, the habit-forming drug does not or at least does so to a very slight degree.

The identification of a narcotic addict is by no means simple. In fact, certain well-known people have used narcotics discreetly for a very long time without causing anyone to suspect their addiction. The popular notion of "dope fiend" is misleading. Many persons think of a drug addict as a pasty-faced, emaciated, nervous individual bent upon any kind of violence or theft in order to procure money to purchase a narcotic. Individuals with such characteristics do exist but they are likely to be addicts of long standing who have not had their "fix," that is their narcotics, and are going through the withdrawal symptoms.

Short of an admission by the individual that he is an addict there are certain signs that indicate but do not necessarily prove his addiction. If he has narcotics in his possession and is unable to give a

---

[2] As quoted in David W. Maurer and Victor H. Vogel, *Narcotics and Narcotic Addiction* (Springfield, Illinois: Charles C. Thomas, Publisher, 1954), pp. 23-24.

satisfactory explanation for them, he may be suspect. Needle marks in the skin which resemble black or blue spots, scars over the veins, abscesses near the place where the drug has been injected, drowsiness, sleepiness or lethargy, and, particularly, the indications of the withdrawal symptoms may seem to indicate that the individual has been using opiates or barbiturates. In the case of opiates, that is, opium or morphine, the pupils of the eye may be contracted, especially immediately following an injection. However, this is usually true of the newer addict only because confirmed addicts eventually attain tolerance and may not have this symptom. If the individual has upon his person or in his living quarters hypodermic equipment such as a needle, eyedropper, syringe, a bent spoon, he is very likely an addict. Certain laboratory tests may also prove that an individual has recently taken an addictive drug, but they do not necessarily prove that he is addicted. As Maurer and Vogel point out, no single sign is conclusive, but if a number of these indications are found, it is highly probable the person is an addict.[3]

## INCIDENCE OF DRUG ADDICTION

According to a report of the Bureau of Narcotics published in 1958, there were 46,266 known addicts in the United States. It should be noted that these are known addicts, and the number of unknown addicts is anyone's guess. It has been claimed that there are 90,000 addicts in New York City alone. This represents a considerable decrease from the past. In 1918, one estimate, probably exaggerated, placed the number of addicts at about 1,000,000. In 1924 they were estimated at 109,000 and by 1937 the incidence rate had dropped to less than one addict per 5,000 persons. Shortly after the war the number of addicts, particularly among youths, rose sharply. In 1951 the Federal Bureau of Narcotics stated:

> The use of narcotic drugs by teenagers is primarily located in large metropolitan centers; there is little of it in small cities and rural areas. Addiction among boys is almost 10 times as great as it is among girls. Many of the young addicts have criminal records before they come to the attention of the Bureau of Narcotics.[4]

[3] Maurer and Vogel, *op. cit.*, pp. 122-23.
[4] Ausubel, *op. cit.*, p. 63.

The number of addicts under 21 years of age in the two U.S. government drug addiction hospitals increased from 22 in 1947 to 440 in 1950. New York City's Bellevue Hospital had no adolescent addicts between 1940 and 1948, but during the first two months of 1951 there were 84 cases of adolescent addicts.[5]

## TYPES OF DRUGS

The type of drug used by individuals shows regional variations. According to the Bureau of Narcotics, of the 46,266 addicts upon which they reported, heroin was used by 92 per cent; morphine by 3 per cent; and synthetic drugs, opium, paregoric, or codeine by the remaining 5 per cent.[7] Ausubel, however, claims that morphine is used most commonly in the United States for addictive purposes, except in the East, where heroin is used more frequently.

Morphine sulfate is an opium derivative. It is an *analgesic*—that is, pain relieving—and acts on the central nervous system. The first reaction to morphine is stimulation, but this is generally followed by a depressant action. Among persons prone to addiction the administration of morphine results in sensations of pleasure or well-being; but others merely find that their pains are relieved, without the accompanying euphoria.

Among addicts morphine is called "M," "white stuff," "junk," and many other names. Heroin, known as "H," or "horse," is a white, crystalline powder that resembles morphine—from which it is derived. Since 1925 it has been banned in the United States because of its dangerous addiction possibilities. It has even greater addictive liabilities than morphine and is twice as potent in the same given quantity. Both of these drugs may be taken orally, or subcutaneously (by injecting them beneath the skin), or intravenously (known as "mainlining"). Heroin, sometimes mixed with cocaine, is also taken by sniffing it up the nose, where it is absorbed through the mucous membrane. The immediate and maximum effect of these drugs is best obtained through intravenous injection. Sometimes a combination of drugs is used, called a "speedball" by addicts. Cocaine is made from

---

[5] Ausubel, *op. cit.*, p. 63.
[7] *Traffic in Opium and Other Dangerous Drugs*, p. 41.

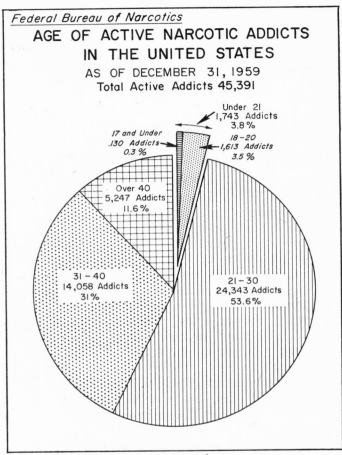

*Federal Bureau of Narcotics*

**AGE OF ACTIVE NARCOTIC ADDICTS
IN THE UNITED STATES**

AS OF DECEMBER 31, 1959
Total Active Addicts 45,391

FIGURE 9-1 [6]

cocoa leaves and is a very strong stimulant. For this reason it is frequently used by addicts; but to counteract the depressant feeling which rather quickly follows the euphoria it is often mixed with heroin or some other opiate.

Marijuana is variously known in the argot of the addicts as "griefo," "greefo," "love weed," or "Texas tea." It is made from various species

[6] Adapted from *Traffic in Opium and Other Dangerous Drugs*, Bureau of Narcotics (Washington, D.C.: Government Printing Office, 1960), p. 37.

of the Indian hemp plant. This weed grows readily in most parts of the United States and has been found on the vacant lots of large cities as well as in the back yards of homes. In the United States the use of marijuana is most common among teenagers or younger people. It is almost invariably smoked although it can be eaten in the form of a cake. The actual effects of marijuana are variable and cannot be predicted. It is believed that they depend in part upon the personality of the user, the amount taken, the area from which it comes, and the method of administration.

However, in order to achieve the effect, the cigarette must be smoked in a certain way. If so, the user at first finds his pulse beating more quickly, blood pressure is raised, the pupils of the eye may dilate and the face flush. Hunger is noticeably increased and there is some loss of coordination. A room will seem to be considerably larger and in going down steps the individual takes bigger steps than necessary. Marijuana smokers under the influence of the drug feel that their arms and legs are longer and that the head is considerably larger than it should be. Since it does distort the sense of space, driving an automobile under the influence of this drug is highly dangerous.

It has been widely believed that marijuana is a sexual stimulant. Actually, this is not true. On the contrary, an individual who continually uses marijuana soon becomes disinterested in sexual activity. However, under the influence of marijuana, the suggestibility of the individual becomes very great, and if he believes that marijuana is an aphrodisiac, this may have some psychological influence upon him in the beginning. It also lowers the inhibitions, and this too may lead to sexual activity.

Some addicts begin their careers as marijuana smokers. Later they graduate to morphine, heroin, or some combination of drugs. At first the drugs may be taken orally or sniffed up the nose. Later, addicts move to "mainlining." The dangers of such administration are obvious. While some addicts do attempt to observe sterile techniques, others will use needles which have been used by other persons. Sometimes a needle is brushed through their hair in the belief that this will lubricate it, making it easier to enter the vein. The danger of infection is high, as well as the possibility of thrombophlebitis, i.e., inflammation of the vein from a blood clot. Repeated punctures of the same vein eventually make it useless and the addict must find a vein somewhere else in his body. Drugs purchased illegally are rarely pure. They have been cut many times in order to provide a greater profit to the seller. Therefore, the user is completely unaware of what impure ingredients may be mixed with the drug he injects. Neither does he know the exact amount of the drug he is using, and the results are unpredictable.

## HISTORY OF DRUG ADDICTION

It is not known when man first began to use drugs, but a description of the cultivation and preparation of opium was found on clay tablets left by the Sumerians in 7000 B.C. The consumption of dangerous drugs such as opium, hashish (a type of marijuana), and cocaine seems to have a long history. Hashish was used to stimulate warriors before battle, and other drugs were used in puberty rites, religious ceremonies, and to allay the fears caused by the countless taboos typical of preliterates.

The growing, preparation, and sale of opium have proved a profitable enterprise in the past and remains so today. Britain fought the Opium War with China to protect commerce between India and China in that drug. Opium was used widely in the American colonies, apparently as a panacea for almost any illness. Opium smoking, a culture complex of the Chinese, was brought to California by them in the latter part of the 19th century and eventually became popular. Heroin was discovered by the Germans in 1898 and was first hailed as a cure for addiction, although ultimately it proved the most addictive of all drugs. Use of the hypodermic needle for intravenous injection of narcotics began about the mid-nineteenth century and was employed during the Civil War. As a result a number of veterans became addicts. The hemp plant from which marijuana is derived was grown in the American colonies, but the smoking of marijuana did not begin until after the turn of the 20th century, when the custom seems to have been imported from Mexico.

Prior to the passage of the Harrison Act in 1914, narcotics could be sold by pharmacists without a prescription. Many of the patent medicines of that period contained relatively large amounts of both alcohol and narcotics. Drug addiction was apparently considered a personal rather than a social problem and addiction was probably fairly widespread.[8] Professor Alfred R. Lindesmith states that originally the Harrison Act was a revenue measure, and made no reference to addicts or addiction. But it did attempt to make distribution of drugs a matter of record. It did not prevent registered physicians and dentists from dispensing narcotics in their legitimate professional practice, and failed to define "legitimate professional practice." [9]

Confusion arose over U.S. Supreme Court decisions. In the Webb case, an early ruling, it was stated that a physician who prescribed drugs for an addict merely to make him comfortable was not operating within the law. Later, in the Linder case, the court modified its stand, admitting that addiction is a disease and permitting a physician to prescribe moderate amounts of drugs to relieve withdrawal distress. On the other hand Regulation 85 of the Federal Bureau of Narcotics (1938) forbids prescribing drugs for an addict or a habitual user of narcotics if not in the course of professional treatment but rather to keep him comfortable by maintaining his customary use. In view of these contradictory regulations, Lindesmith believes that a physician does not know whether he will be prosecuted under one rule or exonerated under another if he prescribes narcotics for an addict. As a result, physicians have shunned the problem of addiction.[10]

In 1937 the Marijuana Tax Act placed the growth, sale, transfer and use of marijuana under federal control. It is likewise banned by most states under the Uniform Narcotic Drug Act, and since it is cited in the Geneva Drug Convention of 1925, as are cocaine and derivatives of opium, it is also under the control of the United Nations bodies which regulate narcotics. Marijuana addicts are likewise eligible for admission to the federal hospitals at Lexington and Fort Worth, which treat drug addiction.[11]

---

[8] Maurer and Vogel, op. cit., pp. 3-6.
[9] Alfred R. Lindesmith, "General Law and Drug Addiction," Social Problems, 7 (Summer 1959), p. 48.
[10] Lindesmith, op. cit., pp. 52-53.
[11] Ausubel, op. cit., p. 96.

SOCIAL CHARACTERISTICS OF ADDICTS

In attempting to determine the causal factors involved in drug addiction, the various social characteristics such as race, ethnic origin, religion, sex, education, occupation, and age at the beginning of addic-

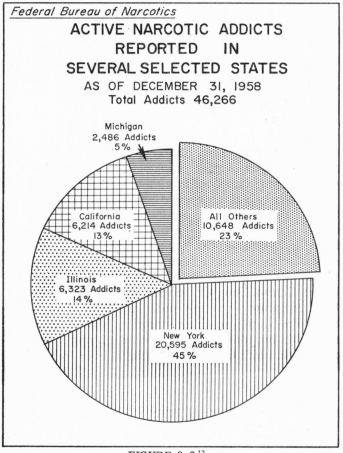

FIGURE 9-2 [12]

[12] Adapted from *Traffic in Opium and Other Dangerous Drugs*, Bureau of Narcotics, p. 36.

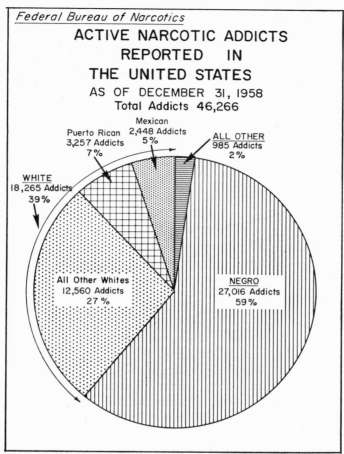

Federal Bureau of Narcotics

# ACTIVE NARCOTIC ADDICTS
# REPORTED IN
# THE UNITED STATES
## AS OF DECEMBER 31, 1958
### Total Addicts 46,266

Mexican
2,448 Addicts
5%

Puerto Rican
3,257 Addicts
7%

ALL OTHER
985 Addicts
2%

WHITE
18,265 Addicts
39%

All Other Whites
12,560 Addicts
27%

NEGRO
27,016 Addicts
59%

FIGURE 9-3 [13]

tion are important clues. Any association between race, residence, religion, and other factors and a high incidence of addiction is not in itself a causal factor but it does raise the question whether such conditions tend to make individuals more prone to addiction. According to Figure 9-2, 45 per cent of the addicts known to the Federal Bureau of Narcotics are found in New York State, 14 per

[13] Adapted from *Traffic in Opium and Other Dangerous Drugs*, Bureau of Narcotics, p. 37.

cent in Illinois, and 13 per cent in California. Thus New York State with about 10 per cent of the population has four-and-one-half times as many addicts as might be expected. Illinois and California also exceed the expected proportions, although not nearly to the degree that New York does. Within these three states are found the three largest cities in the country, respectively New York, Chicago, and Los Angeles. Two of these states are coastal, with large ports. They are undoubtedly ports of entry for smuggled narcotics. Addiction seems to be primarily an urban problem.

A study of addicts in Chicago by Bingham Dai published in 1937 showed that those areas with the highest rate of addiction were typical interstitial areas with many more men than women, few married persons, a high degree of mobility, and a high rate of disorganization.[14] While such a distribution of narcotic addicts would be sociologically expected, it should be noted that these studies are based upon known addicts. Lower-class addicts are more likely to come to the knowledge of law enforcement officers. Since the sale of illegal narcotics is very largely in the hands of the underworld, which operates in such areas, statistics may merely reflect that addicts tend to live close to their supply.

A striking feature of Figure 9-3 is that 59 per cent of known addicts are Negroes, although Negroes constitute only about 10 per cent of the U.S. population. Puerto Ricans and Mexicans likewise have a disproportionately high rate of addiction according to this figure. Since these minorities live for the most part in slum areas or lower income sections of the city, they are undoubtedly more exposed to narcotics. It is also true that minorities more frequently run afoul of the law. So again, caution is indicated in assessing these statistics. Some of the earlier studies with small samplings do not reveal a high proportion of Negroes or other minorities as addicts. Michael J. Pescor who studied 47 physician drug addicts in the Fort Worth hospital, found that they had practiced for the most part in a small urban or rural community.[15]

Men appear to be more prone to narcotic addiction than women, and the Federal Bureau of Narcotics report stated that 80 per cent

[14] Alan S. Meyer, ed., *Social and Psychological Factors in Opiate Addiction* (New York: Bureau of Applied Social Research, Columbia University, 1952), pp. 42-43.
[15] Meyer, *op. cit.*, p. 43.

of the known addicts were males. It also found that 60 per cent of the addicts were between 21 and 30 years of age, and 12 per cent under 21. Most of the minors, however, were at least 18. These findings are in general agreement with older studies dealing with the age and sex of addicts. The explanation appears to be that men are more exposed to the possibilities of narcotic addiction than women and, since narcotics are usually taken the first time for the sake of the thrill ("kick") or a new experience, such behavior is most typical of younger persons. There is also the impact of group pressure, particularly powerful during the teens and the early twenties.

Studies dealing with the religion of addicts are both dated and confusing. In fact, it is impossible to draw any conclusion from them. A 1930 study of addicts voluntarily committed to Bellevue Hospital in New York showed that of 318 patients, 193 were Catholic, 63 Protestant, and 62 Jewish. A 1951 study of 75 addicts voluntarily committed to the New York hospital between 1930 and 1950 found 43 Protestants, 22 Catholics, 9 Jews, and one Quaker.[16]

A number of older studies done mainly in the twenties and thirties show an inverse relationship between the amount of education and the incidence of drug addiction. The relationship between marital status and drug addiction is not clear from data presently available. Addicts are likely to be unemployed, or employed irregularly. One notable exception here, of course, is the physician. A disproportionately high number of addicts are employed in the field of personal service, recreation, or amusement. There is reason to believe that physicians, and possibly nurses, have a higher rate of addiction than others. The reason is quite clear since narcotics are more available to such persons. But they likewise have a greater knowledge of the psychological and physical influence of drugs than most other persons do. There is no research available on the attitudes of these groups toward the use of narcotics.

Generally speaking, on the evidence available it appears that a narcotic addict is most likely to be an urban male between the ages of 21 and 30 who lives in an interstitial area and is a member of the Negro race, a Puerto Rican, or Mexican. But again it should be recalled that all of the studies cited here have been based upon known addicts, that is, persons who voluntarily committed themselves for

---

[16] Meyer, *op. cit.*, pp. 36-37.

treatment, or were arrested and committed for treatment. There is practically no information about addicts who have not been identified by the authorities voluntarily or otherwise. Perhaps it is for this reason that Ausubel claims addicts and nonaddicts show no significant differences ethnically, racially, or educationally. He attributes the fact that a greater number of addicts is in the lower class to the fact that drugs are more readily available in slum areas rather than to lower-class status. He likewise points out that religious affiliation shows no consistent relationship to addiction, and claims that the geographical distribution of addicts is the same or is similar to the geographical distribution of the population at large. The low number of foreign-born addicts at the Lexington hospital, Ausubel claims, is merely a reflection of the low incidence of addiction in Europe.[17]

## PSYCHOLOGICAL FACTORS IN ADDICTION

Studies of addicts reveal no association between the level of intelligence and addiction. Among 318 addicts voluntarily committed to Bellevue Hospital, most appeared to be of average intelligence, a few were intellectually superior, and 14—less than 5 per cent—were mentally inferior. Judgments, however, were based merely on observation of addicts' behavior. Another study of 37 women addicts at the Illinois State Reformatory, in which the revised Army Alpha Intelligence test was used, found that they scored close to the mean of the general population. The IQ scores in these studies seem to be related much more to the characteristics of the sample studies than to narcotic addiction.[18]

In attempting to assess the personality characteristics of an addict, it would be essential to know something about the individual prior to his addiction. At present such data are inadequate, although Kolb claims that some addicts had social problems prior to addiction.[19] The personality of addicts is studied after they have become addicted

[17] Ausubel, *op. cit.*, pp. 64-65.
[18] Meyer, *op. cit.*, p. 71.
[19] Alfred R. Lindesmith, *Opiate Addiction* (Bloomington, Indiana: Principia Press, 1948), p. 142.

to drugs and it is reasonably certain that in a culture in which drug addiction is socially unacceptable and illegal, such persons might well develop personality defects as a result of guilt feelings and fear of detection. Ausubel points out that all persons who are exposed to drugs do not become addicted. For example, persons who are hospitalized for a period of time and whose condition necessitates the use of opiates do not necessarily become drug addicts. Those who do, he believes, associate euphoria with the drug. Those who do not become addicted have no such association. He asks whether or not there is some personality characteristic which predisposes an individual to seek and associate this euphoria with a narcotic.

Ausubel mentions the two types of individuals for whom addiction to drugs has specific adjustive value. They are the inadequate personality and those suffering from anxiety and reactive depression states. Of these two he considers the first, that is, the inadequate personality (the maladjusted individual), the more numerous. He thinks this is a predisposing personality factor to opiate addiction. Among those suffering anxiety and reactive depression states he believes the adjustive value of addiction is less efficient, and as a result the incidence is lower and the prognosis better. In support of this he cites clinical studies of adult drug addicts at U.S. Public Health Service Hospital and Bellevue Hospital.[20] Dai, who interviewed more than 40 addicts from the Chicago area, found that almost all of them had an infantile type of personality with excessive dependence on other people and a persistent tendency to escape social responsibilities. He classified 92.6 per cent of addicts in the Women's Reformatory as psychopathic, that is, inadequate or unstable; 6.3 per cent as psychotic; and 1.0 per cent as having mental deficiency as a result of injuries. The total cases studied numbered 95.[21]

Professor Lindesmith cites the work of Dr. Lawrence Kolb and Dr. Charles Schultz on psychopathy and addiction. In Kolb's study of 225 addicts, he classifies them as follows: Normals who are accidently or necessarily addicted in medical practice (14 per cent); carefree individuals, devoted to pleasure, seeking new sensations (38 per cent); definite neuroses (13.5 per cent); habitual criminals—always psychopathic (13 per cent); inebriates (21.5 per cent). In another study by Kolb of 119 cases addicted in medical practice he rated

[20] Ausubel, op. cit., pp. 37-41.
[21] Meyer, op. cit., p. 75.

only 67 per cent as psychopathic, and in a third study he found that 91 per cent of 210 cases were defective prior to addiction. He claims that students have long been aware that persons who become addicted are generally abnormal from the nervous standpoint before they acquire the habit. Schultz listed 318 cases of addiction as unclassified (13.2 per cent). By this he meant that in 13.2 per cent of the patients treated, he could find little or no evidence of psychopathic personality besides drug addiction itself. He found that 30 per cent were inadequate personalities and the majority in this group were probably psychopathic types before they became addicted. Twenty per cent he claimed were emotionally unstable. It is not certain whether the instability was present before or came as a result of addiction, although he seems to feel the majority were unstable before using drugs.

Lindesmith correctly points out that in no case was any use made of control groups and "incredible as it may seem, the desirability of control groups is not even suggested despite the fact that that the percentage of psychopaths in the general population may exceed that among the addicts." Because of the failure to use control groups, comparative statements are unjustified on the basis of the information given by these two authors. Moreover, neither offers any exact criteria for the classification of addicts. In Kolb's scheme, the largest percentage of cases is made up of "carefree individuals, devoted to pleasure, seeking new sensations," and according to Schultz the largest class is composed of those with inadequate personalities. "These terms are too loose to permit any exact classification and, therefore, are scientifically almost useless." [22]

While narcotic addicts may or may not be neurotic or psychopathic depending upon how one evaluates the evidence presented, there is little indication that any large number of them is psychotic. Out of 125,000 admissions to state mental hospitals in New York between 1946 and 1951 only 55 were believed to have become psychotic from the use of opiates.[23]

Contrary to popular belief and dramatic treatment in the newspapers, there is no sound evidence that narcotic addiction leads to violent crimes. While the Bureau of Narcotics reports a number of cases in its "Traffic in Opium and Other Dangerous Drugs" involv-

---

[22] Lindesmith, *op. cit.*, p. 146.
[23] Ausubel, *op. cit.*, p. 32.

ing murder, prostitution, theft, and rape, these are scarcely statistically conclusive. A distinction must be made between addicts and
those who traffic in drugs. The latter may not be users of narcotics
at all and their crimes can scarcely be attributed to addiction. As
a matter of fact, continued use of narcotics tends to make the
individual unaggressive. When an addict is suffering withdrawal
symptoms, it is quite true that he or she may engage in theft or
prostitution to obtain money to purchase drugs. A distinction must
be made, however, between the opiate drugs such as opium and
derivatives of opium, and cocaine and marijuana. The latter two
drugs are stimulants and may directly or indirectly be responsible
for an individual's aggressiveness. Neither are addicts found among
the ranks of organized gangsters because there is a well-founded
fear that if the addict finds his supply of narcotics cut off, he will
do anything to obtain them, including turning informer.

## THE SITUATIONAL-VALUE APPROACH

While the physical and psychological effects of narcotics are
relatively well known, the social and psychological characteristics
of individuals prior to addiction are relatively unknown. Persons
living in certain situations are exposed to narcotics. This would
include slum dwellers, physicians, nurses, pharmacists, and dentists.
In other words the social situation itself may facilitate addiction.
However, despite the fact that large numbers of persons are in a
position to acquire narcotics, and even to become addicts, relatively
few appear to do so. While specific proof is lacking, it seems logical to
assume that the particular values of those persons who do become
addicts differ from those who do not. It may well be that the use
of narcotics in the beginning for some persons is a kind of escape,
just as is alcohol. For others, social pressure may initiate them into
the use of narcotics, and once "hooked" they become confirmed
addicts.

Howard Becker claims that the motivation to engage in marijuana
smoking occurs while learning to use it and does not precede this
introduction. He believes it is unnecessary to attempt to identify
traits which bring about addiction but rather an effort should be

made to describe the behavior sequence in an individual's conception of marijuana smoking and of the experience it provides for him.[24] However, marijuana does not produce addiction as the opiate drugs do and there is no withdrawal sickness nor strong craving for the drug. On the basis of research available at this time, it is only possible to conclude that availability of narcotics and some kind of psychological, social, or physical proneness to addiction can explain it.

## WITHDRAWAL SYMPTOMS

There seems to be considerable contradiction about how painful withdrawal symptoms of narcotics are. They depend in part upon the type of drug used. The abstinence syndrome for an individual who has been using methadone, for instance, is mild but prolonged in comparison to those who have used morphine. Ausubel describes withdrawal symptoms as "yawning, sneezing, lacrimation, a running nose, goose flesh, rapid pulse, sexual orgasm, increased blood pressure, dilated pupils, hot and cold flashes, nausea, vomiting, diarrhea, loss of appetite, weight loss, and muscular twitches." [25] However, he also says that while these symptoms are uncomfortable they are rarely more severe than a bad case of gastro-intestinal influenza. Unless the individual is old, feeble, or suffering from a heart condition they do not endanger life. There is no doubt that the basis of the withdrawal symptoms are physiological, although it seems probable that they may be increased or decreased by psychological factors.

In Sunday supplements and popular books the withdrawal symptoms are described in dramatic and probably exaggerated language. In some cases such books or articles are written by addicts or are the results of interviews with addicts. It is obvious that such persons will make every attempt possible to obtain drugs and may considerably rationalize the painful symptoms which they undergo as a result of withdrawal. But withdrawal symptoms are apparently painful enough to bring about death among those who are debilitated or suffering from cardiac conditions.

---

[24] Howard S. Becker, "Becoming a Marijuana User," *The American Journal of Sociology*, 59 (Nov. 1953), p. 235-42.

[25] Ausubel, *op. cit.*, p. 23.

## NARCOTIC ADDICTION AS A SOCIAL PROBLEM

Since a social problem has already been defined as a social situation confronting a relatively large number of people and constituting a threat to them according to their definition of the situation, and dealt with in an organized way, it appears that the only question to be raised here is whether or not a sufficiently large number of persons are addicts to label narcotic addiction a social problem. As pointed out earlier, it is absolutely impossible to get accurate statistics on the incidence of drug addiction in the United States. While the known number of addicts has decreased considerably even in the last eight years, no information about addicts who have not been arrested or voluntarily submitted to treatment is available. Furthermore, it is generally believed that addicts tend to lead others into drug addiction. Even if addicts didn't do this, it is quite true that peddlers for the sake of profit do. The danger does exist that if narcotic addiction were legalized, the number of addicts would rise.

Neither is there much question about what ultimately happens to the addict himself or what would happen to a nation in which addiction became a widespread problem. The history of China in the past is ample testimony to the degrees this problem can reach. Just as alcoholism involves the wife, children, relatives, and friends of the alcoholic, so too narcotic addiction involves those close to the addict. It cannot be gauged solely by the number of known addicts, or even those who are not known (if such information were to become available). Narcotic addiction may be considered an overt social problem and it is dealt with in an organized way.

## TREATMENT OF NARCOTIC ADDICTION

Dr. P. O. Wolff of the World Health Organization says, "It is scarcely a paradox to say that the best way to be cured of addiction is not to become an addict, and the best weapon against addiction is possession of a normal psyche." [26] Some believe that psychiatry and mental hygiene must be emphasized in order to eliminate addiction from that section of the population which is prone to it. Others believe that if the addict can be prevented from securing drugs he will cure himself.

Maurer and Vogel suggest the following steps to prevent narcotic addiction. First, they call for education programs designed to reach all persons who might become addicts, but concentrated particularly on youth in school. It is hoped that this would make people less vulnerable to the persuasion of addicts or peddlers. Second, there should be careful law enforcement at the state and local levels as well as at the federal level. Third, there must be control of the international production of narcotics through the United Nations. And fourth, there must be a long range attack on those social and economic conditions which tend to break down the personality. They believe that the very best answer would be the discovery of a drug which would relieve pain as effectively as morphine or heroin without producing euphoria. However, they admit that the relief of physical pain may be so closely associated with the relief of emotional distress that such a drug may never be found.[27]

In addition to the two U.S. government hospitals for the treatment of drug addiction at Lexington, Kentucky and Fort Worth, Texas, some states and communities provide facilities for the treatment of addicts. Treatment in private institutions is also available. However, the relapse rate in all cases seems to be rather high. In a study of 318 addicts who had voluntarily committed themselves to Bellevue Hospital, 88 per cent had previously suffered relapses after having been cured. Out of 193 patients who received an honorable discharge after eight months of treatment plus sixteen months of parole in California Spadra Hospital, 27½ per cent had not relapsed at the time they were studied.[28]

While there is considerable disagreement as to whether addicts really want to be cured or not, practically all of them at some time or other do take the cure. Sometimes they attempt to carry it out themselves and are not very serious about it. Other times they voluntarily commit themselves to institutions, while on still other

---

[26] Maurer and Vogel, op. cit., p. 150.
[27] Maurer and Vogel, op. cit., pp. 150-51.
[28] Meyer, op. cit., p. 23.

occasions they may be committed as a result of arrest. Following their release they may suffer periods of depression and anxiety, as practically all people do at times, and under such circumstances decide to take a shot. They falsely believe that they can take that one shot and quit. Almost inevitably it turns out that this shot is the beginning of their relapse. This makes it quite clear that the addict who has taken a cure should be under some kind of supervision for a long period of time following his release. While some addicts are able to overcome the habit, it seems clear that prevention is the most important factor in the control of narcotic addiction.

One of the most controversial issues in the whole matter of narcotic addiction is the so-called British Plan. Lindesmith strongly recommends certain changes in the laws in order to permit physicians to prescribe drugs to addicts. He claims that this is the way in which English drug laws are interpreted. His basic argument is that in England, where doctors do prescribe for addicts, the addiction problem is much smaller than it is in this country, and smuggling is at a minimum. He cites the late August Vollmer, formerly police chief of Berkeley, California and an outstanding authority on police problems, who agrees with this argument. Vollmer emphasizes the fact that drug addiction is not a police problem but a medical problem. Under this plan it is believed that new addicts would immediately be recognized, treated, and, hopefully, cured before their addiction became too severe. Furthermore, drugs would be dispensed at cost either via the public health service or ultimately by physicians in private practice and thus the profit would be taken out of traffic in narcotics. It would likewise end some of the brutal and cruel methods of handling addicts which exist today.[29] It should be noted that these reforms do not extend to cocaine and marijuana, which are not opiate drugs.

But there is strong opposition in some quarters to the British Plan—in fact it is denied that such a "plan" exists as such. M. L. Harney, superintendent, Division of Narcotic Control in the State of Illinois, claims that the United Kingdom subscribes to the same international agreements as the United States and that their system of law enforcement does not differ greatly from that of this country and Canada. Based on a publication of the United Kingdom Home Office of February, 1956, he states that under no circumstances are

---

[29] Lindesmith, *op. cit.*, pp. 205-8.

physicians or dentists permitted to use dangerous drugs for any purpose other than caring for the strictly medical or dental needs of patients. He says that the continued use of dangerous drugs solely for the gratification of addiction is not regarded as a medical need. However, he does admit that in the fine print of this publication it points to cases

> . . . . where it has been similarly demonstrated that the patient, while capable of leading a useful and relatively normal life when a certain minimum dose is regularly administered, becomes incapable of this when a drug is entirely discontinued.[30]

He doubts that such people exist. If they do, he says that the number is so small that they should have no influence in the determination of such a program. It is likewise pointed out that English culture differs considerably from that of the United States. The per capita crime rate in the United States is almost five times as high as it is in England and Wales, and the divorce rate is almost two and one-half times as high. The rate of alcoholism in the United States, it is claimed, is almost four times as high as it is in England.[31] Other arguments maintain that if the British Plan were adopted in the United States, the government would be aiding and abetting addiction.

With today's limited knowledge of drug addiction, it seems impossible to reach any conclusion as to the adoption of the British Plan in the United States. If drug addiction is really a disease, as claimed, then it should not be considered a crime. Strictly speaking, addiction in itself is not considered a crime, but the possession of narcotics is. This is a rather fine and, in the case of the addict, meaningless distinction. If it is legally possible, experimentation might be carried on in this country in certain states or communities where the addiction rate is high to assess just how well the British Plan might succeed in the United States.

---

[30] M. L. Harney, "The British System," in *Comments on Narcotic Drugs,* Interim Report of the Joint Committee of the American Bar Association and the American Medical Association on Narcotic Drugs by the Advisory Committee to the Federal Bureau of Narcotics (Washington, D.C.: U.S. Treasury, Bureau of Narcotics, 1958), p. 1.

[31] Harney, *op. cit.,* p. 10.

# REVIEW QUESTIONS

1. What is "drug addiction?" What are the three characteristics associated with it?
2. While narcotic addicts are difficult to identify, what are some of the factors that may indicate addiction?
3. Is there agreement on the number of drug addicts in the United States? Explain the reason for your answer.
4. Geographically, where are most drug addicts found?
5. What are the common drugs used by addicts in the United States?
6. How are narcotics usually taken? What dangers exist in some methods of administration?
7. What are the social characteristics of addicts?
8. How do you explain the unusually high incidence of narcotic addicts among certain categories of people?
9. Many persons, while patients in hospitals, are given narcotics over a long period of time. Some become addicts, some do not. How do you explain this difference?
10. Evaluate studies which attempt to explain narcotic addiction on a psychological basis.
11. Should the law permit physicians to administer narcotics to addicts?
12. How painful are withdrawal symptoms?
13. Is the treatment of narcotic addicts usually successful?

# SELECTED READINGS

*Articles*

Becker, Howard S., "Becoming a Marihuana User," *American Journal of Sociology*, 59 (Nov. 1953), 233-42.

Lindesmith, A. R., "General Law and Drug Addiction," *Social Problems*, 7 (Summer 1959), 46-52.

————, "The Drug Addict as a Psychopath," *American Sociological Review*, 5 (Dec. 1940), 914-20.

Winick, Charles, "The Use of Drugs by Jazz Musicians," *Social Problems*, 1 (Winter 1959-60), 240-53.

## Books

Ausubel, B. B., *Drug Addiction: Physiological, Psychological and Sociological Aspects*. New York: Random House, 1958.

Hoch, Paul H., *Problems of Addiction and Habituation*. New York: Grune and Stratton, 1958.

Lindesmith, Alfred R., *Opiate Addiction*. Bloomington, Indiana: Principia Press, 1948.

Maurer, David W. and Victor H. Vogel, *Narcotics and Narcotic Addiction*. Springfield, Illinois: Charles C. Thomas, Publisher, 1954.

Meyer, Alan S., ed., *Social and Psychological Factors in Opiate Addiction*. New York: Bureau of Applied Research, Columbia University, 1952.

Traffic in Opium and Other Dangerous Drugs, Bureau of Narcotics. Washington, D.C.: Government Printing Office, 1960.

# 10

# Alcoholism

D RINKING of alcoholic beverages is an important part of the culture in the United States, Canada, and most of the Western world. Professor J. P. Shalloo has pointed out:

> In our times it is culturally imperative to toast the bride, christen the ship, seal the bargain, welcome a guest, speed the friend, salute the New Year, celebrate good fortune and wake the dead . . .[1]

Actually, occasions for drinking have been multiplied since Professor Shalloo wrote the above passage in 1941. The cocktail party is a contemporary social device serving many functions. Once more or less an upper-class phenomenon, it is now fairly common among the upper-middle class as well. It almost invariably precedes dinners given by various organizations. It is a method of paying off social obligations to a large number of persons at the same time. In addition to this the custom of having a cocktail or some type of drink before dinner seems to have

---

[1] J. P. Shalloo, "Some Cultural Factors in the Etiology of Alcoholism," *Quarterly Journal of Studies on Alcoholism*, 2 (1941), p. 467.

grown among business and professional men and women. Spectorsky describes a hilarious scene in a New York, New Haven and Hartford railroad baggage car which had been converted into a bar through commuters' demands.[2] In large cities the plushier bars are crowded with well-dressed patrons during the "cocktail hour," while more modest establishments are dispensing beer and "shots" to "working-men."

Today it is estimated that sixty-eight million persons—or about two-thirds of the population fifteen years of age and older—drink. Of these about forty million are men and twenty-eight million are women.[3] But while drinking is widespread there are various sub-cultures in which drinking is frowned upon. Certain Protestant sects vigorously oppose drinking. According to an investigation carried on at the then Yale Center for Alcohol Studies (now located at Rutgers University) only 13 per cent of Jews and 21 per cent of Catholics are teetotalers, as compared to 41 per cent of Protestants.[4]

But compared to the past both the types and amounts of alcoholic beverages consumed show some variations. In 1850 about 90 per cent of alcoholic beverages consumed in the United States was in the form of distilled spirits and only about 7 per cent in the form of beer. In 1950 only 38 per cent was spirits and 51 per cent beer. Since domestic beer averages about four and one-half per cent alcohol, a considerable amount must be consumed to result in intoxication, although it is possible. Mark Keller claims that if the actual number of drinkers in 1850 were known as compared to the present, the actual per capita intake of alcoholic beverages would show a decline. In other words, the increased volume of drinking is shared by many more people.[5]

## WHAT IS ALCOHOL?

Ethyl alcohol, the type used in beverages, results mainly from the action of yeast on saccharine substances. As a result of fermenta-

---

[2] A. C. Spectorsky, *The Exurbanites* (Philadelphia: J. B. Lippincott Co., 1955), p. 128.

[3] Mark Keller, "Alcoholism: Nature and Extent of the Problem," *The Annals, 315* (Jan. 1958), p. 3.

[4] Charles R. Snyder, *Alcohol and the Jews* (New York: The Free Press of Glencoe, 1958), p. 4.

[5] *The Annals, 315* (Jan. 1958), p. 4.

tion or distillation various types of beverages are produced—wine, beer, and spirits. The percentage of alcohol in beer and wine varies from 2 per cent to 20 per cent or more in fortified wines, and in distilled spirits from 35 per cent to 75 per cent.

Alcohol does not require digestion, but goes directly from the stomach to the blood stream. It travels to the liver, where it is oxidized—although some is absorbed in the small intestine—and returned to the blood which then distributes it to the various tissues of the body. How rapidly alcohol is absorbed depends upon two factors: first, the percentage of alcohol in the drink consumed—the higher the concentration of alcohol, the more rapid its absorption into the blood stream; and second, the presence of other substances in the stomach, particularly fats, which slow down the rate of absorption.[6]

In the past it was believed that alcohol was a stimulant which later had depressant effects. Today, it is agreed that alcohol is a depressant only. A drinker is led to believe that alcohol stimulates because it releases the lower nerve centers from the control of the higher by its narcotic effects on the latter. The individual is relaxed, loses whatever tension he may have, and feels temporarily "pepped up." Ultimately, however, if enough alcohol is consumed its narcotic effects become obvious.[7]

But while alcohol does not require digestion, and enters the blood stream rapidly, the body can only oxidize between five and ten grams an hour. The "hangover" suffered the day after heavy drinking is caused by this lag in oxidization, as well as by the presence of fusel oil (a by-product of fermentation) in drinks.


ALCOHOLISM AS A SOCIAL PROBLEM

Is drinking of alcoholic beverages a social problem? Moderate use of alcoholic beverages by adults under most circumstances cannot be considered a social problem because it does not constitute a threat

---

[6] James M. Reinhardt, Paul Meadows, and John M. Gillette, *Social Problems and Social Policy* (New York: American Book Co., 1952), pp. 503-4.
[7] Edward A. Strecker and Francis T. Chambers, Jr., *Alcohol: One Man's Meat* (New York: The Macmillan Co., 1949), p. 5.

to the welfare of the individual or to that of the society. But alcoholism—which is temporarily defined as the habitual, excessive use of such beverages—is a social problem. It impairs the health of the drinker; probably shortens his life span; often results in alcoholic psychoses, cirrhosis of the liver, and other disabilities; seriously disturbs his ability to work and even to hold a job; impairs his family relationships; and undoubtedly contributes to the divorce rate. Not infrequently it impoverishes the alcoholic and his family. The physical abuse of wife and children sometimes occurs as a result of drinking.

However, even moderate drinking may prove a social problem under certain circumstances. The National Safety Council in its fact sheet points out that "social drinkers" who drive are a greater menace than commonly believed because their critical judgment is impaired by even a fairly low alcohol concentration, although they are unaware of it. They vastly outnumber intoxicated drivers. In 1957 a drinking driver was involved in at least 30 per cent of all fatal traffic accidents. Over the Labor Day weekend of 1956, 48 per cent of fatal traffic accidents involved a drinking driver. "Drunkometer" tests have been devised by which the concentration of alcohol in the blood stream can be measured by analysis of a driver's breath, which has been blown into a balloon, or by analysis of an actual blood sample from the driver.

Drinking also contributes to industrial accidents. In one study of male "problem drinkers"—who were not alcoholics—eighty-two accidents of all types were recorded for the drinkers. This was three times as many as were found in the control group, which did not drink. Among women there were 17 recorded accidents in the drinking group against none among those who abstained. Sickness payments in one U.S. company with over 10,000 employees were over three times as frequent among problem drinkers as in the control group.[8]

The true extent of physiological, psychological, economic, and social damage resulting from excessive drinking probably cannot be calculated. It is useless to make an estimate merely in dollars and cents—its real penalties go much further. Perhaps one of the most distressing aspects of frequent, excessive drinking is that the victims include not only the drinker himself but also his wife, children,

---

[8] An Observer and Milton A. Maxwell, "A Study of Absenteeism, Accidents, and Sickness—Sickness Payments to Problem Drinkers in One Industry," *Quarterly Journal of Studies on Alcoholism*, 20 (June 1959), p. 302.

relatives, and friends. For every true alcoholic in society, somewhere between three to ten other persons must also suffer. This makes the probable magnitude of the problem tremendous.

## WHO IS AN ALCOHOLIC?

So far, the terms "alcoholic" and "problem drinker" have been used with no attempt to define them adequately. Actually, despite the fact that such expressions are used widely in literature and popular conversation, clear definitions of either are difficult. One of the early attempts to define alcoholism was made by Thomas Trotter, an Edinburgh physician, who in 1804 wrote: "In medical language, I consider drunkeness, strictly speaking, to be a disease, produced by remote cause, and giving birth to actions and movements in a living body, that disorder the functions of health." [9] At a time when it was customary to think of alcoholism almost entirely as a moral problem, it is noteworthy that Dr. Trotter recognized the medical aspects of it. But the meaning of alcoholism still remained vague, and still is vague, as Strecker and Chambers indicate:

> The term alcoholic has become as vague and meaningless as the words "nervous breakdown." To the public an alcoholic presents a picture of a bleary-eyed, bulbous-nosed, shaky creature, disheveled and uncombed, often in the hands of a burly policeman, who is ushering him none too gently into the depths of the patrol wagon. While this man may be a drunk, he may not fundamentally be an alcoholic at all. In fact, he may be mentally ill or he may belong to the nomadic type, a group of homeless men with no home ties found in large cities.[10]

To dismiss this stereotype of an alcoholic, it must be pointed out that alcoholism attacks all kinds of persons: clergymen, physicians, pickpockets, judges, teachers, artists, salesmen, laborers—even psychoanalysts! [11]

---

[9] Juan T. Marconi, M.D., "The Concept of Alcoholism," *Quarterly Journal of Studies on Alcoholism*, 20 (June 1959), 223.

[10] Strecker and Chambers, *op. cit.*, p. 21.

[11] Ruth Fox, "Treatment of Alcoholics" in *Alcoholics, Basic Aspects* and *Treatment*, ed. Harold E. Hinwich (Washington, D.C.: The American Association for the Advancement of Science, 1957), p. 163.

Perhaps it will facilitate the definition of an alcoholic to begin with the "normal drinker." This is an individual who uses alcohol as a socially accepted gesture and never gets into serious trouble from drinking. Strecker and Chambers state that the border line between normal and abnormal drinking is passed when a person begins to use alcohol to adjust to reality.[12] It has been popularly said that it is normal when one drinks to make reality more pleasant; it is abnormal when one drinks to make reality tolerable.

Some of the danger signals of incipient alcoholism are displayed when a person who is usually quite reserved becomes embarrassingly indecent after a few drinks; or when a retiring, modest individual becomes excessively boastful after drinking. In other words, when there is a complete personality and behavior reversal after several drinks, or when a person's drinking becomes a problem to his family, his friends, and himself, he is in—or on the way to—trouble.[13]

One of the indications of a tendency toward alcoholism is "morning drinking." Some men and women cannot face day-to-day tensions without a morning "nip," and must fortify themselves frequently throughout the day with alcohol. A tragic aspect of the alcoholic is that he can give up drinking for protracted periods of time. Family and friends are encouraged and hopeful. But when the individual becomes intoxicated again, their despair is deepened.[14] The real alcoholic cannot drink in moderation. It has been said of him that one drink is too much and a thousand drinks are not enough.

One of the most detailed definitions of an alcoholic has been offered by Seldon Bacon. To paraphrase his words, alcoholism within an adult individual is a disease, characterized by a compulsion to drink in order to face ordinary life problems. Drinking is associated with blackouts, secret drinks, guilt feelings, solitary imbibing, and tremors. Psychologically there is a state of pain and insecurity, a sense of immaturity, and increasing maladjustments clear to observers. Finally— although not always—there is accompanying physical disease or damage.[15]

A shorter but still useful definition is provided by Mark Keller, who says:

---

[12] Strecker and Chambers, *op. cit.*, p. 32.
[13] Strecker and Chambers, *op. cit.*, p. 32.
[14] Strecker and Chambers, *op. cit.*, p. 34.
[15] Fox, *op. cit.*, p. 163.

pear to be the basic characteristics of:

1. Alcoholism is a psychological and physiological illness with or without complications such as delirium tremens (a temporary mental illness, characterized by tremblings and hallucinations), cirrhosis of the liver, and such.
2. Alcoholism is characterized by a compulsion to drink in order to face the ordinary tensions of life, although periodic abstinence is possible. Drinking in moderation is impossible for the alcoholic. Once he starts, he cannot stop.

Omitting the psychotic, psychopathic, and "skid-row" drinkers, Dr. Ruth Fox has identified three types of alcoholics. One is the *situational drinker*, who because of a catastrophe may take up heavy drinking for a short time as a solace. She believes that some—but not all—may eventually be able to resume controlled social drinking. Another type is the *secondary addict*, who has not been neurotic in early life but slips into pathological drinking later from habit. Frequently, these are persons of talent and ability who have been heavy social drinkers for years, and they are usually capable of recovery. The third type—the *primary addicts*—have been emotionally maladjusted since childhood. Drinking has helped them resolve their social and psychological problems. Their condition is largely one of immaturity.[17]

### INCIDENCE OF ALCOHOLISM

The actual number of alcoholics in the United States and Canada simply is not known. Estimates are based upon the Jellinek formula. According to this there were 4,712,000 alcoholics in the United States in 1955. Of these, 4,002,000 were men and 710,000 were women.[18] According to this formula:

---

[16] *The Annals*, 315 (Jan. 1958), p. 4.
[17] Fox, *op. cit.*, p. 163.
[18] *The Annals*, 315 (Jan. 1958), p. 6.

...and women, ... the ... of cirrhosis of the liver and the proportion of all deaths from cirrhosis attributable to alcoholism. Once the number of alcoholics with complications is thus calculated, another constant is required to allow the addition of alcoholics without complications. This latter varies from country to country. In the United States and Canada, according to Jellinek, it is four; that is, there are three alcoholics without for every alcoholic with complications—hence the number with complications must be multiplied by four to obtain the total number of alcoholics.[19]

Many difficulties are involved in the application of this formula. First of all there is a matter of accurate diagnosis, and, associated with this, the adequate reporting of such deaths. Whether it is always possible to separate deaths from cirrhosis of the liver in any year caused by alcoholism and those not caused by alcoholism is likewise debatable. But in every country that has instituted prohibition of liquor consumption, the death rate from cirrhosis of the liver during the prohibition period dropped below the general mortality rate. John R. Seeley claims that Jellinek has used this rate to indicate the difference between deaths from cirrhosis of the liver caused by alcoholism and those not caused by alcoholism.[20]

Seeley concludes that statements about the magnitude of alcoholism based upon this formula are misleading, and scientific studies using such data probably are not valid. He feels that it would be wise to declare a moratorium on conclusions as to the incidence of alcoholism based upon such data.[21]

Because of the inadequacies of the Jellinek formula, it is not scientifically possible to state as he does that we have between four and five million alcoholics in the United States. The actual number may be larger, smaller, or about the same. It is impossible at this point to be certain.

---

[19] *The Annals*, p. 5.
[20] John R. Seeley, "Estimating the Prevalence of Alcoholism: A Critical Analysis of the Jellinek Formula," *Quarterly Journal of Studies on Alcoholism*, 20 (June 1959), p. 245.
[21] Seeley, *op. cit.*

## OTHER  TYPES  OF  DRINKERS

Aside from the alcoholic at least two other types of drinkers are usually distinguished. As mentioned, the "social," or controlled drinker is one who uses alcohol in keeping with social conventions. This actually means two things. First, he drinks because it is the socially approved thing to do, and second, his drinking does not result in intoxication. He is entirely capable of not drinking if he so desires. Among social drinkers, Professor Clinard mentions two types: the occasional social drinker, who drinks only sporadically, and the regular social drinker, who may drink several times a week. These are the categories in which most drinkers will be found.

Another type is the ordinary excessive drinker who from time to time—particularly when he is under stress—may drink too much. He is likely to drink more than others in his group, and occasionally will sneak a drink. Such a person may continue this drinking pattern for the rest of his life, or he may reduce his drinking, or he may become an alcoholic.[22]

## THE  ETIOLOGY  OF  ALCOHOLISM

In the United States, unlike Europe, it is still necessary to repeat that alcoholism is a sickness. This is the modern approach to the problem. It arises, as Dr. Wexberg has pointed out, from "a strong need to contend with the anti-therapeutic effects of a viewpoint, represented mainly by Puritans, drys, and temperance unions, which considers drinking as nothing but a vice." [23] In view of this it is interesting that not a few sociology texts in social problems continue to list alcoholism under the heading of personal vices. If alcoholism is truly a sickness, and this is generally accepted in scientific circles today, it can scarcely be a vice.

[22] Marshall B. Clinard, *Sociology of Deviant Behavior* (New York: Holt, Rinehart & Winston, Inc., 1957), pp. 298-99.

[23] Leopold Erwin Wexberg, "Alcoholism As a Sickness," *Quarterly Journal of Studies on Alcoholism*, 12 (June 1951), p. 217.

The actual causes of alcoholism are not really known. Theories about its etiology are both numerous and conflicting. A great deal of reputed theories of causality have come from psychiatry and psychoanalysis. However, it is important to note that such studies generally lack a control group. The clinical approach to the etiology of alcoholism—which is the approach of the medical profession generally—is based upon the dealings of physicians, psychiatrists, or psychoanalysts with alcoholics. They are not systematic studies because they have not included non-alcoholics from the same cultural backgrounds. While such studies should not be neglected, projection of their conclusions on the entire population is questionable. The causes of alcoholism may be divided into at least three general aspects: the psychological, which includes the psychiatric and the psychoanalytic, the physiological, and the sociological.

One does not become an alcoholic overnight. The process usually extends over a period of from ten to twenty years and can be traced to the drinking histories of a number of alcoholics. Most of them became intoxicated for the first time at about the age of eighteen or nineteen. Regular drinking began about five years later, and by the age of twenty-nine most of the individuals had begun excessive drinking and had first begun to experience blackouts during intoxication. At this time they also sneaked drinks, lost control of themselves, engaged in extravagant behavior, and went on weekend drunks.[24]

## PSYCHOLOGICAL FACTORS IN ALCOHOLISM

One of the most important but unresolved questions regarding alcoholism is whether it should be viewed as a symptom of some underlying personality disturbance which results in alcoholism, or whether excessive drinking is alone a cause of alcoholism. Harriet R. Mowrer has said: "That marital discord is not the result of alcoholism but that both are the result of the same etiological factors, research has demonstrated.[25] According to Strecker and Chambers,

---

[24] E. M. Jellinek, "Phases in Drinking History of Alcoholics," *Quarterly Journal of Studies on Alcoholism,* 13 (1952), p. 301.
[25] Harriet R. Mowrer, "The Psychocultural Analysis of the Alcoholic," in *Analyzing Social Problems* (New York: The Dryden Press, 1950), p. 75.

when one observes the various stages of intoxication, one can note a progressive psychological descent, or regression. In other words, this is a psychoanalytic theory, which attempts to explain alcoholism by means of *regression*—that is, a reversion to an earlier and less mature stage of life.

> One could almost judge at which time the individual rebelled at growing up emotionally by the degree to which he habitually allows himself to become intoxicated or drunken. Most individuals seem satisfied to regress to some stage of the teen age, which was probably an enjoyable and carefree time, deeply implanted on the unconscious. Others seem satisfied with a very slight descent, and still others are never satisfied until they have reached an infantile level.[26]

According to Strecker and Chambers, the incentive for alcoholism is the unconscious desire to regress—to return to an earlier stage of life when the alcoholic was presumably happier or better adjusted.

Generally speaking, the psychiatric and psychoanalytic theories on alcoholism tend to associate it with neuroses and psychoses. Chambers has said that an underlying neurotic condition makes alcoholism possible in certain individuals. They have an *alcoholic compulsion neurosis*.[27] As new theories have been developed in the general field of psychiatry and analysis, efforts have been made to apply such theories to the alcoholic. For instance it has been claimed that alcoholism is a defense against homosexuality. But Botwinick and Machover, in a study of thirty-nine male patients diagnosed as alcoholics, concluded that on the basis of tests employed (the Terman and Miles Attitude-Interest-Analysis Test and a version of the Minnesota Multiphasic Personality Inventory) that homosexuality—latent or otherwise—cannot be, or rather is not an essential factor in alcoholism, although in individual cases it may play an important part.[28] Others have attempted to associate alcoholism with the sex drive and the Oedipus complex.

So far as can be determined at present there is no such thing as a "pre-alcoholic" personality. However, once alcoholism has developed, there is a cluster of personality traits which show or reveal a sur-

---

[26] Strecker and Chambers, *op. cit.*, pp. 15-16.
[27] Mowrer, *op. cit.*, p. 71.
[28] Jack Botwinick and Solomon Machover, "Psychometric Examination of Latent Homosexuality in Alcoholism," *Quarterly Journal of Studies on Alcoholism*, 12 (June 1951), pp. 268-72.

prising similarity. Among these is an extremely low frustration-tolerance point, that is, an inability to endure anxiety or tension, accompanied by feelings of isolation and inferiority. There is likewise an undue sensitivity, coupled with a tendency to act compulsively and extreme narcissism and exhibitionism. There is also a tendency toward self-punitive behavior and hypochondria.[29]

## PHYSIOLOGICAL FACTORS IN ALCOHOLISM

Efforts have been made to explain the causes of alcoholism physiologically. Some kind of a biochemical defect is supposed to exist, resulting in a craving for alcoholic beverages which the individual cannot control. Roger J. Williams has blamed it on nutritional deficiencies. Others have explained it as the result of defects in the endocrine glands. However, if this is the case, then the correction of such a defect or defects would result in a cure of alcoholism. As Mark Keller points out, to date very few such cures have been demonstrated and none of the defects have been proved to exist among persons prior to their becoming alcoholics.[30]

## THE SOCIOLOGICAL FACTORS IN ALCOHOLISM

In searching for sociological theories explaining alcoholism, one attempts to discover whether or not membership in one group or another, in one sub-culture or another, more readily gives rise to alcoholism. One of the best analyses from this viewpoint is that of Harriet R. Mowrer. She studied three groups, each consisting of twenty-five married individuals and their marital partners. While some have claimed that the alcoholic is more likely to be the only, or the youngest child, Mowrer found that ordinal position within the family was not significant except as it was a factor in determining role. In her study, the alcoholic was more likely to be the next to the oldest, the youngest, or the next to the youngest. In family interac-

---

[29] Fox, op. cit., p. 164.
[30] The Annals, 315 (Jan. 1958), p. 10.

tion she found the most significant factors were a dislike or hatred of the father, dislike or jealousy of a brother who was believed favored by the father, and a strong attachment to the mother or sister—who in turn favored them. She states that if a conclusion is at all possible from such material it would be that ambiguity in role is a factor in alcoholism.

As pointed out earlier, there are two situations in which an individual suffers frustration. One is the case in which his role is disliked and he cannot escape from it, and the other is when his role is ambiguous—that is, not well defined. Mowrer's findings also seem to correlate well with psychiatric findings that the alcoholic is an individual with a very low tension point.

Another of her interesting findings was "that fathers of the alcoholic group are less often alcoholic than those of the non-alcoholic organized group." [31] This she considered an additional indication that alcoholism is not inherited. Furthermore, alcoholism may have different meanings for various persons reared in a home by an alcoholic parent. Some may reject it for this very reason, while others may accept it.

Another finding of Professor Mowrer that fits in very well with the statements of Strecker and Chambers is that the alcoholic becomes the center of attention by drinking. To the extent that he feels inferior and desires a higher status, he indirectly obtains this status by becoming a problem to his family and friends who then center attention on him. As a result he temporarily abandons drinking. When the attention focused on him is removed, however, he reverts to it. She states: "The behavior of the alcoholic cannot be understood except with reference to the basic pattern of personality developed in early familial interaction. Alcoholism provides a way of recapturing at least temporarily the attention-receiving role of the early familial group." [32] The approach used in this book is the situational-value approach. To what extent can this be applied to the social problem of alcoholism? It seems impossible at this point to offer any single causality theory of the disease of alcoholism. The incipient factors and the continued motives that make an alcoholic undoubtedly vary from person to person, although one may detect categories which are similar.

---

[31] Mowrer, *op. cit.*, p. 74.
[32] Mowrer, *op. cit.*, p. 77.

Group associations and cultural factors undoubtedly play an important part in determining who becomes an alcoholic and who does not. Professor Clinard has pointed out that in our society group patterns of excessive drinking, of companions, of social class, and of religious and ethnic groups are important. At this point, therefore, two questions are raised. What are the common situational factors which appear to be associated with alcoholism, and what are the particular sets of values which seem common to many alcoholics?

### THE SITUATIONAL-VALUE APPROACH

The consumption of alcoholic beverages is socially approved in the upper class and, as indicated earlier, increasingly so in the upper-middle class. In the lower-middle class there is much less acceptance of alcohol, and women generally do not drink at all. But drinking, even in the upper class and to some extent the middle class, is done with some restraint. One is more or less expected to drink but one is also expected not to drink to excess. This is in sharp contrast to the lower classes, where restraints on drinking are not so marked. This does not mean that persons in the lower class necessarily become alcoholics but it does mean that a negative attitude toward excessive drinking is less pronounced.

Some business men find drinking associated with their work. Luncheons are preceded by one or two martinis, and after a leisurely lunch a deal may be concluded. Salesmen, who must be absent from home for long periods, frequently find life lonely. One solace for loneliness is the hotel bar or tavern. Here they find drinking companions and conversation. This is also true of homeless men. Straus, in a study of two hundred homeless men, found that only seven did not drink at all and only seventeen were moderate drinkers.[33]

It was already pointed out that there are sharp differences in drinking patterns among the various religious groups. The same is true of ethnic background. The Irish tend to drink more than others, especially whiskey, because their culture approves of it. It seems clear then that those persons who because of social class, occupation, re-

---

[33] Robert Straus, "Alcohol and the Homeless Man," *Quarterly Journal of Studies on Alcoholism*, 7:360-404.

ligion, or ethnic background are members of groups which tend to drink are likely to engage in it. Those who for the same reasons find themselves associated with persons who drink not at all or drink very sparingly are likely to do so too. Obviously there are certain individual exceptions in both cases.

Drinking then is a learned reaction. Some persons use alcohol to reduce tensions which arise from many sources, among which are role conflicts—particularly when the role is disliked or when it is ambiguous. Alcohol may ultimately become a value in itself if the individual faces situations which he considers overwhelming. He could, of course, turn just as readily to narcotics or some other form of escape if they were as available or as socially approved among his group. There may be certain physiological factors predisposing an individual to become an alcoholic, but if this is so, to date it has not been adequately proved.

### TREATMENT OF ALCOHOLISM

The alcoholic tends to live in a world of self delusion. Even after years of excessive drinking, most will maintain that they can take it or leave it alone. In reality, however, it seems clear that very few if any can leave it alone. Eventually, however, the alcoholic generally "hits the bottom" as Alcoholics Anonymous puts it. This occurs when the individual either loses or is about to lose something which he regards as highly important because of drinking. It may be the threat of a divorce, the loss of a job, or the loss of his self-respect because of his excessive drinking.

Many states today have committees on alcoholism and have established clinics in order to help the excessive drinker readjust. Thus, society indicates that alcoholism is an overt social problem because it does make an effort to deal with it in an organized way. Perhaps the best known organization for dealing with alcoholism is Alcoholics Anonymous (A.A.). It was organized in 1935 and now has about two hundred thousand members, having spread throughout the world. In the United States alone there are four thousand groups. It is a type of group therapy in which members meet and quite honestly tell their drinking histories, explaining how Alcoholics Anonymous helped them recover. Family auxiliaries are formed and various social affairs are held. It was originally associated with the Oxford Group, a religious movement, but has since separated itself from it. It likewise eschews temperance and political movements. It is an informal organization and it can perhaps best be described by citing its twelve suggested steps for recovery from alcoholism:

1. We admit we were powerless over alcohol—that our lives had become unmanageable.
2. Came to believe that a Power greater than ourselves could restore us to sanity.
3. Made a decision to turn our will and our lives over to the care of God as we understood Him.
4. Made a searching and fearless moral inventory of ourselves.
5. Admitted to God, to ourselves, and to another human being the exact nature of our wrongs.
6. We were entirely ready to have God remove all these defects of character.
7. Humbly asked Him to remove our shortcomings.
8. Made a list of all persons we had harmed, and became willing to make amends to them all.
9. Made direct amends to such people wherever possible, except when to do so would injure them or others.
10. Continued to take personal inventory and when we were wrong promptly admitted it.
11. Sought through prayer and meditation to improve our conscious contact with God as we understood Him, praying only for knowledge of His will for us and the power to carry it out.
12. Having had a spiritual awakening as a result of these steps, we tried to carry this message to alcoholics and practice these principles in all our affairs.[34]

One study has discovered that a considerable difference exists between those alcoholics who become members of A.A. and those who do not. The former are able to share their basic emotional experiences rather readily with others and they also can adapt themselves to the casual association that develops before and after A.A. meetings. Generally they have had considerable experience within small informal groups. It is believed that those who join A.A. regard their drinking as symptoms of a problem. They understood their alcoholic excesses as a threat to their homes, families, jobs, and status in the community. In other words they had developed considerable emo-

---

[34] From *Marty Mann's New Primer on Alcoholism* by Marty Mann. Copyright 1950, © 1958 by Marty Mann. Reprinted by permission of Holt, Rinehart and Winston, Inc. Pp. 175-76.

tional conflict about their drinking. Those who failed to join A.A. associated the pleasures of living with their drinking. Even such things as blackouts and delirium tremens were not indicative to them of an illness. They likewise achieved a certain prestige among their drinking friends because of their excesses. While Alcoholics Anonymous has enjoyed considerable success, it must be pointed out that not everyone can recover through it. Some would find adjustment to its intense group life very difficult.

This is, of course, not the only method employed to combat alcoholism. Psychiatric treatment in institutions is also utilized. Antabuse is a popular and effective remedy. After a person has taken this—and he should only do so under the care of a physician—he cannot drink alcohol in any form without becoming violently ill. Within a matter of ten or twenty minutes after drinking he suffers flushing, palpitation, pounding headaches, finds it difficult to breathe, and experiences nausea and vomiting.

Another method is the conditioned reflex. Ematin is injected into the individual's bloodstream, producing nausea and vomiting when the individual tries to drink. Hopefully, this results in a strong distaste for alcohol. Of course the individual must be willing to follow such medication, since eventually its effects wear off. Finally, as Alcoholics Anonymous discovered, it is absolutely essential that the organization or the physician work with wives, parents, and family. Sometimes a wife, mother, father, or family member has become extremely punitive. They hold to the former view that drinking is a vice and the individual himself is entirely responsible for it. They refuse to accept the concept that this is an illness. In such cases alcoholism may be partly the result of the attitudes of family members toward the drinker. Unless these are changed there is little hope for change in the drinking behavior of the alcoholic.[35]

## REVIEW QUESTIONS

1. What is the estimate as to the number of persons in the United States who consume alcoholic beverages? What is the estimate of the number of actual alcoholics?

2. What is alcohol and how does it act on the system?

[35] Fox, *op. cit.*, p. 170.

3. What is the difference between the alcoholic and the problem drinker?
4. Explain the natural history of the alcoholic as depicted in sociological and psychological literature.
5. What is the Jellinek formula? Discuss its validity.
6. Should alcoholism be considered a medical problem or a matter of weakness? Explain.
7. Is there a pre-alcoholic personality?
8. Have physiological explanations for the cause of alcoholism proved satisfactory?
9. What is Alcoholics Anonymous? Is it effective for all types of alcoholics?
10. Does American culture contribute to the incidence of alcoholism?

## SELECTED READINGS

*Articles*

Demone, Harold W., Jr., David J. Pittman, and Austin L. Porterfield, consulting eds., "Social Disorganization and Alcoholism: A Review of Significant Research Since 1940" by Harrison M. Trice and David J. Pittman, *Social Problems*, 5 (Spring 1958), 294-338.

Efron, Vera, "The Society Approach to Alcoholism," *Social Problems*, 7 (Spring 1960), 307-15.

Gottlieb, David, "The Neighborhood Tavern and the Cocktail Lounge: A Study of Class Differences," *American Journal of Sociology*, 62 (May 1957), 559-62.

McGenty, Denis, "Family Relationships Contributing to Alcoholism," *American Catholic Sociological Review*, 19 (Mar. 1958), 13-23.

Rettig, Salomon and Benjamin Tasmanick, "Changes in Moral Values as a Function of Adult Socialization," *Social Problems*, 7 (Fall 1959), 117-25.

*Books*

*Alcoholism, Conference on Community Mental Health,* Washington University, Springfield, Illinois: Charles C. Thomas, Publisher, 1959.

Fox, Ruth, *Alcoholism.* New York: Random House, 1956.

Free, James L., *Just One More: Problem Drinker.* New York: Coward-McCann, Inc., 1955.

Kruse, H. D., ed., *Alcoholism as a Medical Problem.* New York: Harper & Brothers, 1956.

produce this result."[2] Ruth Cavan considered suicide the intentional taking of one's life or failure to save one's life when death threatens.[3] Both of these definitions require some qualification. A negative action or failure to save one's life when death threatens may not always be suicide. If one dies in an effort to save another, a double effect is present. One's first intention is to preserve the life of another even though as a result he, the rescuer, will die—such a situation would not constitute suicide. Neither is it considered suicide if one fails to take extraordinary measures to save his life. Unless a person has as his primary motive the taking of his own life, his failure can scarcely be considered suicide.

There are certain habits which tend to reduce the life-span, such as chronic alcoholism, drug addiction, and, possibly, excessive smoking. Do persons who retain such habits despite knowledge that they may lead to a premature death have an unconscious desire to commit suicide? Some persons are "accident-prone," and Karl A. Menninger, a psychoanalyst, believes such individuals have a conflict between the will to live and the will to die.[4] If this is the case, however, the wish or desire for death is probably unconscious and, again strictly speaking, does not constitute the deliberate act of suicide.

Suicide then would seem to be limited to those who deliberately, consciously, and successfully bring about death at their own hands. Attempted suicides also require some qualifications. Most persons who attempt suicide fail to achieve it, and strong suspicion exists that the failure may be quite deliberate. The attempt is made either by means not likely to succeed or is made at a time or place when help will quickly rescue them from death. While it is practically impossible to do more than conjecture, the probability also exists that some who do achieve suicide may have intended only to attempt it. Their deaths may have been accidental—not truly suicidal. Finally, those who are mentally ill when they kill themselves—about 20 per cent of the cases—are technically suicides but are not morally responsible because of mental imbalance.

Is suicide a social problem? In other words, is suicide a social situa-

[2] Emile Durkheim, *Suicide*, trans. John A. Spaulding and George Simpson (New York: The Free Press of Glencoe, 1951), p. 44.

[3] Marshall B. Clinard, *Sociology of Deviant Behavior* (New York: Holt, Rinehart & Winston, Inc., 1957), p. 348.

[4] Paul H. Landis, *Social Problems in Nation and World* (Philadelphia: J. B. Lippincott Co., 1959), p. 190.

tion involving a relatively large number of persons which constitutes a threat to the common welfare as defined by the society and should therefore be dealt with in an organized way? Suicide, of course, is a social situation which threatens group welfare, and as will be pointed out later, definite methods are employed to prevent it. The basic question, however, seems to be whether a sufficiently large number of persons is involved to warrant its being considered a social problem. Since suicide is among the first twelve causes of death in the United States and since at least 20,000 persons commit it annually (actually the number may be much larger), and, particularly, since 100,000 persons attempt suicide each year, there seems to be a sufficiently large number to answer this question affirmatively. Furthermore, Ruth Cavan in her study found that more than half the persons in this country had at one time contemplated suicide.[5]

On the basis of the number of suicides annually, the number of attempted suicides annually, and, particularly, the number of persons contemplating suicide according to the Cavan study, there is no doubt that this should be considered a social problem.

## SUICIDE AND CULTURE

The oldest historical record of suicides appears in the Old Testament, in which seven people killed themselves. When King Saul was wounded by the Philistines he ordered his armor bearer to kill him in order to avoid capture by the enemy. When the man refused, Saul fell upon his sword, and his armor bearer, seeing that the king was dead, likewise killed himself. But suicide was apparently relatively rare among the Jews of the Old Testament. However, during the seige of Jerusalem in 70 A.D. by Titus, Josephius Flavius states that when the fall of the city was imminent many preferred suicide to falling into the hands of the enemy.[6]

In the earlier history of ancient Greece, suicide was not common.

---

[5] Clinard, op. cit., p. 357.

[6] Adolph Domonic Frenay, The Suicide Problem in the United States (Boston: Richard G. Badger, 1927), p. 30; and Lewis I. Dublin and Bessie Bunzel, To Be or Not To Be (New York: Harrison and Haas, 1933), p. 173.

Four kinds of arguments were used against it, the most important being the religious one. Plato objected to suicide as an unnatural act because man is his own closest friend and therefore has no right to injure himself. He likewise considered suicide a cowardly act and an offense against the State because it thus lost a citizen. Aristotle condemned suicide severely because he too argued it was an injury against one's native land. In the early days of ancient Rome suicide was likewise rare. It was opposed on the basis of the concept of the high dignity of man held by Plutarch and other aristocratic Romans. But despite all these arguments, it seems likely that the Greeks and Romans took a more lenient view of suicide than contemporary moralists do.

It was with the development of the Stoic philosophy founded by Zeno in Greece toward the close of the fourth century B.C. that a new attitude toward suicide developed, particularly in Rome. Stoics believed that one should live according to nature or right reason. But this was impossible if the body were afflicted by a disease, the reason impaired, the will coerced by a tyrant or the spirit crushed by actual tortures. In such cases they considered suicide a welcome deliverance and actually consistent with proper self-respect. But suicide was to be committed only after careful deliberation, when all of the arguments for and against it had been thoroughly weighed. Nevertheless, a number of outstanding Greeks and Romans committed suicide.[7]

In the Orient, especially in India, there was a custom known as "suttee," by which a widow committed suicide at her husband's funeral, usually by throwing herself upon the funeral pyre. This was believed to be a certain passport to paradise and by it the wife atoned for the sins of her husband and opened to him the gates of heaven. Children whose mother had committed suttee achieved social distinction. This custom was forbidden by the English in India, but even in 1828 when this legislation was passed there were 463 cases of suttee. As late as 1932, when an Indian woman refused to throw herself upon a roaring funeral pyre some villagers attempted to force her into it and rioting occurred. In the course of this disorder three persons were killed and five were wounded.

In China, suicide was used for revenge. A man might kill himself in order to embarrass his enemy and to haunt him after death. The

---

[7] Dublin and Bunzel, *op. cit.*, pp. 183-96.

laws of China placed a responsibility for the suicide on the person who had occasioned it. Suicide was well institutionalized in Japan. The samurai practices "hara-kiri" (a type of ritualistic suicide in which the person disembowels himself with a sword) not to escape suffering but to die for a principle. There are two kinds of hara-kiri, compulsory and voluntary. Hara-kiri originally was permitted only to the nobility for expiating a crime while avoiding an ignominious death at the hands of a public executioner. Estimates claim that for centuries, about 1500 hara-kiris occurred each year, and half of them were entirely voluntary.[8] During the Second World War, Japanese soldiers committed suicide by rushing forward in what could only prove a fatal and unsuccessful attack, crying "Banzai." The "kamikaze" (divine wind) pilots who flew loaded with bombs into American ships in suicide runs were another example of a type of institutionalized suicide.

Christianity has strongly opposed suicide and has preached that human life is valuable. The fathers of the Church, the doctors of the Church, St. Augustine, and St. Thomas all vigorously opposed suicide and emphasized its sinfulness. The Church legislated against suicide as early as 452 in the Council of Arles. Penalties against suicide were renewed in the Synod of Braques (563) and of Auxere in 576. During the Middle Ages Christian burial was denied to all suicides and their goods and property were confiscated by the civil authorities. Since the person committing suicide could not be buried in a Christian cemetery, he was buried on the highway with a stake driven through his body. This remained true in England until 1824 when an act of Parliament permitted burial in churchyards without religious rites between 9 and 12 P.M. In 1882 burial was permitted at any hour with the usual rites.[9]

This opposition to suicide is characteristic of Western European and American society. Christian reasoning holds that no man possesses such absolute jurisdiction over himself as to be at liberty to put an end to his own existence.[10] The effectiveness of the Church's stand against suicide is illustrated by the fact that it was extremely rare during the Middle Ages. Even in times of warfare and extreme stress, there is little record of suicide.

---

[8] Dublin and Bunzel, *op. cit.*, pp. 154-69.
[9] Frenay, *op. cit.*, p. 31.
[10] Frenay, *op. cit.*

By the 17th century, following the Protestant Reformation, some entirely new attitudes toward suicide began to develop. John Donne, the Anglican Bishop of St. Paul's, wrote in 1644 on the subject and strongly objected to the notion that it is an irremissible sin because it was committed at the moment of death, when repentance would be impossible. He believed this challenged the infinite mercy of God. David Hume in his essay on suicide argued that men should have the liberty to commit suicide without guilt or blame. Rousseau also attempted to justify suicide. Thus, for the first time since the ascendancy of Christianity a defense of suicide was proposed. Part of this defense undoubtedly stemmed from the very harsh measures taken against the suicide himself (by denying him decent burial, etc.) and sometimes against his family. Furthermore, with the development of psychiatry it was realized that at least some suicides are mentally ill and therefore not responsible for their actions. This number however, is relatively small. So far as accurate statistics are available, it is clear that the number of suicides has increased since the Middle Ages. But in the United States the number has been relatively constant over the years in terms of population.[11]

It is clear that the incidence of suicide is closely associated with a culture. There are societies which tolerate suicide, societies which actually compel suicide under certain circumstances, and societies which reject suicide under almost all circumstances. Suicide still carries a stigma in American society. While the suicide himself escapes such stigma—in this world, at least—his family, relatives, and friends suffer from it. It is usually considered a cowardly and selfish way out of one's difficulties. Judaism and Christianity both oppose suicide, but the ecclesiastical penalties against it are much less severe than in the past. Furthermore, since the possibility of mental illness cannot always be ruled out, the suicide frequently receives the benefit of this doubt.

## WHO COMMITS SUICIDE?

In the United States, suicide is most common among white, urban, unmarried males 45 years of age or over who are Protestant or without religious affiliations. More women than men attempt suicide.

---

[11] Hirsch, *op. cit.*, pp. 516-17.

But more men than women succeed. In a study of 1,000 attempted suicides in Detroit there were two attempts on the part of women for every one attempt on the part of men.[12] In 1953 there were 16.1 suicides by males for every 100,000 persons compared with 4.3 by females for every 100,000 persons. Clinard points out that this seems to indicate that women use attempted suicide as a means to attain some other end.[13]

Generally speaking, the rate of suicide increases with age. Suicide is relatively rare up until the age of 15. In the five-year period between 15 and 19, about 3 per cent of all deaths occurring in this category are from suicide. This is one age category, by the way, in which female suicides are somewhat higher than those of males, although both are relatively low. More than half of all suicides are committed by persons who are 45 years of age and over, although they constituted only a little over one-fifth of the population in 1929.[14]

But while the suicide rate is not so high among young people, it should be noted, for example, that it is the second most common cause of death among the student body at Yale University. A survey of the 209 deaths of students at Yale between 1920 and 1955 revealed that accidents claimed 92 students, or 43.8 per cent, while suicide claimed 25 students, or 12 per cent. The national suicide death rate for this age group (which averages about 20 years) is 6.6 per 100,000, but the Yale rate was 9.0 per 100,000.[15] It should be pointed out that Yale is not unique in this respect. Emile Durkheim in his famous study *Suicide,* found that among 1,000 young Catholics attending institutions of higher learning of every sort there were only about 1.3 suicides, while among Protestants the number was 2.5. For Jews this figure reached 16.[16] At one of the largest Catholic Universities in this country, there has not been a single student suicide in the last 15 years.

The rate of Negro suicide is far lower than that of white persons. Out of over 16,000 suicides in 1929, fewer than 600 were colored, and this included Orientals as well as Negroes. The suicide death rate for white persons was 15.0 per 100,000, while that for colored persons was only 5.0. In 1953, 15,307 white persons committed suicide, com-

---

[12] Clinard, *op. cit.,* p. 355.
[13] Clinard, *op. cit.*
[14] Dublin and Bunzel, *op. cit.,* p. 40.
[15] *Newsweek* (July 15, 1957), p. 78.
[16] Durkheim, *op. cit.,* p. 167.

pared to 640 nonwhites. Among the factors cited by Clinard to explain the lower incidence of Negro suicides is the predominantly rural background of the Negro, which will be seen to be a factor decreasing the suicide rate, and the fact that the severity of racial discrimination may lower Negro expectations and consequently raise the tolerance point for frustration.[17] Japanese and Chinese, who are listed in the Census as colored, have a very high suicide rate—and their expectations, as a rule, are higher than those of the Negro. This means that the Negro suicide rate is even lower than statistics based on the suicides of all colored persons would indicate.

While the ethnic diversity of the American population has become much less important since large-scale immigration was discontinued in 1924, some earlier studies indicate that immigrants from Germany had a much higher proportion of suicides than would be expected by their numbers in the population. In the period previous to 1920, their rate in New York State was twice as high as that of the native white population. In Pennsylvania it reached the figure of 80 per 100,000 among German males of all ages, and 141 in the age group between 65 and 84. Scandinavian and Russian-born males in Pennsylvania also had a very high rate of suicide, but those of Italian birth had the lowest suicide rate of all nationalities. Dr. Starns found that, generally speaking, foreign-born persons in the State of Massachusetts had approximately the same suicide rate as such persons did in their native land. One startling exception was the Irish, who had a higher suicide rate than their numbers in the Massachusetts population would warrant. This is more striking because the suicide rate in Ireland is extremely low.[18]

Marital status and occupation also reveal some interesting differences in the suicide rate. The highest completed and attempted suicide rates are found among the divorced, according to a study carried on in Seattle between 1948-1952. The white-collar occupations have a lower rate of both completed and attempted suicides than the blue-collar occupations.[19] A Metropolitan Life Insurance Company study based on differential suicide rates among those holding policies in the industrial department—generally wage earners of relatively

---

[17] Clinard, *op. cit.*, pp. 355-56.

[18] Dublin and Bunzel, *op. cit.*, pp. 33-34.

[19] Calvin F. Schmid and Morris T. Van Arsdol, Jr., "Completed and Attempted Suicides: A Comparative Analysis," *American Sociological Review*, 20 (June 1955), pp. 273-83.

lower income—and those holding policies in the ordinary department—who come from a higher economic group—agrees with the Seattle findings.[20] Contrary to what is generally claimed, it seems that persons in the higher socio-economic brackets commit suicide to a less extent than those in the middle and lower socio-economic brackets. However, there is a possibility that suicides among those more highly placed may be better concealed.

These data are supported by the ecological studies of the suicide rate in cities. In a study of Chicago, Cavan found that a high suicide rate occurs in socially disorganized areas. In other words, in the interstitial areas of the cities, where institutional controls are poor and group relations strained, the incidence of suicide tends to rise. In view of this it is not surprising that suicide rates in rural areas are lower than in urban areas. In 1940 the rural rate was 12.9, in cities of 100,000 or more the suicide rate was 15.6.[21]

Ever since the time of Durkheim students have been involved with the incidence of suicide against religious backgrounds. Overwhelmingly, studies reveal that Catholics have a lower suicide rate than Protestants and Jews. On the basis of foreign data, Prussia in 1925 had a suicide rate of 13.5 among Catholics, 28.0 among Protestants, and 53.0 among Jews. Earlier, Jews had a lower suicide rate than Catholics, but recently as a result of persecution the Jewish rate has risen. Durkheim and others have explained the lower suicide rate among Catholics by the fact that Catholicism tends to integrate the individual into the group to a greater extent than most Protestant denominations do.[22] Undoubtedly, Catholic teaching on life after death and Catholic penalties against suicide are effective in lowering Catholic suicide rates.

ETIOLOGY OF SUICIDE

Durkheim believed that the sociological study of suicide was justified, because suicides in a given society over a definite period of time, rather than being viewed as separate, unrelated occurrences, should

---

[20] Dublin and Bunzel, *op. cit.*, p. 98.
[21] Landis, *op. cit.*, pp. 197-99.
[22] Durkheim, *op. cit.*, p. 44.

be analyzed as a whole. His explanation of suicide was largely based on the structure of a society. He pointed out that the rate of suicide remains relatively constant from year to year, providing another indication that suicide is a social fact. If suicide is studied over a long period of time, changes do occur; but to him these changes merely indicate alterations in the structure of society.[23]

He identified three types of suicide: the egoistic, the altruistic, and the anomic. The *egoistic suicide* is committed by a person who is not adequately adjusted to his society. It is a secret and selfish act, prompted by personal motives that usually involve avoiding a serious crisis or what the individual thinks is a serious crisis. Thus, an individual facing social or economic disaster and unable to cope with it is actually deserting his family, relatives, and friends for his own personal motives by doing away with himself.

*Altruistic suicide* occurs when the individual is very well integrated into a society, which expects him, in the face of certain crises, to give up his life. In fact failure to commit suicide under such circumstances would constitute a social disgrace for him, his family, and his friends. This is the type of suicide which the Japanese know as hara-kiri. Among military men in some societies, it has been customary to commit suicide if defeated. It has even been suggested, as a result of the last World War and the Korean conflict, that highly placed military personnel who might be captured should carry cyanide pills so that they can commit suicide instantaneously before they are compelled to reveal military secrets through torture. The moral implications of such an act have not as yet been thoroughly discussed, but this type of suicide socially—albeit not morally—would fit into the altruistic pattern of Durkheim.

The third type of suicide—*anomic*—occurs in the face of grave, personal disorganization which alienates the individual from other persons.[24] This is the kind of suicide that apparently occurs in urban interstitial areas where social disorganization is at a maximum. This too may help to explain the higher incidence of suicide among divorced persons.

If attention is focused upon the structure of society, one should find a low rate of suicide in those societies which are relatively small, stable, characterized by a predominance of primary group relation-

[23] Durkheim, *op. cit.*, p. 46.
[24] Durkheim, *op. cit.*, pp. 152-276.

ships, and where suicide is opposed under almost all circumstances. This is the type of society that apparently existed in the early days of ancient Greece and Rome, when the suicide rate was relatively low, and during the Middle Ages, when the suicide rate was insignificant. On the other hand even if a society were relatively small, stable, and characterized by primary group relationships—yet had a socially approved pattern of suicide—there would be a fair incidence of it. This seems to have been the case with Japan prior to the latter part of the 19th century.

In a large, complex, and swiftly changing society, where secondary groups are more numerous than primary groups, the possibilities of a high suicide rate are greater, whether suicide is institutionalized or forbidden. This seems to have been the case in the latter days of ancient Greece and Rome and to some extent in contemporary Europe and America. In other words it is difficult in such societies for an individual to be well integrated into his society, particularly in the large urban areas. If one attempts to apply these aspects of Durkheim's theory to the data cited in the section "Who Commits Suicide," it seems to offer a reasonably good explanation in many but not in all cases.

For example, it was pointed out that persons most likely to commit suicide are white, urban, unmarried males, 45 years of age or over who are either Protestants or have no religious affiliation. Attempting now to apply Durkheim's principal of *anomie*, it is clear that most married males are likely to be better integrated in their society because of the bonds of marital life. Admittedly, there are exceptions to this, but insofar as the marriage is a relatively happy one, this is more rather than less likely to be the case. To the extent that primary group relationships prevent the development of anomie, it is obvious that married women generally are deeply involved in the primary rather than the secondary group realtionships. It is likewise true that the close, permanent, face-to-face relationships of the primary group are more typical of the rural area or the small town than of the large metropolitan area. Consequently there is a higher incidence of suicide in the urban area. Age too is an important factor because as persons reach their later years, children have normally left home, the death of a spouse has often occurred, and their ties with other persons are likely to be lessened. The possibilities of both anomie and anomic suicide increase.

Religion is an important factor because upon it will depend one's philosophy of life. Protestantism is much more individualistic than Catholicism. In the Catholic Church there is a doctrine of the Mystical Body of Christ, of which all men are members, and there is the flow of Grace through the Sacraments of Penance and the Holy Eucharist. There is likewise a strong prohibition of suicide. Together, these factors probably help to decrease anomie and at the same time to lower the suicide rate. The person with no membership in a religious denomination lacks one of the bonds that can help tie a man to his fellow men. To some extent at least, therefore, Durkheim's theory of anomie seems helpful in attempting to understand the causes of suicide.

But while such an explanation may be used generally, there is still the difficulty that persons who are below the age of 45, women, rural dwellers, Catholics, Jews and devout Protestants—all commit suicide.

Ruth Cavan suggests that the popular idea of a crisis being a sudden catastrophe needs extension. According to her, a crisis may be a situation into which some new element enters to which one cannot adapt. To her, disorganization occurs only when that area of life which has now become chaotic is thought of as essential to an individual's happiness. Thus a person who thought very little of money would not be sorely disturbed if he had to live on a much lower income. The person who has little regard for his wife and family may not suffer acutely if he loses both. In other words, it is a matter of the definition of the situation against the individual's perception of it as colored by his values.[25]

## THE SITUATIONAL-VALUE APPROACH

Aside from those individuals suffering acute depression or some other type of mental illness, factors contributing to suicide seem to involve both the situation and the values of the person contemplating suicide. Situationally, it would depend first on the type of society in which an individual lives. As pointed out, if it

---

[25] Ruth Cavan, *Suicide* (Chicago: The University of Chicago Press, 1928), pp. 148-49.

is a very well integrated society with strong prohibitions against suicide, the crisis prompting it would have to be unusually strong for the individual. On the other hand if the person finds himself in a society in which there is little or no prohibition against suicide or one in which suicide is institutionalized under certain conditions, he may resort to it in a less severe crisis. Thus the values of the society or culture contribute to the possible incidence of suicide.

## PREVENTION OF SUICIDE

Folklore has it that persons who threaten suicide rarely if ever do so. This is entirely inaccurate, as Dr. Edwin S. Shneidman and Dr. Norman L. Farberow point out in their study "Clues to Suicide." Three-fourths of their subjects who committeed suicide had previously threatened or attempted to do so. In other words, a suicide threat is rarely an idle threat. Furthermore, they found that almost half of the individuals who took their lives did so within three months after they appeared to have passed an emotional crisis successfully. This means that individuals suffering acute depression, or having undergone a highly acute crisis, should be kept under observation for a period of 90 days.[26]

A number of voluntary societies exist, such as the "Save-A-Life League" in New York, London's "Anti-Suicide Bureau," Vienna's "Advisory Center for Those Weary of Life," and Berlin's "Suicide Aid Society." The earliest of these is believed to be the "Anti-Suicide Bureau," which was founded by the Salvation Army in 1906.

An excellent illustration of a remedial measure against suicide is the work of Father Kenneth B. Murphy of the archdiocese of Boston, founder of "Rescue, Inc." About 8:00 A.M. on St. Patrick's day in 1959, the police came to St. Francis de Sales' rectory to inform Father Murphy that a young man in his twenties was threatening to jump from an eighth-floor window. Father Murphy recalls that he went to the building and found that a large crowd had

---

[26] Edwin S. Shneidman and Norman L. Farberow, "Clues to Suicide," *Public Health Reports*, 71, No. 2 (Feb. 1956), pp. 109-14.

gathered—since many persons were on their way to work. Some of the people were urging the young man to jump. Father Murphy was able to talk him out of it, and discovered that the cause of the man's suicide threat was a marital problem. He was a seaman whose wife had become pregnant by another man after she had left him.

After several other such police calls, Father Murphy approached Cardinal Cushing, who enthusiastically gave him $5,000 to establish Rescue, Inc. Today, Father Murphy maintains offices in the Boston Fire Department and the Boston City Hospital. He has a radio-equipped car and a special emergency telephone with a twenty-four hour answering service. Over three thousand calls have been made in the last two years. He has a staff of seventy members, including rabbis, ministers, psychiatrists, psychologists, physicians, nurses, a Trappist monk, and a handwriting expert. To Father Murphy every call is a serious one, and competent help is obtained for the individual as soon as possible.[27]

Another precautionary measure that might well be taken is the careful observation of certain well-known suicide spots. One of these is the Golden Gate Bridge in San Francisco. Almost every large city has a bridge, a high building, a river, or a lake which is a favorite suicide spot. An example of such a precautionary measure was a squadron of boats called the "Suicide Flotilla" which patrolled the Danube River in order to rescue would-be suicides. In April and May of 1928 there was an epidemic of suicides in Budapest which resulted in 150 deliberate drownings. Since the boat service was started, it has been able to save 9 out of 10 of those persons attempting suicide.

Obviously, it is not enough to prevent the suicide attempt alone. Persons who make such an attempt should be referred to adequate psychiatric care. But what is basically needed is a change in American culture. To the extent that our society is one which creates anomie, which fails to recognize as early as possible those suffering from mental illness and to take steps to provide for them, suicide is likely to remain a social problem. Furthermore, the lowering of prohibitions against suicides by churches or other social organizations will certainly not help reduce them. While the family, relatives, and friends of a suicide should certainly not be

---

[27] Catherine Hughes, "Rescue, Inc.," *St. Jude*, 27 (Nov. 1961), pp. 12-15.

punished, society must make it clear that it vigorously opposes suicide.

## REVIEW QUESTIONS

1. What limitations exist in the definitions of suicide provided by Durkheim and Cavan?
2. What is the estimated annual incidence of suicide in the United States? How realistic is this estimate?
3. How does a specific culture contribute to the suicide rate? Give examples.
4. On what basis does Christianity usually oppose suicide?
5. Historically, what measures were employed to indicate society's opposition to suicide in England?
6. In the United States, what are the most common social characteristics of those who commit suicide?
7. What is the estimate of annual attempted suicides in the United States? Are attempted suicides more common among men or women?
8. Can the high rate of suicide among some university students be explained?
9. What impact does religion appear to have on suicide?
10. What are Durkheim's three types of suicide? Explain each.
11. Using the situational-value approach, analyze the factors which appear to contribute to suicide.
12. What are some of the remedies employed to prevent suicide?

## SELECTED READINGS

*Articles*

Gibbs, Jack B. and Walter T. Martin, "Status Integration and Suicide in Ceylon," *American Journal of Sociology*, 64 (May 1959), 585-91.

Gold, Martin, "Suicide, Homicide, and the Socialization of Aggression," *American Journal of Sociology*, 63 (May 1958), 651-61.

Harsh, Joseph, "Suicide," *Mental Hygiene*, 43 (Oct. 1959), 515-17.

Mihanovich, Clement S., "Who Commits Suicide?" *American Catholic Sociological Review*, 8 (Dec. 1947), 281-84.

Porterfield, Austin L., "Suicide and Crime in a Social Structure of an Urban Setting: Fort Worth, 1930-1950," *American Sociological Review*, 17 (June 1952), 341-48.

————, "Indices of Suicide and Homicide by States and Cities," *American Sociological Review*, 14 (Aug. 1947), 481-89.

Schmid, Calvin F. and Morris T. Van Arstol, Jr., "Completed and Attempted Suicides: A Comparative Analysis," *American Sociological Review*, 20 (June 1955), 273-83.

Selvin, Hannan C., "Durkheim's Suicide and Problems of Empirical Research," *American Journal of Sociology*, 63 (May 1950), 607-19.

Schneidman, Edwin S. and Norman L. Farberow, "Clues to Suicide," *Public Health Reports*, 70 (Feb. 1955), 109-14.

*Traffic in Opium and Other Dangerous Drugs*, Report by the Government of the United States of America for the year ended Dec. 31, 1958. Washington, D.C.: Government Printing Office, 1959.

### Books

Cavan, Ruth S., *Suicide*. Chicago: The University of Chicago Press, 1928.

Conannan, Paul, ed., *African Homicide and Suicide*. Princeton, N.J.: Princeton University Press, 1960.

Dublin, Lewis I. and Bessie Bunzel, *To Be or Not To Be*. New York: Harrison & Robert Haas, 1933.

Durkheim, Emile, *Suicide*. New York: The Free Press of Glencoe, 1951.

Freney, Adolph Domonic, *Suicide Problem in the United States*. Boston: Richard G. Badger, 1927.

Schneidman, Edwin S. and N. L. Farberow, eds., *Clues to Suicide*. New York: McGraw-Hill Book Co., Inc., 1957.

# PART FOUR

# Problems of America's Minorities

T HE question of racial, religious, and ethnic relationships remains an important problem in a democratic society. While race relations, particularly Negro-white relations, provide one of the most challenging problems today, interreligious and ethnic group difficulties cannot be ignored. The inequality of American Negroes in such areas as education, housing, and occupations stems from prejudice and discrimination against them stemming from their status as slaves but perhaps even stronger since they became freedmen. Considerable progress has been made in recent years but desirable, democratic goals are still distant. An understanding of the Negro's plight today cannot be divorced from his history, and for this reason considerable historical background has been provided. The contemporary aspects of the problem in specific areas are likewise discussed.

The inclusion of American Catholics as a minority group is not usual in social problems texts. Yet adequate evidence is offered that, sociologically, Catholics in the United States both historically and contemporaneously are a minority. Some of the historical aspects of Protestant-Catholic relations in this country may come as a surprise to many students. Some will find it difficult to accept the proposition that Catholics are a minority at all. This reaction can be traced to the fact that prejudice and discrimination against Catholics is more subtle than that against Negroes and Jews and actually does not even exist in some sections of the United States where Catholics both numerically and sociologically are now or are becoming a majority group. But if this situation is viewed nationally, the minority status is clear. Furthermore, as Catholics emerge from a minority status it seems likely that interreligious tensions may at least temporarily increase, as was evidenced in objections to the nomination of the first Catholic (Alfred E. Smith) to the U.S. Presidency and the subsequent attacks made during the campaign of the second Catholic presidential nominee (John F. Kennedy), who was ultimately elected.

The minority status of American Jews is much clearer. They have suffered and continue to suffer certain types of obvious discrimination in education, occupations, housing, and exclusive clubs. While they do not undergo the privations and discrimination typical for most Negroes, and generally enjoy a higher economic, occupational, and educational status than Catholics, their problems are quite real and severe, partly because their social structure is such that discriminations against them occur in areas in which persons of equal economic and social standing would otherwise be entirely acceptable. Futhermore, throughout history they have undergone frequent and severe persecutions in many parts of the world, the last being the cruel attempts to exterminate them in Europe during the Hitler regime.

Other minority problems are present in the United States, notably those of the Indian and the Puerto Rican, but these have been omitted in the interest of space. The reason for grouping minority problems is obvious. All of them have one aspect in common, namely prejudice on the part of the out-group, but it will be clear that the expression of such prejudice and discrimination varies among the groups treated.

# 12

# The Negro in America

R ACE is basically a biological matter. As the
result of heredity a person may be born
into one of three major races, Caucasoid,
Negroid, and Mongoloid. While skin color is generally
used as an index of race, anthropologists distinguish
many other characteristics, such as the shape of the
hair, shape of the nose, type of head, distribution of
body hair, physical size and shape of the lips as well as
the eyes. In addition to these three major races there are
various sub-races, such as the Nordic, the Alpine, and the
Mediterranean. There is, however, no such thing as a
pure race. Throughout the centuries persons from various
races have intermarried, and one can find some Negroes
who are lighter than many white persons and whose
other physical characteristics are more Caucasoid than
some who are classified as Caucasian. If members of
various races were plotted on a normal curve of distribution there would tend to be an overlap, so that at each
extreme it would become difficult to determine whether a
person was a Mongolian, Caucasian, or Negro.

While all of this is quite true, unfortunately race has become a social rather than a biological concept in the United States. Whether a man is to be classified legally as a Negro or not depends as much upon state legislatures as it does upon his physical appearance, if indeed not more so. In some states if a man is 1/32 Negro he is classified as a Negro. In other states he must be 1/16 or 1/4. While it may be simple enough to identify most Negroes, Caucasoids, and Mongolians in terms of race, there are borderline cases which defy categorization. As a result of this it is known that a certain number of Negroes "pass" over into the white race each year. Some pass permanently, others temporarily. When a Negro's skin is light enough and his other features close enough to those of the whites he may simply disappear into white society and be accepted as a Caucasian. In other cases he may pass temporarily in order to gain admission to a college or a university, or to secure employment which would otherwise be denied him. The exact number of Negroes who "pass" each year cannot be determined and estimates run from as low as 70 or 80 thousand to 200,000 or more.[1]

Sometimes such Negroes marry white persons, and folklore has it that on such occasion a child may be born who is entirely black. Genetically speaking, there is a rule of thumb that if a pure white person marries a "mulatto"—that is a Negro with mixed white and Negro blood—the child will never be darker than the darker parent. If, however, two mulattoes should marry it is possible that one of the offspring may be much darker than either of the parents. In other words, when a very dark child is born, it is clear that both parents carried Negro genes.

## HISTORY OF THE NEGRO IN AMERICA

The first Negroes to enter what is now the United States were brought here in 1619 by a Dutch vessel and sold as slaves. By 1790 there were more than 750,000 Negroes in this country, about 60,000 of them free. Almost all of them were involved in plantation

---

[1] E. W. Eckard, "How Many Negroes 'Pass'?" *American Journal of Sociology*, 52 (May 1947), pp. 498-500.

work in the South.[2] But at this period of American history, the use of slaves for raising cotton was becoming increasingly unprofitable. As a matter of fact the importation of slaves was forbidden in 1808. But two great changes occurred which made slavery profitable. One was the invention of the cotton gin by Eli Whitney. Prior to this, the cotton in the coastal area was unsatisfactory because it contained large numbers of seeds which had to be picked out by hand. The cotton gin facilitated the mechanical removal of seeds and thus made cotton a profitable crop in the coastal areas. At about the same time the cotton textile industry in England boomed and the demand for raw cotton increased. This in turn made slaves more valuable. Despite the prohibition of slavery, slaves were still smuggled into the United States. Because of their economic value efforts were made to justify the exploitation of Negroes, and literature began to appear depicting them as an inferior race.

Contrary to Harriet Beecher Stowe's *Uncle Tom's Cabin*, slaves were generally not mistreated. In fact, they were so valuable that they were handled with consideration in most cases. But the cruelty of the institution itself was undeniable. The relatively stable organization which Negroes knew in their tribes in Africa was destroyed. Most plantation owners did not allow Negroes to develop any kind of family life, and husky males were used for breeding purposes. As a matter of fact the Negro family, insofar as it existed, became a matriarchal family through the loss of so many fathers and in some cases still remains so.

## THE RECONSTRUCTION PERIOD

Since the close of the Civil War the history of the Negro in American society can be divided roughly into three phases: from the reconstruction period until America's entry into World War I; the period of World War I, the depression of the thirties, and World War II, ending with the historic decision of the United States Supreme Court in 1954; and from 1954 until the present. While it would be entirely feasible to divide the history of the

[2] Earl Raab and Gertrude J. Selznick, *Major Social Problems* (Evanston, Illinois: Row, Peterson & Company, 1959), p. 188.

American Negro since the Civil War into six or more periods, the three phases suggested seem suitable for the analysis here undertaken.

On January 1st, 1863, President Lincoln issued his Emancipation Proclamation, which declared that all persons held as slaves within states that were in rebellion against the United States were free. It likewise provided that these freed men could be received into the federal armed forces. Legally then, all Negroes had been freed in those states which had joined in the Confederacy. In reality, however, such freedom existed only in those states or sections of those states which were occupied by the Union Forces. Slavery could still be continued with de facto legality in those states which were not in rebellion. In December of 1865 the 13th Amendment to the U.S. Constitution, abolishing slavery throughout the United States, had been ratified by a sufficient number of states to become the law of the land. In 1866 the 14th Amendment was passed by the U.S. Congress but rejected by a number of southern states. In order to secure its adoption the first Reconstruction Act was passed in March of 1867 converting ten southern states into five military districts, in which Negroes were granted the right to vote and civil and military officials of the Confederacy were excluded from participation in the election of the state conventions organized under the Act.[3] In this way the 14th Amendment was adopted in the ten southern states before the Federal forces were removed. By means of this legislation, slavery was completely abolished and suffrage was granted to Negroes.

Actually, the southern Negro became the pawn of the northern "carpetbagger" (an opportunist Northerner who moved into the South) and the southern "scalawag" (a Southerner sympathizing with Northern political objectives). The Negro, as a result of this lack of education, was generally in no position to exercise his voting franchise intelligently. This was not true of all Negroes, especially some of the freedmen in Louisiana. But it is undeniable that in some sections of the South ridiculous excesses were perpetrated by state legislatures, composed largely of Negroes. Ultimately the blame for this was placed upon the Negro, not upon the northern politicians who had as their ultimate goal the establishment of the

[3] E. Franklin Frazier, *The Negro in the United States* (New York: The Macmillan Co., 1957), p. 131.

Republican party as the supreme party in the South. Retaliation by the whites was not long in coming and, as Federal forces were withdrawn, the Ku Klux Klan was formed to terrorize Negroes and prevent the exercise of their franchise. In addition to this, state legislation known as "The Black Codes" was enacted, dealing with such matters as apprenticeship, labor contracts, migration, vagrancy, and civil and legal rights. This was simply an effort to re-establish the former master-slave relationship. Most of these laws remained in effect long after the Reconstruction period, and in Mississippi almost until the beginning of the 20th century. White supremacy was restored and has in effect remained so until the present in most of the South.

Not suffrage but ownership of farmland and an adequate education were the Negro's major needs. In fact, General Sherman had confiscated some southern plantations and redistributed the land among Negroes, but President Johnson seemed unwilling to carry out such a policy, and, generally speaking, it became impossible for most Negroes to own land. However, opposition to the education of Negroes was not strong, and some southern states made provisions for a school system. It was even expected that such school systems would eventually be integrated. A number of Northerners flocked to the South to staff these schools and southern antagonism was aroused because they believed the ultimate effect of educating the Negro would be his seeking social equality. But if the Negro retained the right to vote, it became clear that he could become a political force and perhaps achieve some of the ends he sought. As a result legislation was passed between 1890 and 1910 to disenfranchise the Negro. The 15th Amendment had been adopted to assure the Negro's right to vote, which had been provided for in the 14th Amendment. To bypass the 15th Amendment laws were enacted requiring a voter to pay poll and other taxes, and to register months in advance of voting. Sometimes ownership of a small piece of property was likewise included in voting qualifications. But at this point a problem arose regarding the poor white who would likewise be disqualified. As a result the so-called "grandfather clause" was included in most of the new state constitutions. If a person had served in the armies of the United States or the Confederacy, or was the descendant of such a person, or had a franchise before 1867, he still remained eligible to vote even though he owned no property.

Literacy was another qualification, and it was most effectively employed. Even educated Negroes who were quite literate were required to read sections of the Constitution in various foreign languages, some of which those presenting the test were probably unable to translate themselves. A story is told of a Negro Doctor of Philosophy who had successfully passed a literacy test in English, French, and German, and was then offered a copy in Chinese. He is reputed to have said, "It says here that no Negro can vote in the State of Mississippi."

Furthermore, considerable power was left to local school boards so that in the distribution of funds, Negroes were given a very slight share. The school year of the Negro child was usually less than that of the white child, and the actual money appropriated per Negro pupil (as opposed to a white pupil) was ridiculously low. Thus, through successful disenfranchisement, the Negro lost the right to vote and with it whatever influence he may have had politically in improving his status. Inability to secure ownership of land turned him into a tenant farmer, utterly dependent upon the owner. His poverty became acute. An inferior educational system made it impossible for him to acquire the knowledge and skills that might enable him to rise. Consequently, certain stereotypes of the Negro became commonplace. It was believed that he was mentally inferior, that social equality was impractical if not impossible, that Negroes were lazy and shiftless, incapable of self-discipline, criminally inclined, satisfied with their present status, and that segregation was essential. Five different studies of the attitudes of whites towards Negroes report the prevalence of such attitudes in at least four of the studies.[4] Through such stereotypes and through the law itself, there emerged in the South a type of racial etiquette between Negroes and whites exemplified by the "Jim Crow" laws, regulations requiring Negroes to ride in certain sections of streetcars, to drink only from fountains designated "Negro," to have their own restrooms, to attend their own theaters, or to sit in designated places in theaters attended by whites. Even if churches were bi-racial, Negroes were directed to certain pews. The school system was entirely segregated

---

[4] Edward McDonagh, *Ethnic Relations in the United States* (New York: Appleton-Century-Crofts, Inc., 1953), p. 101.

at all levels. One never addressed a Negro as "Mister," and even if he were a person of some importance, the term "professor" was used. He never went to the front door of a white man's home, but always to the rear and removed his hat. Sociologically, of course, these indignities have all been indices of the subservient position of the Negro in the South and to some extent in the North.

One of the great fears of the white race, especially in the South, seems to have been that Negroes would attain social equality. For this reason the greatest taboo existed against interracial marriage and, in fact, laws against miscegenation exist in most of the southern states. In a famous study by Gunnar Myrdal, *An American Dilemma*, it was found that the strongest opposition toward the Negro on the part of whites was in the field of intermarriage. On the other hand the Negro's greatest desire was not intermarriage (which actually ranked last in his order of desired privileges) but an opportunity to earn an adequate living.

Prejudice and discrimination against the Negro have at times taken violent forms. Lynching is the murder of a person by a group of individuals without legal authority and with no legal determination of a person's guilt. Since the beginning of this century about 2,000 persons have been lynched in the United States, of which approximately 90 per cent were Negroes. Although it is commonly believed that Negroes are lynched most frequently on the accusation of rape, this is not true. Only in about one-third of the cases has this been the charge. In fact, the accusation is sometimes very trivial, such as being "uppity." Often, later investigation reveals that the individuals were guilty of no offense at all.[5] Another form of violence which seems to be more frequent than lynching is the race riot. In these cases two mobs of people attack each other. Individuals are killed and sometimes severe property damage is sustained. Two of the most serious race riots have occurred since 1919: one was in Chicago in that year, and the other in Detroit in 1941.[6]

---

[5] John L. Gillin, Clarence G. Dittmas, Roy J. Colbert, and Norman M. Castler, *Social Problems* (New York: Appleton-Century-Crofts, Inc., 1952), p. 90.

[6] George Easton Simpson and J. Milton Yinger, *Racial and Cultural Minorities: An Analysis of Prejudice and Discrimination* (New York: Harper & Brothers, 1953), pp. 448-49.

## NEGRO LEADERSHIP AND MOVEMENTS

A number of Negro leaders have attempted to secure some measure of interracial justice and to alleviate interracial strains. One of the earliest of these was Booker T. Washington. His attitude is best described as conciliatory. Perhaps he could have been nothing else during his period of history—he himself had once been a slave. He believed that Negroes should accept segregation and not push too hard for the franchise. In his opinion they could elevate themselves by securing an education, particularly a technical education, and thus gain positions in trade and industry. By these means he hoped that Negroes could become successful businessmen, skilled tradesmen, and, through thrift, improve their positions until they actually reached the level of captains of industry and middle-class respectability. At this point he expected that Negro discrimination would largely disappear.

But Washington tended to place much of the blame for the Negroes' condition on themselves, although he did attempt to inculcate a pride in their race and a spirit of racial cooperation. Today, Booker T. Washington's methods would be repudiated by contemporary Negro leadership. In fact, W. E. B. DuBois was more nearly a forerunner of the kind of Negro leadership that exists today. DuBois became convinced that only a higher liberal education would produce intelligent Negro leadership, and that elementary schools and industrial training alone would never solve the racial problem. For some years he had vacillated between the position of Booker T. Washington and a more radical point of view. Ultimately, he rejected Washington's proposed solutions and became a leading spokesman in opposition to the conservatism at Tuskegee. He was mainly responsible for inaugurating the "Niagara movement."

Dubois called a meeting of Negro leaders at Niagara Falls in 1905 to organize a social movement in defense of Negro rights. The first official conference of the movement was held the following year, significantly enough at Harpers Ferry, West Virginia, the scene of John Brown's Raid. In effect, it demanded equal civil and social rights including suffrage, equal treatment in public accommodations, equality before the law and the right to associate with white people who wished to befriend Negroes. It also demanded adequate education for Negro children.[7]

The Niagara movement was handicapped by a lack of money, but a spontaneous race riot in Springfield, Illinois in 1908 focused national attention upon the plight of the American Negro. A conference was held in New York City in 1909 at which DuBois was present, and resulted in the establishment of the National Association for the Advancement of Colored People (NAACP) in the same year. The basic platform demanded that all forced segregation be abolished, equal educational advantages be provided for both races, the Negro should be enfranchised, and the 14th and 15th Amendments should be enforced.[8]

## WORLD WAR I TO 1954

Just as the Civil War had radically altered the status of the American Negro, the First World War caused further radical change. Labor needs in the northern industries had been largely met by immigration from Europe. In fact, northern employers had actually sent recruiters to Europe to find workers. The opening of hostilities virtually cut off immigration to the United States and a new source of labor—particularly cheap labor—had to be found. The southern Negro was the answer, and more than half a million Negroes moved into northern cities during World War I alone (whereas from 1900 and 1930 over two million left the South to settle in northern cities). At the start of the depression there was some tendency to return south, but some Negroes later came north because it was easier to obtain public relief there.

By 1929 European immigration was restricted to about 154,000 persons annually, and the Second World War thus resulted in an even more dramatic influx of southern Negroes to the North.

Between 1940 and 1950 the non-white population more than doubled in thirty of the metropolitan areas of the United States, all

[7] Frazier, *op. cit.*, pp. 523-24.
[8] Frazier, *op. cit.*, p. 525.

but one of these being in the North or West rather than the South, the historical region of Negro concentration.[9]

The Detroit metropolitan area had an increase of 109.5 per cent in its Negro population between 1940 and 1950. At the same time New York, Philadelphia, St. Louis, and other northern cities were likewise experiencing an upsurge of Negro immigrants. Prior to World War I the Negro populations of large northern cities had been relatively small. This sudden mass migration made the Negro highly visible. Furthermore, many of these Negroes were from the rural South and entirely unaccustomed to urban living. As a result, social problems occurred in the areas of settlement, involving living accommodations, education, health, and crime.

HOUSING

Adequate housing for all Americans has yet to be realized. Unsightly slums are more conspicuous in large cities but they are far from absent in rural areas. For example, in 1950 over one-third of American dwellings did not have hot running water, a private toilet, or a bath which was not dilapidated.[10] But Negroes and other nonwhites feel the need for adequate housing facilities most acutely. The major reasons for this situation are overcrowding, particularly in northern cities; segregation policies, which attempt to restrict Negro residences to limited areas within the city; and the difficulties that many Negroes experience when they apply for mortgage loans.

It has already been pointed out that millions of Negroes have moved north and settled in metropolitan areas since the beginning of this century. For the most part they have had to accept menial positions with low wages, which compelled them to find the cheapest housing available. Very often this housing was in an area already occupied by Negroes. But even when their income was sufficient to purchase or rent better housing, in other areas they came into conflict with white owners or realtors. There is a widespread rationaliza-

---

[9] Reprinted from *The Negro Population of Chicago* by Otis Dudley Duncan and Beverly Duncan by permission of The University of Chicago Press. Copyright 1957 by The University of Chicago. (p. 1).

[10] *Statistical Abstract of the United States, 1954*, Bureau of the Census, Washington, D.C., 1954, p. 792.

tion that when Negroes move into an area, it begins to deteriorate. This is not necessarily so, and the extent to which this decline has occurred can be blamed partly on overcrowding. It is not uncommon to find that four or five Negro families are forced to occupy a residence which at one time housed only one white family.

Furthermore, some white owners have exploited Negroes by converting a relatively small house into a number of apartments and charging each Negro family almost the same price they once charged a white family for the entire premises. This has proved a highly profitable venture, but the social price paid for it has been devastatingly high. Lack of space within the apartment has pushed Negro youths into the streets. These areas have generally lacked playgrounds and other recreational facilities. With nothing to do, time hangs heavily on the hands of such boys and girls. In some cases antisocial gangs have been formed.[11] A complete lack of privacy within the home has exposed Negro youngsters to a very early knowledge of sex. Since these sections are usually slum areas, Negro youths soon become acquainted with the various rackets and other criminal activities common to such parts of any large city.

In the past, segregation in housing was accomplished by means of the *restrictive covenant*. This was an agreement entered into by the purchaser of a home that he would never sell it to Negroes or members of other minorities. The United States Supreme Court will no longer uphold such agreements, but this has by no means solved the problem. When middle-class Negroes do succeed in purchasing a home in a white district, their lives have been threatened, their homes have been bombed or set afire, and they have become the target for continual petty annoyances. The Negro who wishes to rear his children in a decent residential area generally faces a dilemma. If he moves into a white area he may place the lives of his family in jeopardy or risk the destruction of his property. If he remains in the slum area, he may see his children exposed to the vice that exists there. As a result the vast majority of Negroes find themselves confined to what are sometimes called "black belts," either through lack of funds to move elsewhere or, if possessing the money, because of the discriminatory practices of some white persons.

---

[11] John J. Kane, "The Tops and Bottoms: A Study of Negro Boys' Gangs in West Philadelphia," *American Catholic Sociology Review*, 60 (June 1948), pp. 74-83.

Many whites have accused Negroes of a technique known as "block busting." It is believed that a carefully laid plan exists for a Negro family to move into a block which is completely white, create panic among the residents and compel them to flee. In certain sections of Chicago white residents have been harassed by telephone calls day and night from persons asking them if they cared to sell their homes. This has gone so far that in some areas of this city notices are posted on properties stating that they are not for sale. There is reason to believe that this technique can be laid to a few real estate speculators, who thus repurchased property at a very low price from white residents fearing a Negro invasion, selling it to Negroes at a much higher price. In this case both the white owners and the new Negro owners are exploited. The obvious answer to the problem is a firm refusal by white persons to panic merely because a Negro family moves to the street.

Recently, when a builder proposed to construct homes in the suburbs of a large city and set aside a certain number of them for Negro families, many of the residents protested vigorously. It was decided to rezone that particular tract of land so that no homes at all could be built there. Thus far, this action has been upheld by the courts.

In 1950 the proportion of owner-occupancies of houses by whites was 55 per cent, compared to a 35.2 percentage of Negroes.[12] Part of this difference may be explained by the generally lower income of Negroes, but some of it must also be traceable to the difficulties Negroes encounter when they attempt to secure mortgage loans. Even Negro veterans who had the benefit of the G.I. Bill found borrowing money a problem.

However, there are some hopeful signs. Banks and loan associations are becoming increasingly aware of the Negro market and the Negro's desperate plight in the field of housing. One builder, who has erected large numbers of prefabricated homes, recently announced that in his new project provision will be made for Negroes. It seems entirely likely that Negroes and whites can live together harmoniously, and, recently, some Negro leaders have been talking about a quota system by which 10 or 20 per cent of all housing would be occupied by Negroes, the rest by whites. But until the present stereotype of the

---

[12] *Notes on the Economic Situation of Negroes in the United States* (Washington, D.C.: U.S. Bureau of Labor Statistics, 1958), p. 45.

Negro and the belief that his entry into a neighborhood means its deterioration are broken down, integrated housing will be difficult. Perhaps integration can be accomplished most readily as a larger middle class of Negroes emerges and as white people learn to make the same distinctions regarding Negroes that they now make regarding members of their own race.

EDUCATION

In American society one of the best methods of vertical mobility is believed to be a formal education. The lower income and occupational status of the American Negro as well as the inferior housing in which he lives are all in part associated with the fact that his educational opportunities are considerably more limited than those of whites. In 1940, the median years of school completed by white persons 25 years of age and over was 8.6; for nonwhites, it was 5.8. By 1950 this figure had risen to 9.3 for white persons and to 6.9 years for nonwhites.[13] But median years of education in themselves tell relatively little. There is the question of the type of education available to the individual. Most Negroes reside in the South, which spends less for public education than all other parts of the country combined. In 1951, the current average expenditure per pupil in average daily attendance (minus dropouts, etc.) at public, elementary, and secondary day schools for the country at large was $224. In Florida, it was $196; in Virginia, $157; in North Carolina, $155; in Tennessee, $138; in Georgia, $133; in South Carolina, $132; and in Alabama, $126. Mississippi, with the lowest amount for the entire country, spent $93 per pupil.[14] On the other hand the South spends proportionately more of its income on education than many northern states such as New York—but since this income is low to begin with, the actual amount is considerably smaller.

In view of this situation it may appear surprising that the South attempts to operate two separate school systems, one for whites and one for Negroes. Furthermore, there is an unequal division of funds between the races. In 1952 the expenditure per Negro student

---

[13] *Statistical Abstract of the United States, 1954*, p. 121.
[14] *Statistical Abstract of the United States, 1954*, p. 116.

in nine southern states was 70 per cent of that for a white student. The length of the school year for Negro pupils is somewhat shorter than for whites, although it has recently been increased. Various other inequalities have existed or continue to exist in Negro and white schools, such as differing teachers' salaries, library facilities, laboratory facilities, buildings, and equipment. In other words the so-called separate but equal facilities are considerably more separate than they are equal.

Professor E. Franklin Frazier has pointed out the economic futility of attempting to maintain separate schools for each race. He states that Missouri had built a new school of Journalism on the Lincoln University campus for Negroes which cost $65,000 in 1941 and employed a faculty costing $13,000 annually. Between 1941 and 1943 the student body increased from 2 to 14 and then declined.[15] In the state of Oklahoma, $15,500 was spent for the salaries of a dean and two professors in the law school established for Negroes, although the young woman for whom the school had been established refused to attend.[16]

In the North the situation is somewhat different. While many public schools have both Negro and white students, school districts are often set up in such a way that there will be no Negro pupils in certain schools. In other cases the enrollment may be over-whelmingly Negro or overwhelmingly white. The heavy migration of southern Negroes to northern cities during and after the Second World War has likewise created problems in schools. A fourth-grade Negro student from a southern school may not be capable of carrying on the work required in the fourth grade of a northern school. At times, such students become disciplinary problems and arouse invidious comments about members of their race. Occupational discrimination against Negroes is no secret to colored students, and in some cases militates against their taking school work seriously. Neither are the social disorganization of the slum areas in which many Negroes live and the resultant family problems conducive to study.

Negroes likewise encounter discrimination in graduate and professional schools, particularly medical schools. Most Negro physicians are graduates of Howard University Medical College or Meharry Medical College in Nashville, Tenn. About 70 Negro physicians are

---

[15] Frazier, *op. cit.*, p. 487.
[16] Frazier, *op. cit.*, p. 487.

graduated from each of these two schools and about 12 come from northern medical schools. E. Franklin Frazier states that the relatively small number of Negro graduates from northern medical schools is the result of a policy of excluding or discouraging the attendance of Negroes. He likewise claims that medical education at Negro institutions is inferior, and, over a period of 44 years between 1903 to 1946, the graduates of Howard and Meharry had a record of 16.7 per cent and 28.9 per cent failures respectively in state board examinations as compared with 3.1 per cent failures for graduates of Harvard and Washington University in St. Louis.[17]

## ECONOMIC STATUS

For most Americans regardless of race, economic status depends upon the amount of the income they receive and the security of the jobs they hold. But money and steady employment are related to the kind of work one does, whether he be employed by someone else, operates his own business, or has a private professional practice. Certain other factors are closely allied with economic security, such as age, health, and education. What then is the economic status of the American Negro?

The median wage or salary income of male whites in 1952 was about $3,400; the income of nonwhite males in the same year was $2,000. White women in 1952 had a median income of $2,000; nonwhite women a little less than $1,000.[18] It is clear that Negroes generally earn considerably lower incomes than whites. But this does not tell the complete story because Negroes are much more likely to be unemployed than white persons.

In April of 1959 there were 700,000 unemployed Negro workers. They comprised one-fifth of all unemployed—about twice their proportion in the labor force. Among Negro men 25 to 44 years of age, the rate of unemployment was three times as high for Negro as for white workers.[19] It still remains a truism that the Negro is the "last hired and the first fired."

---

[17] Frazier, op. cit., pp. 588-89.
[18] Statistical Abstract of the United States, 1954, p. 297.
[19] The Unemployed, Spring 1959 (Washington, D.C.: Bureau of Labor Statistics, Bureau of Employment Security, 1959), p. 30.

Some of these differentials may be explained in part by the lower educational level of American Negroes. However, if the educational level is held constant, there is still a considerable difference in income. In 1940, for example, native white males 25 to 29 years of age who had completed college had a median income of $1,567. Negro males in the same age group with the same education had a median income of $882. Even when his educational background is approximately the same as that of a white person, the Negro apparently earns a considerably lower salary.[20]

There are also striking differences between the percentages of whites and nonwhites in the various occupations. In April of 1959 about 12 per cent of professional and technical workers were whites, compared to less than 5 per cent nonwhites. In managerial positions, about 12 per cent of the persons were white, while less than 3 per cent were nonwhite. In both sales and clerical work the number of nonwhites is disproportionately low, but nonwhites are almost three times as numerous among nonfarm laborers and over three times as numerous in service occupations, including household work.[21] If the Negro is a professional man, he is most likely to be a schoolteacher and most likely on the faculty of a colored institution. The profession with about the second largest number of Negroes is the ministry. For many of these, however, the ministry is a sideline for men who have other occupations. There are relatively few Negro physicians and attorneys.

## THE NEGRO AND CRIME

Practically all studies dealing with the Negro crime rate are in agreement on two points: first, that the Negro crime rate is considerably higher than that of whites and second, that the types of crimes most frequently committed differ with each race. In *An American Dilemma*, Myrdal, using 1939 census data, found that 42.4 native whites and 23.6 foreign-born whites per 100,000 population were received from courts by state and federal prisons, as compared

---

[20] Frazier, *op. cit.*, pp. 606-7.
[21] *The Unemployed, Spring 1959*, p. 33.

to 134.7 Negroes.[22] In 1948, according to the F.B.I.'s Uniform Crime Reports, 73 per cent of the arrests reported were white and 25 per cent were colored. Since nonwhites in the United States at that time were approximately only 10 per cent of the population, the arrest rate was disproportionately high. The rate of juvenile delinquency among urban Negro boys and girls is much higher than that to be expected on the basis of their proportion of the population. In the District of Columbia in 1945, about 73 per cent of the juveniles arrested were Negroes.[23]

Among specific offenses in which the Negro rate considerably exceeds that of the white are homicide, assault, carrying and possessing weapons, receiving or buying stolen goods, gambling, and violation of liquor laws. There are other offenses, however, in which the Negro arrest rate was considerably lower than that of the white. Among these are driving while intoxicated, auto theft, forgery and counterfeiting, drunkenness, embezzlement, and fraud. Behind these differences in specific crime rates are the sub-cultural differences between whites and Negroes in the United States. Counterfeiting requires certain skills which Negroes are not likely to possess. Fraud and embezzlement are frequently a type of white-collar crime committed by a person in his occupational role. Relatively few Negroes find themselves in occupations which make such crimes possible. Auto theft is much more common among white youth than Negro youth and at least one probable reason is that police are more likely to stop and question Negro youths driving an expensive, late-model car than they would whites.

As pointed out, statistics on crime are notoriously inaccurate. The F.B.I.'s Uniform Crime Reports list total crimes known to the police by those jurisdictions reporting. But not all jurisdictions report, some crimes are more likely to be reported to the police than others, and the actual categorization of the offense varies from one place to another. Of all the crimes known to the police, only a small percentage result in arrest, and an even smaller percentage result in conviction. Such factors must be kept in mind in any attempt to assess the Negro crime rate.

---

[22] Gunnar Myrdal, *An American Dilemma: The Negro Problem and Modern Democracy* (New York: Harper & Brothers, 1944), Vol. 2, pp. 966-67.

[23] Frazier, *op. cit.*, p. 651.

Criminologists generally agree that the Negro is more likely to be arrested than the white person, and if arrested more likely to be convicted. If convicted, his chances for probation rather than commitment to a prison are usually lower than those of the white person. When the percentage of commitments to prison of Negroes is considered, the fact of race prejudice cannot be ignored.

But race prejudice alone will not explain the higher Negro crime rate for certain offenses. As a matter of fact the Negro arrest rate as compared to the white is much higher in the North than in the South, even though race prejudice is generally believed to be higher in the South. The reason is that many southern Negroes live in rural areas, and the national crime rate for most offenses is higher in urban than in rural areas. Most northern Negroes are city dwellers. Furthermore, the vast majority live in those areas of the city in which the crime rate remains high regardless of the racial or ethnic background of the people living there. Such areas are usually centers of social disorganization, in which racketeering and vice flourish. The Negro is exposed to opportunities for criminal activity, and his inability to obtain work, his poverty, and his insecurity are probably factors that facilitate anti-social behavior. But no single factor here should be considered a simple explanation of crime causation. Rather all these factors may constitute a syndrome which motivates criminal activity.

It is also worth noting that the Negro crime rate in northern cities seems to increase as masses of southern Negroes move north. Many of these are young males in the age brackets where the crime rate for both the white and Negro races is highest. Adjustment to life in northern cities is not easy for southern Negroes, and may be another factor which influences their crime rate.

### FROM 1954 TO THE PRESENT

In 1954 the U.S. Supreme Court declared that in the field of public education the doctrine of "separate but equal" (i.e., having separate but equivalent, often parallel facilities for each race) has no place. While this marked a change in the legal aspects of race relations in the United States it was more of an evolution than a revolution because in the years prior to 1954 Supreme Court decisions had increasingly been spelling out the basic civil rights of minorities. At this time, however, the Supreme Court did not indicate how states were to carry out its decision regarding desegregation in public schools. But about a year later the court ruled that desegregation should proceed with "deliberate speed." In 1956 the Supreme Court affirmed the decision of a lower court against racial segregation in tax-supported colleges and universities and thus in effect extended its decision of 1954 to institutions of higher learning as well as elementary and secondary schools.

But after almost six years and a number of law suits the Southern Education Reporting Service in April of 1960 stated that of the 17 affected states and the District of Columbia only West Virginia and the District of Columbia had been completely desegregated. Out of 3,039,133 Negroes in southern public schools, only 6 per cent are attending integrated classes.[24] Nevertheless, progress in desegregation did occur in Baltimore and St. Louis. Generally, the border states cities were able to integrate their schools, and in those states where the Negro population was relatively low, such as West Virginia, integration did occur.

Despite the South's general failure to implement the decision of the U.S. Supreme Court, Negroes have pressed forward for such civil rights as voting and the removal of Jim Crow regulations in public restaurants and transportation. They have employed such tactics as boycotts, picketing, "sit-ins" at lunch counters and public places, and demonstrations. White southerners in turn have established White Citizens' Councils, revived the Ku Klux Klan in some sections, and employed violence. In Little Rock, Arkansas, President Eisenhower sent in troops to compel Governor Faubus to open the high school to Negro students.[25]

A commission on Civil Rights was appointed by President Eisenhower to investigate disenfranchisement of Negroes, and, while it encountered considerable difficulty, civil rights legislation was introduced into the Congress in 1960. Although this resulted in the longest filibuster in the history of the U.S. Senate, the bill was passed in April of 1960.

---

[24] *Time* (Apr. 18, 1960), p. 16.
[25] James W. Van der Zanden, "The Klan Revival," *American Journal of Sociology*, 65 (Mar. 1960), pp. 456-62.

## THE BLACK MUSLIMS

From time to time throughout American history Negro protest movements of a militant nature have appeared. During slavery some took the form of actual rebellions. The National Association for the Advancement of Colored People, The Urban League, and certain aspects of Father Divine's religious movement also have protest aspects. Marcus Garvey's efforts during the 1920's to establish Negro business enterprises as well as a steamship company by which Negroes could return to Africa would also fit into this category. However, perhaps the most militant organization ever established by Negroes is the "Black Muslims." It is believed to consist of 100,000 militant Negroes who have as their goal the treatment of the white man in the United States as they feel he ought to be treated. In 1960 there were 69 temples, or "missions," in 27 states. The leader is Elijah Muhammad and the demand of his organization is that this country establish a separate Negro state which would occupy about one-fifth of American territory. The rationale for this demand is that the Negro was deprived of his rights during the period of slavery, was not reimbursed for his services, and has suffered so much at the hands of white men that this would be just restitution.[26]

While they claim to be neither pacifists nor aggressors, and generally observe the letter of the law (avoiding "sit-ins," for example), they still maintain that if anyone attacks a Negro the Negro must lay down his life. There have been some tense situations but to date little violence. Police authorities maintain a careful watch on this sect as does the F.B.I. But C. Eric Lincoln believes there is a widespread view among Negro youth associated with this movement that ultimately the white man should be physically attacked by Negroes. The following statement of a New York youth is considered by Lincoln to be typical:

> Man, I don't care what those (Muslims) cats say *out loud*—that's just a hype they're putting on for The Man (i.e. the white man). Let me tell you—they've got some stuff for The Man even the Mau

---

[26] From *The Black Muslims in America*, by C. Eric Lincoln. © 1961 by C. Eric Lincoln. (Boston: Beacon Press, 1961), pp. 4-22. Reprinted by permission of the Beacon Press.

Mau didn't have . . . I grew up with some of the cats in that temple—went to school with them; ran around with them. Man those cats have changed. They ain't for no light playing. Those cats are for real, and you had better believe it! [27]

The emergence of this movement in the United States is probably associated with the world-wide attempts of nonwhite colonial people to attain freedom and equality. It is believed that American Negroes have a strong sense of identification with them.

The racial and national identity of the leader, Elijah Muhammad, is unknown. He first appeared in Detroit in 1930 as a peddler, claiming to be an Arab. He was known as "The Prophet" and began warning Negroes against the use of certain foods and giving other health advice. At first he used the Bible for religious instruction, but his interpretation was that it would only serve until Negroes were introduced to the "Holy Qur'an" (or Koran). He became increasingly bitter toward the white race, began to attack the teachings of the Bible, and stimulated emotional crises at his meetings in which people underwent sudden "conversions" and became his followers.

His income comes from contributions totaling one-third of all earnings by the Muslim members, and there is some question as to the potential political power of this group. But it is extremely difficult to obtain accurate information about the Muslims. White persons are not admitted to their meetings, and Negroes who attend are carefully searched before entering. It is impossible to predict the future of this movement. At present it appears to be relatively small, if 100,000 members constitute an accurate figure.[28] It has many characteristics of a colorful religious sect. It may simply die out, or it may develop into a more formal, restrained, and dignified organization. At present the latter possibility seems remote. However, it is another indication that the pacifism of the American Negro in seeking equality is diminishing.

## SITUATIONAL-VALUE ANALYSIS

Race relations in the U.S. constitute one of the major social problems of the 20th century. The situation of the American Negro

---

[27] Lincoln, *op. cit.*, p. 5 (from a series of street interviews by the author).
[28] Lincoln, *op. cit.*

in the past and present has already been discussed at length. It is clear that in some sections of the country he is denied the civil rights granted him through amendments to the Constitution. In certain places he is denied his right to vote and discriminated against in public transportation, restaurants, hotels, housing, education, and occupational opportunities. Denial of these rights has been termed the "American Dilemma" because according to the law of the land Americans shall enjoy equal rights under the law. This is part of the democratic tradition and continual refusal to grant such equality represents a value conflict.

Many white Americans freely admit as much and strongly support all measures to insure interracial justice. Many, however, do not, and all of those who oppose equal rights for the Negro are not confined to the southern states. Many of the rationalizations used in the past, such as the reputed intellectual inferiority of Negroes, their happiness in a subservient position, and others, have been refuted by scientific research or by the actual demands of American Negroes. Even the legal devices used to deny the Negro his basic rights have either been rejected by the courts or apparently soon will be.

By 1945, 12 states and 37 cities had enacted statutes against racial, religious, or ethnic discrimination. Some cities have established commissions to enforce these laws, among them being Chicago, Minneapolis, New York, Philadelphia, Cincinnati, and others. They vary in effectiveness, depending upon the kinds of sanctions employed. Some of them attempt to use persuasion only and this apparently is not entirely ineffective since many businesses prefer not to have it known publicly that they are discriminating against any minority group.

In addition, a number of societies, organizations, and associations have been formed to help the Negro. The Catholic Interracial Society was established about a quarter of a century ago and now has units in a number of cities. American college students in the North have demonstrated in behalf of Negro rights. The NAACP has done outstanding work in the fight for desegregation in education and in other areas. The Urban League, another Negro organization, has sought occupational opportunities for Negroes. The National Conference of Christians and Jews, by means of educational methods such as workshops, literature, and films, has attempted to change public opinion in America. The effort to secure equality of opportunity for the Negro is no longer confined to members of that race or to a few white leaders.

Very recently, new organizations have emerged to fight for civil rights in a highly direct fashion. One of these is the Student Nonviolent Coordinating Committee (SNICK) led by James Forman of Chicago. Its members are the "shock troops" on the civil rights front in "sit-ins," boycotts, and other demonstrations. Another organization is the Southern Christian Leadership Conference, consisting of 65 local civil rights groups in the South and headed by the Reverend Martin Luther King, Jr., who became nationally well known for leading a successful effort to integrate buses in Montgomery, Alabama in 1956. The third organization is the Congress of Racial Equality (C.O.R.E.), composed of Northern whites and Negroes under the leadership of James Farmer. This group organized the first "Freedom Ride" from Washington to New Orleans, but withdrew after mob violence in Birmingham.[29]

The situation of the American Negro has improved considerably since 1940. While complete attainment of Negro rights is not in the immediate offing, it is probably closer than at any time in American History. As more Negroes are offered adequate educational facilities, better economic opportunities, and decent housing, it is inevitable that a larger middle-class Negro society will emerge and discrimination will lessen. Sociologically, the situation is changing for the American Negro and to the extent that the value system of American society actually does believe in equality of opportunity, it will probably be extended to American Negroes.

REMEDIAL MEASURES

While the American Negro has made considerable progress educationally, economically, politically, and socially in recent years, he has yet to attain the equality which is due him in a democratic society. The situation is considerably more hopeful today than it was 20 or 30 years ago. Various approaches may be employed to help American Negroes attain their deserved status in American society.

[29] *Time* (Jan. 12, 1962), p. 15.

Perhaps the most important are: equal educational opportunities, equal political opportunities, and equal social opportunities.

The legal approach to this problem is best exemplified by legislation in the field of civil rights and attempts to enforce laws regarding the franchise of Negroes. Desegregation of interstate travel and use of such facilities associated with it as bus terminals, railroad stations, and restaurants is now underway. While these are proceeding more slowly than many would desire, such desegregation seems ultimately inevitable.

Desegregation of schools, also proceeding slowly, presents certain problems in some communities. These communities are not exclusively located in the South. As pointed out earlier, desegregation in education itself is meaningless unless economic opportunities to apply such education exist. But again, serious efforts have been made in many cities and states to accomplish this.

But another kind of education, aside from the formal, is necessary if the laws of the land are to be truly meaningful. This may be better accomplished by volunteer organizations such as the National Conference of Christians and Jews, the Catholic Interracial Society, and similar groups which attempt to persuade Americans that racial discrimination is both undemocratic and immoral. Perhaps the basic situation of the American Negro today is best summed up by stating that he is on his way, but he has a long way to go before he secures his full democratic rights and privileges, and all legitimate avenues to facilitate this goal should be employed.

## REVIEW QUESTIONS

1. Define "race." Is there a "pure" race?
2. What was the condition of American Negroes between their arrival in America and the end of the Civil War?
3. Were reconstruction measures successful in establishing a democratic status for the American Negro?
4. What is meant by "racial etiquette"? What was the purpose of the grandfather clauses?
5. How has Negro leadership changed its goals in attempting to secure improved conditions for American Negroes?
6. What caused the movement of Negroes from the South to Northern cities? How has this resulted in interracial problems in the North?

7. Do racially segregated schools hamper the education of American Negroes?

8. How do prejudice and discrimination against American Negroes influence their income?

9. The Negro has a higher crime rate, according to statistics, than white persons. Are there any adequate explanations for this difference?

10. Who are the Black Muslims? To what extent does this movement reflect a new attitude toward American Negroes?

11. In terms of situational factors and American values analyze the factors which resulted in the present status of the American Negro.

12. List some remedial measures which may be employed to improve the situation of the American Negro.

## SELECTED READINGS

*Articles*

Antonovski, Aaron and Melvin J. Lerner, "Occupational Aspirations of Lower Class Negro and White Youth," *Social Problems,* 7 (Fall 1959), 132-38.

Augustine, Brother Dominick, "The Catholic College Man and the Negro," *American Catholic Sociological Review,* 8 (Oct. 1947), 204-8.

Campbell, Ernest Q. and Thomas F. Pettigrew, "Racial and Moral Crises: The Role of Little Rock Ministers," *American Journal of Sociology,* 64 (Mar. 1959), 494-504.

Eckard, E. W., "How Many Negroes Pass?" *American Journal of Sociology,* 52 (May 1947), 498-500.

Foley, Albert S., "The Status and Role of the Negro Priest in the American Catholic Clergy." *American Catholic Sociological Review,* 15 (June 1955), 83-93.

E. Franklin Frazier, "Race Contacts in the Social Structure," *American Sociological Review,* 14 (Feb. 1949), 1-10.

Golden, Joseph, "Characteristics of Negro-White Intermarriage in Philadelphia," *American Sociological Review,* 18 (Apr. 1953), 177-83.

Harte, Thomas J., "Scalogram Analysis of Catholic Attitudes Toward the Negro," *American Catholic Sociological Review,* 12 (June 1951), 66-74.

Herr, David M., "The Sentiment of White Supremacy: An Ecological Study," *American Journal of Sociology,* 64 (May 1959), 592-98.

Kephart, William M., "Is the American Negro Becoming Lighter? An Analysis of the Sociological and Biological Trends," *American Sociological Review,* 13 (Aug. 1948), 437-43.

Lee, Oscar J., "Protestant Churches and Public School Desegregation," *Social Problems*, 2 (Apr. 1955), 212-14.

Mihanovich, Clement S., "Characteristics of the Negro Family in St. Louis, Missouri," *The American Catholic Sociological Review*, 7 (Mar. 1946), 53-57.

Monahan, Thomas P. and Elizabeth H. Monahan, "Some Characteristics of American Negro Leaders," *American Sociological Review*, 21 (Aug. 1956), 589-95.

Turner, Ralph H., "The Relative Position of the Negro Male in the Labor Force of Large American Cities," *American Sociological Review*, 16 (Aug. 1951), 524-29.

*Books*

Campbell, Ernest Q., *When a City Closes its Schools*. Chapel-Hill University of North Carolina Press, 1961.

Drake, St. Clair, *Black Metropolis*. New York: Harcourt, Brace & World, Inc., 1945.

Glazer, Nathan, ed., *Studies in Housing and Minority Groups*. Berkeley: University of California Press, 1960.

Reitzers, Dietrich C., *Negroes and Medicine*. Cambridge, Mass: Harvard University Press, 1958.

Rudwick, Elliot T. and W. E. B. DuBois, *A Study in Minority Group Leadership*. Philadelphia: University of Pennsylvania Press, 1961.

Shuey, Audrey M., *The Testing of Negro Intelligence*. Lynchburg, Va.: The J. P. Bell Co., 1958.

# 13

# The Jews as a

# Minority Group

J UDAISM is a religion. Israel is a nation. But all Jews do not belong to the Jewish faith and most Jews do not live in Israel. Therefore, it is not possible to define "Jews" as a nationality or a religious group. Efforts to categorize Jews as a race are also useless. Race is the common possession of certain physical characteristics transmitted through heredity. In the course of centuries Jews have wandered throughout most of the world and have intermarried with various peoples. Jews as a religious group can be found in various races other than the Caucasoid. Neither is there any common physical characteristic which make Jews easily identifiable. If it is possible to categorize Jews at all, it seems best to use the term *ethnic group*. An ethnic group is usually defined as a number of people who retain their culture—or perhaps better, their sub-culture—in the face of an alien culture. Milton L. Barron says that practically speaking the Jews are those people who either consider themselves Jews or are so considered by others regardless of the criteria of identification.[1] The rabbi who described Jews as a people in quest of a definition may have defined them rather well.[2]

Despite the fact that Jews are not a race, it is still true that many Jews in the United States are identifiable as such. The basis of the identification, however, is complex. It may be accent, although this is not always true. It may be gestures, although gestures of American-born Jews are quite different from those of Jews born in Eastern Europe. The shape of the nose, usually considered an index of Jewishness, may not be at all "Jewish," and if it is, it is equally characteristic of Arabs and certain other peoples. Dress has ceased to be any indication of Jewishness and the ear locks worn by the Orthodox are rarely found today. Family names may give more clue but in many cases these have been anglicized. In other words there are no wholly reliable criteria by which American Jews can be recognized. But despite this, it is still possible for many people to point out persons as Jewish, and the more anti-Semitic an individual is, the more likely he is to identify Jews accurately.[3]

## HISTORY OF THE JEWS

Jews were and are a remarkable people. Their original home was in the Near East, a part of the world that was under continual pressure from a number of successive empires.[4] The religions of the ancient world, of which the Jews were a part, were polytheistic. Jews were monotheistic. Friction between Jews and Gentiles apparently resulted from the intolerence with which Jews viewed the religions of other peoples. They also became targets of jealousy when their belief in one God was recognized and they were excused from

---

[1] Milton L. Barron, *American Minorities* (New York: Alfred A. Knopf, Inc., 1957), p. 376.

[2] Reprinted from *American Judaism* by Nathan Glazer by permission of The University of Chicago Press. Copyright 1957 by The University of Chicago. (p. 3).

[3] Theodore Newcomb, *Social Psychology* (New York: The Dryden Press, 1950), p. 577.

[4] George Eaton and J. Milton Yinger, *Racial and Cultural Minorities, An Analysis of Prejudice and Discrimination* (New York: Harper & Brothers, 1953), p. 262.

certain civic duties involving sacrifice and the expenditure of a great deal of money.[5]

On a number of occasions the Jews were forcefully dispersed and ultimately spread throughout Europe. During the Middle Ages they were compelled to live in ghettos and wear prescribed clothing. They became targets of suspicion and violence, two favorite charges being that they practiced ritual murders and poisoned wells to spread disease. Neither of these charges had any basis in fact and the Papacy opposed them.[6] Permission to live in a city depended upon the willingness of the prince, and Jews had to pay for this privilege. From the 12th century onward Jews became royal usurers. At this time Christians were not permitted to lend money for interest since money had a completely different meaning than it has today. As Jews were not Christians they were exempt from this ban.

Jews have been expelled from Spain, Portugal, England, and other countries. It was not until the middle of the 19th century that full emancipation was granted them. However, none of these persecutions deserves to be called anti-Semitism, which originated only in the latter part of the 19th century in Germany, and represented opposition against the social and political activities of Jewish aliens in Europe.[7]

In 1853 Count de Gobineau wrote a book on the inequality of the human races, claiming that everything noble, beautiful, or worth-while was a product of the Aryan race. Heinrich von Treitschke, a German political philosopher, created the slogan, "the Jews are our calamity." In 1899 Houston Stewart Chamberlain published his book, *The Foundations of the 19th Century*, which Parkes says "became the bible of anti-Semites until Hitler's *Mein Kampf* was published.[8] The concept of an Aryan race has no scientific validity. Actually, it refers to a family of languages and not to any specific people. The Aryan race, it was claimed, originated in Germany and nearly every part of that country has been identified as the birthplace of the Aryan.

Toward the end of the 19th century systematic pograms, that is, attacks against Jews, were carried on in Poland, which was part of

---

[5] James Parkes, *The Jewish Problem in the Modern World* (New York: Oxford University Press, Inc., 1946), p. 6.
[6] Parkes, *op. cit.*, p. 13.
[7] Parkes, *op. cit.*, p. 35 ff.
[8] Parkes, *op. cit.*, pp. 44-45.

Russia, and in Russia itself. These attacks, it is believed, were carried on with the connivance of the Russian government. At any rate the police did very little to prevent or stop them until they had been underway for several days. Finally, however, the government did announce that the Western frontier of Russia was open and a large number of Jews began immediately to leave for the United States.[9]

JEWS IN AMERICA

In 1654 a number of Jewish families fleeing persecution in Brazil landed in New Amsterdam and founded the first American Jewish community. While some Jews had been in the North American colonies prior to that date, Nathan Glazer says they were not the founders of the Jewish community in this country.[10] There were three waves of Jewish immigration to the United States. The first was composed of *Sephardic* Jews, that is, those of Spanish background who had been expelled from Spain in the year that Columbus discovered America. Most of these came before the end of the 18th century, and Jewish settlements were established in New York, Newport, Charleston, Savannah, Philadelphia, and Richmond. These were followed by the *Ashkenazin*, that is, Jews from Germany and their descendants in other lands. Many of these came to the United States as a result of the revolution of 1848 in Germany. The third great wave of Jewish immigrants occurred in what is described as the new immigration, beginning about 1882. Most of these persons came from Eastern Europe, mainly Poland and Russia. In fact, their movement into the country, interrupted temporarily by World War I, continued until cut off by the immigrant quota system of the twenties.

In 1840 the American Jewish population was estimated at 15,000, and by 1880 it had grown to 250,000. By this time the Jewish community in the United States was very largely a German community.[11] By 1914 about a million and a quarter Jews from Eastern Europe

---

[9] Parkes, *op. cit.*, pp. 64-65.
[10] Glazer, *op. cit.*, p. 12.
[11] Glazer, *op. cit.*, p. 23.

had entered this country.[12] There were certain differences between Sephardic and Ashkenazic Jews and the later immigrants from Eastern Europe. Even before the German Jews came, the Spanish Jews had been well acculturated to American Life. The German Jews, who arrived toward the middle of the 19th century, found excellent opportunities in this country and rather quickly achieved vertical mobility upward. They settled in communities in the Middle West and in other sections of the country. This was not to be the case with the latest wave of Jewish immigrants, most of whom were extremely poor, and took up residence in the eastern seaboard cities. They belonged to Orthodox Judaism which is based upon strict interpretation of the Talmud and rigorous adherence to the dietary laws. It is this last group which forms the stereotyped image of the Jew held by many Americans.

## THE DIVISIONS OF JUDAISM

While Jews are usually lumped together as a homogenous group, this is far from the truth. There are really three divisions of the Judaic religion: Orthodox, Reformed, and Conservative. The Orthodox, as explained above, adhere more or less to the traditional Judaism of the past. The Reform movement, traceable to the German Jews, was an effort to adjust Judaism to the contemporary American life of the last century. Many of these people had achieved some economic success and had improved their social status. They wanted a religion which was in keeping with their newly acquired social class. The synagogue became the temple, services were held on Sundays and a Sunday school was established. Conservative Judaism, which arose later, is a sort of middle way between the Orthodox and Reformed version. Jews do seek affiliation with the Jewish community through synagogues and temples, although this identification could be avoided if Jews desired. Today about 50 per cent of America's Jews refrain from this commitment.[13] Despite the

---

[12] Glazer, *op. cit.*, p. 60.

[13] Albert I. Gordon, *Jews in Suburbia* (Boston: Beacon Press, 1959), pp. 152-53.

fact that there are differences among the Orthodox, Reformed, and Conservative Jews, Jews in suburbia decide which type of congregation they will establish by a majority vote.[14]

## SOCIAL CHARACTERISTICS OF AMERICAN JEWS

Jews are a predominantly urban people. Today they make up between 5 and 6 million of the U.S. population, or roughly between three and four per cent. About one-third of American Jews live in the New York metropolitan area and most of the others live in large cities or suburbs of such cities. Occupationally, Jews are most likely to be in small business enterprises, the clothing trade, and to some extent motion picture production and the professions. In a study of Jewish communities carried on in the thirties the following occupational distribution was found in San Francisco:

> Eighteen out of every 1,000 gainfully employed Jews were lawyers or judges, 16 were doctors (among non-Jews 5 out of every 1,000 were lawyers and judges; the same doctors). In Pittsburgh, 14 out of every 1,000 gainfully employed Jews were lawyers or judges, 13 were doctors (among non-Jews, the figures for each of these occupations was 4).[15]

Respect and love of scholarship are a well-known Jewish characteristic and are underscored by the high percentage of Jewish youth which finishes high school and college. In Howard Bell's study *Youth Tell Their Story,* published in 1938, 65 per cent of Jewish youth in Maryland—as compared with 40 per cent of Protestant youth, and 28 per cent of Catholic youth—completed high school. A national study made in 1947 by Helen Davis found that out of 10,063 high school seniors, male and female, 68 per cent of Jewish students had applied for admission to college. The national norm for such application was 35 per cent. Other studies of college youth revealed that, generally speaking, Jews tend to complete college to a much greater extent than Protestant or Catholic youth.[16]

---

[14] Gordon, *op. cit.,* p. 97.

[15] Glazer, *op. cit.,* p. 82.

[16] John J. Kane, *Catholic-Protestant Conflicts in America* (Chicago: Henry Regnery Co., 1955), pp. 74-75.

In the study *They Went to College* it was found that one-third of Jewish college graduates became proprietors, managers, and executives. Forty-five per cent of Jewish graduates entered the non-teaching professions.[17] Contrary to popular belief, however, Jews are not found in large numbers in the field of banking, and they are not as a rule top-flight executives in large corporations. Jews have fewer than their expected numbers in heavy manufacturing, and less than 2 per cent of the Jewish population is in agriculture, whereas 17.5 per cent of the gainfully employed are in that field.[18]

It is quite clear that American Jews, including those who came in the new immigration after 1882, are to be found in the middle class, particularly in the upper-middle class. They have successfully used the various roads to vertical mobility upward, particularly college, graduate work, and professional schools. They seem to have risen more rapidly than certain other immigrant groups, and this no doubt is one factor in American anti-Semitism.

## ANTI-SEMITISM

Anti-Semitism is a prejudice against Jews which is revealed in discriminations against them in economic, political, and social life. It is not directed against Judaism as a religion, and in fact some anti-Semites claim they behave so only because some Jews are irreligious. While Negroes are criticized for their failure to compete successfully, Jews are criticized because they compete too successfully with gentiles. While this is obviously illogical, no one should expect to find much logic behind prejudice and discrimination. The forms that anti-Semitism takes are various. Among them are exclusion of Jews from select residential areas, the denial of membership in certain country clubs and other organizations, and the use of quota systems in colleges and, particularly, professional schools, especially medical colleges.

In 1877 a Jewish banker, Joseph Seligman, was refused admission to the Grand Union Hotel in Saratoga. This caused widespread indignation, and newspapers published editorials criticizing the hotel. It is claimed that by 1880 private schools in New York began to close their

[17] Kane, *op. cit.*, p. 78.
[18] Simpson and Yinger, *op. cit.*, p. 384.

doors to Jewish children, and advertisements for summer resorts began to indicate that Jews would be unwelcome.[19] A well-known novel, *Gentleman's Agreement*, depicted the plight of a man who pretended to be a Jew. He soon discovered that the exclusive country clubs and exclusive resort hotels were exclusively gentile.

In the United States, anti-Semitism had never taken the acute form that it did in Europe, particularly in Germany under Hitler, when it became the overt policy of the government. It reached its apex in Europe during the Second World War when Germany and countries under its domination literally murdered millions of Jews in concentration camps and gas chambers. When anti-Semitism first broke out in the earlier days of the Hitler regime, it was not immediately and vigorously opposed by all Americans. As a matter of fact, certain anti-Semitic movements began in this country and, incidentally, still exist.

Jewish synagogues and temples have been defaced, Jewish youths physically attacked, and Jewish cemeteries desecrated. The notorious "Protocols of the Elders of Zion," a fraudulent document in which it was claimed that a meeting of Jewish leaders had planned to seize control of the world, was first circulated in Europe. It was written in French and translated into Russian by Sergei Nilus, a fanatic. Later, a New York Times correspondent in Constantinople found the original document, which was a satire on the autocracy and ambitions of Napoleon III. Despite this fact it was circulated in the United States by a well-known automobile manufacturer, who later retracted it. But it still appears from time to time.

Some of the most overt discrimination against Jews has occurred in American medical schools. Frank Kindon found that the percentage of Jewish graduates of the City College of New York admitted to medical school dropped from 58.4 per cent in 1925 to 15.0 per cent in 1943. B'nai B'rith found that the percentage of Jewish students in graduate and professional schools had dropped from about 14 per cent in 1935 to about 10 percent in 1946. Dental colleges had dropped their Jewish enrollment by about one-third within the same period of time.[20] Recently this discrimination seems to have decreased.

---

[19] Glazer, *op. cit.*, p. 45.

[20] Edward C. McDonagh, "Status Level of American Jews," in *American Minorities*, ed. Milton L. Barron (New York: Alfred A. Knopf, Inc., 1957), pp. 397-98.

## SOCIAL BACKGROUND IN ANTI-SEMITISM

To what extent are educational, occupational, social class, and religious backgrounds associated with anti-Semitism? Various studies have attempted to investigate the influence of such factors.[21] The author attempted to measure anti-Semitism among Catholic college students by means of a questionnaire study. The respondents were overwhelmingly undergraduate male students in a small Catholic college in the East. A few women in the evening school and a small number of students at a nearby school of industrial relations were likewise included but there were not enough such respondents to warrant a separate breakdown for them. The first 17 items of the questionnaire dealt with various background factors such as age, presence or absence of siblings, father's occupation, etc. The last 12 items are presented in Table 13-1.

Responses to Question 27 varied so much that its inclusion was useless. It inquired about the total Jewish population of the United States and most respondents had no idea of what it was.

On the basis of this questionnaire it is clear that among the Catholic students responding the majority did not believe that there was an excessive number of Jewish physicians, or that most Jews were communists, wealthy, or draft-dodgers. More than half of the respondents did not dislike Jews. More than two out of three were willing to entertain Jews in their homes, and to have Jews as friends on the same basis as non-Jews. But these Catholic respondents showed a fairly highly prejudiced attitude in such areas as business (Question 18), influence (Question 24), and immigration (Questions 25 and 26).

In "A Public Opinion Study on anti-Semitism in New York" by Duane Robinson and Sylvia Rhode, administered to a random sample of the population, it was asked: "Do you think that the Jews have too much power in the U.S.?" This is similar to Question 24 in table 13-1. Seventeen per cent of total responses to the Robinson-Rhode study were "yes," but 53 per cent replied in the affirmative to Question 24. This seems to indicate that male Catholic college

---

[21] Simpson and Yinger, *op. cit.*, pp. 294-300.

TABLE 13-1[22]

GENERAL SUMMARY*

(This table includes all the responses made to the questionnaire)

| | Yes | No | Don't Know |
|---|---|---|---|
| 18. Do you think that the Jews own too many stores in Philadelphia? | 195 53.0% | 101 27.0% | 67 20.0% |
| 19. Do you think that there are too many Jewish doctors? | 67 18.0% | 214 61.0% | 89 21.0% |
| 20. Do you think that most Jews are Communistic? | 59 13.0% | 245 69.0% | 68 18.0% |
| 21. Do you generally dislike Jews? | 151 42.0% | 204 58.0% | — — |
| 22. Do you think that most Jews evaded the draft? | 118 32.0% | 178 48.0% | 73 20.0% |
| 23. Do you think that most Jews are wealthy? | 125 33.0% | 195 53.0% | 52 14.0% |
| 24. Do you think that the Jews have too much influence in the U.S. | 198 53.0% | 126 34.0% | 45 13.0% |
| 25. Should the U.S. admit 100,000 refugees to the U.S., including Jews? | 106 26.2% | 228 68.0% | 41 7.8% |
| 26. Would you be willing to admit 100,000 refugees, if not Jewish? | 135 36.5% | 185 50.1% | 49 13.4% |
| 28. Do you think that the Jews are a real threat to the U.S.? | 72 11.3% | 248 67.0% | 50 11.7% |
| 29. Would you be willing to entertain Jews in your own home? | 257 69.4% | 83 22.4% | 30 8.2% |
| 30. Would you be willing to have Jews as friends on the same basis as non-Jewish friends? | 256 69.3% | 94 25.4% | 19 5.3% |

* The total number of questionnaires studied was 374. In some cases as many as nine or more failed to reply to a specific question, so the total number of cases varies for each question.

On many of the tables that follow, the total number of questionnaires studied drops considerably. In some cases the necessary information, such as age or residence was not provided. In all tables except this one, women's responses were omitted because there were so few women in the study.

[22] Adapted from John J. Kane, "Anti-Semitism Among Catholic College Students," *American Catholic Sociological Review,* 8 (Oct. 1947), p. 211.

288

students in this area express considerably greater anti-Semitic attitudes than a random sampling of the New York population, which, incidentally, included Jews. However, the New York study was broken down in terms of Jews, Catholics, Protestants, and others, and also according to three economic classes. In the upper economic class 33 per cent of Catholics thought that Jews had too much power in the United States; in the middle economic class 27 per cent; and in the lower economic class 29 per cent. Most of the Catholic students in the study cited here came from the middle economic class. Yet their percentage of affirmative responses regarding Jewish influence was almost twice as great as the percentage of Catholics in the middle economic class in the New York study.

According to the breakdown by father's occupation in Table 13-2, sons of those in the professional and unskilled groups showed the least prejudice generally. Breaking it down further, however, the unskilled group showed the least dislike of Jews, probably because they are rarely in competition with them. This does not mean that they do not have contact with Jews. The salesman group ranks first in prejudice in this table, the business group second. This may be explained on the basis of competition. Salesmen and skilled worker groups rank first and second respectively in thinking that the Jews have too much influence in the United States. The skilled group and the business group lead in thinking that the Jews evaded the draft.[24] It seems that those groups whose fathers compete with Jews economically—that is, salesmen and businessmen—are rather prejudiced. It is more difficult to explain the attitude of the skilled worker group. It should be noted that the students themselves are not in economic competition with Jews, but they are in contact with their fathers, who probably are in such competition. This underscores the point that it is not contact with a minority itself which is frequently the cause of prejudice but rather contact with prejudice toward the minority.

The findings of this study, of course, do not prove that Catholics or Catholic college students are necessarily more anti-Semitic than other persons. It does indicate, however, in the sample studied that some of the students are rather highly prejudiced in certain areas.

In the Robinson-Rohde study the lower economic level and the educated Protestants expressed more anti-Semitism than other groups

---

[24] Kane, "Anti-Semitism Among Catholic College Students," p. 215.

TABLE 13-2[23]

RESPONSES ACCORDING TO OCCUPATION OF FATHER*

(Affirmative Responses except as noted.)

| | Un-skilled | Skilled | Sales-men | Busi-ness | Profes-sional |
|---|---|---|---|---|---|
| 18. Do you think that the Jews own too many stores in Philadelphia? | 45 59.2% | 54 51.9% | 9 47.4% | 28 52.7% | 11 44.0% |
| 19. Do you think that there are too many Jewish doctors? | 15 19.1% | 13 12.2% | 4 21.0% | 12 23.0% | 7 27.9% |
| 20. Do you think that most Jews are Communistic? | 15 19.1% | 18 16.8% | 5 26.3% | 5 9.2% | 1 — |
| 21. Do you generally dislike Jews? | 27 35.0% | 42 41.1% | 12 63.1% | 26 48.1% | 11 39.3% |
| 22. Do you think that most Jews evaded the draft? | 16 20.5% | 41 37.7% | 5 29.4% | 19 35.1% | 8 29.7% |
| 23. Do you think that most Jews are wealthy? | 26 33.3% | 43 40.5% | 5 27.7% | 17 31.4% | 6 21.4% |
| 24. Do you think that the Jews have too much influence in the U.S.? | 39 50.6% | 57 54.2% | 12 68.4% | 28 50.9% | 12 42.8% |
| 25. Should the U.S. admit 100,000 refugees to the U.S., including Jews? | 27 35.0% | 31 28.1% | 2 10.5% | 15 26.7% | 7 25.9% |
| 26. Would you be willing to admit 100,000 refugees, if not Jewish? | 25 32.4% | 44 40.0% | 6 31.5% | 20 35.7% | 10 37.7% |
| 28. Do you think that the Jews are a real threat to the U.S.? | 10 12.8% | 22 20.7% | 6 31.5% | 8 14.8% | 7 25.9% |
| *Negative Responses* | | | | | |
| 29. Would you be willing to entertain Jews in your home? | 11 14.6% | 30 28.0% | 4 21.0% | 13 23.6% | 7 25.0% |
| *Negative Responses* | | | | | |
| 30. Would you be willing to have Jews as friends on the same basis as non-Jewish friends? | 14 18.1% | 24 23.3% | 5 26.4% | 22 38.5% | 8 28.5% |

* The total number of cases studied was as follows: Unskilled, 77; Skilled, 104; Salesmen, 19; Business, 53; Professional, 25. In some questions the total responses fell below these totals, since some failed to answer some questions. This explains the apparent discrepancies in certain percentages. In some cases the father was deceased or retired, or no occupation was listed. This reduced the number of responses suitable for study.

[23] Adapted from Kane, "Anti-Semitism Among Catholic College Students," p. 214.

studied. It was suggested that in this group "there are many persons whose positions in the dominant religious group, and perhaps as native-born 'Americans,' contrast painfully with the economic disadvantage and insecurity which they experience. Such a position might lead to feelings of frustration and antagonism which could be channelized readily into anti-Semitic views." [25]

Finally, it should be recalled that both of these studies were done in large cities in the East, neither had a large sampling of respondents, and the study of college students was restricted mainly to male Catholics. It is uncertain that findings in either study can be projected nationally.

## CONTEMPORARY ANTI-SEMITISM

Organized anti-Semitic activity today does not resemble the type that prevailed before the Second World War. Emphasis today is on the dissemination of literature rather than on meetings, picket lines, rallies, and similar demonstrations. "There is also a tendency among prominent ultra-nationalist organizations and leaders to accept—or at least tolerate—hate mongers and their propaganda products." [26]

But Jews continue to suffer discrimination, especially in housing. Along Lake St. Clair just east of Detroit there is an exclusive suburban residential area known as Grosse Pointe. No one is admitted to residence there without successfully passing a screening system.

> Minions of Grosse Pointe—they're called investigators—would seek out, through diverse means, information concerning those who wished to breach the wall of sanctity. These dossiers of prospective entrants contained such important listings as the grammar of the candidates, swarthiness of the skin, education, kinds of friends, of dress, of number of children, and all matters of pedigree." [27]

Eligibility for admission to this community depends upon the number of points a person can earn in the investigation. Jews require

---

[25] Duane Robinson and Sylvia Rohde, "A Public Opinion Study of Anti-Semitism in New York City," *American Sociological Review*, 10 (Aug. 1945), p. 514.

[26] *Anti-Semitic Activity in the United States*, The American Jewish Committee, 1954, p. 17.

[27] *What's the Point of Grosse Pointe?* The American Jewish Committee, New York, 1960, 17:22.

85 points; Southern Europeans (including Italians), 65 points; Poles, 55 points; and all others 50 points. Negroes, of course, are completely excluded. If a Jew is American-born he is credited with 7 points, and if his friends are "typically American" he receives an additional 5 points; but a white Protestant with the same American friends acquires as much as 14 points for this choice of associates. In the case of Jews, "swarthiness" meant the degree to which a person resembled the stereotype Jew.

Dr. Jean Braxton Rosenbaum, a direct descendant of one of the signers of the Declaration of Independence, was turned down by Grosse Pointe as undesirable. He is a professor of psychiatry at Wayne State University. Other Jewish psychiatrists from this university were also refused admission. This is not an isolated incident, because the representative of the Brokers' Association informed the Attorney General's Commission of Michigan that this plan is conducted in other respectable residential communities—but in a more informal manner.[28]

Recently, efforts have been made by the American Nazi party to hold public meetings, and neo-Nazi groups have been found among high school students in some sections of this country. In April, 1959, a dozen public and parochial high school boys in a suburb of Paterson, New Jersey were found to be operating the "Nazi Regime of America." They had in their possession swastika insignia, a gun, and a home-made bomb. They were apprehended when a threatening note was received by a teacher. Another group was uncovered in May of 1959 in a Cleveland high school. It had been formed to get rid of Jews and communists. These boys had made over 300 threatening phone calls, and had set fires at the office of a Jewish agency. While gangs and unrest among American youth are not unusual, it is perhaps surprising to find that some of these youthful offenders have chosen neo-Nazi symbols for expressions of their delinquency.[29]

---

[28] *What's the Point of Grosse Pointe?* The American Jewish Committee.
[29] *Anti-Semitic Activity in the United States,* The American Jewish Committee, p. 18.

## ANTI-SEMITISM AS A SOCIAL PROBLEM

Contemporary anti-Semitism is more subtle now than in the past, and its target includes six million Americans. It attempts to deny Jews equality of opportunity reputedly available to all Americans under law. It is potentially dangerous because the sparks of hatred today could become a conflagration tomorrow under different social circumstances. Quota systems in colleges and professional schools serve to waste the ability and leadership of many American boys and girls. Furthermore, although hate organizations may begin with one minority as a target, they usually have a tendency to spread. In Germany, Hitler first attacked the Jews and later the Catholics and Protestants. Morally, legally, and factually, there is neither basis nor room for anti-Semitism in the United States.

## SITUATIONAL-VALUE APPROACH

Certain situational factors undoubtedly facilitate anti-Semitism within this country. The relatively recent immigrant status of many American Jews is one factor, since opposition to immigration was strong in the United States during the twenties and was expressed in a quota system. Furthermore, Jews are mainly an urban people, and almost one-third of the population of the largest American metropolitan area—New York City—is Jewish. The tendency for Jews to concentrate in certain fields of business and professions makes them even more visible. They tend to be liberal and thus an irritant to ultraconservatives. Numerically they constitute the largest non-Christian denomination in a predominantly Christian nation. They are an intelligent, articulate minority which presses strongly for its rights.

Anti-Semitism has proved a valuable scapegoat in many countries. It has resulted in creating stereotypes of Jews. In view of the relatively few Jews living in the United States compared to the total population, it is probably correct to say that more Americans have been in contact with the stereotypes of Jews than with Jews themselves. One, for example, has been the belief that Jews have unusual mental ability, shrewdness, and competitive ability.[30] There is no proof that any ethnic, religious, or racial group possesses more innate intelligence than any other. There is some evidence that Jews, responding to centuries of persecution, have attempted to compensate for this treatment with increased effort. But this generalization cannot be extended to all Jews. However, if men define situations as real these situations in effect seem to become real in their consequences, and as a result a certain fear of Jews may have been engendered among some Americans.

### REMEDIAL MEASURES

In addition to mayor's commissions, committees on human relations, and various other organizations such as the National Conference of Christians and Jews which attempt to combat all kinds of prejudice and discrimination, a rather notable group is the Anti-Defamation League of B'nai B'rith. Its original goal—which is still primary, although not its exclusive goal—is to contain and overcome anti-Semitism. It has a membership of more than 350,000 men and women, a skilled professional staff, and 27 regional offices in addition to its national headquarters.

One of the basic functions of the A.D.L. is research into discrimination against Jews. It attempts to discover who is guilty of such discrimination, where it occurs, the extent, and the method. It has helped eliminate discriminatory questions on admission forms from more than 800 colleges, gained the support of trade and industry associations (who have agreed not to hold conventions in resorts and hotels which discriminate), and, with the cooperation of industry, has sponsored on-the-job human relations programs. It likewise brings discriminatory practices of all types—whether in housing, employment, education, or public accommodation—to the attention of authorities concerned with the elimination of these practices.

The National Conference of Christians and Jews was established in

---

[30] Robin Williams, Jr., *The Reduction of Inner Group Tensions* (New York: Social Research Council, 1947), p. 38.

1929, following Alfred E. Smith's candidacy and defeat. Its original purpose was emphasis upon better interreligious relations, but since then it has spread into a number of other fields. It is not an agency of action, but rather an educational one. It attempts to change attitudes rather than laws. A great deal of its work is done in schools and colleges, but it also works with religious leaders, in the field of management, labor, the community, and the media of communication. Today, it has more than 40 offices throughout the United States.

While all of these organizations are helpful in combatting anti-Semitism and other types of prejudice, the church, school, and home should be particularly utilized for this purpose. The family can generally prevent the development of prejudice toward minorities, the school can combat it if such prejudice has already been established, and the church can utilize religious motivation for its eradication. The late Holy Father, Pius XII, declared that we are all "spiritual Semites." By this he was referring to Christianity's Judaic heritage. Unfortunately, distortions of Christian teaching have sometimes resulted in anti-Semitism. This need not be, and the full implications of Christian teaching, if realized, could only result in a lessening of anti-Semitism.

## REVIEW QUESTIONS

1. Should American Jews be considered a religious group, a race, or an ethnic group? Explain your answer.
2. Most Jews are readily identifiable in this country. What are the bases for such identification?
3. What are some of the historical circumstances which contributed to prejudice and discrimination against Jews?
4. Discuss the three waves of Jewish emigration to the United States.
5. About how many Jews live in the United States today?
6. What are the most common types of discrimination Jews encounter in America?
7. What is "anti-Semitism"? When did it first appear?
8. On the basis of studies, to what extent and in what areas do Catholics seem to be guilty of anti-Semitism?
9. Are Catholics more anti-Semitic than persons of other religions or persons without religion?

10. To what extent is anti-Semitism a social problem?
11. What remedial measures would you recommend to reduce or eliminate anti-Semitism?

## SELECTED READINGS

### Articles

Cahnman, Warner J., "Socio-economic Causes of Anti-Semitism," *Social Problems*, 5 (July 1957), 21-29.

Infield, Henrik F., "The Concept of Jewish Culture in the State of Israel," *American Sociological Review*, 16 (Aug. 1951), 506-13.

Kane, John J., "Anti-Semitism Among Catholic College Students," *American Catholic Sociological Review*, 8 (Oct. 1947), 209-18.

Kaufman, Walter C., "Status, Authoritarianism and Anti-Semitism," *American Journal of Sociology*, 62 (Jan. 1957), 379-82.

Robinson, Duane and Sylvia Rohde, "A Public Opinion Study of Anti-Semitism in New York City," *American Sociological Review*, 10 (Aug. 1945), 511-14.

Savits, Leonard D. and Richard F. Tomasson, "The Identifiability of Jews," *American Journal of Sociology*, 64 (Mar. 1959), 468-75.

### Books

*American Jewish Year Book*. Philadelphia: The Jewish Publication Society of America, 1960.

Fuchs, Lawrence H., *The Political Behaviour of American Jews*. New York: The Free Press of Glencoe, 1956.

Gartner, Lloyd P., *The Jewish Immigrant in England 1870-1914*. Detroit: Wayne State University Press, 1960.

Glazer, Nathan, *American Judaism*. Chicago: University of Chicago Press, 1957.

Gordis, Robert, *Judaism for the Modern Age*. New York: Farrar, Straus and Cudahy, Inc., 1955.

Gordon, Albert I., *Jews in Suburbia*. Boston: Beacon Press, 1959.

Parkes, James, *The Jewish Problems in the Modern World*. New York: Oxford University Press, Inc., 1946.

Sherman, C. B., *The Jews Within American Society*. Detroit: Wayne State University Press, 1961.

Sklare, Marshall, *Conservative Judaism: An American Religious Movement*. New York: The Free Press of Glencoe, 1955.

# 14

# The American Catholic

# Minority

O N January 1, 1959 there were 39,505,475 Catholics in the United States, including Hawaii and Alaska, armed forces personnel, and other overseas services.[1] They constituted more than 22 per cent of the population, or better than one out of every five persons in this country. Catholics are America's largest minority. While many Americans, including Catholics, may not consider this faith a minority, it does have most of the characteristics of minority status. Louis Worth has defined a minority as a group of people singled out from others in a society for differential and unequal treatment because of special physical or cultural characteristics. Minorities are excluded from full participation in the life of a society.[2]

The minority status of American Catholics has been

---

[1] *National Catholic Almanac*, ed. Felician Foy (Paterson, N.J.: St. Anthony's Guild, 1960), p. 354.

[2] Simpson and Yinger, *Racial and Cultural Minorities*, p. 21.

historically and to some extent still is associated with their immigrant backgrounds and with their social structure within American society. But even native-born Catholics of the upper middle class experience certain kinds of discrimination occupationally, educationally, and politically. Catholics are accused of belinging to an alien religion whose head is the ruler of a temporal state and to whom, it is claimed, they owe political as well as religious allegiance. The Catholic educational system is labeled divisive, since it is claimed that only secular public education can maintain the "American way of life." [3] The Catholic hierarchy is sorely criticized. V. Ogden Vogt has said that a church whose leaders assume the style and title of "prince" cannot teach the democratic way of life.[4] Because of the interpretation of the First Amendment to the Constitution dealing with Church-State relationships and state constitutions, many parochial school students do not have access to tax-supported bus transportation or other fringe benefits usually provided for public school children. While American Catholics and Catholicism have always suffered some prejudice and discrimination, even from colonial days, Protestant-Catholic tensions became acute following World War II. At the risk of over-simplification, the basic reason for this increase appears to have been a fear that American Catholics are growing too rapidly both in number and in power and, should they become a majority group the United States will become less democratic. As Vogt put it, "When the Catholic Church was a small minority, the meaning of this political antipathy was insignificant; now that it has become a large minority, it constitutes a major threat to American unity and peace." [5]

On the basis of a content analsis of the *Christian Century*, a nondenominational Protestant magazine, and *America*, a Jesuit publication, during the first six months of 1939, 1944, and 1949 certain areas of interreligious tension were found. These are listed in Table 14-1.

Major criticisms of the Catholic church in international affairs centered around the case of Cardinal Mindszenty and the treatment of Protestants and Jews in Spain, Italy, and Colombia. Under federal

---

[3] *Public Education and the Future of America* (Washington, D.C.: National Education Association of the United States, 1955), p. 98.

[4] V. Ogden Vogt, *Cult and Culture* (New York: The Macmillan Co., 1951), p. 195.

[5] Vogt, *op. cit.*, p. 195.

TABLE 14-1[6]

AREAS SHOWING THE HIGHEST FREQUENCY OF CRITICISMS OF
CATHOLICISM OR PROTESTANTISM IN THE *CHRISTIAN CENTURY*
AND *AMERICA* DURING THE FIRST SIX MONTHS OF
1939, 1944, AND 1949.

| | *1939* | *1944* | *1949* |
|---|---|---|---|
| Interna-tional | 14—Christian Century<br>0—America | 8—Christian Century<br>1—America | 16—Christian Century<br>5—America |
| Federal Aid to Edu-cation | 0—Christian Century<br>2—America | 0—Christian Century<br>2—America | 11—Christian Century<br>3—America |
| Religious Beliefs | 0—Christian Century<br>1—America | 0—Christian Century<br>0—America | 9—Christian Century<br>4—America |
| Censorship | 0—Christian Century<br>0—America | 2—Christian Century<br>0—America | 4—Christian Century<br>0—America |

[6] Adapted from John J. Kane, "Protestant-Catholic Tensions," *American Sociological Review*, 16 (Oct. 1951), p. 669.

aid to education, charges were made that Catholic efforts to secure "fringe benefits" were merely an entering wedge by which they hoped ultimately to get complete support of their educational system. Catholic religious beliefs were criticized because of their marriage legislation, particularly on mixed religious marriages and the doctrine that there is no salvation outside the Church. In this latter instance the *Christian Century* admitted that, while the Church did not teach this doctrine, it implied it. Under censorship, Catholics were blamed for the exclusion of the magazine *The Nation* from the New York City public schools. At that time the magazine was running a series of articles by Paul Blanshard critical of Catholicism.[7]

Obviously a mere content analysis of two magazines cannot be considered adequate proof that interreligious tensions exist. However, in 1947 Francis Cardinal Spellman stated, "Bigotry once again is eating its way into the vital organs of the greatest nation on the face of the earth, our own beloved America. Once again a crusade is being preached against the Catholic Church in the United States." Bishop G. Bromley Oxnam, then president of the Federal Council of Churches, said in 1945 that "serious tension is developing between Roman Catholics and Protestants in the United States." Here are

[7] Kane, *op. cit.*, p. 666.

two outstanding leaders of Catholics and Protestants emphatically admitting the existence of tensions.[8] Other evidence is not lacking. Since 1950, for example, litigation begun in New Mexico and North Dakota to stop Catholic nuns and brothers from teaching in their habits in public schools has been successful. In a suburb of Cincinnati, both legal and physical conflicts developed over efforts of a predominantly Catholic school board to change a Catholic school into a public school while continuing to employ Catholic sisters as teachers.[9] Former President Truman's attempts to appoint an official Vatican envoy from the United States aroused serious controversy, and "Protestants and Other Americans United for Separation of Church and State," an organization claiming to be a self-constituted watchdog over separation of church and state, threatened a march on Washington.

In July of 1960 Senator John F. Kennedy was nominated for the presidency of the United States by the Democratic convention. At that time three Baptist clergymen attempted to place a petition before the convention claiming that they had 500,000 signatures opposing any Catholic for President or Vice President.[10] The Reverend Dr. W. A. Criswell, pastor of the largest all-white Baptist congregation in the nation, said that the election of a Catholic as President would "spell the death of a free church in a free state . . . and our hopes of continuance of full religious liberty." In Greer, South Carolina, the state conference of the Wesleyan Methodist Church of America adopted a resolution expressing the strongest opposition to the election of a Catholic as president. Dr. O. H. Hovey of Minneapolis, general secretary of the three million-member American Lutheran Church, said that it is the American ideal to keep religion out of politics but admitted that Protestants would feel easier about voting for a Catholic if the Church made an authoritative statement on the issue. But Rabbi Albert Minda of Minneapolis, Vice President of the Central Conference of American Rabbis, said that voters should judge candidates by their stand on political issues, not by their religious background.[11]

---

[8] John J. Kane, *Catholic-Protestant Conflicts in America* (Chicago: Henry Regnery Co., 1955), p. 7.

[9] Kane, *Catholic-Protestant Conflicts in America*, pp. 7-8.

[10] *The South Bend Tribune* (July 13, 1960), p. 2.

[11] *Our Sunday Visitor*, Fort Wayne Diocesan Edition, 49, No. 13 (July 24, 1960), pp. 1a-2a.

## HISTORY OF PROTESTANT-CATHOLIC
## RELATIONS IN THE UNITED STATES

Contemporary Protestant-Catholic relations can only be understood in the light of American history. While a number of European countries founded what later became the 13 colonies, England eventually prevailed. Opposition to Roman Catholicism was imported from England and manifested itself in the colonies. Jesuits were forbidden entry into the Massachusetts Bay Colony. If they were found therein they were expelled. If they returned a second time, the penalty was death. Until the start of the Revolutionary war, Boston mobs annually celebrated Guy Fawkes Day, a commemoration of the Gunpowder Plot in England, by burning in effigy their two most hated figures, the Devil and the Pope. General George Washington forbade celebration of this day because the Catholic French allies might be affronted. In Massachusetts, an established Protestant church persisted until 1833. The United States was predominantly a Protestant country, although since 1636 there had been an English Catholic minority. This minority numbered about 30,000 out of 3,000,000 in 1790, but they were accepted as Americans, although their Catholicism was not approved.[12]

Anti-Catholicism was revived as Irish Catholics, fleeing famines in their native land, poured into the United States. Between 1847 and 1854 the annual arrivals of Irish immigrants never fell below 100,000. Opposition to them was not entirely based upon their religion. They were poverty-stricken, poorly educated if not illiterate, a rural people who settled in urban areas for lack of money to take them further west. They congregated within ghettos in the large Eastern seaboard cities and became conspicuous by reason of their dress, their brogue, and their behavior. At this period in American history Catholicism became identified with the Irish, and to a large extent still is, despite the fact that many other immigrants, such as Germans, Italians, Poles and others, have largely belonged to the same faith. In his

---

[12] Thomas T. McAvoy, "The Formation of the Catholic Minority in the United States, 1820-1860," *The Review of Politics*, 10, No. 1 (Jan. 1948), p. 15.

native land the Irish Catholic had lived under penal laws which discriminated against him economically, socially, and politically because of his religion. He was strongly anti-Protestant and his American experience scarcely assuaged this attitude. With few exceptions, the clergy were the only educated persons among the Irish and they became their leaders in almost all aspects of life. Through fraudulent procedures, "cradle of liberty" immigrants (newly arrived persons who became naturalized without waiting for the required period of residence in the U.S.) were "rocked" into U.S. citizenship almost immediately upon arrival and tended to vote as a bloc at the orders of Irish wardheelers. As their numbers increased and as spires of Catholic churches rose in what had been considered a Protestant country, conflict became almost inevitable.

In 1834 an Ursuline Catholic convent and boarding school for girls was burned by a Protestant mob in Charlestown, Massachusetts. In 1844 a week of rioting between Irish Catholics and some Protestants occurred in Philadelphia in which two Catholic churches, a convent, a rectory, and a seminary were burned to the ground. Volunteer fire companies called to the scene made no efforts to extinguish the blazes out of fear of the mob. The militia was belatedly summoned and eventually took control of the situation.

The immediate cause of these riots was a request by Bishop Kenrick of Philadelphia that Catholic children in public schools have the Catholic version of the Bible instead of the St. James version read to them. In Baltimore, a similar request had been granted, but in Philadelphia it was resisted as an attempt by Catholics to replace the Protestant Bible with their own. This probably marked the zenith of anti-Catholic activity in this country, and during the riots Bishop Kenrick suspended all public worship in Catholic churches.

## TO THE CATHOLICS OF THE CITY AND COUNTY OF PHILADELPHIA[13]

Beloved Children,—

In the critical circumstances in which you are placed, I feel it my duty to suspend the exercises of public worship in the Catholic Churches, which still remain, until it can be resumed with safety, and we can enjoy our constitutional rights to worship God according to the dictates of our conscience. I earnestly conjure you to practice unalterable patience under the trials to which it has pleased Divine

---

[13] Kane, *Catholic-Protestant Conflicts in America*, p. 1.

Providence to subject you—and remember that affliction will serve to purify us, and render us acceptable to God, through Jesus Christ, who patiently suffered on the cross.

May 12, 1844

Francis Patrick Kenrick
Bishop of Philadelphia

In light of contemporary attitudes, Catholic complaints were justifiable. Textbooks used in public schools were anti-Catholic and anti-Irish. Priests were forbidden to enter public orphanages to instruct Catholic children in their faith and denied admission to public hospitals to administer the last rites to dying Catholics. Public funds were voted for the maintenance of Protestant institutions but denied Catholic institutions. In 1850 a petition signed by 3,000 ladies was presented to the Pennsylvania legislature asking it to pass laws to restrain and control establishment of nunneries in the state. The legislature referred this petition to the Committee on Vice and Immorality!

Various nativist movements opposed to the foreign-born as well as to Catholics also developed. The "Know-Nothing" movement of the 1850's grew out of the "Supreme Order of the Star Spangled Banner," an earlier nativist organization which believed that Catholics voted as ordered by their priests and that a Papal plot existed to seize the country. It attained success in certain states but never on a national level. The American Protective Association of the 1890's and the Ku Klux Klan (revived in the 1920's) were other examples of prejudice and discrimination against Catholics. In 1928 anti-Catholicism was again aroused when Alfred E. Smith, a Catholic, was nominated for the presidency on the Democratic ticket. He suffered a sound defeat, carrying only 8 states and receiving 15,000,000 popular votes to Hoover's 40 states and 21,000,000 votes. Several factors undoubtedly contributed to Smith's defeat, such as his affiliation with Tammany Hall, his opposition to prohibition, and the prosperity which the country enjoyed at that time. However, his religion also was an important factor.

The kinds of charges leveled against Catholics and Catholicism in the last century in this country were not very different from current ones. Arguments centered around the belief that Catholics voted as a bloc, never completely true even in the past and much less true today; the belief that priests strongly influenced Catholic votes; the difficulties over public funds being used by Catholic institutions; and the fear that Catholics were growing in numbers and power. A question-- naire submitted to 104 Protestant ministers in a middle-western U.S. county in 1953 through the local Council of Churches (to which 49 ministers replied) found:[14]

|  | Percentage "Yes" |
|---|---|
| Are pronouncements of the Catholic hierarchy, even outside the realm of faith and morals, almost rigidly followed by the laity? | 40.0% |
| Do Catholic schools tend to violate the democratic traditions? | 62.5% |
| Do priests strongly influence the vote of the Catholic laity? | 68.1% |
| Are Catholics becoming more prominent and powerful in national politics? | 75.0% |
| If Catholics became a majority group, would they strongly influence American society toward less democratic principles and practices? | 91.9% |

## SOCIAL STRUCTURE OF AMERICAN CATHOLICS

The position of American Catholics in the middle of the twentieth century differs from that of the nineteenth century. The majority are native-born Americans, their educational level is considerably higher, they no longer reside in ghettos, and they have ceased being the "hewers of wood and drawers of water" for a white nordic Protestant America. While the educational and occupational status of American Catholics has improved, they have not as a rule moved ahead as far and as fast as Protestants and Jews. Catholics are found mainly in the middle class and below.

"In a national study made in 1947 of 10,063 high school seniors, male and female, it was found that 68 per cent of the Jewish high school seniors and 36 per cent of the Protestant high school seniors but only 25 per cent of Catholic seniors entered college. But Catholics are predominantly an urban people and a study of exclusively urban high schools may prove more meaningful. Such a study of 5,564 high

---

[14] Kane, *Catholic-Protestant Conflicts in America*, p. 10.

school seniors was made. It showed that 64 per cent of Jewish seniors, 43 per cent of Protestant seniors but only 26 per cent of Catholic seniors tried to enter college. In Connecticut, 85 per cent of Jewish seniors, 63 per cent of Protestant seniors but only 50 per cent of Catholic seniors applied for college." [15]

Possession of a college degree is one method of achieving vertical mobility upward in American society. Catholics, it appears, do not employ this means nearly so much as Jews and somewhat less than Protestants. But how successful are Catholic college graduates in utilizing formal education for upward vertical mobility? In the study *They Went to College*, one-third of the Jewish college graduates and just slightly better than one-third of the Protestant graduates (34 per cent) became proprietors, managers, and professionals. Only about one out of every four Catholic college graduates attained such positions (26 per cent). At the other end of the scale (white-collar, manual work, and farm labor) the figures were fewer than one out of every six Jewish graduates and about one out of every five Protestant graduates, but almost one out of three Catholic graduates.

Income and occupation generally show a positive association, and figures on income from the same study revealed what might be expected. In cities with a population of half a million or more, the group of college graduates receiving an annual income of $7,500 or more was composed of one out of every four to five Jewish graduates and one out of every five Protestant graduates, but only one out of every six Catholic graduates. Among those receiving less than $3,000 a year, the figures were one out of every five Jewish graduates and one out of every four Protestant graduates, but one out of every three Catholic graduates.[16]

In comparing the occupations of fathers of male high school Juniors in both a public and a Catholic mid-western high school (according to religious affiliation), researchers found that 10 per cent of the Protestant public-high-school fathers, but 21 per cent of the Catholic public-high-school fathers were factory workers. Fourteen and one-half per cent of Protestant fathers were executives compared to 0.71 per cent of the Catholic fathers whose sons were in public high school.

---

[15] John J. Kane, "The Social Structure of American Catholics," *American Catholic Sociological Review, 16*, No. 1 (Mar. 1955), p. 25.

[16] Ernest Havemann and Patricia Salter West, *They Went to College* (New York: Harcourt, Brace & World, Inc., 1952), pp. 187-88.

In the Catholic high school only one per cent of the boys' fathers were executives.[17]

The smaller percentage of Catholic students entering college may be the result of lower incomes, but it more likely represents the value orientation of many Catholic families. It was stated above that American Catholics tend to be found in the middle and lower classes. A number of indices may be employed to determine social class but one of the most important is the value system. Included in this system is a family's attitude toward higher education. Upper- and upper-middle-class families provide about 10 per cent of the children in this country but send 80 per cent of their children to college. The lower middle class produces about 30 per cent of American children but sends only 25 per cent of them to college. Class levels below this provide 60 per cent of the children but send only 5 per cent of them to college.[18] Insofar as education is a status index, Catholics are a very poor third among the major religions.

Another method of examining the social structure of Catholics is to inspect listings of persons found in *Who's Who in America* and *The American Catholic Who's Who*. In a 1928-29 survey of the frequency with which graduates of specific colleges appeared in *Who's Who in America* only two Catholic institutions were found among the first 150: Notre Dame ranked 137th, Xavier University in Cincinnati 138th. In a second study done in 1932-33, five Catholic schools were found among the first 200 institutions in the order of frequency with which their graduates appeared: St. Louis ranked 139th; Notre Dame, 155th; Georgetown, 161st; Holy Cross, 171st; and Xavier University, 200th.[19] A 10 per cent random sampling of the *American Catholic Who's Who*, 1954-55 edition, revealed the following frequency of selected occupations:

"Clerics" included cardinals, bishops, priests, nuns, and brothers. "Lawyers" included judges as well as attorneys. The most striking feature of this table is that almost half of the names—48.6 per cent—are those of clerics and lawyers. On the basis of this listing, it appears

---

[17] Kane, *Catholic-Protestant Conflicts in America*, pp. 75-76.

[18] Robert H. Havighurst and Robert R. Rogers, "The Role of Motivation and Attendance at Post High School Educational Institutions," in *Who Should Go To College*, ed. Byron S. Hollingshead (New York: Columbia University Press, 1953), p. 139.

[19] B. W. Kunkel and D. B. Prentice, "The College's Contribution to Intellectual Leadership," *School and Society*, 50, No. 44 (1939), pp. 601-2.

FREQUENCY OF OCCUPATIONS, based on a selected sample of the *American Catholic Who's Who*, 1954-55 edition:*

|  | Percentage |
|---|---|
| Clerics | 29.0 |
| Lawyers | 19.6 |
| Educators | 9.0 |
| Business executives | 6.0 |
| Writers | 5.0 |
| Bankers | 4.0 |
| Natural scientists | 2.0 |
| Social scientists | none in sample |

* John J. Kane, *Catholic-Protestant Conflicts in America* (Chicago: Henry Regnery Co., 1955).

that clerics are still the most numerous leaders in American Catholic society. A comparison with the 1954-55 edition of *Who's Who in America* in 1954 showed that the distribution of occupations in this listing was just about the same as in the *American Catholic Who's Who*. Clerics account for 29 per cent of the names, lawyers for 19.6 per cent. When Catholics achieve eminence, insofar as these listings are concerned, they apparently do so mainly in two fields: religion and law.[20] The low number of Catholics eminent in the natural and social sciences is also notable. Other studies have noted the dearth of outstanding Catholics in the field of natural science and the unusually large number of those who studied law.[21]

On the basis of material presented here, it is clear that American Catholics have historically suffered prejudice and discrimination, and to some extent still do today. The dearth of Catholic executives mentioned above was also remarked by Havemann & West in *They Went to College*. They said that perhaps Catholics in the business world encounter subtle and unspoken obstacles, and it may be that business firms have a type of unwritten quota system for Catholic executives, just as political parties limit the number of Catholics appearing on the ticket in any given election.[22] Signs formerly hung outside of factories stating "Help wanted—no Irish need apply" are no longer

---

[20] Kane, *Catholic-Protestant Conflicts in America*, pp. 83 and 86.
[21] Robert H. Knapp and Joseph J. Greenbaum, *The Younger American Scholar* (Chicago: University of Chicago Press, 1953), p. 1; R. H. Knapp and H. B. Goodrich, *Origins of American Scientists* (Chicago: University of Chicago Press, 1952), p. 24.
[22] Havemann & West, *op. cit.*, p. 190.

found, and today it is relatively rare to read want ads which specify
Protestants. Catholics are still denied fringe benefits for their children
attending parochial schools in many areas of the country. But discrimination against Catholics is more subtle than that against Negroes
and Jews, probably because Catholics are usually less conspicuous.
Nevertheless, it does exist and does constitute a social problem in the
United States. There are areas of the country, however, in which
Catholics are in a numerical majority. As a consequence, their minority status in other parts of the country tends to be overlooked. There
is a great deal of difference between being a Catholic in South Boston
and being a Catholic in rural Mississippi, so far as minority status is
concerned.

## SITUATIONAL-VALUE APPROACH

As pointed out, the same types of charges are made against Catholics today that were made in the last century. The fear among
Protestants and other non-Catholics that growing Catholic power and
influence will cause the United States to become less democratic
stems particularly from a confusion over the concept of separation of
Church and State. Again and again there are quoted in Protestant
literature a statement by Cardinal Ottiavini appearing in 1948 in
*Civilita Cattolica,* a publication of the Society of Jesus; and an earlier
view of Fathers Ryan and Bolyan that if Catholics become a majority
group in society, the Church would require that legal existence be
denied to Protestants. If other religious minorities legally existed,
they should only have a *de facto* existence. Despite the assertions of
Catholic bishops and theologians that the Catholic Church in America has flourished under a policy of non-union with the State, and
that authors have pointed out the religious freedom of non-Catholics
in Ireland, Protestant fears on this score have not been relieved.

Opposition to a Catholic president on the part of Protestants and
others is the result of faulty perception or a distorted value orientation
regarding Catholicism. David Danzig, the American Jewish Committee program director, has stated:

> A Catholic's acceptance of papal authority on religious matters does
> not relieve him of his individual obligations of conscience in civic

matters, nor does it qualify his oath of office. We do not question the sincerity of others who swear to defend and uphold the Constitution; why assume a Catholic would take the oath with secret reservations? As for the political pressure of the Roman Catholic hierarchy, it is one of the cherished principles of democratic society that religious groups are entitled to speak out on public issues, and that their pronouncements mingle and contend with the pronouncements of other special interest groups.[23]

Fears that a Catholic president would work for the union of the Catholic Church and the United States Government are groundless. First, this would require an amendment to the U.S. Constitution, which can only be effected by Congress and the votes of the states or the state legislatures. Even if it is argued that a Catholic president might somehow or other give the Catholic Church a favored position, this possibility is belied by the actions of the various Catholic governors—who, incidentally, in some highly controversial areas such as education actually have more authority than the President. President Kennedy's stand on federal aid to education in 1961 may have largely reduced such Protestant apprehension. Mr. Danzig has pointed out that in the creeds of Quakers and Christian Scientists there are tenets which, if applied with equal rigidity, would create a similar controversy about their fitness to serve as President. President Herbert Hoover was a Quaker. Yet there was no national questioning of his loyalty to the United States. Criticism of a Catholic presidential nominee for these reasons has been either the result of a misunderstanding among those who are sincere or the product of bigotry among those who are not.

How realistic are fears of the so-called Catholic vote? Historically, it is true that Catholics, more specifically Irish Catholics, tended to vote the Democratic ticket. They did so because the immigrant vote was cultivated by the Democratic party and largely neglected by the Whigs. In the beginning of the twentieth century many immigrants from eastern and southern Europe who were Catholics tended to vote the Republican ticket. It was not until the twenties that its platform of nativism, reaction, and prohibition alienated these ethnic groups from the Republican party.[24] The Catholic vote in the presidential

[23] David Danzig, "Bigotry and Prejudice," *Committee Reporter*, American Jewish Committee, *17*, No. 3 (May 1960), p. 20.

[24] Moses Rischin, *Own Kind—Voting by Race, Creed or National Origin: A Report for the Center for the Study of Democratic Institutions*, Santa Barbara, California, 1960, pp. 8-9.

election of 1952 was just about evenly divided between Republicans and Democrats.

Voting behavior is a complex affair and involves many motives other than racial, religious, and ethnic background. Attitudes toward business and labor are important. In a somewhat narrow study of Philadelphia voters in the 1948 and 1952 presidential elections carried on by Oscar Glantz, such differences were clearly revealed. Among upper- and middle-strata Protestants who had a strong loyalty and orientation toward business, 97 per cent of the vote was Republican, compared to 80 per cent of the Catholic vote in the same strata. In 1952, the respective percentages were 97 per cent and 92 per cent. On the other hand, in 1948 13 per cent of the middle- and lower-strata Protestants with a loyalty and orientation favorable to labor voted the Republican ticket as compared to 4 per cent of Catholics in the same group. In 1952, the respective voting percentages were 25 per cent and 21 per cent.[25]

Age is another factor in voting and a study of student preferences at the University of Connecticut showed that young Catholics whose fathers were 80 per cent Democratic voted 50 per cent Republican.[26] But in the Glantz study in Philadelphia, there was less Republicanism among younger Catholics than among older Catholics.[27] This is a good illustration of the complexity of voting behavior even among persons of the same religion and of about the same age. Certainly since the 1930's, the economic status of a voter has been one factor motivating his choice. While, as pointed out, Catholics have moved ahead neither so fast nor so far as Protestants and Jews, certain changes in the economic and social status of younger Catholics have been occurring since the close of World War II.

The G.I. Bill opened the doors of colleges, universities, and professional schools to many young men and women who would otherwise never have entered them. This has been particularly true for Catholics and first-generation immigrants as well as others. Young Catholics have moved to suburbia, acquired ranch-type and split-level homes, and sometimes membership in modest country clubs.

[25] Oscar Glantz, "Protestant and Catholic Voting Behavior in a Metropolitan Area," as reported in *Religion and Politics*, ed. Peter H. Odegard, The Eagleton Institute of Politics at Rutgers (New York: Oceana Publications, Inc., 1960), p. 135.

[26] Rischin, *op. cit.*, p. 37.

[27] Glantz, *op. cit.*, p. 137.

Their identification with and loyalty to organized labor are somewhat less than that of their fathers. While their fathers may have been members of the A.F. of L. or the C.I.O., these sons may belong to the County Medical Society, the Bar Association, Rotary, Kiwanis, or some other service organization, business, or professional group. Samuel Lubell claims that an almost even split between Democratic and Republican voting occurs in the $10,000 to $15,000 housing areas. Most suburbanites, including Catholics, have such housing and it seems probable that residence, occupation, and income will be factors in their future voting preferences.

Furthermore, voting behavior cannot be disassociated from the kinds of issues that confront the nation. The two highly important domestic issues today are racial integration and the matter of Church-State relationships. On the international level the Cold War—which periodically becomes warmer—also influences voting. In the last 20 years, the "Catholic vote" has become a myth. Obviously, a Catholic vote or any other kind of minority vote can be developed in the face of certain specific issues touching that minority. This may be done directly or indirectly. For example, in 1948 when the great majority of Catholic voters in Massachusetts were Democrats, more than the usual number went to the polls because of a referendum on the dissemination of birth control information. Negroes would certainly vote, if possible, against any law which would deny them their civil rights. Catholics would certainly oppose a law in favor of euthanasia (so-called mercy killing) because it is contrary to their moral principles. All minorities can be aroused by a campaign in which one side is overtly guilty of religious, racial, or ethnic prejudice.

However, as minorities emerge from the difficult position of being denied certain social, economic, or political rights, they are less likely to prefer a candidate simply because he happens to be a member of their religious, racial, or ethnic group. Jews in New York voted for Robert Wagner, Sr. and against a Jewish candidate for the Senate. Negroes in Philadelphia preferred a white candidate to Congress over a Negro candidate. Today large numbers of well-educated and economically secure Catholics are occupied with the major problems facing the nation and not preoccupied with narrow sectarian differences.

The charge that parochial schools are divisive factors in American society has been made by a number of non-Catholic spokesmen.

Actual empirical evidence to prove or disprove this charge has been lacking. In order to investigate it, questionnaires were sent to 120 Catholic school and 120 public school superintendents throughout the United States. Among other questions, one specifically asked: Is the presence of private and/or parochial schools within your community a cause of interreligious tension? Sixty-five public school superintendents responded to this question but only eight of them— or about 12 per cent—answered affirmatively. An overwhelming majority—88 per cent—stated that the presence of private and/or parochial schools did not cause interreligious tensions within their community. This was one of the most amazing responses in the entire questionnaire, and one can only wonder what motives or rationalizations lie behind this oft-repeated charge against Catholic education. On the basis of this study it has little foundation in fact. Perhaps attention has been focused upon the few communities in which such divisiveness has occurred. The cases are infrequent and such tension is relatively rare.

Some situations may occur which cause disagreement in a community between Catholics and Protestants, or between Catholics and non-Catholics. In a culturally pluralistic society, some of this is almost inevitable. But it is not just what happens but rather how people perceive what happens that counts. Tension-provoking incidents are publicized and magnified and, because some Americans fear that Catholics and Catholicism are threats, prejudice and discrimination are aroused. Some Catholics are highly defensive about their Church and needlessly construe objective criticism by Protestants or other non-Catholics as prejudice.

## REMEDIAL MEASURES

On the Catholic side two major steps can be taken to alter the present situation. First, there is a need for the development of strong Catholic lay leadership in almost all areas of American life. The distribution of eminent Catholics, as pointed out above, into certain selected occupations is typical of minority status. When clerical leadership is the exclusive leadership in certain areas which should at the very least be shared by the laity, non-Catholics suspect clerical domination in every aspect of life. Such leadership is now emerging and will probably be an important factor in the future development of American Catholicism.

But lay leadership should not be confined within a real or psychological ghetto as it has so often been done in the past. It is essential that Catholics, particularly lay Catholics, participate with persons of other faiths in the various civic affairs of the community. Close association and cooperation with all Americans under favorable circumstances will decrease the prevalent ignorance about Catholics and Catholicism and increase the understanding of the Catholic Church and her people.

But all Americans, Catholics included, must fully appreciate the implications of cultural as well as religious pluralism in this country. Some disagreements will naturally occur, but there must be a recognition that Catholics have a right to their viewpoints. Catholic pronouncements should not be considered foreign, subversive, or anti-American. Ironically enough, Catholics today are criticized for threatening to do what their Protestant counterparts have done for so long and so successfully within this society. While Catholics have frequently been accused of being undemocratic, the same question could be raised about those who wish to deny any minority, religious, racial, or ethnic, the equal opportunity of expression which is rightfully theirs under the Constitution.

# REVIEW QUESTIONS

1. Are American Catholics sociologically a minority group?
2. Do American Catholics suffer discrimination?
3. What factors brought about serious Catholic-Protestant conflicts in this country during the last century?
4. What are some of the major factors in Catholic-Protestant tensions today and in the immediate past?
5. What is meant by the social structure of American Catholics? Provide some empirical evidence of the Catholic social structure in the United States.
6. Is Catholic education divisive?
7. What remedial measures would reduce tensions between Catholics and other religious groups?

## SELECTED READINGS

*Articles*

Butler, John J. and Edna M. O'Hern, "Medical Education and Research in Catholic Medical Schools and Hospitals," *American Catholic Sociological Review*, 19 (Oct. 1958), 224-37.

Cross, Joseph L., "The American Protective Association: A Sociological Analysis of the Periodic Literature of the Period 1890-1900," *American Catholic Sociological Review*, 10 (Oct. 1949), 172-87.

Donovan, John B., "The American Catholic Hierarchy: A Social Profile," *American Catholic Sociological Review*, 19 (June 1958), 98-112.

Fichter, Joseph H. and T. W. Facey, "Social Attitudes of Catholic High School Students," *American Catholic Sociological Review*, 14 (June 1953), 94-106.

Kane, John J., "Social Structure of American Catholics," *American Catholic Sociological Review*, 16 (Mar. 1955), 23-30.

————, "Protestant-Catholic Tensions," *American Sociological Review*, 16 (Oct. 1951), 663-71.

Thomas, John L., "The Urban Impact on Catholic Families," *American Catholic Sociological Review*, 10 (Dec. 1944), 258-67.

Van der Zanden, James W., "The Klan Revival," *American Journal of Sociology*, 65 (Mar. 1960), 456-62.

*Books*

Bach, Marcus Louis, *Report to Protestants*. Indianapolis: The Bobbs-Merrill Company, Inc., 1948.

Kane, John J., *Catholic-Protestant Conflicts in America*. Chicago: Henry Regnery Co., 1955.

O'Dea, Thomas, *The American Catholic Dilemma*. New York: Sheed and Ward, 1958.

Pelikan, Jaroslav, *The Riddle of Catholicism*. Nashville: Abingdon Press, 1959.

Powell, Theodore, *The School Bus Law: A Case in Education, Religion and Politics*. Middletown, Conn.: Wesleyan University Press, 1960.

Sharfer, Philip, ed., *American Catholics: A Protestant and Jewish View*. New York: Sheed and Ward, 1959.

Underwood, Kenneth W., *Protestant and Catholic*. Boston: Beacon Press, 1957.

# PART FIVE

# Problems of American
# Social Institutions

S OCIAL institutions are organized systems by which and in which certain human needs are met. The most common are the family, religion, education, and political and economic institutions. In this section certain problem aspects of three major social institutions are discussed: the family, religion, and education. Changes in the average marrying age; in the roles of husbands, wives, mothers, and fathers, as well as children; the reputed religious revival; and the increased birthrate, which has taxed educational facilities—all have prompted this discussion.

To no small extent the family, religion, and education are closely related and interdependent. They are the foundations of much of the American value system. For example, the types of schools to which children are sent are influenced by their families and the respective religious affiliation of the family, if any. The extent of formal education is largely the result of the social class of the family. Children are generally reared in the religion of their parents. Furthermore, some education and some religious training occur within the family and prior to the child's contact with school or church.

The present crisis in education is not limited to its ability or inability to accommodate the future increase in population. There are sharp debates over curriculum content, including the matter of religious instruction within public schools. Some private school administrators sense a growing concern over the impact of federal aid to education—when or if it comes—on the private institution. This concern is closely associated with religion, since many private schools are maintained by religious denominations.

It is obvious then that inclusion of the family, religion, and education in Part Five heightens continuity and should facilitate students' appreciation of the close ties among these institutions and the interrelationships of the problems in each institution to those of the others.

# 15

# Marriage and the Family

M ARRIAGE, John P. Marquand once remarked, is a serious business, particularly
around Boston, and Professor James H. S.
Bossard has added that so far as marriage is concerned,
we all live around Boston.[1] It may be trite but it is true
that the family is the basic social institution within any
society, and the family in American society begins with
the marriage of one man to one woman. From this permanent union, to be broken only by the death of one of
the spouses, will likely issue children whose entire lives
will be strongly influenced by their early rearing. The
image of America's tomorrow is now being formed in
millions of homes by parents of small children. While
many other institutions, such as church, school, and
government, will also impinge upon children, their direct
influences will usually come later and, to no small extent,
will be filtered through values and attitudes already acquired within the family. Exceptions, of course, are children orphaned early in life; but in these cases, absence of

---

[1] James H. S. Bossard and Eleanor Stoker Boll, *Why Marriages
Go Wrong* (New York: The Ronald Press, 1958), p. 4.

parents and family life (if these children are in institutions) will also influence them. But marriage and family life affect not only children.

When men and women become husbands and wives they enter into the most intimate, sustained, and critical human interaction possible. They are mutually modified by their close personal relationships. Marriage is truly for better or worse. The happiness of one depends upon the happiness of the other. They are likely to be mutually happy or mutually miserable, so long as they live together. The husband's success or failure on his job; the wife's role of homemaker, mother, and/or career; the economic plight of the family; its status within the community; and the very atmosphere of the home cannot be entirely disassociated from the satisfactory or unsatisfactory adjustments the spouses are able to make toward each other.

What then is the situation of the American family in the latter half of the twentieth century? How well does it fulfill its traditional functions? What are some of the new demands being made upon it? Is its future rosy or dim?

## THE FAMILY, PAST AND PRESENT

Societies may be roughly classified as static or dynamic. A *static* society is one in which social change is either extremely slow or practically nonexistent. A *dynamic* society is one characterized by rapid social change. Obviously, these are only rough classifications, since they do not indicate the degree or rapidity of social change— the range of which should be thought of as a continuum. At one extreme there is literally no change, at the other there is nothing but change. In fact, no extreme really exists because either situation would be nearly impossible. It is more accurate to say that a static society is one found toward that end of the social-change continuum representing no change and a dynamic society one found near the opposite end of the continuum.

The United States is a dynamic society. For this reason it is necessary to outline some of the characteristics of the American family in the past in order to compare and contrast them with the present. In terms of the situational-value approach, the family of the colonial period was largely a rural, farming, patriarchal one, with many children. Divorce was almost unknown. Marriage was based in no small part upon economic considerations, and a wife was truly a helpmeet on the farm. So too were children. Homes were large and the three-generation family not unusual. Children were to be "seen and not heard," and physical punishment was a generally accepted type of discipline. Religion as a social institution was quite important. Roles of husband, wife, father, mother, and children were rather rigidly defined, with few deviations accepted. There were solid reasons for all of these family characteristics. Life was hard compared to contemporary standards and family cooperation was essential to wrest a living from the soil and to preserve life itself against hostile Indian attacks.

Gradually but inevitably this pattern of family life changed. No doubt Cassandras existed who mourned its passing, but the Industrial Revolution had reached America. It caused families to move into cities where factories were located. Father lost his farm, or sold it if he had owned it, and became an industrial employee. Just forty years ago the U.S. Census revealed that more Americans lived in urban than rural areas. The type of family life suitable for a rural, farming, colonial, or frontier people was not suited to an urban people. But while the situation had changed, values had not changed, and efforts were made to cling tenaciously to traditional values of family life preserved from the past. It was at this point that the American family became an institution in trouble, and the problem today, far from being solved, is perhaps even more critical than then.

Her entrance into the First World War marked a turning point in the history of America and the American family. Only a few of the highlights can be cited. After a long battle, women won the right of suffrage. Married women appeared more frequently in the working force. Between 1890 and 1950, their number had increased 500 per cent.[2] The younger generation of the twenties, pathetically if somewhat erroneously labeled "The Lost Generation" by F. Scott Fitzgerald, staged a revolt against the mores and morality of their age. Women bobbed their hair, smoked cigarettes in public, and wore shorter and shorter skirts. The collegian appeared, with pennant, raccoon coat, and hip flask, the latter in defiance of the 18th amendment to the Constitution, which, in effect, prohibited the consumption of

[2] U.S. Census Bureau Press Release, Dec. 30, 1955.

alcoholic beverages. "Cake-eaters," the lower middle-class opposite number of the collegian, wore tight-fitting coats and trousers.

It was as though a dam had been holding back the volume of value change in American society and then had suddenly burst. For a while Americans seemed carried away by the flood. But actually, although tongues clicked and heads wagged about the younger generation, things were not as bad as they were painted. (This is frequently the case in most ages.) Then America was suddenly sobered by the depression of the thirties. The rates of marriages and births dropped. And the last vestiges of the old patriarchal family were lost when a wife or child was forced by the husband's unemployment to become the breadwinner.

Beginning about 1940—but particularly after the Second World War—marriage and family life began to assume its present form, largely among those now under fifty years of age. Today, the normal American family is equalitarian rather than patriarchal, and if anyone has the edge in terms of authority it is more likely to be the wife than the husband. The divorce rate, which had been increasing more or less steadily since statistics were first collected in 1887, took an upward swing in 1946, reaching an all-time high of 610,000—including annulments. Today, about 400,000 divorces are granted annually. The ratio of divorce to marriage, which prior to World War II was about one to six each year, is now one to four.

Another change occurring after the war has been the age at marriage. One-third of all first marriages for women occur at ages eighteen or nineteen. The favorite age for first marriages of men is 21 or 22, and one out of every four marries at these ages. Today the median age for first marriages of women is 20, and of men, 22.8. This is a decrease since 1890 of two years for women and four years for men, respectively.[3]

But Americans not only marry earlier than most peoples in the world but they also marry to a greater extent. In 1890 only 53 per cent of the population over fourteen was married. In 1949 this had risen to 67 per cent.[4] This can be explained in part by the earlier marriage age. By age 45 over 90 per cent of Americans are or have

---

[3] Bossard and Boll, op. cit., p. 103.
[4] U.S. Bureau of the Census, Current Population Reports, Population Characteristics, Marital Status and Household Characteristics: April 1949, Series P, pp. 21-26.

been married. In fact Americans are the most married, the earliest married, and the most frequently divorced people in the world.

There has been still another change in American family life following World War II. If deaths are subtracted from births the population of the United States is increasing at the rate of almost three million persons per year. In 1957 over four million babies were born. Not only do more couples have one child, but more couples have more children. "In 1951 third child births were 80 per cent more numerous than in 1940 and about 31 per cent more numerous than in 1947, and fourth child births were 63 per cent more numerous than in 1940 and 32 per cent more numerous than in 1947." [5]

The contemporary American family is either urban or suburban. Almost 60 per cent of Americans are now urban dwellers. In fact, one out of every five Americans lives within the metropolitan areas of New York, Chicago, Philadelphia, Los Angeles, and Detroit.[6] In contrast to the past, less than 12 per cent of the labor force is in agriculture. The farm too has been mechanized, and fewer hands are required. This change is more dramatic when it is realized that even as late as 1910, almost one-third of the American labor force was engaged in agriculture.

The typical American family in 1960 is the *conjugal* type, consisting of husband, wife, and their children. It is a two-generation rather than a three-generation family. In-laws are welcome but usually only as temporary visitors. The reduced size of the average home leaves little or no room for other than family members as permanent dwellers. Horizontal as well as vertical mobility upward may place both physical and social distance between the conjugal family and its relatives. Rapid social change also creates strains between generations as they attempt to bridge a widening gulf in mores and folkways. This strain becomes apparent even within the conjugal group itself as children reach their teens.

While the "permissive" aspect of child rearing common in the twenties and thirties is somewhat less pronounced today, the stern disciplinary attitude of the past is practically nonexistent. A democratic or equalitarian type of relationship tends to develop between

---

[5] Sumner H. Slichter, "The Prospects Are Bright," *The Atlantic, 193* (June 1954), p. 32.

[6] John F. Cuber, *Sociology: A Synopsis of Principles* (New York: Appleton-Century-Crofts, Inc., 1959), p. 413.

parents and children, especially as the latter become older. Religion is not an unimportant social institution for the family, but it seems to influence it less than in the past. Investigations reveal that relatively large numbers of Catholic children enter the first grade of parochial school unable to recite Grace before meals, the Hail Mary, or the Our Father.[7] Whether the present reputed religious revival has altered this situation is not yet clear.

To summarize, the current American family tends to be conjugal in structure, equalitarian in interpersonal relationships, and urban in residence. It is characterized by marriage at an early age, likely to produce more children than families did in the thirties and forties, frequently devoid of close ties with its kinship groups, and plagued by high rates of divorce, separation, and desertion.

## ANALYSIS OF THE CONTEMPORARY FAMILY

So far in this discussion little effort has been made to analyze the sociological and social-psychological reasons underlying the state of the contemporary family. Sociologists are fond of saying that the American family is in transition. This is quite true, and the chief reason given for it—rapid social change—is also correct. But the family as a social institution is not mere putty to be molded by other institutions and agencies. Many American parents are far from inarticulate—especially mothers—and while present patterns are partly the result of circumstances, they also result in part from voluntary acceptance of the situation.

There are various ways to approach an analysis of the family. One may begin with the impact of economic institutions, as mentioned previously, or of education or government. It would be quite feasible to explain changes in American family life, for example, through the higher level of American education. This is certainly part of the story. Instead, however, an attempt will be made to analyze the family from the viewpoint of the institution itself. Here the concepts of status and the roles of father, mother, husband, wife, and child will be useful.

---

[7] John L. Thomas, "Religion and the Child," *Social Order*, 1 (May 1951), pp. 206-7.

*Status* is one's position in society. Since a person has a number of statuses—father, husband, occupation, club, etc.—all of these are combined into what is termed a *total status*. Status is likewise a collection of rights and duties. *Role* is the acting out of one's status, i.e., playing the part of wife or husband, son or daughter. Furthermore, roles are interlocking. One cannot play the role of wife unless someone also plays the role of husband.

One of the most far-reaching changes in family life has been the alteration in the status and role of women in American society. The wife of the last century was very definitely subordinated to her husband, legally, economically, and socially. When she married, her property became her husband's, to be handled as he wished. She had to be represented by him in the courts if she sued. The husband was lord of the home and master of all he surveyed. Many women seemed to accept this role, but some rejected it. The battle for equality of women has been waged for over a century. If it has not yet been won, victory seems clearly in sight.

Since roles are interlocking, a change in the role of the wife could only occur along with changes in the husband's role. If women were to achieve equality, then the patriarch had to go. And go he did. But equality requires a balancing of the scales, and this is not simple. As the husband lost his rights, he tended to relinquish his duties. These duties were either assumed by some wives or they were left floating in air. As a result, one sociologist described the American family as matricentric.[8] From a father-dominated family, it became a mother-centered family. Today it may even be a child-centered family.

This transitional stage of the family has been one in which the respective roles of the spouses could not be adequately defined. A great deal of this has been facetiously illustrated by the plight of father as depicted in comic strips, television shows, and other media. He is shown as befuddled, bewildered, and not so much bemused by his current role as helpless to alter it. But these are merely superficial indices of role conflicts which lie well below the surface. A more penetrating analysis was made by Dr. Maria Farnham, a woman psychiatrist, in *Modern Woman: The Lost Sex*. Her basic thesis was that modern American woman had relinquished her most important role in life—that of mother—for a mere false goal—a career. But in

---

[8] Ernest W. Burgess and Harvey J. Locke, *The Family* (New York: American Book Co., 1945), pp. 131-34.

1960 she seems only partially right. Although women have careers, or at least jobs, to a greater extent than in the past, they are also having more children than in the past.

## MODERN MEN: THE LOST SEX

Perhaps the basic differences between the sexes today is that women seem to know what they want. Men don't. Margaret Mead has aptly expressed it:

> Men may flounder badly in these periods, during which the primary unit may again become mother and child, the biologically given, and the special conditions under which man has held his social traditions in trust are violated and distorted.[9]

When father was a patriarch, he was held in high esteem for being "a good provider." In many cases today, he shares this role with his wife and sometimes she may provide better than he. Thus, the traditional division of labor between the sexes has changed. Even when father is the sole provider and even a very good provider, he has found his traditional authority gone or considerably diminished. Furthermore, in order to be "a good provider" he finds himself drawn more and more out of the home into his business or profession. Under these circumstances women have not so much usurped authority as they have had it thrust upon them. Some, no doubt, enjoy this new position; but many suffer a sense of dismay when they find the partnership of marriage a one-woman enterprise.

Two major situations in which individuals suffer severe frustration are (a) when their role is uncongenial and they cannot escape from it and (b) when their role is ambiguous.[10] American males tend to suffer from one or the other, and perhaps at times from both. Traditional values tend to persist, sometimes fortunately, when they are vital, sometimes unfortunately when they are still considered vital but have really become peripheral.

The American husband who defines his role as head of the family—

---

[9] Margaret Mead, *Male and Female* (New York: William Morrow & Co., 1949), p. 193.

[10] Theodore Newcomb, *Social Psychology* (New York: The Dryden Press, 1950), pp. 416-19.

which indeed he is, or at least ought to be—in terms of the traditional authoritarian father or husband usually runs into a head-on conflict with his wife. The role of husband and father as his wife tries to define it is an uncongenial one for him and one from which he either cannot escape or escape is a price as yet too high for him to pay. If he attempts to vacillate between extremes of authoritarianism and permissiveness, he finds his role ambiguous. In either case he becomes frustrated and tension-prone.

Frustrations of men or women, of course, may stem from many aspects of life. But few married men or women fail to experience some frustrations within their marriage. An interesting item from the field of psychosomatic medicine may illustrate this point. Peptic ulcers are generally considered to be caused by tension which results from frustration. A study in a New York hospital reveals that the incidence of peptic ulcers over most of the last half-century has increased for men and decreased for women.

> In New York Hospital between 1900 and 1939, the male-female ratio of perforated ulcer cases changed from a ratio of 7 to 6 to a ratio of 31 to 3 . . . (this) ailment has become more significantly a male disorder and . . . the severity of the illness, as indicated by perforation, is no longer as common among young women.[11]

This is not offered as definitive proof of the changing male role but rather as a possible illustration of it.

But another aspect of the contemporary family merits analysis. Demographers had predicted not so long ago that the American population would reach a maximum about 1970 and then gradually decline. The birth rate since the war has caused them to revise their estimates and, while there may be an ultimate leveling off of the population, it will not occur in 1970. Population experts have been puzzled by this upsurge in the birth rate. In the beginning it appeared to be quite logical that it was due to delay of marriages during the war. When the veteran returned, he married and had children. But the problem is that the non-veterans who had not left home married earlier and also had a high reproductive rate.

What do early marriage and high reproductive rates mean? What do they tell us about the future of the American family? First, they may mean a more generalized acceptance by men of the changed

---

[11] Leo Simmons and Harold G. Wolff, *Social Science in Medicine* (New York: Russell Sage Foundation, 1954), pp. 129-30.

roles of husbands and wives. In many cases early marriage is possible only if the wife works, which she often does until she becomes pregnant. Another interesting example in this respect is the number of college students, even on the undergraduate level, who marry and continue their education. For a wife to help a husband through graduate or professional school today is common. Here is a real break with tradition. It is too early to evaluate its ultimate result. It will be pointed out later that marriage at an early age is not believed conducive to happy and successful marriages. Yet it does seem to indicate an acceptance of a changing pattern in husband-wife relations. The role of a wife as a breadwinner, albeit temporary, seems acceptable to the young men and women of America today.

The desire for children as exemplified in the increased birth rate indicates another change. No longer, apparently, do spouses, when listing their needs in married life, place refrigerators, cars, homes, and other material possessions before children. Furthermore, while "Togetherness" has become a somewhat sticky and maudlin phrase, it seems real enough in the case of young couples who have outlived the anesthesia of the honeymoon. Perhaps men are learning to redefine their roles successfully and women are modifying their roles to fit into the new family more adequately.

## EVERYCHILD: THE ALL-AMERICAN BOY OR GIRL

But the roles of parents cannot be divorced from the roles of children. These certainly merit consideration. Among the many other roles they portray, contemporary American parents are also chauffeurs for their children (not to mention their children's friends), den mothers, Blue Bird leaders, Boy Scout masters, coaches of little league baseball, Campfire Girl leaders, classroom mothers, and, in fact, group social workers for the multitudinous organized activities in which American children apparently suffer an obsessive-compulsive neurosis to participate. If most American urban children are lonely, they are indeed lonely in a crowd.

But American parents' participation is not limited to seasonal stints as coaches or weekly meetings of the Cub Scouts, Girl Scouts, or whatever. There seem to be more rituals and rites of passage associated with some of these organizations than are found in the entire Cross Cultural Index (a file of preliterate cultures) at Yale. Parents dutifully play, pray, and pay at these meetings. They buy excessive amounts of candy to support camps to which they will later send their children for a fee. Fathers may assist in collecting old paper and rags for drives to raise money for such activities.

Then there is the birthday complex. Each child must have a party complete with cake, ice cream, paper hats, and crepe paper decorations. Coke is drunk with abandon as the small fry cavort. Father, if humanly possible, will be present, equipped with a motion-picture camera to record the historic event for frequent, subsequent showings. When birthdays are not being celebrated at home, the children are almost certain to be invited to one. Harried parents scurry around to purchase suitable gifts and then wrap them appropriately.

There are father-son, mother-daughter, father-daughter, and mother-son Communion breakfasts at church, as well as P.T.A. meetings at school or individual sessions with teachers, at which reports are received and parents are counseled about their children's class work. Athletic events command parental attendance and dances demand them as chaperones. At least twice a year American families overspend for their children. At Christmas they exhaust their money and credit to perpetuate belief in a Santa Claus who is far from a myth among American youngsters. Whether financially recovered or not by Easter, they go on another spending binge to dress their children magnificently for the Easter "parade."

The American middle-class home is truly a child-centered one. The authority father has lost and some that mother has gained is increasingly usurped by children, and to no small extent they not only help define but actually do define the roles of mothers and fathers. An interesting illustration of this point is provided by a recent advertisement in a national magazine which dealt the *coup de grâce* to whatever paternal prestige remained—or at least any that father thought remained. There is a touching picture of a teen-age girl, her face furrowed with grief and eyes brimful with tears, asking her mother, "Please, Mother, can't Daddy stay upstairs when my date comes?" The reader is informed that Daddy is careless about his dress. His clothes do not measure up to the standard expected by his teen-age daughter and will probably make a very unfavorable impression on her date. At first, in view of the usual dress of teen-age boys and girls, one is tempted to think of this as satire. Apparently it is merely one of a series of advertisements to make father buy clothes and thus become sartorially splendid.

But the problem of paternal etiquette towards daughter's date is not confined to advertisements. A case history revealed that recently a thirteen-year-old girl was having her first date. All her brothers and sisters were confined to the basement prior to the boy's arrival. Daddy came home just fifteen minutes before the date's scheduled appearance, and was required to shave and dress before he met the boy friend, although this father was a white-collar worker. Unlike the ad, however, he was permitted to meet the young man.

Behind this there loom some strange attitudes among American parents. This behavior is most typical of the middle class, particularly of the upper-middle class, many of whom have achieved vertical mobility upward. Sometimes despite severe financial worries they smile bravely and assure each other that their children will have a better life than they did. Associated with this attitude is one of fierce competitiveness. Their children will be smarter, will be better dressed, and will be superior athletes to all other children. Their child or children will be the All-American boy or girl. If a husband and wife have nothing else in common—and some do not—they can usually agree on this one theme. Perhaps this is the basis of the folk belief that children will hold a marriage together, a conviction not capable of generalization in social science. Sometimes they do and sometimes they don't.

At any rate parent-child relations today are a far cry from the past. Despite inflation and continually increasing taxation the standard of living has been raised considerably. It is possible to do more for children in a material way but, as pointed out, parental concern is not limited to lavishing material goods upon children. There is a whole-hearted, continuous psychological support afforded, generally speaking, and children reared in such a style come not only to expect it as a privilege but to demand it as a right. Again it is too early to predict just what the ultimate effect of this type of child rearing may have. To some extent it has characterized American life for over half a century but the intensity and extent of it seem to have increased notably since World War II.

In writing of the American family, however, it is necessary to point out that this is an ideal construct. Social class, ethnic, racial, religious, and regional backgrounds do make a difference, and these differences have not been explored. The family under discussion here is the white, urban, middle-class one.

Finally, while this analysis has been approached via status and role, many other factors have played a part. A redefinition of woman's role has occurred in occupational, educational, and governmental spheres. Some of these changes have placed women in competition with men, and a number of authorities have underscored the fact that women may learn how to compete with men in business, industry, and the professions and then face the problem of how to cooperate with a man in marriage. Marriage at an early age may decrease this competitive aspect.

### DIVORCE

Despite certain indications of increased unity, or "togetherness," in the newer American families, the increasing incidence of divorce emphasizes a tendency toward a fundamental instability in American family life. There are two types of divorce: *Absolute* divorce, with a right to remarry, as recognized in state laws, and *limited* divorce, or separation, with no right to remarry. In addition to this there are annulments, in which it is held that no marriage actually occurred for various reasons. In certain states where divorce is granted only on a single ground, such as adultery (as for example in New York State), the rate of annulments is likely to be high.

In the Roman Catholic Church absolute divorce is forbidden. Limited divorce or separation with the approval of the bishop may be permitted for grave reasons. Annulment is also possible in the Roman Catholic Church if no valid contract ever existed, or if one or more of thirteen impediments to marriage are present.[12] When divorce is referred to in this section, it means absolute divorce. Limited divorce will be discussed later.

Some perspective of the extent of divorce in the United States can

---

[12] Clement S. Mihanovich, Gerald J. Schnepp, and John L. Thomas, *Marriage and the Family* (Milwaukee: The Bruce Publishing Co., 1952), pp. 168-78.

be gained by comparing it with other countries. Professor Bossard states:

> Approximately one-half of all divorces reported in the world each year are granted in the United States. Selecting a year at mid-century (1950), the United States with 381,000 reported divorces, exceeded by 235,000 the total number granted in Canada, England, Wales, France, West Germany, Yugoslavia, Sweden, Switzerland and Japan. In other words, the United States, with a population three-fifths as large as the combined total for the countries just named, granted one and three-fifths times as many divorces as they did.[13]

War and depressions have influenced the divorce rate. During the depression years of the early thirties the divorce rate declined. Immediately after World War II it showed a very sharp upsurge. Since then it has declined a bit. But the over-all trend has been upward from 1887, when it was 0.5 per 1,000 persons, to 1955, when it was 2.3 per 1,000 persons. As indicated earlier about 400,000 divorces are granted each year in this country, and the ratio of divorces to marriage within a given year has almost doubled since 1940.

### ATTITUDES TOWARDS DIVORCE

Whether divorce is actually accepted as a social problem in the United States is debatable. For this reason it was earlier classified as a covert social problem. Many authorities consider it a serious social problem and so do some persons who have been involved in it. Yet a recent, although somewhat limited, survey of 600 teen-agers found that 77 per cent would not "stick out an unhappy marriage," but preferred divorce. Even if children were present, more than half— 57 per cent—would seek divorce.[14] Sociological research in general seems to indicate that divorce carries relatively little social stigma today.

Here obviously is one factor in divorce that must be recognized. A value change has occurred among Americans who in the last century socially stigmatized divorce. Furthermore, a conflict of values is clear

---

[13] Bossard and Boll, *op. cit.*, p. 12.
[14] "Gilbert Research Company," in the *South Bend Tribune* (Mar. 29, 1959), Section 2, p. 25.

in this area. On the one hand the family is hailed as the basis of society, on the other, the breakdown of the family is accepted or at least tolerated. Persons who failed so miserably in almost any other aspect of their lives would suffer a lowered status and very likely a loss of their own self-respect.

The tragedy of divorce is amply attested to by those involved in it. Children generally suffer, most families undergo some economic privations, and many former husbands and wives cannot forget that they have repudiated solemn vows made to each other. However, it must be admitted that divorce is the ultimate, overt indication of family disorganization that has persisted over a long period of time.

The Roman Catholic Church sometimes permits legal divorce proceedings following separation in order to protect property rights, inheritance, etc. But it does not permit remarriage while both spouses are alive. If this occurs it is viewed as an adulterous relationship on the part of the previously married party. The Catholic Church almost alone today adheres to the words of Christ, "What God hath put together, let no man put asunder."

## DIVORCE LAWS

Widespread toleration of divorce is associated with divorce laws. Judge Paul W. Alexander of the Court of Common Pleas, Toledo, Ohio, has written: "Seldom has any branch of our jurisprudence set such an example of ineffable ineptitude and brought upon itself such serious censure from such varied sources as has the law of divorce." [15] Legally, a divorce is granted only when one party is guilty. Thus it is a trial by combat, if contested. Frequently, divorces are not contested. Grounds for divorce, as indicated earlier, show tremendous variations from one state to another. All fifty states grant divorces on the basis of adultery. Forty-three permit it for cruelty, which has a very wide range of interpretations. Desertion may be used in forty states and drink in forty-one.

The courts foster the legal fiction that only one party is guilty. In

---

[15] Paul W. Alexander, "Therapeutic Approach to the Problem of Divorce," in *Readings in Marriage and the Family*, eds. Judson T. and Mary G. Landis (Englewood Cliffs, N.J.: Prentice-Hall, Inc., 1952), p. 360.

most cases wives sue for divorce and a husband's chivalry, reputedly, permits it, whether he considers himself the guilty party or not. Yet it is extremely debatable if one party is ever exclusively guilty. Such cases may, of course, exist, but it seems more likely that both parties contribute—albeit one may be *more* responsible for it than the other. Under these circumstances both spouses can get "off the hook." The wife has court proceedings to prove her innocence, the husband, his sense of chivalry, which forbade his telling his side of the case, although he may intimate to friends that he has a side which if made public would clearly exonerate him. In the last analysis it is made to appear that both parties are innocent or only mildly guilty. It is not difficult to understand why divorce no longer carries a social stigma among many persons.

Furthermore, actual collusion is practiced. If the court knows this, or admits it, the proceedings should legally be thrown out. In at least one state a racket is carried on with the assistance of private detective agencies to prove adultery by arranging to find a husband with another woman in a compromising situation, even though no actual adultery occurred. At the outset one factor in divorce today is the present legal system regulating it and the actual court procedures.

## CAUSAL FACTORS IN DIVORCE

The real reasons for divorce are not the reasons offered to the courts. If this were so one would have to explain why citizens obtaining divorces in New York State always allege adultery while citizens in other states, where the law permits more grounds for it, give a variety of reasons. Grounds for divorce given to the courts are those which are acceptable within the given jurisdiction and least socially reprehensible to the complaining party.

It is difficult to disentangle the skeins of an unhappy marriage. Sometimes the parties involved do not actually know the true reasons why a divorce is sought. They tend to employ rationalizations, and the cumulative effect—i.e., repeated misbehavior or a series of misbehaviors—prove to be the "straw that breaks the camel's back." In pursuing the situational-value approach three generalizations may be made. First, changing marital roles make their mutual definition difficult. Second, the economic emancipation of women, provisions for alimony for the wife, and payments for support of children by the ex-husband make wives less dependent financially. Third, as has been said, attitudes toward divorce have softened and it is now socially acceptable, or at least tolerable.

To provide continuity, the status-role approach is used to analyze causal factors in divorce. Social change, personality differences, horizontal and vertical mobility, and ethnic, religious, regional, and racial backgrounds all make role-defining difficult. It should be recalled that neither husband nor wife define their roles alone, but rather together, and against their respective backgrounds within the society in which they live. The changing roles of spouses have already been discussed at length. Here, emphasis will be placed on those differences which seem to provoke maladjustments in marriage.

Romantic love, or the notion that there is a one and only person destined for an individual through all eternity who is ideal in all respects permeates American literature and other media of communication. To some extent it tends to influence a number of young men and women, particularly in their teens and early twenties. They enter marriage with extremely high expectations, and not infrequently individual happiness is the major goal. Romantic love is valuable in that, within limits, it often eases the strain of the newlyweds' adjustment. But only too soon the more mundane aspects of marriage descend on a couple and, unless the roots of their love are deep, disillusionment usually sets in. Real love involves sacrifice for the loved one, a notion not generally prevalent despite bombastic promises during courtship.

Marriage at an early age—in the past at least—has not been conducive to marital adjustment. The ability to face domestic problems such as money, in-laws, occasional quarrels, and the comparatively unexciting life after marriage, as compared to courtship, engagement, wedding, and honeymoon demand emotional maturity. While emotional maturity and chronological age are not identical, there is an association in most cases. Teen-age couples find in-law attempts to manage or dominate rather common. Male adultery is also somewhat high.[16] The youthful husband cannot adequately define his role,

---

[16] Judson T. Landis, "Time Required to Achieve Marital Adjustment," *American Sociological Review*, 11 (1946), pp. 666-77.

which now involves considerable responsibility, and he is not prepared to have his wife help define it for him.

All studies that attempt to predict success or failure in marriage reach the conclusion that the more a husband and wife possess a common social, economic, educational, religious, and ethnic background, among other factors, the more likely are the chances of marital adjustment. Put a little differently, this simply means that a boy and girl who both come from the middle class, have approximately the same educational level (although the husband's having more formal education than the wife does not create significant problems), belong to the same religious denomination, and, if members of an ethnic group, are members of the same one, can more readily define their marital roles.

To illustrate this point, a middle-class girl married to a lower-class boy discovers that his values are not her values. She will most likely expect an equalitarian relationship in marriage, he something more akin to the patriarchy. A Protestant mother, despite her prenuptial promises, may consider it annoying, if not downright unfair, to rear her children in a faith to which she does not belong. Her role in the religious education of her children is just about nil, and she may resent it. There is a tendency, despite the gulf between generations, to base role portrayal in part upon what was observed in the family in which one was reared.

Even when husband and wife begin with the same backgrounds, horizontal and social mobility may affect them differently. A new community may pose real problems of adjustment, particularly for a wife who is not, will not, or cannot become a part of it. Some women will not leave their home towns regardless of a husband's opportunity because they will not leave their mothers. If as a result of a college degree and ability a man rises in the socio-economic system, he will take on the values and behaviors of the new membership group. His wife may not be assimilated and, left behind socially, is incapable of assuming the new role essential to their changed status. This may be especially acute if a husband's success was made possible by his wife's assistance through college.

It is generally believed that husband and wife make the best adjustments when their personalities complement each other. If both are dominant, conflict is almost inevitable. It is only too obvious how a dominant wife and a dominant husband would define each other's roles.

Regardless of reasons alleged in a divorce court the basic problem in marital breakup is one of disagreement between spouses in one or more areas of life. It should be noted that for every couple that obtains a divorce for adultery, drink, non-support, cruelty, or almost any other reason, there are probably other couples who face the same difficulties, perhaps even more acutely, yet do not seek divorce. From the viewpoint of social psychology, it is not what happens to an individual alone which is important but how he defines what happens to him. Thus, there is a personal aspect to divorce. Individuals vary in their tolerance of a spouse's misbehavior. Perhaps those with low tolerance points are most likely to seek divorce, and given the situational and value changes in American society in recent years, this tolerance point seems to have been lowered.

TABLE 15-1[17]
FACTORS PRECIPITATING MARITAL DISRUPTION

| | *Irving* Five Dioceses (548 cases) | | *Thomas* (1580 cases) | | *Brinkman* (518 cases) | |
|---|---|---|---|---|---|---|
| | *Per cent* | *Rank* | *Per cent* | *Rank* | *Per cent* | *Rank* |
| Drink | 27.9 | 1 | 29.8 | 1 | 31.8 | 1 |
| Adultery | 27.2 | 2 | 24.8 | 2 | 20.3 | 2 |
| Temperament* | 16.8 | 3 | 12.1 | 4 | 10.2 | 3 |
| Irresponsibility* | 13.1 | 4 | 12.4 | 3 | — | — |
| Sex | 4.7 | 5 | 5.4 | 6 | 4.6 | 5 |
| Religion | 3.3 | 6 | 2.9 | 8 | 4.2 | 6 |
| Mental | 2.6 | 7 | 3.0 | 7 | 3.0 | 7 |
| In-laws | 2.0 | 8 | 7.2 | 5 | 4.8 | 4 |
| Money | 1.1 | 9 | .8 | 9 | — | — |
| Unclassified | 1.3 | | 1.7 | | 7.6 | |
| Total | 100.0 | | 100.0 | | 86.6 | |

* Includes abuse under temperament and desertion and non-support under irresponsibility and immaturity.

[17] Adapted from Gordon Irving, "Factors in Marital Breakdown in Five Midwestern Dioceses" (Unpublished doctoral dissertation, University of Notre Dame, 1959), pp. 258-60.

TABLE 15-2[18]

FACTORS PRECIPITATING SEPARATION IN TWO STUDIES
ACCORDING TO TOTAL FREQUENCY

| | Irving (548 cases) | | Brinkman (518 cases) | | |
|---|---|---|---|---|---|
| | Per cent | Rank | Per cent | Rank | |
| Drink | 42.2 | 1 | 30.1 | 2 | |
| Adultery | 39.9 | 2 | 20.3 | 4 | |
| Temperament | 25.5 | 7 | 11.9 | 6 | (incompatibility— nagging) |
| Irresponsibility | 26.1 | 5 | 11.8 | 7 | (infidelity) |
| Sex | 13.1 | 8 | 4.6 | 10 | |
| Religion | 8.0 | 9 | 8.1 | 8 | |
| Mental | 4.2 | 11 | 3.5 | 11 | |
| In-laws | 7.4 | 10 | 4.8 | 9 | |
| Money | 3.7 | 12 | — | — | |
| Desertion | 25.6 | 6 | 18.8 | 5 | |
| Non-support | 28.7 | 4 | 22.6 | 3 | |
| Abuse | 32.8 | 3 | 33.8 | 1 | |
| Other | 2.9 | | 25.3 | | |

[18] Adapted from Irving, *op. cit.*, pp. 258-60.

## SEPARATION

Separation is limited divorce in which the spouses are permitted to live apart but the marital bond is not legally dissolved. Sometimes this is done by mutual agreement without any recourse to the courts. Catholics are required to secure ecclesiastical permission through the chancery court.

Three studies of alleged factors in such separations have been made. The first was a study done in Chicago by Reverend John L. Thomas, S.J., who attempted to discover what he termed the "precipitating factor," that is, the factor that was in his estimation the one which sent a spouse to the chancery to petition for separation. In all three studies it should be noted that drinking, i.e., drinking of alcoholic beverages excessively, ranks first as a precipitating factor. In all three studies in Table 15-1, adultery is second in rank as a precipitating factor. However, Reverend Gordon J. Irving, O.M.I., who studied five midwestern dioceses, found adultery only seven-tenths of one per cent below drinking, while Reverend Gabriel Brinkman, O.F.A., who made his investigation in four eastern archdioceses, found adultery 11.5 per cent below drinking.

While there may be, or at least appear to be to those involved, a single pertinent factor, sociologists are inclined to agree that factors involved in divorce or separation are multiple. In fact, Father Thomas admits that even where drinking is the precipitating factor it is not uncommon to find drinking, non-support, and other factors associated with it.

In Table 15-2 where the *total frequency* of factors is listed, Father Irving found drink first, but Father Brinkman found that abuse outranked drink, which in his study was second. Since these studies were carried on in different parts of the United States and involved persons of somewhat different social backgrounds, discrepancies in results should not prove surprising.

But the listing of drink as first among precipitating factors merits examination. Excessive use of alcoholic beverages is usually considered a symptom of some deeper maladjustment which may stem from the marriage itself or from other sources. But there is no doubt that such drinking constitutes a real threat to marital adjustment. Cruelty, abuse, non-support and adultery may be associated with it, and together may constitute a syndrome which can destroy a marriage. But before drinking is accepted as a major factor in marital breakdown it would be desirable to determine, if possible, what basic motivations lead to excessive drinking.

Here it is clear that sociological studies of "causes" of divorce and separation, as well as desertion, do not go deeply enough. Professor Claude Bowman has aptly pointed out the need for depth analysis to uncover the real factors associated with the breakup of marriages. At present chancery courts and, for that matter, almost any courts are not equipped to carry on such intensive studies.

Finally, factors alleged as causes in these studies of diocesan chancery courts cannot be projected onto all American Catholics—differences between the Irving and Brinkman study alone prove this—and certainly not to all Americans. They are helpful in assessing the situation and should direct future research of a psychological nature into a deeper investigation of the factors listed.

## DESERTION

Desertion is the abandonment of children and/or a spouse. It is usually the husband who deserts, but wives too have done so. Reliable figures on the extent of desertion are simply impossible to obtain. One estimate is that the rate of desertion is one-half that of the divorce rate.[19] Other estimates claim that the desertion rate is only one-fourth as high as the divorce rate.[20] Desertions come to light only when appeals are made to courts or social agencies, usually to compel support by the absent spouse.

Since reliable statistics do not exist on desertion it is not possible to determine whether or not it is increasing. But a study in Philadelphia found that over the past thirty years, new desertion and non-support cases had almost doubled the number of divorces granted within that period.[21] The deserting husband usually makes no economic provision for his family, placing his wife and children in a dubious position. Since he has disappeared, it is not certain whether or not he is even alive. Yet some deserters make periodic reappearances and are accepted back into the family, only to disappear again later.

But there are cases of "fictitious" desertion, in which spouses continue to live together, or at least the husband's whereabouts is known. Since desertion is a ground for divorce in some states, it may be done through collusion of husband and wife who use this device to obtain a divorce.[22] While desertion has been called "the poor man's divorce," there is some evidence that it is also used when spouses wish to avoid the publicity attendant upon divorce but do not care to remain together.

---

[19] Kingsley Davis, "Divorce and Its Effects," in *Modern Marriage and Family Living*, eds. Morris Fishbein and Ruby Jo Reeves Kennedy (New York: Oxford University Press, Inc., 1957), p. 109.

[20] Ray E. Baker, *Marriage and the Family* (New York: McGraw-Hill Book Co., Inc., 1953), pp. 493-94.

[21] William N. Kephart and Thomas P. Monahan, "Desertion and Divorce in Philadelphia," *American Sociological Review*, 17 (Dec. 1952), p. 719.

[22] Kephart and Monahan, *op. cit.*, p. 719.

## REMEDIAL ACTION

Before collective remedial action to prevent or decrease the incidence of divorce and separation can occur there will have to be wider acceptance of the conviction that divorce and separation are really overt social problems. Obviously there are marriages where provision for separation will have to be made, but it is possible to decrease the rate.

First, a change in values is essential. Marriage must be recognized as a sacred, solemn contract to be broken only by the death of one spouse. At present it seems unlikely that such a value is acceptable to a relatively large number of Americans.

Second, changes in the situational aspects of marriage are necessary. One undeniable factor in divorce is hasty marriage, in which the parties do not know each other well, have little or nothing in common and under the influence of romantic love become husband and wife "till divorce do them part."

Third, the question of age at marriage should be carefully evaluated. There is at least some doubt that many teen-agers in American society have achieved enough maturity to enter the married state. Furthermore, many husbands, especially in the middle class and above, have years of schooling ahead of them. Some of these marriages are successful but in others disillusionment follows quickly on the heels of the honeymoon, and particularly after the birth of the first child, when the husband realizes that his professional or occupational aspirations are either doomed or will be achieved only with very great effort and sacrifice.

Fourth, changes in the divorce laws are clearly indicated. The variations from one state to another are bizarre and bewildering. In some states divorces are granted on very flimsy grounds and within a relatively short period of time. When necessary and possible, some couples will resort to these divorce mills.

Fifth, divorce court procedures should not be a trial by combat. It should be recognized that there is rarely only one guilty party. Efforts at reconciliation should be made through marriage counseling.

Sixth, marriage counseling should be developed on a wider scale so that couples with problems which they cannot solve alone will apply for help, and do so long before the problem becomes so acute that they seek divorce or separation.

Seventh, prospective husbands and wives should make efforts to define their roles prior to marriage, although this is difficult. Yet only mutually satisfactory definitions of such roles make a happy and successful marriage possible.

Eighth, individual happiness as the exclusive goal in marriage is an unrealistic ideal. As pointed out earlier, only mutual happiness is possible and mutual happiness will involve sacrifice from time to time on the part of husband, wife or both.

Finally, it should be clearly recognized by both parties that quarrels, disagreements and disappointments are inevitable in any marriage. The frequency and degree of these will vary but they will invariably be present. In other words, marriage is truly for better or worse and those who enter this state of life with realistic expectations and work together to make it better will usually make it so.

## REVIEW QUESTIONS

1. The American family is often said to be in a state of transition. What does this mean?
2. What changes have recently occurred in the age at which Americans marry?
3. The typical American family today may be described as "conjugal." What does this mean?
4. How has the status and role of women been altered in American society?
5. What has happened to the traditional role of the father in the United States?
6. What is the attitude of the average middle-class American family toward child rearing?
7. What is the extent of divorce in the United States today?
8. Does the Roman Catholic Church oppose all types of divorce?
9. Studies by Father Thomas and others seem to indicate that drinking is a major factor in marital breakup among Catholics. Evaluate this finding.
10. Desertion has been called a "poor man's divorce." Is this currently true?

11. What remedial measures could be taken to increase the stability of the American family?

## SELECTED READINGS

*Articles*

Barta, Russell and Charles T. O'Reilly, "Some Dating Patterns and Attitudes Toward Marriage of 174 Catholic College Students," *American Catholic Sociological Review,* 13 (Dec. 1952), 240-48.

Bukowski, F., "The Stability of the Marriages of Catholic College Graduates," *American Catholic Sociological Review,* 12 (Mar. 1951), 11-16.

Goode, William J., "Problems in Post Divorce Adjustment," *American Sociological Review,* 13 (Aug. 1948), 394-400.

Huth, Edward A., "America's Challenge: The Divorce Problem," *American Catholic Sociological Review,* 8 (Dec. 1947), 275-80.

Kane, John J., "The Changing Roles of Father and Mother in Contemporary American Society," *American Catholic Sociological Review,* 11 (Oct. 1956), 140-51.

Kephart, William M., "Occupational Level and Marital Disruption," *American Sociological Review,* 20 (Aug. 1955), 456-65.

Landis, Judson T., "Marriages of Mixed and Non-Mixed Religious Faith," *American Sociological Review,* 14 (June 1949), 401-6.

Rooney, Elizabeth, "Polish Americans and Family Disorganization," *American Catholic Sociological Review,* 18 (Mar. 1957), 47-63.

Thomas, John L., "Theory and Research in Family Sociology," *American Sociological Review,* 15 (Mar. 1955), 6-18.

*Books*

Bandura, Albert, *Adolescent Aggression: A Study of the Influence of Child Training Practices and Family Inter-Relationships.* New York: The Ronald Press Company, 1959.

Bernard, Jesse S., *Dating, Mating and Marriage: A Documentary-Case Approach.* Cleveland: Howard Allen, Inc., 1958.

Bossard, James H. S., and Eleanor Stoker Boll, *Why Marriages Go Wrong.* New York: The Ronald Press Company, 1948.

Duvall, Evelyn Ruth, *The Art of Dating.* New York: Association Press, 1958.

Kane, John J., *Marriage and the Family.* New York: The Dryden Press, 1952.

Strecker, Edward A., *Their Mothers' Daughters*. Philadelphia: J. B. Lippincott Co., 1956.

Thomas, John L., *The American Catholic Family*. Englewood Cliffs, N.J.: Prentice-Hall, Inc., 1956.

Werth, Alvin and Clement Mihanovich, *Papal Pronouncements on Marriage and the Family from Leo XIII to Pius XII*. Milwaukee: The Bruce Publishing Co., 1955.

# 16

# Religion in American Society

I N a discussion of social problems it seems appropriate to consider the influence of religion as expressed through the churches in alleviating social problems or in sometimes contributing to them. In many of the social problems considered in this text, American churches have played an important role in attempting to eliminate or reduce them. Both Catholic and Protestant churches have sponsored temperance movements in an effort to combat excessive drinking or to prevent drinking of alcoholic beverages entirely. Protestantism was largely responsible for the 18th Amendment to the Constitution, which outlawed the manufacture or the importation of alcoholic beverages. Recently, most of the churches have taken a forthright stand against racial discrimination. The Catholic Church especially, although not exclusively, has fostered the right of employees to bargain collectively with an employer. Needless to say, organized religion has shown a real concern over crime and juvenile delinquency. The Catholic Church has established reformatories for the wayward, while hospitals, founded and maintained by various churches, are common throughout this country. The same may be said of schools and colleges. Care of the poor and the aged is another function performed by the churches. Furthermore, most of this was done long before the state assumed some of the work.

While the contribution of the churches toward the alleviation of social problems considerably outweighs their contribution to them, in all fairness such occasions ought to be mentioned. When churches have contributed to social problems, it has usually been through the action of a few clergymen or the official stand of one of the smaller sects. During the twenties, and particularly at the time Alfred E. Smith, a Catholic, was campaigning for the presidency of the United States, some ministers apparently supported the Ku Klux Klan by inviting Klan members to attend the services in their regalia. The Ku Klux Klan was openly and avowedly opposed to Negroes, Catholics, and Jews. Insofar as these ministers upheld the ideals of the Klan, they appeared to give church approval to it and thus to racial, ethnic, and religious prejudices. During the thirties it was claimed that a nationally known priest and radio orator was anti-Semitic. While John F. Kennedy was campaigning for the presidency of the United States, certain Protestant churches issued public statements against the election of a Catholic to this office, and in Indianapolis the candidate was picketed by members of one church group. Refusal by Christian Scientist parents to permit necessary operations on their children have brought them into conflict with the law. The same is true of some small sects which prohibit their children from attending school until the required maximum age. In fact, the sheer number of diverse religious denominations in the United States, with their sometimes conflicting value systems, stimulates interreligious tensions and conflicts. But this is inevitable in a democratic society, and is by no means an insurmountable difficulty.

Opportunities for the churches to lead or assist in the alleviation of social problems now seem to be unparalleled. Challenges in the form of crime and juvenile delinquency, so far as available statistics are correct, are unprecedented. At the same time during the fifties and sixties, a religious revival has been sweeping America. Church spires are rising almost as rapidly as the birth rate. Nine hundred and thirty-five million dollars were expended in construction of religious buildings in 1959, as compared to $593 million in 1954. In 1954 over 112 million persons belonged to some religious body, which was 63.4 per cent of the population, the highest in history. In 1930, for example, only 47 per cent of the population claimed membership in some church. According to a poll by the American Institute of Public Opinion 47 per cent of the persons interviewed had attended church during the week preceding the interview. A poll conducted in 1939 showed that only 41 per cent had attended during the week prior to the interview. Between 1952 and 1959, Protestant church-related day schools increased from 3,000 to 4,794. In the latter year a total of 358,739 students were enrolled in some type of Protestant day school below the college level. Roman Catholic enrollments at that time amounted to more than 4,000,000.[1]

Statistics on church membership are far from accurate. The Church of Christ, Scientist, has a rule which forbids collection of church membership statistics. In the figures cited there are probably many omissions, and church membership may actually be larger than statistics reveal. Furthermore, in many Protestant denominations children below the age of fourteen are not counted, although they do attend church and Sunday school services. But church membership alone does not necessarily indicate a religious revival. There are certain indications, as Will Herberg has stated, that secularism is not an unimportant factor in American life.

Herberg believes that secularism in America is covert, that is, a somewhat unconscious attitude which influences life and thought. To illustrate, he states that Ignazio Silone, an Italian writer and socialist, when asked to mention the most important date in the history of the world cited the 25th of December in the year zero. On the other hand, when 30 outstanding Americans were asked to rate the 100 most significant events in history, they gave first place to Columbus' discovery of America but 14th place to the birth and crucifixion of Christ. These received no higher rating than the discovery of the X ray or the Wright Brothers' first flight. Despite the fact that the Bible has become an increasing best-seller in the United States, and that more than 80 per cent of adults said they considered it the revealed word of God and not merely a great piece of literature, more

---

[1] *The Yearbook of American Churches*, Bonson Y. Landis, ed. (New York: Office of Publication and Distribution, National Council of the Churches of Christ of the U.S.A., 1960), pp. 278-84.

than one-half of them could not name any of the first four books of the New Testament.[2] Thus, religion in America is something of a paradox. On the one hand church edifices, church membership, and church attendance are booming. On the other hand crime, scandals in public office and among college athletes, violence against Negroes, and a pervasive secularistic attitude are all common.

Religion in America presents another interesting phenomenon. There are over 250 different denominations, sects, and cults. They vary from such organizations as "Two-Seed-in-the-Spirit Predestinarian Baptist," with sixteen churches and 201 members in 1945, to the Roman Catholic Church, with 23,346 churches and over 40 million members. While it is customary to think of three great religious bodies in the United States—Protestant, Catholic, and Jewish—this is an oversimplification. Very many different kinds of denominations with varied theological viewpoints are grouped under the name of Protestantism. Some, such as the Unitarians, are not even considered Protestant by some Protestant spokesmen. Among Catholics in this country all do not belong to the Roman rite. While they hold the same theological beliefs and are in union with Rome, their rituals vary from those of Roman Catholics. And, as pointed out, the Jews consist of three groups, Orthodox, Conservative, and Reformed.

Among Christians there are also the Eastern Orthodox churches, usually with some national prefix—such as the Greek Orthodox, the Romanian Orthodox, the Ukrainian Orthodox, the Russian Orthodox Church outside Russia, and others. Some of the Asiatic churches have likewise been established in the United States. The Buddhists have 52 churches and a total membership of 7,700. In 1953 the Moslems erected a mosque in Washington, D.C., but to date they appear to have no formal general organization. Their membership is estimated at between 10 and 20 thousand persons.[3] Compared to certain European countries, such as Sweden, the variety of religious denominations in the United States is great.

---

[2] Will Herberg, *Protestant, Catholic, Jew* (Garden City, N.Y.: Doubleday and Company, Inc., 1955), pp. 13-14.

[3] *The Yearbook of American Churches*, pp. 29 and 82.

## RELIGIOUS REVIVALS

The present religious revival is not altogether novel. In the history of religion in America it is customary to think of three or four important religious revivals, usually identified by outstanding preachers. For the most part these refer to Protestantism because during the colonial period and the early days of the republic, Catholics were few. The large waves of Jewish immigration did not reach these shores until the latter 1840's, and particularly after 1880. While any sociological rule of thumb regarding religious revivals is not feasible, it is possible to generalize to the extent that at certain periods of history there has been a vigorous renewal of interest in religion. Generally, this has been followed by a decline of religious fervor—until the next revival.

The "First Great Awakening" occurred in the colonial era and is associated with an eminent early preacher, Jonathan Edwards. But later, Rationalism, Deism, and Unitarianism became prevalent. The "Second Great Awakening," beginning about 1800, was characterized by Western camp meetings, revivals in Eastern colleges, the establishment of a new tract, and revival and home mission societies. The name of Charles G. Finney is associated with this revival. But popular interest subsequently turned to industrialization, westward expansion, the Mexican War, and the increased struggle between North and South over the slavery issue. Following the Civil War Dwight L. Moody was the leader and spokesman of the third great religious revival. About this time, however, an interest in science began competing with Evangelical Christianity, causing it to be displaced among Protestants by the new "social gospel," a concern for the socio-economic plight of workers. Despite the colorful behavior of an ex-baseball player turned Evangelist, Billy Sunday, who held meetings throughout the United States around the turn of the last century, urged people to "hit the sawdust trail," and "wrestled" with the devil on the public platform, it was believed that the day of important revivalists was past.[4]

---

[4] Timothy L. Smith, "Historic Waves of Religious Interest in America," *The Annals*, 332 (Nov. 1960), p. 10.

During the twenties there was a decline in religious enthusiasm and interest as the behavioral sciences—including Freudian psychology—seemed to threaten the "old-time religion." The high point in this new conflict was reached in Dayton, Tennessee in 1925 with the Scopes trial. A popularized knowledge of Darwin's theories of evolution had reached the masses. The State of Tennessee passed a law forbidding the teaching of evolution in the schools, fearing that it threatened the Christian concept of the universe. Scopes, a high school teacher, taught this theory and was brought to trial. He was defended by Clarence Darrow, a famous criminal lawyer, and prosecuted by William Jennings Bryan, a three-time unsuccessful candidate for the presidency on the Democratic ticket and a Fundamentalist in religion. The trial attracted national and international attention and made some of the Protestant Fundamentalist beliefs on the literal interpretation of the Bible appear ridiculous. Bryan "won the battle but lost the war," and there followed a period in which many intellectuals left Protestantism, and church contributions and attendance declined.

The Scopes trial did not have this impact on Catholicism because the Catholic Church did not insist upon a literal interpretation of the Bible. For example, the six days in which the world was created in the Catholic interpretation did not necessarily mean six periods of 24 hours. However, the Scopes trial was an unnecessary and unfortunate blow to religion. Darwin had never claimed that man descended from an ape but rather that man and the ape had a common ancestor. The Scopes hearing has sometimes been referred to as the "monkey trial," mostly because Darwin's theories had been badly misconstrued.

Toward the end of the depression of the thirties, and particularly since 1940, there has been an upsurge in religious interest and activity. Church membership, as pointed out, has increased notably. Among Protestants this revival has been spearheaded by such spokesmen as Reinhold Niebuhr, Paul Tillich, Karl Barth, and others. It has been called Neo-Orthodoxy, "a self-conscious movement of Christian thought, drawing deeply from traditions that had been spurned for two centuries, invigorated by fresh concern for the Biblical message, and determined to speak relevantly to the total human situation." [5]

---

[5] Sidney E. Ahlstrom, "Theology and the Present Day Revival," *The Annals*, 332 (Nov. 1960), p. 22.

The social gospel of Protestantism began toward the end of the 19th century and to some extent continues today. Basically, it was an attempt at humanitarian reform. Ministers have attempted to promote policies in the business and social world which are in conformity with their religious principles. It has not always enjoyed the unqualified approval of the laity, particularly those whose vested interests are imperiled by it. Neither has it seemed entirely relevant to some of the laity. The best example today is racial equalitarianism, and the clergy, in this case both Catholic and Protestant, sometimes encounter stiff opposition from laymen in this area.[6]

Explanations for the current religious revival are varied. Will Herberg views it in relation to immigration. According to him the first generation of immigrants arriving in the United States had to redefine their roles. Unsettled through immigration, they found security and solace within their ethnic group. They had their newspapers, their societies, and, particularly, their churches. But for the second generation this was untrue. Some became "professional" Italians, Poles, or whatever, assuming a position of leadership within their ethnic group. Others, unwilling to do this, found themselves in an ambiguous role: not quite able to be genuine Americans and not quite willing to remain ethnically separated. Most of the second generation, however, took neither of these courses, but remained somewhat confused, anxious and discontented, without any true awareness of what the trouble was. Herberg believes that the "professional ethnic" remained a member of his church and supported it but his interest was rather casual. Those who rejected their ethnic background tended to reject their religion too. He believes that the second generation by and large tended to drift away from the church. But the third generation is quite different. They reject ethnic pluralism but they do not hope for the melting-pot solution by which all cultures are subordinated to the American. To them the newcomer is expected to change many things as he becomes Americanized—but not his religion. This then is one explanation of the religious revival.[7]

While such a thesis may be plausible enough for those who are third-generation Americans, it does not cover the large numbers who are of the fourth, fifth, or even later generations. After 1880 most of

---

[6] Richard D. Lambert, "Current Trends in Religion: A Summary," *The Anals*, 332 (Nov. 1960), p. 152.

[7] Herberg, *op. cit.*, pp. 28-35.

the immigrants were Jews or Catholics. While the Herberg theory may fit American Jews, its application to Catholics appears somewhat tenuous. Furthermore, the religious revival is quite strong among Protestants, large numbers of whom are not third generation.

Reasons for the religious revival are undoubtedly numerous and complex. But as Sidney E. Ahlstrom has put it:

> Most would probably agree . . . that the post-war American situation—its affluent society, its lonely crowds of gray-flanneled organization men, its vast numbers of upwardly mobile status seekers, fruitless and insecure, its trembling awareness of hydrogen bombs, fallout, and the fact that a blow at the enemy would be suicide—all this has created religious needs both shallow and deep.[8]

While the social scientist seeks sociological reasons for the religious revival, supernatural aspects, although not amenable to empirical research, also play their part.

## CULTS AND SECTS

Another aspect of the growing religious revival is the increase of sects and cults in America. Among the sects are the historic Adventist bodies, the Jehovah's Witnesses, the Pentecostals, the Assemblies of God, and others. Among the cults would be the Father Divine movement, the "I AM" movement, to some extent the Oxford Group, and others.[9] *Sects* are religious ingroups characterized by social isolation or exclusiveness and a strict adherence to credal tenets. They have been thought of as a type of accommodation against assimilation into the larger outgroup.[10] Generally, the sect attracts members of a minority group or the under privileged segments. Later, as it develops a larger membership, it may become a denomination.

The term *cult* has a variety of meanings, but generally it refers to a rather small group characterized by mysticism, little formal organization, and a charismatic leader. Its creed and rituals differ sharply from those prevalent in the culture, and, because it is normally built around

---

[8] Ahlstrom, *op. cit.*, p. 26.
[9] Martin E. Marty, "Sects and Cults," *The Annals*, 332 (Nov. 1960), p. 130.
[10] Henry Kraft Fairchild, *Dictionary of Sociology* (Ames, Iowa: Littlefield, Adams and Company, 1955), p. 268.

the leadership of one person, it usually disbands at his death. Cults rarely develop into established sects or denominations.[11] It is believed that the number of sects and cults has grown considerably in recent years, although reliable statistics are not available. Some sects and cults keep their membership figures a secret, while others may exaggerate to gain greater prestige. It is likewise believed that economic support for these organizations is considerably higher than that given to the more prosperous established churches.[12] If this is the case it may indicate a growing insecurity among some of the recent in-migrants to metropolitan areas—particularly southern Negroes and poor southern whites—or perhaps a reaction against conformity even in areas of religion among some of America's population. Of course, all sects and cults are not found in urban areas. Some of them thrive in rural areas, particularly in the South. At any rate, they seem to be another indication of the increased interest in religion among Americans.

## THE RELIGIOUS REVIVAL AMONG CATHOLICS

The religious revival among Catholics—if indeed it can even be thought of as such—takes an entirely different form. The growth of the Catholic Church in the United States during recent years can be traced chiefly to the Catholic birth rate and, to a much lesser extent, conversions. While many of the displaced persons or refugees arriving in this country since the end of World War II have been Catholics, their numbers do not compare with the rate of immigration prior to the 1920's. Generally, the Catholic birth rate is somewhat higher nationally than the Protestant and Jewish rates, and the Catholic Church counts as members all those who are baptized. Since among Catholics, infants are baptized within a few weeks after birth, the increased U.S. birth rate would be reflected more quickly in Catholic membership statistics. Catholics, like many other Americans, have been moving to the suburbs. But this general movement is particularly noticeable among Catholics because they are inherently an

---

[11] J. Milton Yinger, *Religion, Society and the Individual* (New York: The Macmillan Company, 1957), pp. 154-55.

[12] Marty, *op. cit.*, p. 129.

urban people. This transition has necessitated the erection of churches and—since more than one-half of Catholic elementary school children are in parochial schools—the building of schools.

It is not possible to distinguish any three or four "great awakenings" in American Catholicism. The growth of the Catholic Church in the United States has been consistently upward, although there have been periods in which spurts occurred because of heavy Catholic immigration. The Catholic immigrant, his children, and his grandchildren for the most part retained the faith. There are no historical statistics to indicate church attendance in the past but the fervor of American Catholics seems amply attested to by the spread of their religion in America. For years Catholicism was an immigrant religion and relegated to at least a second-class status. Sociologically speaking, this may have cemented the ingroup feeling and deepened Catholic loyalty, but the economic and social discriminations suffered were trying.

But within contemporary Catholicism there is a certain ferment which may be considered roughly akin to the revival occurring in other religious bodies. Perhaps it can be categorized most readily by the movement known as Catholic Action, which is the apostolate of the laity under the direction of bishops. One expression of this apostolate is the Christian Family Movement, composed of small groups who meet for study, prayer, and action. It is active in over 100 dioceses and has another 250 regional leaders. Another recent movement is the Cana Conference. While it is not nationally organized, in 1950 it existed in 87 dioceses out of 122 in the nation. It usually consists of a one-day conference for married couples, with lectures by priests, physicians, and others, followed by small discussion groups. The Pre-Cana Conference has been established to help prepare engaged couples for marriage.[13] While the Catholic Church has always been interested in the welfare of the family, it is notable that these two movements are relatively recent and to no small extent have been actively co-sponsored by the laity.

Another example of recent action by the Church is the modification of the Eucharistic fast prior to the reception of Holy Communion, making the prolonged fasting from midnight until the reception of Communion no longer necessary. Also, with the permis-

---

[13] Alphonse E. Clemens, *Marriage and the Family* (Englewood Cliffs, New Jersey: Prentice-Hall, Inc., 1957), pp. 325-26.

sion of the bishop, Mass may be celebrated in the afternoon or evening. The time of Holy Week services has likewise been changed, returning to a system common in the earlier days of Christianity. The summoning of an Ecumenical Council by Pope John XXIII is a milestone in contemporary Catholicism.

## PARISH SOCIOLOGY

Over the last 20 years, Catholics in the field of sociology have investigated many areas of parish life. Brother Augustine McCaffrey published his study of youth in a Catholic parish in 1941. He found that 51 per cent of the adult men and 60 per cent of the adult women practiced their faith, while a total of 44 per cent of the adults did not. In 1942 Brother Gerald J. Schnepp's doctoral dissertation, "Leakage from a Catholic Parish," appeared. He found that 80 per cent of the parishioners practiced their faith regularly, 4 per cent were lax, and 16 per cent did not practice at all. Father Schuyler states that this was the first parish study of its type, "more detailed and analytic than any of the European studies have yet been; and it is a veritable gold mine of statistical data for parish research." [14] Father George A. Kelly studied white, English-speaking Catholics in the diocese of St. Augustine, Florida. He found that 75 per cent of these people attended Mass regularly on Sunday. Twelve per cent attended irregularly.

Reverend Joseph H. Fichter has carried on a number of studies of Catholicism in America. His first book, *The Southern Parish; Dynamics of a City Church*, appeared in 1951. While Brothers Augustine and Gerald had studied parishes on the eastern seaboard, Father Fichter selected New Orleans. He found that somewhat less than 60 per cent of the parishioners attended Mass regularly on Sunday, but did not make any adjustment for those who would be legitimately excused. In his second book, *Social Relations in the Urban Parish*, he constructed ideal types of parishioners, such as the "nuclear parishioner," or the ideal Catholic; the "modal parishioner," or average Catholic; the "marginal parishioner," or lax Catholic; and the "dor-

---

[14] Joseph B. Schuyler, *Northern Parish* (Chicago: Loyola University Press, 1960), pp. 292-93.

mant parishioner," or lapsed Catholic. He found that the marginal Catholic remains a church member but is on the fringe. His reference group is more likely to be that of his business associates and his value systems are more in conformity with secular institutions than with the church. At times he is even somewhat anti-Catholic. According to a Catholic Digest sample of American Catholics, between 57 per cent and 67 per cent of them (if the sample had been projected onto the entire population) would have attended Sunday Mass on each of the 12 Sundays preceding the interview.[15]

While even the lowest percentage cited in any of the above studies —57 per cent—is higher than the national percentage of 47 per cent who attended church on the Sunday preceding the American Institute of Public Opinion interview, it should be remembered that Catholics are obliged to attend Mass every Sunday unless excused for a serious reason, as long as they have reached seven years of age. A more recent study by Father Joseph Schuyler in New York City, where allowances are made for children under seven and it is estimated that about 10 per cent of the parishioners had a legitimate excuse for not attending Sunday services, it was found on the basis of census returns that 79.6 per cent of the parishioners were regularly present at Sunday Mass, 9.8 per cent attended irregularly, and 10.6 per cent did not attend at all.[16]

While attendance at Sunday Mass is not an exclusive indication of the extent of Catholic practice, it is certainly a fundamental one. Differential figures on Sunday Mass attendance reported by the various investigators can be explained in part by the particular methods of computation they employed, the period during which the study was conducted, and the section of the country considered. Even the type of parish would probably alter the findings. For example, Irish Catholics and Catholics of Irish descent are usually believed to be more faithful in Sunday Mass attendance than certain other ethnic groups. In the study conducted by Father Schuyler, 49.1 per cent of the parishioners born outside the United States came from Ireland. Probably the most logical conclusion to be drawn from these studies is that Sunday Mass attendance will reveal variations between one parish and another, variations among dioceses, and variations in periods of time. Nevertheless, it seems clear that the majority of

---

[15] Schuyler, *op. cit.*, pp. 295-97.
[16] Schuyler, *op. cit.*, p. 200.

American Catholics do attend Mass regularly, although the percentage absenting itself may be greater than was realized prior to these studies.

## AMERICAN JEWS

Rabbi Albert E. Gordon has studied Jews in 89 suburban communities in the United States. He points out that according to estimates 60 per cent of the entire American Jewish community was affiliated with synagogues in 1956-57. On the basis of his study he suggests that the percentage of Jewish membership in synagogues matches that of the nation as a whole with regard to religious affiliation. However, he finds some differences in the percentage of membership in synagogues. Where low-housing predominates, Jewish families join the synagogues when their children are old enough to attend Hebrew or Sunday school. He also discovered an association between income and affiliation. When basic family financial obligations can readily be met, there is a greater tendency to join the synagogue. Synagogue membership is also associated with crisis situations, and when there is an increase in prejudice and intolerance in the suburb the Jews tend to seek the security of the synagogue. Rabbi Gordon believes that denominational differences among the Conservative, Reformed, and Orthodox Jews have lessened in the synagogue. In fact, some Jewish families join several synagogues and temples—Conservative, Reformed, and Orthodox—within the same community. The traditional role of the rabbi as a learned and pious Jew has been changed somewhat in suburbia, where the rabbi is likely to be something of a pastor, counselor, and guide to moral and ethical living.[17]

Just as attendance at Sunday Mass is scarcely an exclusive indication of the practice of Catholicism, affiliation with a synagogue or temple itself would probably not alone indicate a sincere practice of Judaism. But, on the other hand, the synagogue or temple is the center of Jewish life, and is probably as good an index as can be found for estimating religious practice among Jews.

---

[17] Albert I. Gordon, *Jews in Suburbia* (Boston: Beacon Press, 1959), pp. 85-88.

RELIGION AND ECONOMIC LIFE

It appears that there is a religious revival among Protestants, that the majority of Catholics are faithful in attending Sunday Mass, and that most Jews, at least in suburbia, are affiliated with synagogues. What impact, then, does this religiosity have upon these people in their economic and political lives? Shortly after the turn of the century Max Weber published *The Protestant Ethic and the Spirit of Capitalism*. In his essays, he attempted to explain why the spirit of capitalism, as found in Western Europe and the United States, had developed. To him, this spirit of capitalism was epitomized by some of the aphorisms of Benjamin Franklin regarding the spending, saving, and investment of money, as well as diligence at work.[18] His general conclusions were that the Protestant Reformation, while not actually causing the development of capitalism, facilitated it through what he termed the "Protestant ethic." Martin Luther had raised the status of business to that of a sacred calling. This concept was further developed by John Calvin and others, who promoted a type of ascetical worldliness by which a person worked hard, practiced frugality, and did not spend his money on luxuries, or even a highly comfortable living. If one became a financial success, he could be reasonably sure that somehow God was "on his side" and that he had probably gained salvation in the afterlife. This represented a break in the traditional attitude toward business, which had seen it only as something transacted rather casually over five or six hours of the day.

This new spirit of capitalism was not typical of all Protestant denominations but was particularly prominent among such groups as the Puritans in New England, the Calvinists in Europe, and the Methodists and some of the Baptist sects.[19] Weber states that a study of the distribution of occupations among religious groups in any country of mixed religious composition reveals that business leaders and owners of capital, higher grades of skilled labor and to

---

[18] Max Weber, *The Protestant Ethic and The Spirit of Capitalism*, trans. Talcott Parsons (New York: Charles Scribner's Sons, 1930), p. 50.
[19] Weber, *op. cit.*, pp. 98-154.

an even greater degree the higher technically and commercially trained personnel are mostly Protestants. He also mentions that the number of Catholic students in and graduates of higher educational institutions was lower than that of Protestants, according to their proportion in the respective population.[20]

Although Weber made his study more than half a century ago, a number of studies in the 1950's and 1960's in the United States reveal a somewhat similar pattern. (This matter has been discussed at length in the section, "The American Catholic Minority.") All students of this subject do not agree that Catholic aspirations and attainments are less than those of Protestants. Raymond Mack, Raymond Murphy, and Seymour Yellin in their article, "The Protestant Ethic, Level of Aspiration and Social Mobility," claim that there are no statistically significant differences between these two religious categories, either in aspirations to advance or in actual occupational achievement.[21] Gerhard Lenski, however, takes issue with this conclusion and is critical of the statistical procedures used. He likewise rejects the statements of Lipset and Bendix that the rates of mobility between Catholics and Protestants on the basis of a national sample of American men interviewed during the 1952 presidential election are the same. He points out, for example, that they fail to consider the size of the community. Upward mobility is more difficult in a smaller town than in a large city and a quarter of white Protestants in the United States live in communities of a quarter of a million or less, whereas Catholics tend to live in larger communities. Under these circumstances he believes that Protestants in this sample were competing under a handicap.[22]

In a 1958 Detroit-area study based on 750 cases, Lenski states, "when white Protestants were compared with Catholics who began life in the same point in the class system, the former rose to (or stayed in) the ranks of the upper middle class more often than the latter." At the opposite extreme, Catholics wound up in the lower half of the working class more often than Protestants three out of

---

[20] Weber, *op. cit.*, pp. 35 and 38.

[21] Raymond Mack, Raymond Murphy, and Seymour Yellin, "The Protestant Ethic, Level of Aspiration and Social Mobility," *American Sociological Review*, 21 (June 1956), pp. 295-300.

[22] Gerhard Lenski, *The Religious Factor* (Garden City, N.Y.: Doubleday and Company, Inc., 1961), pp. 76-77.

four times. Differences were especially marked among the sons of middle-class men and farmers.[23]

Despite some conflicting findings regarding the aspirations and attainments of American Catholics and Protestants, an assessment of available data seems to indicate that such differences do exist. While there are notable exceptions it is possible to state generally that the educational and occupational aspirations and attainments of American Catholics are lower than those of Protestants on the basis of their respective numbers in the U.S. population. The general impression has been that time will erase such differentials. However, Neil J. Weller in an unpublished doctoral dissertation, "Religion and Social Mobility in Industrial Society," compared Catholics and Protestants above the age of 40 and those under the age of 40. He found the differences equally great between the two age categories, and in fact even somewhat greater among the younger men.[24]

But equally important is the reason for these differences. Can they be explained by original social-class membership, or do the religions themselves enter into them? Lenski's respondents were offered five criteria by which they could determine the desirability of a job. These were high income, no danger of being fired, short working hours, much free time, chances of advancement, importance of the work, and a feeling of accomplishment. The differences among the religious categories were small, although Jews rated opportunities for advancement higher than any of the others. As a result he concluded that whatever differences in aspiration and ambition may exist among these religious categories, only a small part of their variations in vertical mobility can be explained.

He then attempted to explore attitudes that people have toward work by inquiring whether they would really be happy unless they were working or whether they would be much happier if they didn't have to work and could take life easy. He concluded that some persons had positive, neutral, or negative attitudes toward work. The largest number with a negative attitude involved Negro Protestants (22 per cent), closely followed by white Protestants and white Catholics, each with 21 per cent. Only 8 per cent of the Jews expressed a negative attitude. But only 23 per cent of white Catholics, the lowest percentage, had a positive attitude toward work followed

---

[23] Lenski, *op. cit.*, p. 77.
[24] Lenski, *op. cit.*, p. 80.

by 24 per cent of the Negro Protestants, 30 per cent of white Protestants, but 42 per cent of Jews. More than half of the white Catholics, 57 per cent, and the highest holding such an attitude were neutral toward work. Fifty-four per cent of Negro Protestants and 50 per cent of white Protestants and Jews also held neutral attitudes toward work. When the class positions of respondents was held constant, Protestants holding responsible positions more frequently had positive attitudes toward work and less frequently negative attitudes, while the reverse relationship was true of Catholics.[25]

As a result of this he believes that more than the Protestant doctrine of the calling, as treated by Weber, is involved. However, it should be noted that the total number of cases in some of these categories was relatively small. There were only 12 Jews and 41 Negro Protestants. Among white Protestants he had 111 respondents, and among white Catholics, 106. When social class was held constant, he had only 16 white Catholics in the upper middle class. While his findings are undoubtedly correct for the sample under study, the projection of such findings onto the entire Jewish, Protestant, or Catholic categories in America may not be warranted. Only further research can answer this question.

In an effort to throw more light upon religious differences in aspiration and attainments, Lenski proposed a series of questions about child rearing. The two most pertinent to this discussion were one regarding obedience and one regarding teaching children to think for themselves as the most important thing to give a child for his future life. Teaching a child to think for himself he labeled "intellectual autonomy," and obedience to the dictates of others, "intellectual heteronomy." Upper-middle-class Jews and white Protestants place a high emphasis on intellectual autonomy. Upper-middle-class Catholics place less emphasis upon it; and middle-class Catholics placed the least emphasis on it of all four categories. Generally speaking and regardless of social class, the differences between white Protestants and Catholics on this question were fairly large—13.5 percentage points. Lenski believes that the upper middle class overwhelmingly accepts the notion of personal autonomy and as a consequence those who would rise in this system are handicapped by a heteronomic orientation. He likewise finds that those who have succeeded in moving upward are likely to have had an autonomic orientation,

[25] Lenski, op. cit., pp. 81-87.

while those who are moving downward are most likely to have had the heteronomic.[26]

In research of this type it is always difficult to be certain that such questions mean the same thing to all respondents. Obedience of children is stressed among all Protestant, Catholic, and Jewish groups. The actual meaning of obedience and its degree of emphasis undoubtedly show variations from one family to another. If many observers of the contemporary scene are correct, obedience would undoubtedly mean conformity, and, reputedly, conformity today is a means of gaining acceptance. But thinking for oneself is also considered a favorable characteristic. Within the area of faith and morals, Catholics are required to give obedience to the teachings of the Church. But this need not discourage thinking for oneself in many other areas of life. At this point, it appears that Professor Lenski's findings are stimulating and possibly somewhat controversial, yet also somewhat less than conclusive. They merit respectful attention but scarcely unqualified acceptance. It is quite probable that differentials in aspiration and attainment among America's religious groups have many and more complex causes than have yet been uncovered.

Churches have made other efforts to influence the economic order, particularly through pronouncements by organized church bodies such as the Council of Churches, the annual meeting of Catholic bishops in Washington, and the Papal encyclicals. Reference has already been made to the Protestant social gospel. Thomas Ford Hoult believes that this reached its height of success and aggressiveness with the publication of *Christianity and the Social Crisis* by Walter Rauschenbusch in 1907. This book claimed that the "real" Christianity as based on the teaching of Christ and the apostles basically dealt with social justice. Other Protestant spokesmen espousing a similar position were Sherwood Eddy and Norman Thomas. The latter abandoned his role as a Presbyterian minister to lead the socialist party.[27] In 1891 Pope Leo XIII issued his famous encyclical,

---

[26] Lenski, *op. cit.*, pp. 200-202.
[27] Thomas Ford Hoult, *The Sociology of Religion* (New York: The Dryden Press, 1958), p. 270.

"Rerum Novarum," defending the workers' right to bargain collectively with employers through labor unions. At that time the document was considered radical, apparently even in certain Catholic quarters. However, the position of the Catholic Church was established by this pronouncement, reaffirmed in the encyclical of Pope Pius XII forty years later, "Quadregismo Anno," and again in 1961 by Pope John XXIII in "Mater et Magistra."

However, the attitude of churches toward labor unions was by no means so favorable in the middle and latter part of the last century and even, for that matter, as late as the 1920's. Liston Pope in his study, *Millhands and Preachers*, an investigation of the relationship between churches and cotton mills in Gastonia, North Carolina, revealed that during the strike of 1929, Protestant ministers tended to defend the status quo.[28] T. V. Powderly, a Catholic and an early leader of a labor organization known as the Knights of Labor, encountered opposition from some American Bishops. In fact, one member of the hierarchy, the Most Reverend James Bailey, said that no Catholic with any idea of the spirit of his religion will encourage the Knights of Labor. This labor organization was a secret society, as were some of the earlier labor organizations, and its broad program apparently involved social and economic heresies. In some quarters it was viewed as nothing more or less than a conspiracy to overthrow the state. Finally, Elzear Cardinal Taschreu of Quebec obtained from Rome a disapproval of the "knights" in his province. But when Cardinal Gibbons was assured by Powderly that the organization was law-abiding and the oath of secrecy did not interfere with the sacrament of Penance, he summoned the American hierarchy and found that nine out of eleven agreed with him that censure of this society was undesirable. The matter was taken to Rome and Cardinal Gibbons presented Powderly's statement to the College of Propaganda. In view of this new evidence the congregation ruled that the Knights could be approved if minor changes were made in their preamble. This was done, and approval was subsequently granted.[29]

---

[28] Liston Pope, *Millhands and Preachers* (New Haven: Yale University Press, 1942), pp. 187-205.

[29] Robert B. Cross, *The Emergence of Liberal Catholicism in America* (Cambridge, Mass.: Harvard University Press, 1958), pp. 115-18.

## THE CHURCH AND POLITICS

In the United States the relationship between churches and the political order in recent times has been colored by the so-called wall of separation between Church and State. While no such "wall of state" was ever expressly written into the Constitution, the average American appears to believe it was. Actually, under the First Amendment to the Constitution freedom of worship was promised to all. There was to be no established church and no favoring of one church over the other. Yet established churches in certain states persisted well into the 19th century. During most of the last century Protestant churches and organizations were both vocal and powerful in securing funds for some of their institutions. Protestant churchmen were outstanding spokesmen on both sides of the slavery issue. In 1886 the Lord's Day Alliance was formed, representing Protestant efforts to enact legislation making Sunday a day of rest and worship. Such laws, usually known as "blue laws," still remain in the statutes of a number of states. In 1874, the Women's Christian Temperance Union began a campaign for prohibition and, as noted earlier, Protestant efforts were largely responsible for the passage of the 18th Amendment. Many churches and church agencies maintain offices in Washington, some of which are claimed to be merely channels of information regarding legislation, while others are obviously lobbies.[30]

Catholics and Jews have not been aloof from efforts in the political field. The American Jewish Congress has expressed particular concern about the teaching of sectarian religion in public schools. Local Catholics, aided by the Knights of Columbus, and joining with a non-Catholic private school carried a law of the State of Oregon (which would, in effect, have prohibited private and parochial schools) to the Supreme Court of the United States. More recently, through the National Catholic Welfare Conference, attempts have been made to secure some kind of federal assistance for Catholic schools. (This is discussed at greater lengths in the chapter on education.)

---

[30] Luke Ebersole, "Religion and Politics," *The Annals*, 332 (Nov. 1960), pp. 102-103.

In contemporary America there seem to be two attitudes toward the relationship between churches and the political order. Some apparently believe that churches should eschew all connection with politics. Others believe that churches as a moral power cannot and should not be oblivious to legislation with moral implications, nor ignore social problems which legislation could ameliorate. Furthermore, in a nation with over 250 different religious denominations, sects, and cults, fear is expressed that a powerful religious organization, even though numerically a minority, could impose its will upon all Americans. That this has occurred in the past certainly seems clear in the case of Prohibition.

## SITUATIONAL-VALUE APPROACH

In a rapidly changing society, the influence of various religious denominations and the impact of religion itself, as already indicated, will vary from time to time. Certain other social changes, such as a greatly increased birth rate and alterations in values and attitudes, are bound to bring certain church pressures on federal, state, and local governments. Rapidly growing school populations have resulted in direct requests for federal assistance. The economic plight of public schools is shared by parochial and private schools. Until now, public schools have been for the most part supported by local and state governments. The request for federal funds reflects a value change. As a consequence, a social problem arises as parochial and private schools seek such funds.

In the economic sphere, the rapid increase of wealth in the United States during the latter half of the nineteenth century was not shared equally by all persons. As a matter of fact, a disproportionately low share of it filtered down to the worker. Both his living and working conditions became miserable as he left the farm and settled in the slum areas of large cities. This situational change created altered attitudes towards collective bargaining and labor unions, to which the churches responded. Again, critical attitudes toward the churches developed among workers either because the churches failed to employ their moral persuasion to assist the workingman or did so too late. Others criticized the churches because they did so at all.

Among Catholics there has been a certain ferment as their lower social and economic positions became apparent. Perhaps it is too early to assess the ultimate effect this will have. In fact, this situation has not yet reached the stage where it is even generally admitted, and it must still be considered something of a covert social problem. When it does emerge, it may have far-reaching effects upon Catholic education, family values, and ambitions. If Catholic upward striving is suddenly and acutely increased, renewed fears of Catholic domination among non-Catholics will be revived or more emphatically emphasized.

The reputed religious revival is a cyclical situational change. Behind it is an enhanced evaluation of religion. If this can be interpreted as more than casual lip service to creeping conformity, its eventual implications for society could be profound. This new religious interest would certainly lessen some of the contemporary social problems. But it may also take a turn toward narrow parochialism and a cementing of ingroup loyalty and outgroup hostility, no small disaster in a nation with so many different religious bodies. And it may also decline in strength.

The ecumenical movements, already taking place in Protestantism and now being planned in Catholicism, may reduce the diversity of churches, and in the most optimistic—although scarcely practical—vein, they may be the beginning of a reunited Christendom. Viewed pessimistically, the ecumenical drive may reduce the number of religious bodies but may also increase social distance and suspicion among them toward outsiders.

In today's America, religion seems to have a more powerful and pervasive influence than it did in the thirties. Starting from a social institution lower in prestige than other economic, political, and educational institutions, it seems to be gaining momentum. Its strong opposition to communism makes it a welcome ally of political and economic institutions, but it must be hoped that this is not its exclusive claim to existence or extension. While religion has been analyzed sociologically, as may quite legitimately be done, its supernatural implications and its mission of salvation are even more important. Father Gustave Weigel has expressed the function of religion most forcefully. He states:

> Hence the role of the churches in America is not to save America. The day they make their purpose, they have failed as churches. The

role of the churches is to be the locus where man meets God and dedicates himself to do His purposes. When I see a flag in a church, though not against it, I often wonder if its presence is not a sign that we are more anxious about the fatherland than the Father's will.[31]

It may be hoped that this nationalistic anxiety is not the explanation for the presently strong position of the churches in the United States and the reputed religious revival.

# REVIEW QUESTIONS

1. Is there a religious revival in the contemporary America?
2. What is meant by the "social gospel" of Protestantism? Define a "cult" and a "sect." Under what circumstances do they arise, and what is their usual development?
3. What is "Catholic Action?" Are there any new elements in Catholic Action of recent origin?
4. What are the conclusions in recent studies of parish sociology regarding the number of persons who attend Mass regularly, irregularly or not at all on Sunday?
5. What circumstances appear to operate in Jewish families' joining Synagogues and Temples?
6. There are three great divisions of Judaism in the United States. Name and explain the more salient characteristics of each.
7. What is meant by the "Protestant ethic?"
8. What was Professor Lenski's finding regarding a Catholic attitude toward work? Do you consider this finding valid? Discuss.
9. What impact have American churches had upon politics?
10. What impact have American churches had upon economic life?
11. What is the "ecumenical movement?" Give some recent examples of it.
12. Secularism is usually considered an important value in American society. To what extent do you accept or reject this idea? Give your reasons.

---

[31] Gustave Weigel, *Faith and Understanding in America* (New York: The Macmillan Co., 1959), p. 50.

## SELECTED READINGS

*Articles*

Eister, Allen W., "Some Aspects of Institutional Behavior with Reference to Churches," *American Sociological Review*, 17 (Feb. 1952), 64-69.

Fichter, Joseph H., "Religious Values and the Social Personality," *American Catholic Sociological Review*, 17 (June 1956), 109-16.

———, "Urban Mobility and Religious Observance," *American Catholic Sociological Review*, 11 (Oct. 1950), 130-39.

Hoult, Thomas Ford, "Economic Class Conciousness in American Protestantism," *American Sociological Review*, 15 (Feb. 1950), 97-100 and 17 (June 1952), 349-50.

Johnson, Benton, "A Critical Appraisal of the Church-Sect Typology," *American Sociological Review*, 22 (Feb. 1957), 88-91.

Liu, William T., "The Marginal Catholics in the South—A Revision of Concepts," *American Journal of Sociology*, 65 (Jan. 1960), 383-90.

Schuyler, Joesph B., "Religious Behaviour in Northern Parish: A Study of Motivating Values," *American Catholic Sociological Review*, 19 (June 1958), 134-44.

Wilson, Bryan R., "The Pentecostalist Minister: Role Conflicts and Status Contradictions," *American Journal of Sociology*, 64 (Mar. 1957), 494-504.

*Books*

Cross, Robert B., *The Emergence of Liberal Catholicism in America*. Cambridge, Mass.: Harvard University Press, 1958.

Fichter, Joseph A., *Religion as an Occupation*. Notre Dame, Indiana: Notre Dame University Press, 1961.

Herberg, Will, *Protestant, Catholic, Jew*. Garden City, N.Y.: Doubleday & Co., Inc., 1955.

Hoult, Thomas Ford, *The Sociology of Religion*. New York: The Dryden Press, 1958.

Lenski, Gerhard, *The Religious Factor*. Garden City, N.Y.: Doubleday & Co., Inc., 1961.

Pope, Liston, *Millhands and Preachers*. New Haven: Yale University Press, 1942.

Schuyler, Joseph B., *Northern Parish*. Chicago: Loyola University Press, 1960.

Weber, Max, *The Protestant Ethic and the Spirit of Capitalism.* New York: Charles Scribner & Sons, 1930.

Weigel, Gustave, *Faith and Understanding in America.* New York: The Macmillan Co., 1959.

Yinger, J. Milton, *Religion, Society and the Individual.* New York: The Macmillan Co., 1957.

# 17

# Education in America

ALL societies from the simple to the highly complex have some methods by which they induct their children into the culture. Among preliterates this must be done by word of mouth. It is carried on by the parents, siblings, and, especially, the elders of the society, through admonitions, precepts, folk tales, and example. In more sophisticated societies, knowledge is also transmitted by parents, older siblings, peer groups, schools and others, but particularly through mass media of communication, including newspapers, magazines, comic books, books, radio, television, and motion pictures. In the United States the term "education" is almost synonymous with formal schooling. This is scarcely an accurate definition of it because most children learn a great deal from sources other than the school, and some probably learn much more from these sources than from school.

*Education* is the transmission and acquisition of factual knowledge, values, motives, attitudes, and techniques of performance. This last type of knowledge is sometimes described as training, but it is part of the curriculum in schools, as shown by the presence, in addition to the traditional three R's of typing, shorthand, cooking, sewing, automobile driving, and the teaching of other skills. In this chapter, formal education, as transmitted through the schools, is the major topic of discussion; but it is important to remember that this is not the exclusive source of education in this country or in any country.

Within American society there is generally a firm belief in the value of education, at least until the end of high school. But this is not a universal belief throughout American society because different attitudes toward the extent of formal education are found among the various social classes.[1] Furthermore, while lip service is paid to the conviction that formal education is desirable, American attitudes toward it may be better described as ambivalent. Stiff opposition is encountered from certain quarters toward any effort to increase school taxes, although there is a widespread belief that educational opportunities should be readily available to all persons. There is also a conviction, rather freely expressed and, in fact, supported by research, that education will result in better jobs and higher incomes. But the belief that education is a good thing in itself is neither universally nor even generally accepted. Widespread differences of opinion also exist regarding the functions of formal education.

Disagreements over the functions of formal education became sharper—and even bitter—with the successful launching of *Sputnik I* by the Soviet Union in 1957. Since the Russians beat the Americans to the punch on the satellite launching pad, heated controversies over the content of American school curricula became commonplace. A reputed dearth of American engineers, mathematicians, and nuclear physicists was claimed and the blame placed on the failure of American "progressive" educational institutions, although most of the persons with responsible positions in the development of outer space vehicles had probably attended school before many of the recent curricula changes to which such failures were traced had been brought about.

Inability of many Americans to speak a foreign tongue and to understand other cultures, it is charged, has proved a diplomatic liability to the United States. This charge was dramatized in a best-

---

[1] Robert J. Havighurst, "Social-Class Influences on American Education," in *Social Forces Influencing American Education*, ed. Nelson B. Henry (Chicago: University of Chicago Press, 1961), p. 123.

selling novel, *The Ugly American*. The situation depicted in this book may be entirely accurate. But whether this situation is typical of the American diplomatic service throughout the world is at least debatable. Furthermore, the situation is more directly traceable to the system by which ambassadors and policy-making diplomats are selected, i.e., by the amount of their contributions to presidential campaign funds, more than a failure to teach languages adequately in American schools. Characteristically enough, American success in the locale of this novel was achieved by a "hard-bitten, two-fisted, practical" businessman. But criticisms of the schools go well beyond the teaching of mathematics and foreign languages. Another bestseller, *Why Johnny Can't Read*, claimed that schools failed to teach even the reading of English adequately.

As a result, strident charges have been made that American education is inferior to European education. Crash programs have been initiated to "catch up." The federal government and various foundations have poured funds into the schools for the teaching of mathematics, foreign languages, and guidance programs. President Kennedy has initiated a "Peace Corps," through which young Americans, following intensive, albeit brief, training in the languages and cultures of certain underdeveloped countries, will go to these countries, work and live with the people, and, hopefully, expedite their development. Behind much of these criticisms and efforts is the fear that the communist world will bring these newly developing, independent countries over to its side, and they will thus be lost to the free world.

## HISTORY OF EDUCATION IN AMERICA

A full understanding of contemporary American education is impossible without some reference to its origins and developments during the colonial period and since the founding of the republic. Motives for the initiation of some kind of formal elementary education are usually dated from the "Old Deluder Satan Act" passed in the Massachusetts Bay Colony in 1647. Its basic function was to teach men to read so that they could acquire a knowledge of the scriptures. It provided that within every township of fifty householders a person should be appointed to teach those children who came to him to read and write. The wages of this teacher were to be paid by parents, or the masters of such children, or by the inhabitants generally. This, it was hopefully believed, would frustrate the efforts of Satan to keep men from a knowledge of the Bible. It provided for free general education but not of a compulsory nature.

As New Englanders spread westward, they carried this idea with them and attempted to duplicate the New England village school. During the colonial period other types of schools emerged, such as the charity and pauper schools, and private schools at which tuition was paid. Some of the latter were secular, others religious. There was also an apprentice system by which boys were "bound out" to a master tradesman. In the southern colonies many children went abroad for their education.[2]

These origins of formal education within New England have not entirely lost their influence on the contemporary scene. While the basic reason for establishing schools was religious, there were economic and political objectives as well. Responsibility for the establishment and maintenance of these schools was placed in the hands of the local community and the curricula were designed to assure conformity with the prevailing ethos. This was simple in a small, relatively homogeneous community strongly influenced, if not completely dominated, by congregationalism. Harvard College was established in 1636 largely for the training of ministers. Ideological unity, particularly in matters of religion, was a major function of early American schools.

But certain changes were in the offing. Even in New England there had been some dissenters. Roger Williams, looking for religious freedom, fled the Massachusetts Bay Colony and established what is now Rhode Island. In the middle of the last century large-scale immigration from Europe brought persons of diverse nationalities and religious beliefs to these shores, but the public schools remained largely Protestant. (See Chapter 14.) In 1852 Massachusetts had passed the first compulsory school attendance law, and the last state to do so was Mississippi in 1918.[3] While Horace Mann had somewhat modified the Puritan attitude toward education he still believed that ideological unity within a society was an absolute neces-

---

[2] H. Otto Dahlke, *Values in Culture and Classroom* (New York: Harper & Brothers, 1958), pp. 16-18.
[3] Dahlke, *op. cit.*, p. 20.

sity. It should create among all persons a common faith, common interests and devotion for the political order serving these faiths and these interests.[4] Partly as a result of compulsory attendance at public schools by non-Protestant students, and partly as a result of the First Amendment, providing for freedom of worship, the influence of sectarian religion on public schools was modified.

Two other trends in the history of American education merit attention. While Thomas Jefferson believed in a system of public education, he advocated a rather rigid selection of students so that only the most qualified would enter higher education. In contrast to this, Andrew Jackson held a more equalitarian view of education. He placed particular emphasis upon vocational training in order to produce better farmers, skilled tradesmen, and merchants. Merle L. Borrowman contrasts what he terms the "Hebraic-Puritan attitude" with the "Hellenic attitude." While the Puritan-Hebraic attitude became secularized, he believes it has been expressed by the "survival of the fittest" concept, as set forth by the Darwinists. This emphasizes the desirability of hard work and the student's obligation to serve his society according to its standards. In contrast, the Hellenic attitude would encourage the child to follow his own native bent, which would ultimately lead to a knowledge and realization of himself. John Dewey, who has probably made the greatest impact on contemporary education, did not quite accept the unfolding of the natural self, but he advocated starting with activities in which students had a lively interest and pleasure and on these bases other knowledge could be built.[5]

This very brief summary of certain aspects of the origin and development of the American school system reveals some of the problems confronting contemporary education in the United States. First, there is a question regarding the function of education. Shall it be the development of a common ideology in matters of religion, economics, and political life? The public schools are prohibited from teaching sectarian religion, so the transmission of a single or common religion is impossible for them. But they do attempt to advocate a common economic and political "faith." Generally, this is a firm

[4] Merly L. Borrowman, "Traditional Values and the Shaping of American Education: Social Forces Influencing American Education," in The 60th Yearbook of the National Society for the Study of Education, ed. Nelson B. Henry (Chicago: University of Chicago Press, 1961), pp. 151-52.
[5] Borrowman, op. cit., pp. 153-56.

belief in democratic traditions and principles and, within limits, the capitalistic economic system. On the other hand, private schools of a sectarian nature can and do transmit the dogmas and practices of their respective denominations.

The second major controversy dominating contemporary education is the means by which knowledge shall be transmitted to students. Shall it be done in a highly permissive or an authoritarian manner? The third controversy is who shall be educated? Should more than the absolutely minimal education be offered to other than the brighter students or the elite? At present there is a great ferment in American educational circles and American society generally about such matters. They are far from resolved, and efforts to resolve them have taken various directions. Some private institutions of higher education and a few on the elementary and secondary level cater to the intellectually elite, while many state universities are required to take all high school graduate residents within the state who apply. The mortality in such cases is usually high. There are smaller community colleges whose standards generally are not so high as private colleges and universities, and there are junior colleges which extend education beyond high school for a period of about two years.

On the high school level various types of courses, such as the academic, the commercial, and the vocational exist, and in some cities there are vocational high schools. In other words, in the United States secondary and higher education are quite diversified. Compulsory laws on school attendance keep youths in classrooms until they are fourteen or sixteen. Since individuals vary tremendously in talent and motivation, it appears unlikely that any really revolutionary changes on a wide scale can be made on the secondary level of education. Curricula for brighter and exceptional students can be improved, but some seem to oppose this as undemocratic. At any rate, recent increases in the birth rate demand a realistic evaluation of American educational policies.

## THE WAVE OF THE FUTURE

In the fall of 1959 35,286,177 students were enrolled full time in public elementary and secondary schools in the United States.

At the same time 3,402,297 men and women were attending higher educational institutions. On April 14, 1960, Roman Catholic elementary and high school enrollments had reached 5,090,012. (These figures do not include some seminaries and other types of schools.) Almost 44 million students out of a population of approximately 180,000,000 persons were in classrooms. This was a little more than 23 per cent, or more than one out of every five persons in the population.[6] To these may be added those attending private elementary and secondary schools, secular schools, or religious schools other than Catholic. During the last ten years total school enrollments have increased by about 15,000,000, or 50 per cent. In 1900, 94,833 students were graduated from high school. In 1956 this had risen to 1,414,800. In 1900, 27,410 persons were graduated from college; in 1956, 308,812.[7] In 1940 the average adult 25 years of age or over had completed only eight years of school, but by 1959 he had completed eleven years. In 1940, 5 per cent of the population had completed college. By 1959 this had risen to 8 per cent.[8]

Increases in school population are traceable to two factors. First, between 1950 and 1960 the U.S. population increased by more than three million persons a year, which far exceeds the rate of any prior decade in this nation's history. The second factor is that more children remain in school for a longer period of time. Christopher Jencks has pointed out that the average American left school in 1900 at the age of 12, having completed his elementary education. But by 1930 students remained in school until about the age of 15, and by 1960, four out of five young persons were securing high school diplomas, two out of five were enrolling in college, one out of five was completing college, and one in twenty was going on for graduate degrees.[9]

Reasons for attending and/or completing high school and college vary, but perhaps the major motivation is to obtain a higher social and economic status—the sociological term "vertical mobility up-

---

[6] *The 1961 World Almanac and book of facts* (New York: New York World-Telegram and The Sun, 1961), pp. 507 and 706.

[7] *Statistical Abstract of the United States, 1960,* U.S. Dept. of Commerce, Bureau of the Census, Washington, D.C., 1960, p. 109.

[8] Eleanor H. Bernard and Charles B. Nam, *Demographic Factors Affecting American Education,* ed. Nelson B. Henry (Chicago: University of Chicago Press), pp. 109-11.

[9] Christopher Jencks, "The Next Thirty Years in College," *Harpers Magazine,* 223, No. 1337 (Oct. 1961), p. 120.

ward." Toward this goal formal education is the most heavily traveled road. Since 1950 the total number of higher positions available in American society has increased rapidly. But opportunities in some occupations have expanded quickly, while others have contracted. For example, job opportunities have increased in professional, technical, and other similar kinds of work, as well as clerical and service work (excluding household tasks). On the other hand job opportunities among farmers, farm managers, farm laborers, foremen, and laborers—with the exception of farm or mine laborers—have decreased.[10] As automation becomes common, job opportunities for the unskilled and semi-skilled will decrease. In fact, this has to some extent already occurred.

Those who fail to complete high school find themselves in a disadvantageous position in the labor market. In October of 1959 about 800,000 students aged sixteen and seventeen dropped out of school. About one-fourth of these were unemployed in October of 1959, compared with one-eighth of the June high school graduates of the same period. These two categories obtained different kinds of positions. About half of the high school graduates were in office, clerical, or sales jobs, but only 6 per cent of the dropouts obtained such work. Lower paying, unskilled, semi-skilled, and farm-laborer jobs claimed 44 per cent of the dropouts, but only 18 per cent of the graduates.[11]

In view of this, it seems likely that a larger percentage of American youth in the future will enter and complete high school and, to a lesser extent, enter and complete college. It is likewise probable that larger numbers will enter and complete professional and graduate schools. Short-term, national forecasts of future school enrollments on the national level can be made with considerable accuracy for those children already born. Their mortality rates are low, and few will emigrate from the United States.

But even short-term projections are difficult if made for states or specific cities. Horizontal mobility is common within this country, and certain sections are developing more rapidly than others—for example, California, the Southwest, and Florida. Other areas, such as New England, are losing population. Even if an adequate number of classrooms were provided on the national level, they might not be

---

[10] Bernard and Nam, *op. cit.*, pp. 93-94.
[11] Bernard and Nam, *op. cit.*, p. 108.

located in areas where needed. If present fertility rates remain constant, the number of children between five and thirteen would reach thirty-nine million by 1970 and about forty-nine million by 1980. Children of the usual high school age—fourteen to seventeen— would number over fourteen million by 1965, almost sixteen million by 1970, and about eighteen million by 1980. Those of college age will increase from seventeen million in 1960 to twenty-five million in 1970 and approximately thirty million by 1980.[12]

If these projections prove reasonably accurate, the need for more school buildings, teachers, library facilities, and laboratories is obvious. An increase in school taxes likewise appears inevitable. At present the United States spends more per capita on the schooling of students than any country in the world. The national average is $43 but there are great variations from state to state. In 1958 Delaware spent $124 per capita in state expenditures for all public education while Massachusetts was spending only $18 per capita.[13]

## FEDERAL AID TO EDUCATION

In recent years successive efforts have been made to enact federal legislation to aid public education. To date such legislation has proved highly controversial, and none has passed both houses. Some apparently consider federal aid to education an entirely novel idea of recent origin. Actually, there is a long history of such aid in the United States. When the Northwest Territory was opened, Congress set aside one section in each township for schools, and in 1803, a donation of two townships was made to the Ohio Company —which was the original endowment for what later became Ohio State University. As each state was admitted to the union, other such grants were made, so that by 1860 seventeen state universities had been founded.[14] In the 1958-59 school year the federal govern-

---

[12] Bernard and Nam, *op. cit.*, p. 114.

[13] *Research Bulletin*, Research Division of the National Education Association, *38*, No. 3 (Oct. 1960), p. 67.

[14] Harold Underwood Faulkner, *American Political and Social History*, 7th ed. (New York: Appleton-Century-Crofts, Inc., 1957), p. 215.

ment was in fact spending $786,000,000 in support of elementary and secondary schools, and in the 1959-60 school year, the figure was $867,000,000.[15]

President Kennedy's message to Congress on February 20, 1961, however, contained the most extensive proposals for federal aid to education thus far. He recommended a three-year program of direct federal assistance for public elementary and secondary classroom instruction (including raising teachers' salaries), the extension of the current college-housing loan program for five more years, and long-term, low-interest loans for construction of classrooms, laboratories, libraries, and related structures for public and private institutions of higher education. He also asked Congress to amend and expand student loans and other provisions of the National Defense Education Act, and 26¼ million dollars for state-administered scholarships for needy young persons regardless of color, creed, sex, or race, to attend colleges of their own selection and follow programs of their own choosing.[16] However, President Kennedy made it clear that aid at the elementary and secondary level would go only to public institutions, thus ruling out for what he considered constitutional reasons assistance to denominational and private elementary and secondary schools.

The argument in defense of federal aid to education is relatively simple. Economic resources, personal incomes, and state income via taxation vary considerably from one state to another. Wealthier states spend more money per capita on education and a lower percentage of their total revenues than poor states, which spend less money per capita on education but a higher percentage of their revenues. As a result, the level and extent of education vary from state to state. Perhaps the most critical areas are to be found in the South, particularly the southeastern part of this country. But persons born, reared, and educated in the South or other sections in which educational standards are comparatively low do not always remain there. A number migrate to northeastern and central cities as well as to the West Coast. Some individuals may become economic burdens to their adopted places of residence because lack of educa-

---

[15] *School Life*, Official Journal of the Office of Education, 43 (Feb.-Mar., 1961), p. 2.
[16] *School Life*, pp. 3-6.

tion as well as other factors causes them to swell the ranks of the unemployed, especially during periods of recession. Opponents of federal aid to education argue that wealthier states should not be compelled to pay for education in poorer states. But these wealthier states are already either helping to pay for this disparity indirectly, or paying for the relief of unemployed in-migrants within their own borders. Furthermore, since people constitute a major resource of any country, their education can scarcely be considered an exclusively local matter when its condition, good or bad, may have national repercussions.

Bill S-2101, embodying President Kennedy's recommendations, was passed by the Senate but not by the House. One of the major reasons, but not the only reason, for its defeat was the controversy over its failure to provide federal assistance to private and/or religious elementary and secondary schools, at least in the form of long-term, low-interest loans.

## TEACHER SHORTAGE

The most critical need at present and in the years ahead for American education is an adequate supply of qualified teachers. In the school year 1960-1961 there was a shortage of 135,000 adequately prepared teachers on the elementary and secondary levels, although 10,000 more potential teachers received bachelor degrees in 1960 than in 1959. Prospective high school teachers in that year amounted to 80,465, an increase of 12.4 per cent over the preceding year, and qualified new elementary school teachers totaled 48,830, an increase of only 2.1 per cent over the preceding year. Since more elementary school teachers are needed than high school teachers, production in terms of need has been reversed.

But more college graduates in 1960 were qualified to teach in those areas where there is the greatest need. For example, there was an increase of 31.9 per cent in mathematics, 26.4 per cent science, and 21.1 per cent in foreign languages teachers. In other areas, such as social studies, music, home economics, and industrial arts, increases were somewhat below average compared to 1959. But only about 75

TOO MANY QUALIFIED GRADUATES DO NOT ENTER TEACHING

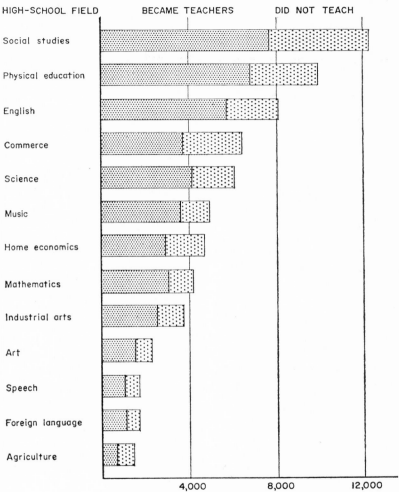

FIGURE 17-1 [17]

---

[17] Adapted from *Research Bulletin,* Research Division of the National Education Association, 38, No. 3 (Oct. 1960), p. 69.

per cent of these newly trained teachers entered school systems after graduation.[18]

It appears that a number of college students take required courses to obtain teaching certificates, but only as a cushion against a possible inability to find employment elsewhere. This is also true of teachers' colleges. Furthermore, the teacher supply problem cannot be adequately estimated on a national level. Young men and women entering the field of education tend to gravitate toward school systems offering the highest salaries, best working conditions, and superior opportunities for advancement. They also tend to head for larger cities, where opportunities for greater personal freedom and cultural advantages exist. Thus, potential teachers with better training and superior talent are more likely to be employed by the best school systems, while those with less adequate training and lower ability enter poorer school systems.

Teachers' salaries have been notoriously low compared to the amount of formal education necessary for qualified instructors. In 1959-1960 the national average salary was $5,025. In California it was $6,525 but in Mississippi only $3,175.[19] While costs of living vary from one locality to another in this country, it is doubtful that teachers in Mississippi cities find their expenses to be one-half those of teachers in California cities.

It may be possible to staff classrooms with many kinds of teachers, but the goal is qualified teachers. One out of four elementary school teachers today are not college graduates. Some of them do not even have two years of preparation beyond high school. It should be noted here that the matter of completion of required courses in the field of education is not being raised. Sharp criticisms have been leveled at certain types of such education courses and not without reason. Certain basic techniques of teaching can be and are taught in some courses of education. Some are perhaps better acquired through on-the-job training. But in today's schools, it appears desirable that all teachers on the elementary and secondary level should at least have a college degree.

In September of 1960 it was estimated that 230,000 new teachers

---

[18] *Research Bulletin*, Research Division of the National Education Association, 39, No. 7 (Oct. 1961), p. 68.

[19] *Research Bulletin*, Research Division of the National Education Association, 39, No. 7 (Oct. 1961), p. 67.

were necessary to staff elementary and secondary schools. About 110,000 were required to replenish those leaving, 30,000 to take care of increased enrollments, 30,000 to relieve overcrowding and eliminate half-day sessions, 20,000 to provide instruction and services presently unavailable, and 40,000 to replace those not adequately prepared. In that year only 95,000 college graduates sought teaching positions. The shortage of 135,000 teachers could only be recruited by employing persons from the general population, some of whom possessed uncertain qualifications.[20] Finally, it should be noted that, while new schools may be erected within a period of one or two years, it requires sixteen or more years to produce qualified teachers, if the years from first grade to graduation from college or graduate school are included.

## SOCIAL CHANGE AND SCHOOL CURRICULA

Content and methods of teaching in American schools have changed tremendously since the early twentieth century. They have been altered partly as a result of changes introduced by John Dewey, and partly from "progressive" education, as exemplified by Columbia University's Teachers College. In some quarters this change is viewed at best as a mixed blessing. In this case professional educators themselves introduced the changes. However, the perennially debated question of whether schools do or should take the lead in effecting social change, or whether they should merely follow social change, is not readily resolved. In some respects, schools do initiate social change, but in many others they tend to follow it. Sometimes a rather invidious tug-of-war develops, with professional educators on one team and school board members and parents on the other. This is something of an oversimplification, because either side may have persons from all three categories. Members of American school boards are elected or appointed. They may or may not include persons knowledgeable about educational content and method. School boards are invariably attuned to the costs of education, which are re-

[20] *Research Bulletin*, Research Division of the National Education Association, 33, No. 7 (Oct. 1961), p. 74.

flected in school taxes. The school superintendent is the key man in whatever struggles develop between opposing parties. Frequently, it is impossible for him to resolve the conflicting demands, and he may have to settle for a compromise, getting less than he wanted but more than what the authorities intended to yield.

About fifty or sixty years ago, as pointed out, the elementary school represented the *terminal,* or highest education level for most Americans. The high school prepared individuals for college, and its curriculum was dictated by college administrators. As the high school increasingly became the terminal education level for most Americans, it was inevitable that its curriculum would be changed. Pragmatism has always colored American education, perhaps never more than at present. As stated, the first schools in the Massachusetts Bay Colony were established for the practical purpose of teaching citizens to read the Bible, and Harvard College was founded primarily to train ministers.

Since most of the new high school students did not plan to attend college (as is still the case today), certain classical subjects, such as Latin and Greek, were either eliminated, decreased from three or four years to one or two, or taught only to a diminishing number of students. When psychologists discovered that "transfer of training," i.e., the carrying over of skills acquired in one subject (for example, Latin) into other areas, was not a tenable concept, a major reason for teaching classical languages was eliminated. Furthermore, methods of teaching the classics in some schools had become nothing more than monotonous drills in vocabulary, declensions, and conjugations. This might have helped students acquire knowledge of English grammar —which should have been learned earlier anyway—but that was not always the case. The truly great contributions of classical Latin literature were neither transmitted to nor caught by most students. To some extent other traditional college preparation courses, such as mathematics and foreign languages, were watered down, and even eliminated for some students.

The majority of high school students, as well as their parents, desired instruction in "practical" subjects, which would help them secure jobs and earn a living, such as shorthand, typing, bookkeeping, industrial arts, and others. Furthermore, since many more children began to attend high school than in the past, there was an influx of the less talented and less motivated, who would never have entered high school at all except for compulsory school attendance laws. This problem, however, may be less hopeless than is usually claimed, as Martin Mayer has pointed out in *The Schools*.[21]

What is true of high schools is only less true of colleges. In the last century many candidates for law and medicine learned their professions by "reading" with a lawyer or serving as an apprentice to a physician. The widespread establishment of schools of law and medicine gradually changed this, but it has only been recently that a college degree or some college preparation has been required for entrance to such professional schools. As a consequence, pre-medical, pre-legal, and other college pre-professional courses were developed. Some of these, particularly the pre-medical and pre-dental preparations, require a heavy concentration in the natural sciences at times, to the detriment of the liberal education usually offered by undergraduate colleges. Lately, this emphasis seems to be shifting back to liberal arts. Colleges of commerce and business administration were likewise established within universities, or major sequences in such subjects were offered in colleges. These too tended to become narrow specializations. The same may be said of many colleges of engineering. Normal schools and colleges of education were also founded to train teachers. These institutions have been viewed rather dimly by many college professors, including some who are faculty members at these institutions.[22]

Response to the increase in students attending high schools and colleges has been a proliferation of high school courses, the establishment of new colleges within universities, and the multiplication of major fields in undergraduate institutions. Oscar Handlin has pointed out that John Dewey's notion of education as an adjustment to life resulted in breaking down the established disciplines and creating the impression that all things were equally worthy of being taught. High schools succumbed to pressures to teach anything that seemed to have immediate urgency and practicality. Faculty opposition to the introduction of new subject matter was dispelled when opponents were assured that their own disciplines would remain intact.[23]

[21] Martin Mayer, *The Schools* (New York: Harper & Brothers, 1961), pp. 120-35.

[22] Miriam Borgenicht, "Teachers' College: An Extinct Volcano?" *Harpers Magazine*, 223, No. 1334 (July 1961), pp. 82-87.

[23] Oscar Handlin, "Live Students and Dead Education," *The Atlantic*, 208, No. 3 (Sept. 1961), p. 32.

## WHO SHOULD BE EDUCATED?

At the outset, sincere questions will have to be raised as to what persons should attend college, since universal high school attendance is now just about taken for granted. It has been said facetiously that the whole difficulty can be eliminated by conferring an AB degree upon every American child at birth. In England and Europe such decisions regarding the future education of children are made through examinations about the age of eleven. These reputedly separate the wheat from the chaff, but they may do so at an intolerable cost. There are "late bloomers" who, through lack of maturity, motivation, or both do not exhibit their potential talents until several years later. In the usual American interpretation of democracy, such distinctions are considered almost totalitarian. Even the European countries which employ them are now concerned about the intolerable strains placed on students of average or even better than average ability by these examinations. Yet even in the more liberal United States, family pressures by upper-middle-class parents for their children to succeed often become most cruel.[24]

## CAN THE SCHOOLS TEACH A COMMON IDEOLOGY?

Ideology, as a core system of values common to a nation, can only be transmitted in a limited fashion through the public schools. Certain basic tenets such as democracy, belief in the profit motive, and private property can be handled in public school classrooms. Even these, however, present problems, since students are drawn from diverse social classes as well as racial and ethnic groups. Family values and school values sometimes conflict. But there is one area—religion—that seems to be an insurmountable obstacle in public

---

[24] Spencer Brown, "Have Our Schools Failed?" *Commentary*, 25, No. 6 (June 1958), pp. 461-71.

education. It is basically a matter of how religious education should be defined. "Education becomes religious, in a formal sense, when instruction is given in tenets of one of the organized faiths." [25] If religion is considered a system of ethics, the limitations of the public school are reduced but not eliminated. The American Council on Education, in "The Function of the Public School in Dealing with Religion," based upon a questionnaire sent to forty-seven chief state officers and 213 superintendents of schools reported:

> The answer to the question, 'How are the public elementary and secondary schools dealing with religion?' is three fold. A few school systems appear to avoid religion deliberately, but they are a small minority of those participating in this inquiry. However, avoidance of a part of the responsibility of the public schools inadvertently through neglect or failure to deal with the facts and implications of religion intrinsic to the curriculum, was found in greater or lesser degree in all replies of material received. Nearly all the school systems participating in this study make some provision for planned religious activity. . . . It should be pointed out, however, that such activities that we have classified as falling within this category may, and perhaps often do, give a false impression that the schools are doing all that needs to be done about religion.[26]

At the present time, according to various decisions of the U.S. Supreme Court, it appears that sectarian religion cannot be taught upon public school premises. "Released time," which is here defined as the practice by which children are excused from classes during regular school hours for sectarian religious instruction elsewhere, and "dismissed time," by which children are permitted to leave the classroom earlier than the usual dismissal hour to attend religious instruction elsewhere, are both employed in various school systems. Public schools cannot enforce attendance at religious instruction nor take roll to see who attends and who doesn't. The National Jewish Congress, as well as other organizations, strongly oppose any effort to introduce almost any kind of sectarian religious instruction into public schools.

---

[25] Rofle Lanier Hund, "Religion and Education," *Annals*, 332 (Nov. 1960), p. 90.

[26] "The Function of the Public Schools in Dealing with Religion," *A Report on the Exploratory Study made by the Committee on Religion and Education* (Washington, D.C.: American Council on Education, 1953), p. 38.

TABLE 17-1[27]

ENROLLMENT IN CHURCH-RELATED ELEMENTARY AND
SECONDARY SCHOOLS IN THE UNITED STATES

| | Enroll. by Type of School* | | |
|---|---|---|---|
| Denominational Control | Kindergarten | Elementary[a] | Secondary[b] |
| *10 Principal School Systems* | | | |
| Roman Catholic | n.r. | 3,400,000 | 690,000 |
| Missouri Synod Lutheran | 1,724 | 130,124 | 7,022 |
| Seventh-day Adventist | — | 42,069 | 13,380 |
| Protestant Episcopal[c] | 3,252 | 12,028 | 17,900 |
| Joint Synod of Wisconsin | — | 21,901 | — |
| Christian Reformed[d] | — | 31,874 | 6,664 |
| Nat'l Assn. of Christ. Schools | 7 | 8,960 | 7,492 |
| Mennonite (including Amish) | 88 | [e] | 5,870 |
| Friends | 221 | 4,978 | 4,940 |
| Jewish[f] | 4,133 | 21,259 | 4,326 |
| *Other Denominations with Schools* | | | |
| American Baptist Convention | — | — | 968 |
| American Luth. Church | 1,236 | 2,765 | — |
| Augustana Luth. Church | — | 259 | — |
| Council of Liberal Churches | — | — | 126[g] |
| Evangelical Luth. Church | — | 1,151[h] | 692[i] |
| Evangelical Mission Covenant | — | — | 944 |
| Latter-Day Saints | — | — | 324 |
| Los Angeles Baptist City Mission Society | — | 2,949 | — |
| Methodist Church, The | 4,018[j] | 244 | 5,003 |
| Moravian Church | — | — | 574 |
| National Evangelical Lutheran | 21 | 38 | — |
| New England Assn. of Christian Schools | 91 | 218 | 173 |
| Norwegian Synod Luth. | — | 379 | — |
| Presbyterian U. S. | n.r. | 1,130 | 970 |
| Presbyterian U. S. A. | n.r. | — | — |
| Reformed Church in America | — | — | 62 |
| Slovak Evangelical Luth. | — | 147 | — |
| Southern Baptist Convention | 7,400[k] | 2,000 | 3,606 |
| United Lutheran Church | — | 625 | — |
| Wesleyan Meth. Church | — | — | 72 |

* Total reported Protestant enrollment: Kindergartens 18,058; Elementary 263,839; Secondary 76,842.

[a] Includes schools with kindergartens but no schools with grades above grade 8.

[b] Includes all schools with one or more grades 9-12, including schools with elementary grades also. Does not include junior colleges or other institutions on college level that offer precollege level courses.

---

[27] Adapted from Hund, *op. cit.*, p. 95.

More law suits are pending on such issues (that is teaching of sectarian religion in public schools) than are pending in the more publicized field of racial desegregation of public schools. It is appropriate to note that in a society in which most children attend public schools, memberships in Catholic, Jewish and Protestant religious organizations have increased to unprecedented proportions.[28]

In the fields of religion and education, this matter is, has been, and will likely remain a continually controversial issue. Since 1946 the percentage of children in non-public schools from kindergarten to the eighth grade has increased from 11.3 per cent to 16.1 per cent. For grades 9 to 12 the percentage has risen from 6.8 per cent in 1940 to 11.9 per cent in 1960.[29] No distinction is made here between private schools of a religious nature and those of a non-denominational nature. However, it seems probable that a large part of this increase may be traced to denominational private schools.

## THE PAROCHIAL SCHOOLS

Strictly speaking, parochial schools are those maintained by a parish or church. The largest of these systems is maintained by the Roman Catholics, but the Missouri Synod, the Lutherans, the Seventh-Day Adventists, the Protestant Episcopals, the Joint Synod of Wisconsin, the Quakers, the Mennonites, and the Jews also maintain some types of elementary schools. Most of these also have secondary schools as well as colleges and universities.

---

[28] Hund, *op. cit.*, p. 100.
[29] Hund, *op. cit.*, p. 94.

---

[c] Enrollment figures for this denomination were for 85 nursery-kindergartens, 112 elementary schools, and 84 secondary schools.

[d] The schools sponsored by this denomination comprise the National Union of Christian Schools.

[e] Included with figures for secondary schools.

[f] Does not include 550 for which level of instruction was not known.

[g] One school only reporting enrollment.

[h] Eight schools only reporting enrollment.

[i] Two schools only reporting enrollment.

[j] Includes 1,992 pupils in nursery schools.

[k] Includes an estimated 600 pupils in nursery grades.

In 1960 the official Catholic Directory reported 8,786,270 students under Catholic instruction. The distribution of such students is shown in Table 17-2.

TABLE 17-2[30]

DISTRIBUTION OF CATHOLIC STUDENTS IN EDUCATIONAL
INSTITUTIONS IN THE UNITED STATES

| Educational Level | Number of Schools | Number of Students |
|---|---|---|
| *Elementary School* | | |
| Parochial and Institutional | 9,897 | 4,195,781 |
| Private | 475 | 90,115 |
| Protective Institutions | . . . | 11,875 |
| Public | . . . | 2,466,386 |
| *Secondary School* | | |
| Diocesan and Parochial | 1,567 | 520,128 |
| Private | 866 | 324,171 |
| Public | . . . | 835,015 |
| *Seminary* | | |
| Diocesan | 96 | 12,763 |
| Religious of Scholasticate | 429 | 19,618 |
| Other | . . . | 7,515 |
| *College or University* | 265 | 302,908 |

[30] Adapted from Hund, *op. cit.*, p. 96.

Catholic schools fall into five categories: elementary, parochial and institutional, private, protective institutions, and public. Secondary schools include diocesan and parochial high schools as well as private and public high schools. The third category is seminaries and the fourth, colleges and universities. On the elementary and secondary level, between fifty and sixty per cent of Catholic students in those age categories are enrolled in Catholic institutions. On the college and university levels only about one of every three Catholic students attending institutions of higher learning is enrolled in a Catholic college or university. But enrollments in elementary schools, parochial or private, show some startling variations from one section of the country to another. For example, in New England, which has the highest concentration of Catholics in the United States, only 43.5 per cent of Catholic students are in Catholic elementary and secondary schools. On the other hand in the east-south-central section

of the country—Kentucky, Tennessee, Alabama, and Mississippi—
90.5 per cent of Catholic children are enrolled in parochial or private
Catholic schools. It is practically impossible to realize the ideal of
having every Catholic child in a Catholic school, and if efforts
to do so were attempted in New England, Catholic elementary
schools would have to be expanded to accommodate more than twice
the number of children now in attendance and Catholic high schools
would have to be enlarged almost three times. On the college and
university level, the problem is more acute. These institutions would
have to accommodate three times as many students as they now do.
Under these circumstances, it seems probable most Catholics attending colleges and universities will continue to enroll at non-
Catholic institutions. On the elementary and secondary level, at
least one-third of the Catholic students will have to be accommodated
by public institutions.

Catholic schools do obtain some state aid in many parts of the
country. In some places as many as three text books other than
religious texts are paid for by the state. Transportation to and from
school is available via state buses in some areas. Catholic schools
are also exempt from taxation. However, despite these types of
assistance, certain questions may be raised concerning the future of
Catholic education in the United States.

## FUNCTION OF CATHOLIC SCHOOLS

The function of Catholic schools was expressed by Pope Pius XII
in his address to teaching sisters:

> . . . according to the Catholic concept, the object of the school and
> of education is the formation of the perfect Christian. Your entire
> school and educational system would be useless were this object not
> the central point of your labor.[31]

While the major goal of Catholic schools is to provide religious
instruction, intensify religious motivations, and thus, through the
intellect and will, enable students to know, love, and serve God, this is
not their exclusive function. They likewise transmit a knowledge of

---

[31] "On Educating Youth," *The Catholic Mind*, 50, No. 1074 (June 1952),
p. 379.

secular subjects, just as do public and other private schools. Whether this latter function is performed better than in public schools, less efficiently, or at about the same level, simply cannot be answered because adequate empirical evidence is lacking. It seems probable, however, that any kind of valid comparison between the two school systems would reveal comparative strengths and weaknesses, depending upon the community under study. In some respects and in some communities, some Catholic schools are probably superior to some public schools, while in other areas and in other communities they may be inferior. Generally speaking, they are probably about equal. But Catholics and other religiously minded persons consider it a distinct advantage that their children receive religious training in their respective faiths within such schools. For this reason Catholics, Jews, and some Protestants support two school systems in the United States: public schools through school taxes and parochial and private schools by means of voluntary contributions.

## THE CRISIS IN CATHOLIC EDUCATION

The economic contributions of Catholic parents and others who pay tuition or otherwise support various types of independent education should not be dismissed lightly. The late Cardinal O'Hara estimated that in the year 1956-57 American Catholics had saved the U.S. taxpayers—including themselves, of course—almost $1.5 billion on the elementary and secondary school levels. If Catholic education alone were suddenly abandoned, school taxes would rapidly rise, although they would become more equitably distributed throughout the population. While it is quite true that Catholic parents enjoy the right under civil law to use public schools, public opinion seems to hold that they must pay for the support of such schools, even though they send their children to a parochial school. Thus, they are doubly taxed for exercising their religious convictions regarding education.

The cost of all education today is spiraling, and this includes Catholic schools. More buildings, libraries, and laboratories are necessary to accommodate the increasing school population, both public and parochial. In the Catholic field perhaps the building crisis

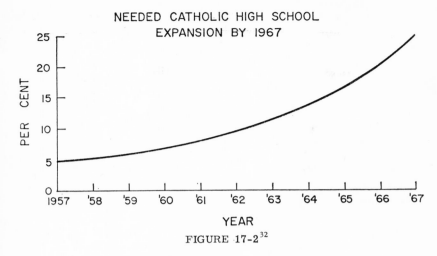

NEEDED CATHOLIC HIGH SCHOOL
EXPANSION BY 1967

YEAR

FIGURE 17-2[32]

is most acute for high school facilities. By 1967 these will have to be expanded by at least 25 per cent to accommodate the estimated enrollment.

But here, as in public schools, the greatest need is an adequate teaching staff. Catholic secondary schools have increased their enrollment between 1947 and 1959 by 68 per cent, Catholic elementary schools during the same period by 77 per cent. Instructional costs in Catholic institutions have been kept down in the past because they were largely staffed by priests, brothers, and nuns. This situation is rapidly changing. Vocations to the priesthood and the religious life have not kept pace with the demand. Some of this is due to the low birth rate in the 30's and early 40's. It is now necessary to employ more and more non-clerical teachers. The National Catholic Welfare Conference, in its survey of 1956, stated that in the last ten years the number of lay teachers had increased by 196 per cent. The largest increase occurred in elementary schools, 409 per cent. In 1956, there were 20,989 lay men and women teaching in elementary and secondary Catholic schools. Estimating their annual salary at $2700 annually (a dismally low income by today's standards) the total cost was $75 million. By now, it has passed that mark.

But education costs for Catholic parents do not end with payment

---

[32] Adapted from *Ave Maria*, 85, No. 17 (Apr. 27, 1957), p. 14.

of tuition and contribution to the church. In some states there are book purchases and book rentals—usually both—and annual raffles, dinners, and other fund-raising devices are common. Extracurricular activities likewise cost money. Activities such as athletic teams and school bands tax the resources of Catholics; and most institutions have fathers' clubs, mothers' clubs, or similar organizations dedicated largely to the raising of money for athletic equipment and so on. The cost of building and maintaining adequate library facilities today is prohibitive. In those states where tax-supported buses cannot transport Catholic children to and from classes, Catholic parents either drive their youngsters or pay for public transportation out of their own pockets. Since public funds, other than noted above, are not now provided nor liable to be provided for Catholic elementary and secondary schools in the near future, questions about Catholic ability to maintain, not to mention expand, Catholic school systems are being raised.

Some have proposed that elementary or parochial schools be abolished completely. Others have suggested the elimination of the first six years of parochial schools and concentration upon junior and senior high schools. Sharp criticisms of such proposals have resulted, and to date there is no meeting of minds. Msgr. Norbert M. Shumaker, Diocesan Superintendent of Schools in Toledo, and Msgr. John C. Harrington, Principal of Central High School in the same city, believe that secondary education can be accomplished in three instead of four years without scholastic harm. No doubt this would effect some saving, but there is the question of how many Catholic children might be lost in the speedup. Certainly, if it resulted in the dumping of slow learners into the public schools, it would arouse criticism.[33]

A more optimistic note was sounded by Msgr. Frederick C. Hochwalt, Secretary-General of the National Catholic Educational Association. He admits the existence of innumerable problems created by the increasing Catholic population, and increasing financial burdens, but he urges that the efforts of early Catholic pioneers in this country should not be forgotten. The Catholic educational system of today is a monument to their work. He believes that

---

[33] John J. Kane, "Can Our Parochial Schools Survive?" *Ave Maria*, 92, No. 11 (Sept. 10, 1960), pp. 5-7.

with modern prosperity and technical know-how there is little excuse to falter, and greater motivation and strength to grow with Catholic educational needs.[34]

## CATHOLIC HIGHER EDUCATION

The situation in Catholic colleges and universities may ultimately prove even more difficult than that described in elementary and secondary schools. First, higher education is considerably more expensive and requires larger libraries and more expensive, well-equipped laboratories. But, above all, it requires trained specialists with graduate degrees. The ratio of nonclerical to clerical teachers in most Catholic colleges is higher than that in the lower schools. Professional schools, teaching medicine, dentistry, law, social service, and so on are almost entirely staffed by lay persons. Salaries of such professors are usually higher than those paid to high school and elementary school teachers, and the scarcity of such personnel in terms of demand is great. To secure them, Catholic institutions must compete with well-endowed private institutions, as well as state colleges and universities supported by public taxation. The situation on the graduate level is already serious.

Catholic colleges and universities not only compete with state and non-Catholic institutions of higher learning, they also compete with each other for students. In one eastern metropolitan area there are two Catholic colleges and one Catholic university for men. Yet their combined enrollments would not equal Catholic enrollments at the two private, nonsectarian universities in the same city. On the other hand, there are certain states in which not a single Catholic college for men exists. Neither is there much pooling of resources, such as already exists among certain small colleges located in the same area. Future needs of Catholic students will compel a rethinking as to the distribution of Catholic colleges and the extent of cooperation possible among them.

---

[34] Gerard E. Sheery, "Catholic Education Today: an Interview with the Rt. Rev. Msgr. Frederick G. Hochwalt," *Ave Maria*, 85, No. 17 (Apr. 27, 1957), p. 15.

## SITUATIONAL-VALUE APPROACH

The increased birth rate, changing attitudes toward the extent of school considered necessary, lack of adequately trained teachers and professors, as well as new directions in curriculum content and methods, are all part of the situational factor, already examined, impinging upon the educational system in the United States today. A population increase was to be expected, but the rate at which it occurred was not. Had the birth rate grown steadily but slowly, all schools would have been better able to accommodate future waves of students. But this was not the case, and the situational aspects of American education have created a problem. This is further complicated by the fact that youths with less talent and motivation now attend high school, partly as a result of compulsory school law attendance, and partly because such education is now considered essential to obtaining a good job—or at least a better job. The number of in-migrants from the South, the rural South, and Puerto Rico likewise presents a challenge to northern educational systems because of the culture or sub-culture of such children. Some of these students have transferred from schools in which educational standards have been below those of northern schools and this sharpens the problem.

Inability to recruit teachers is only partly the result of low salaries. In certain small communities teachers live in "glass houses." Their personal lives are carefully scrutinized and drinking and smoking are frowned upon—although those doing the frowning may both drink and smoke themselves. Prejudice against teacher applicants with minority backgrounds, such as race, ethnic group, or religion likewise operates in some places. It is scarcely surprising that a fair number of persons trained for the teaching profession prefer the economic rewards, the greater freedom, and the lack of discrimination found in other occupations.

Costs of supporting future school systems will be correspondingly great and at present strong opposition to federal aid is encountered because of some Americans' values. They not only oppose an increase in school taxation but fear that local communities will lose control of their schools. As pointed out earlier, local control of school administration and taxation has historically characterized American school systems. Whether federal aid will mean federal control is open to debate, but even the most optimistic are compelled to admit that aid from Washington would probably result in some supervision from Washington. In view of the state of certain American school systems, this should not be entirely deplored. It becomes a matter of the degree and the way in which such control would be exercised. Parents have the primary right and responsibility to educate their children. This is more easily maintained on a community than on a national level simply because locally elected and appointed officials are likely to be more responsive to communities' demands than would senators and representatives.

American value systems also influence curricula content. Again, as pointed out earlier, pragmatism is a strong American characteristic. Consequently, community pressures to include vocational training courses on the secondary level of education are not likely to decline. Most American parents expect that schools will make some direct contribution to training their children for future employment. Few understand and fewer appreciate what kinds of contributions for future employment certain types of courses such as the classics can make. On the other hand, they do not want their children forcibly shuttled into a school or into courses which seem to indicate that they possess only average or less than average ability.

The handling of religion in public schools is likely to remain unresolved. Situationally, childern of many different religious backgrounds—as well as those with none—are enrolled in public schools. In certain localities where one particular religious denomination dominates, such as certain sections of the South, pressures to introduce sectarian instruction will persist and to some extent will be complied with. In large metropolitan areas where the diversity of religious affiliation is great, demands to prohibit sectarian religious instruction are strong, and the schools will have to comply, particularly since this compliance appears to be legally required. Nevertheless arguments over the celebration of Christmas and Easter, as well as baccalaureate addresses in Protestant churches, will cause controversy. Closely allied with this is the whole matter of the existence of parochial schools.

As enrollment in Catholic and other church-related elementary and secondary schools increase, so will greater efforts be made to obtain some sort of state aid other than that now given. Whether or not their requests are ultimately met, some serious problems in the field of interreligious relations may result from this controversy in the field of education.

## REMEDIAL MEASURES

Two approaches may be employed to determine who shall be educated. First, colleges and universities themselves could establish higher admission requirements, as some have done. However, there are always some institutions which do not meet their quotas, and today any American high school graduate of average or even less than average ability can be admitted to some college if he looks hard enough and far enough. This situation may change with increased population pressure, but it is more probable that many more colleges will be established, and some of these, willing or otherwise, will fill their quotas largely with students of below average attainments.

The second approach to the college curriculum problem is more extensive use of junior colleges or community colleges, which help students to reach their highest intellectual attainments but do not confer degrees. Such institutions could be largely vocational in their curricular content, and could provide knowledge and skills for various white-collar positions. Some of this instruction is being given today, and a great deal more will very probably be offered in the future.

On a high school level somewhat similar approaches are indicated. Those of superior talent should be encouraged to enroll in pre-college courses, and provisions must be made for them to attend college even though they are financially unable. Today, a great deal of American talent is lost because some superior students simply cannot afford a college education. A Boston study of 3,348 boys with superior intelligence revealed that 89 per cent of those whose fathers were important white-collar workers expected to go to college, but only 29 per cent of equally talented boys whose fathers were in labor and service occupations expected to do so.[35] Those who lack the intellectual attainments to profit by college should be encouraged to enter terminal courses which will provide them with the basic skills essential for technical positions available in an age of automation. Those who insist on a college preparatory course despite their clearly indicated inability should be discouraged—but not forbidden —from attempting such a course of study. Motivation is an important factor which as yet cannot be reliably measured. If the counselors are correct in their appraisals of such students, results will be obvious and such children can be transferred to other types of courses.

To some this may appear undemocratic. But democracy means equality of opportunity, and was never intended to mean equality of ability. High school teachers can work to avoid the types of insidious distinctions that could well emerge from this system. If democracy is to prevail in the world, and if America is to provide equal opportunities for all students to achieve their highest intellectual attainments, the risk of inequalities will have to be faced realistically.

## SCHOOL BUILDINGS

School facilities could be increased considerably without adding a single classroom. In the United States it has been traditional to hold classes from about 8 or 9 in the morning until 2 or 3 in the afternoon in elementary and secondary schools. Saturday is a traditional free day, so children only attend five days a week. Even some colleges fail to make full use of their classrooms in the late afternoon and evening hours. Furthermore, because education was first established when the United States was a rural economy, provisions for long vacation periods during the sowing and harvesting seasons became traditional. For very young children in kindergarten and the first four grades, no change in schools hours should perhaps be made. But this is not true for older children, particularly in junior and senior high schools, colleges, and universities.

[35] Arnold Green, *Sociology* (New York: McGraw-Hill Book Co., Inc., 1960), p. 487.

When students leave school and take a job, they will find a 40-hour week for at least 50 weeks of the year their usual work load. If the school day for older children were lengthened—or extended to six days—and if long summer, Christmas, and Easter vacations were shortened, more children could be accommodated by present facilities. For example, if a child attends 25 classes a week for a total of some 20 hours or less of school instruction, the same result could be achieved if one group of children attended Monday, Wednesday, and Friday and another attended Tuesday, Thursday, and Saturday. A decrease in lengthy vacation periods could bring about either the three-semester or the quarter system. Perhaps the school population could even be doubled under these circumstances without the addition of a single classroom!

Obviously, time must be left for study, but if children attended class only three days a week this would leave them four days for study. Certain accommodations would have to be made for the summer sessions so that children would be free to accompany their parents on vacations. Such adjustments may be difficult but they would not be insurmountable. Finally, considerable attention might well be given to streamlining the years spent in formal education. For some, this would probably be impossible, and they would have to spend at least twelve years through elementary and secondary schools. Others might well complete such courses in a maximum of 9 or 10 years.

## TEACHER SHORTAGE

The teacher shortage is less readily solvable but use of television and other audio-visual aids could be stepped up. Better salaries will help attract more and better teachers, but they are not a panacea. If a higher social status were attached to the teaching profession, and if teachers in many small communities did not have to live under such rigid supervision, the field would also prove more attractive. Whether or not these possibilities can be realized, however, recruitment of new teachers will have to be attempted; and particular efforts should be made to attract the very best students, or at least some of the very best students, to this field.

## CATHOLIC SCHOOLS

Much of what has been said about education in general also applies to Catholic schools. But certain other changes might be accomplished in this area. Every parish seems to have as its ideal the erection and maintenance of a parochial school. But if such buildings were more fully utilized, one parish school might very well serve two or more parishes, especially since distance is much less of a problem in the day of the automobile and bus. As new parishes are established, it would be wise to consider the erection of one parochial school to serve several parishes. While such a school would be larger and more costly, it would also be maintained by a considerably larger number of people. When the cost of education is increasing, and when Catholic and other religious schools do not receive any direct state aid, particular consideration should be given to decreasing the cost of instruction without decreasing its quality. Fuller ultilization of high school facilities could also be attempted.

On the college and university level, Catholic institutions should especially consider consolidation of efforts. In certain subjects, larger college classes achieve the same results as smaller classes. For example, if three Catholic colleges within the same city are offering a course in American History to three classes, each numbering 40 to 60 students, the same course could be offered to 150 or 180 students at one time. In this way, both building and teacher needs could be met. Another method would be for one Catholic college to specialize in science, another in business, and another in the humanities. A common core of studies for all students might be offered in one of the larger institutions during the first year or two, and, following that, they could be divided into various fields according to their preferences. On the graduate level, some division of effort might also be tried. Strategic location, acquisition of outstanding scholars, and the very best libraries and laboratory facilities for the subjects taught in graduate school could thus be more readily achieved. It must be admitted that the administrative problems associated with these recommended changes are tremendous. And there is also a limit to the number of Catholic universities that can be adequately staffed in the United States. But if the future crisis is to be met, then consideration should be given now to possible solutions of the problem.

Since it seems impossible that every Catholic student in the future, any more than today, can be enrolled in Catholic schools, Newman clubs or Catholic centers of a similar type should be more widely established on all non-Catholic college and university campuses. Possibilities of granting college credit for courses taught in these centers, as is already done in some places, should be more thoroughly explored. Newman clubs or similar facilities might likewise be established on the high school level. On the elementary level, dismissed time is apparently legal, and could be used more widely.

Since Americans do place a high value on education, every effort should be made to make it completely available to any child who can profit from it. Such efforts have to be made, and more money for education must be more readily forthcoming, if and when it becomes clear to the public that existing facilities, teachers, and equipment are being put to their most effective use, and have been utilized to their absolute limits.

## REVIEW QUESTIONS

1. Do Americans generally have a firm belief in education for its own sake?
2. What were the motivations for the original establishment of formal elementary education in this country? To what extent do they play a continuing part in the American attitude towards education?
3. How did Thomas Jefferson and Andrew Jackson differ in their views on education?
4. What are the problems confronting the American school system as a result of the postwar birth rate?
5. Evaluate the advantages and disadvantages to federal education under the proposal made in 1961 by the Kennedy administration.
6. What are the reasons for the reputed lack of teachers in the United States?
7. How has the curriculum of the secondary school and the college been changed in recent years?

8. On what bases shall the determination be made as to what persons should be educated in American colleges and universities?
9. Is the European method of educational selection superior to the American?
10. What are the major problems confronting Catholic education in the United States today?
11. Short of more extensive federal, state, or community aid to Catholic educational institutions, what remedial measures would you propose to ease the present and probable future drain on their resources?

## SELECTED READINGS

*Articles*

Butler, John J. and Edna M. O'Hearn, "Medical Education and Research in Catholic Medical Schools and Hospitals," *American Catholic Sociological Review,* 19 (Oct. 1958), 224-37.

Clark, Burton R., "The 'Cooling Out' Function in Higher Education," *American Journal of Sociology,* 65 (May 1960), 569-76.

Fichter, Joseph H. and Paul P. W. Facey, "Social Attitudes of Catholic High School Students," *American Catholic Sociological Review,* 14 (June 1953), 94-106.

Harte, Thomas J., "Catholic Education as a Factor in Catholic Opinion," *American Catholic Sociological Review,* 10 (Mar. 1949), 15-30.

Mihanovitch, Clement S. and Eugene W. Janson, "Social Attitudes of Catholic High School Seniors," *American Catholic Sociological Review,* 7 (Oct. 1946), 170-73.

Mulligan, Raymond A., "Socio-Economic Background and College Enrollment," *American Sociological Review,* 16 (June 1955), 188-95.

Sewell, William H., Archie O. Haller, and Murray A. Straus, "Social Status and Educational and Occupational Aspirations," *American Sociological Review,* 22 (Feb. 1957), 67-72.

*Books*

Conant, James B., *Slums and Suburbs.* New York: McGraw-Hill Book Co., Inc., 1961.

Dahlke, H. Otto, *Values and Culture in Classrooms.* New York: Harper and Brothers, 1958.

Gordon, C. Wayne, *The Social System of the High School: A Study in the Sociology of Adolescence.* New York: The Free Press of Glencoe, 1957.

Henry, Nelson B., *Social Forces Influencing American Education.* Chicago: University of Chicago Press, 1961.

Knapp, Robert H. and Joseph J. Greenbaub, *The Younger American Scholar.* Chicago: The University of Chicago Press, 1953.

Mayer, Martin, *The Schools.* New York: Harper and Brothers, 1961.

Queen, Stuart A. and Jennette Rowe Gruener, *Social Pathology.* New York: Thomas Y. Crowell Co., 1940, pp. 38-42.

# PART SIX

# Conclusion—Obstacles

# to Solving Social

# Problems

I N the course of this book a number of social
problems have been described and their
causal factors analyzed and explained by
means of the situational-value approach. Possible methods
of solution or reduction of such problems have also been
considered. It was pointed out that the problems covered
in this book by no means exhaust the range of social
problems within American society. Three major social
institutions—the family, religion, and education—have
likewise been discussed, and some of the internal problems
involved with each have been analyzed. This concluding
chapter will examine some of the obstacles which inhibit
or weaken efforts to solve social problems in American
society.

Two major difficulties confront students of social problems as well as various leaders and the public itself, in any
effort to resolve or reduce the extent of these problems.
The first may be subsumed under public knowledge, the

second under the values of American society. Under public knowledge of social problems the following aspects will be considered: first, to what extent society knows of the existence of a problem at all; second, to what extent it has any appreciation of its incidence and causal factors; and third, to what extent it realizes the impact of one social problem upon another. Under values of American society, values, attitudes, and motives of the American public in general as well as powerful groups within American society will be discussed and analyzed in an effort to determine to what degree these interfere with suggested approaches to the reduction or elimination of social problems.

In the first chapter it was indicated that social problems fall into two major categories: overt problems, situations about which the public in general has some knowledge and against which it is willing to mobilize community resources to solve them, and covert problems, about which the public at large has little knowledge, and toward which no organized action is therefore taken, but which nonetheless are considered problems by a sizable number of authorities or by some specific group within the society.

The extent to which American society in general has any knowledge of an existing social problem varies tremendously among social classes, ethnic, racial, and religious groups, as well as by regions. Most Americans know about overt social problems from reading newspapers, magazines, and, to a lesser extent, books. They also learn about them through television, motion pictures, the radio, or, to a much lesser extent, by attending lectures. But these media tend to emphasize the more dramatic types of social problems, or at least the dramatic aspects of them. Sudden and severe catastrophes—such as airplane accidents—in which large numbers are killed, the devastating effects of hurricanes or floods, and murders (particularly those of a sensational type, with sexual aspects) receive wide coverage, large headlines, or, at least, prominent space in newspapers. Television and radio, with their on-the-spot coverage of such news, heighten the dramatic aspect and provide a vivid portrayal of the actual event through verbal descriptions or pictures. As a result of this, the American public is quite aware of certain types of social problems.

On the other hand, they are considerably less aware of certain kinds of problems which fail to receive this attention. The state of physical health and medical care, mental illness, and problems of the aging and aged do not receive the same kind of coverage. As a result, the public's awareness of the field of social problems tends to be directed towards those problems which are highly dramatic, represent serious conflict situations, or which arouse pity and sympathy. The public is also more keenly aware of the kinds of problems which occur within the United States or within their own communities. But this type of coverage, and the resulting increased public knowledge of the problems, gives little indication of the incidence or causal factors involved in social problems. While the number of airplane fatalities, for example, may be cited at length, along with a brief history of such accidents occurring in recent years, emphasis is upon the fatality rate rather than upon the millions of passengers who fly millions of miles without incident. The usual explanation of social problems offered by the media of communication is in the nature of limited, casual discussions, which are inevitably superficial. As a consequence, society at large has little insight into the complexity and depth of the causal factors in social problems.

But even the serious student of social problems, who turns to scholarly books, is not guaranteed a thoroughly adequate analysis of the causes of social problems. For example, it should have become quite apparent to students reading this book that accurate knowledge of the incidence of certain social problems cannot be obtained. Statistics on crime and religious membership are notoriously inaccurate. Sharp differences of opinion on the number of narcotic addicts in the United States has been shown by disagreement between the Federal Bureau of Narcotics and the New York City Police Department. It has been pointed out that we have a much better knowledge of the batting averages of big-league baseball players than we have of some more vital human events.

Students may also be puzzled by the conflicting findings of researchers regarding the incidence and causal factors of any social problem. Disagreement among demographers about the world's ability to support a rapidly growing population has been evident. Causal factors in alcoholism and narcotic addiction show some variation from one study to another. At this particular stage of the development of social science, the desirable level of knowledge about social problems and causes has yet to be reached. While this is annoying to readers, it should be recalled that such disagreements are common in science. Natural scientists cannot seem to agree on the effects of radiation fallout. Yet physics, biology, and medicine are considerably better developed than social science. As man strives to improve his physical, psychological, economic, political, and social conditions he inevitably discovers that the questions are considerably more complex than first believed. He is, therefore, compelled to act upon the best knowledge he can obtain without throwing up his hands in despair and permitting social problems to become worse as he awaits more knowledge.

Discussion and analysis of social problems in this book have been based largely upon sociology and social psychology. But students should not conclude that these are the only two disciplines capable of contributing to the reduction or resolution of social problems. Social philosophy is particularly important to remedial action. Philosophy and theology have notable contributions to make. All of these last three disciplines touch especially upon value systems, and to no small extent help determine whether or not an existing condition is a social problem—and they strongly influence proposed solutions.

But today "science" has become a magic word. To the average citizen, it means the natural, or physical, sciences. Only to a lesser extent does the average person think of social science within this category, and he certainly would not consider the inclusion of philosophy and theology. Yet, in one sense of the meaning of science (a body of organized knowledge), philosophy and theology are sciences. The nature of these disciplines and their methods of investigation are not the same as those of natural or physical sciences. Social science occupies an intermediate position. Insofar as possible, social scientists try to employ the techniques of the natural or physical scientist. However, there are limitations to this approach which are probably not fully appreciated even among some social scientists. A great deal of this attempt undoubtedly stems from the hope that, through the use of such techniques, social science may be identified with natural or physical science and thus enjoy the same level of prestige. On the other hand, it would be foolhardy to pretend that the social scientist cannot and should not employ such techniques insofar as they are feasible.

Despite his awareness of certain social problems and even some knowledge of their causal factors, the average person has little appreciation of the interrelationship and interdependence of such problems. If this interaction is pointed out in the media of communication followed by most Americans, it is done in a most cursory fashion. The full realization that poverty, minority status, lack of education and occupational opportunities, and residence in slum areas may facilitate crime and delinquency is not entirely grasped. Insofar as there is some appreciation of it, all-out attacks on such matters are often urged. Some action may even be taken, usually followed by a swift and severe disappointment that delinquency and crime are not immediately obliterated. On the other hand, those who have no knowledge of the relationship among social problems seek a quick and simple solution to crime and delinquency by urging naive measures such as punishment of parents, the "treat 'em rough" method toward criminals, stringent censorship of the media of communication, and similar measures. Since the public loves a simple explanation and a simple remedy, none of this is surprising.

But ignorance of the incidence, causal factors, and possible approaches to social problems is only part of the story of the inability to solve them. More important is the value system of American society. Even among the overt social problems which are clearly recognized as dangers to society, proposed solutions encounter opposition. First, many of the proposals require the expenditure of money. If they are carried on by a public agency, this usually means an increase in in the tax rate, which is something resisted by most persons with the utmost effort. Yet the very persons who may staunchly resist increased taxation may be the same persons who indirectly underwrite the expense of tolerating such problems.

In the chapter on education it was pointed out that one aspect of resistance to federal aid to education is the belief that citizens in some states should not pay for the education of citizens in other states. Yet these poorly educated, unskilled persons may migrate into the states which resisted federal aid, be placed on relief roles through lack of employment and be supported by public taxes.

Another source of disagreement about solutions to social problems in American society is the question of whether they shall be handled by public or private agencies. Within the American value system there is a strong belief that private methods are superior to government methods. There is also a belief that communities should solve their own problems rather than seek the assistance of state and federal governments. Within limits this dilemma can be resolved if it is made clear that certain social problems are not susceptible to resolution on a private or a local level. Obviously, no single small community can cope with the over-all problem of narcotic addiction. Even a large metropolitan area like New York City must turn to the federal government, which alone, for example, has control of imports. Since most narcotics are imported from other countries, it is only through the action of the U.S. Custom Service that effective controls can be exercised. In the case of narcotics, the case is quite clear; but in many other areas it is less easy to demonstrate that alleviation of social problems requires aid beyond the community level. As a result there is considerable debate about the issue, and in the process of this debate the social problems continue unchecked.

Finally, there are small but powerful groups within the United States which have a vested interest in the status quo. This becomes clearly evident in such measures as slum clearance. Certain real estate owners or operators actually profit financially from slum areas, albeit they pay for them in other ways. The purchase of tracts of land for public housing may be resisted by persons living in or near the area because they fear their own properties will lose value if public housing is erected. In other words, there is a considerable conflict of interest operating to impede proposed solutions to some social problems.

This opposition is carried over into the political arena, where various social problems are turned into political footballs. Invidious terms are invented, usually labeling such measures "socialism." This can be exemplified readily by the opponents of the plan for medical care for the aged through the Social Security system. Attempts to pass this bill have been balked at least in part by propaganda to the effect that such a measure would be "socialized medicine." Many other examples could be provided to indicate that conflict of interests, vested interests, and such ultimately permit the perpetuation of certain social problems. On the other hand, it must also be granted that none of the solutions advanced are really panaceas, and some of them may be sorely inadequate.

Despite these difficulties, notable improvements in the elimination or reduction of social problems have occurred. Narcotic addiction is far less than what it was in the past. While statistics to prove or disprove the fact are unavailable, it seems probable that alcoholism was a more severe problem in the last century than in the present. Poverty is still a social problem but its extent and severity, typical of some groups in the last century and the beginning of this century, are less. But social problems change as a result of social change. Certain other problems appear to be growing in incidence and severity. Positive efforts to reduce or diminish social problems depend upon a fuller knowledge of their incidence, causal factors, and probable solutions. They likewise depend upon certain changes in the value systems of many Americans. The situation is far from hopeless. Rising standards of education, better use of the media of communication, and a frank realization that individual sacrifice for the common good is essential to the welfare of society will help change the present situation. All social problems will not be eliminated, neither will all necessarily be reduced. But if their incidence and severity can be lessened and if new probems can be faced realistically and objectively, all Americans will profit from it.

# REVIEW QUESTIONS

1. About what kind of social problems is the average American likely to have the best knowledge? Are these necessarily the most critical problems?

2. Evaluate the following statement: "The greatest obstacle to the solution or reduction of social problems is the present inadequacy of social science, which is not true of physical or natural science."

3. Why is it impossible to obtain accurate statistics on certain social problems such as alcoholism, suicide, and crime?

4. How does the American value system generally impede the solution or reduction of social problems?

5. Should social problems be handled by governmental agencies or private voluntary organizations? On what basis would you make such decisions?

6. It is sometimes claimed that Americans have a parochial view of social problems. Do you agree or disagree? Explain the reason for your position.

7. What recommendations would you make to see that Americans are more thoroughly informed about current social problems?

## SELECTED READINGS

*Articles*

Burgess, Ernest W., "Values in Sociological Research," *Social Problems*, 2 (July 1954), 16-20.

Furfey, Paul Hanley, "The Social Philosophy of Social Pathologists," *Social Problems*, 2 (Oct. 1954), 71-74.

——, "Value Judgments in Sociology," *American Catholic Sociological Review*, 7 (June 1946), 83-95.

Kennedy, John F., "The Principle of Subsidiary," *American Catholic Sociological Review*, 16 (Mar. 1945), 31-36.

Klob, William L., "The Impingement of Moral Values on Sociology," *Social Problems*, 2 (Oct. 1954), 66-67.

Lane, Robert E., "Government Regulation and the Business Mind," *American Sociological Review*, 16 (Apr. 1951), 163-73.

Lynch, Sister Miriam, "Communication Between Philosophers and Sociologists," *American Catholic Sociological Review*, 19 (Dec. 1958), 290-309.

*Mater et Magistra, Encyclical Letter of Pope John XXIII*. New York: The American Press, 1961.

Dror, Yehezkel, "Knowledge, Social Action and Social Problems," *Social Problems*, 7 (Spring 1960), 356-59.

Young, Kimball, "Society and the State," *American Sociological Review*, 11 (Apr. 1946), 137-45.

# Index of Names

# A

Abbot, Herman, 21, 22, 28, 29
Abrahamsen, David, 190
Ahlstrom, Sidney E., 348, 350, 351
Alexander, Judge Paul W., 158, 331
Anderson, Odin, 81, 82, 93
Antonovski, Aaron, 277
Apple, Dorrian, 93
Aquinas, St. Thomas, 238
Aristotle, 237
Aschaffenburg, Gustav, 174
Augusta, Sister Maria, 19
Augustine, Saint, 238
Ausubel, D. B., 192, 194, 199, 204-206, 208, 214
Averback, Alfred, 113

# B

Bach, Marcus Louis, 314
Bacon, Seldon, 220
Baker, Ray E., 338
Bailey, Most Reverend James, 361
Bailey, Reverend D. Sherwin, 57
Bandura, Albert, 341
Barnes, Harry Elmer, and Teeters, Negley F., 174, 177, 178, 182, 190
Barron, Milton L., 136, 146, 279, 280, 286
Barta, Russell, 341
Barth, Karl, 348
Becker, Howard S., 93, 207, 208, 213
Bell, Howard, 284
Ben-David, Joseph, 93
Bendix, W., 357
Bennett, John, 56-58
Bensing, Robert C., 190
Bernard, Eleanor H., 374-376
Bernard, Jessie, 71, 341
Biren, James E., 136
Blanshard, Paul P., 299
Bloomgarten, Lawrence, 83, 84, 93
Blumer, Herbert, 37
Bobo, James H., 141, 162, 167
Boll, Eleanor Stoker, 317, 320, 330, 341
Bonger, W. H., 174
Borgenicht, Miriam, 383
Borrowman, Merle L. P., 372
Bossard, James H. S., vii, 31, 317, 320, 330, 341

Botwinick, Jack, 225
Bowman, Claude, 37, 337
Bracelend, Francis J., 129, 130
Brinkman, Rev. Gabriel, O.F.A., 337
Breen, Leonard, 118, 119
Brown, Spencer, 384
Bryan, William Jennings, 348
Bukowski, F., 341
Bunzel, Bessie, 236-238, 240-242, 249
Burch, Thomas K., 69
Burgess, Ernest W., 136, 137, 323, 410
Butler, John J., 314, 401

# C

Cahnman, Warner, 296
Calvin, John, 356
Cameron, Norman, 112
Campbell, Arthur A., 59-65, 70
Campbell, Ernest Q., 277, 278
Canisia, Sister Mary, 69
Carr, Lowell Julliard, 38, 142, 162
Castler, Norman M., 259
Cavan, Ruth, 136, 137, 171, 172, 190, 235, 236, 245, 249
Cavanagh, Dr. John R., 155
Centers, Richard, 8
Chamberlain, Houston Stewart, 281
Chambers, Francis T., Jr., 217, 219, 220, 224, 225, 227
Clague, Ewan, 118
Clark, Burton R., 401
Clark, Robert E., 112
Clemens, Alphonse E., 352
Clinard, Marshall B., 7, 223, 228, 235, 236, 240, 241
Cloward, Richard A., 163
Clusen, John A., 101, 102, 112
Cohen, Albert A., 38, 148, 163
Cohn, Melvin L., 112
Colbert, Roy J., 259
Coleman, James C., 96, 97, 99, 105, 107, 108, 113
Cook, Robert C., 49
Cooley, Charles H., 23
Conannan, Paul, 249
Conant, James, 153, 401
Cooper, Clara C., 163
Corbin, S., 162
Cowdry, E. V., 127

# Index of Subjects